UNDERSTANDING PARASITOLOGY

UNDERSTANDING PARASITOLOGY

By

Dr. Amita Sarkar

Dept. of Zoology
Agra College
Agra (U.P.)
(India)

DPH

DISCOVERY PUBLISHING HOUSE PVT. LTD.

NEW DELHI-110 002

Published by:
Namit Wasan
DISCOVERY PUBLISHING HOUSE PVT. LTD.
4383/4B, Ansari Road, Darya Ganj
New Delhi-110 002 (India)
Phone : +91-11-23279245; 23253475; 43596065
E-mail : discoverybooksindia@gmail.com
discoverypublishinghouse@gmail.com
namitwasan9@gmail.com
web : www.discoverypublishinggroup.com

First Edition: **2010**

ISBN: 978-81-8356-520-2

Understanding Parasitology

Preface

The present title "Understanding Parasitology" has been written for those students interested in careers in diverse fields of biological sciences. It provides a structured approach to learning by covering all the important topics in a uniform, systematic format. The book has been comprehensively designed incorporating recent advances in this fast moving field. It also provides accessible information on molecular biology in compact form for undergraduate students in biology and related life sciences. It is intelligible to the educated layman, though it deals with some complex ideas. It is an adequate text for all the requirements of students in this area. In addition, busy lecturers who require a quick reference compendium will find it useful, particularly for tutional planning. Simple, yet hopefully clear figures and tables are provided throughout the book.

The over-riding goal of this book, and indeed of the whole *Understanding series,* is to present the essential information concering molecular biology in a compact, readily accessible form which leads itself to student learning and revision. The convergence of various approaches has generated a rich panorama of detail, the significance of which we are still attempting to unraval. The present text has been written as an introduction to this rapidly growing field.

To make the work more comprehensive and informative, the author has consulted many authoritative books, research journals, abstracts, monographs etc., so there can be no claim to originality except in the manner of treatment.

The author expresses his thanks to his friends and colleagues whose continue inspirations have initiated him to bring out this book.

The author expresses his gratitude to Mr. Wasan and staff of M/s Discovery Publishing House Pvt. Ltd. for their whole hearted cooperation in the publication of this book.

In the mean time, the author will remain sincerely responsible for any shortcomings of the book and be grateful to the readers for their suggestions and constructive criticism for the continuous betterment of the book. He takes this opportunity to appeal to the readers to send their suggestions straightaway to his Publisher.

Author

Contents

1

Malaria Parasite

Plasmodium, the protozoan parasite that causes malaria, exists in a variety of different forms which have successfully adapted to different cellular environments, in both the vertebrate host and the mosquito vector. The parasite develops in a highly regulated manner through three distinct cycles in the vertebrate host and two cycles in the insect. At certain stages of its life cycle, development is intracellular.

In the vertebrate host this protective environment, together with the fact that each stage is antigenically distinct, provides the main strategies for evading the host's immune attack. This chapter reviews the complex process of host cell invasion, the parasite's ability to alter or subvert host cell functions to its advantage, and its ability to subsequently free itself from the intracellular environment, en route to a new host cell.

In biochemical terms we know very little of these events, and experimental investigation of the processes has proved difficult in many cases. Therefore, questions about the suitability and the limitations of techniques applied to the study of the plasmodia will also be considered. The genus *Plasmodium* is a member of the subphylum Apicomplexa. Members of this subphylum include genera of other intracellular protozoa: *Eimeria*, *Toxoplasma*, *Babesia*, and *Theileria*.

A unifying and unique feature of the subphylum is the complex array of subcellular apical structures known as rhoptries and micronemes. These organelles are presumed to be involved in entry into host cells, which for the most part are nonphagocytic.

Entry requires the active participation of the parasite. Rhoptries and microncmes are organelles that are present in both sporozoites and merozoites, the extracellular stages that invade host cells, but they are absent in gametes and ookinetes, stages that do not invade. Over 100 species of *Plasmodia* infect rodents, birds, and primates. The sporozoite is the form of the parasite that the mosquito injects into the vertebrate host and that initiates the intrahepatic cycle. Sporozoites rapidly circulate to the liver, where they invade liver cells and develop into tissue schizonts within hepatocytes.

In the course of 1 to 2 weeks each tissue schizont divides to form at least 10,000 merozoites. On release from the liver into the blood stream, the merozoites invade erythrocytes. The specificity of the interaction between the merozoite and erythrocyte has received considerable attention in recent years because this step is a crucial and potentially vulnerable one for the parasite's survival. Rings and trophozoites are intraerythrocytic asexual stages into which the merozoites develop.

Trophozoites in turn develop into the multinucleated schizonts that give rise to the merozoites that are released by rupture of the infected red cell. These merozoites then invade other red cells. The cyclical development from merozoite to schizont can proceed many times in vivo or until the host succumbs, and it also can be sustained indefinitely in vitro.

Some merozoites develop intracellularly to form male or female gametocytes, which if ingested by mosquitoes, change into male and female gametes in the mosquito midgut; they cause no disease in the vertebrate host. During the parasites sexual cycle, fertilization occurs when gametes unite in the gut to form a unicellular zygote. The fertilized zygote transforms to a motile ookinete and penetrates through the intestinal wall of the midgut, where it forms an oocyst.

The oocyst undergoes a process called sporogony that results in the formation of 10,00020,000 sporozoites, which migrate to the salivary gland. From here sporozoites emerge to infect the host when the vector mosquito takes a blood meal. In summary, there are five distinct extracellular stages: the sporozoite and the merozoite in the vertebrate host and the gamete, zygote, and ookinete in the mosquito. All are unicellular.

The ookinete and the male gamete are capable of multiplication; the latter forms eight motile microgametes. There are three intracellular stages and in two of these, the intrahepatic schizont and intraerythrocytic schizont, asexual division occurs by binary fusion. Only the gametocyte remains uninucleate. Attempts have been made, with varying degrees of success, to culture all stages of *Plasmodium falciparum* and some stages of other species. In vitro cultivation has been most successful for the asexual erythrocytic stages of *P. falciparum*. Production of gametocytes and ookinetes during cultivation of the erythrocytic stages has also been possible.

Recently the complete hepatic cycle of *P. vivax* and *P. falciparum* has been accomplished. The in vitro culture systems will be discussed in more detail in the relevant sections that follow.

THE HEPATIC CYCLE

Ultrastructure of Sporozoites

The sporozoite is an elongated unicellular organism, 11 micrometers (μm) in length. It is covered by a thin surface coat overlying a double unit membrane and a row of subpellicular microtubules. The only surface protein identified to date as a component of the surface coat is the circumsporozoite protein (CS), which probably will prove to be the only one.

Incubation of sporozoite with antisporozoite immune serum results in the precipitation and sloughing off of the surface coat material, in a process called the circumsporozoite precipitation (CSP) reaction. The CS protein was first identified in *P. berghei*. Homologous proteins have also been identified in other species: *P. cynamolgi*, *P. knowlesi*, *P. falciparum*, and *P. vivax*.

The CS protein varies in size from 40 kilodaltons (kD) in *P. knowlesi* to 60 kD in *P. falciparum;* it appears to be synthesized as a high-molecular-weight precursor and is processed during transport to the cell surface. The CS protein of *P. knowlesi* was the first plasmodial protein to be cloned in *E. coil*, and base pair sequence analysis of the cDNA revealed a remarkable feature, the presence of an extensive repeat domain. Subsequent analysis of other plasmodial antigens or the genes coding for them revealed that many parasite proteins share this property, some having even larger repeat domains than the CS protein.

For the CS protein, the number and sequence of amino acids per repeat and the number of repeats per molecule vary between species and in some instances between strains; however, the repeat domain generally constitutes 40 percent and occupies the same location in the molecule.

Flanking the repeat domain at the 3' and Vend of the molecule are regions of highly charged amino acids that are conserved between species. The sporozoite exists in the bloodstream for a maximum of 1 hour. Efficient invasion of hepatic cells is necessary to guarantee protection against host defenses, and generation of the subsequent stages is its major objective. It has been proposed that the function of the CS protein is to mediate the interaction (attachment and entry) with the hepatic cells although there has been little biochemical information available to support this hypothesis.

Recently, however, it has been demonstrated that a region of the CS protein immediately 5' to the repeat domain is conserved in different species and apparently is responsible for binding to hepatoma cells in vitro (a culture system believed to mimic in vivo conditions).

Rhoptries and micronemes are also present in the sporozoite and probably have an important role in invasion as well.

Sporozoite Invasion of Hepatocytes

Electron microscopic studies of the in vivo entry of *P. berghei* sporozoites into hepatic cells have been performed after sporozoite attachment. The hepatocyte plasmalemma invaginates at the point of attachment and creates a parasitophorous vacuole in which sporozoites reside.

An active involvement of the sporozoite during this invasion is postulated. Because the proteins of the sporozoite rhoptries have not yet been identified, it has not been possible to directly examine their fate during invasion. If a monoclonal antibody to a rhoptry protein were available, it would be possible to follow the movement of its contents by immunofluorescence during invasion.

It has been assumed that the sporozoite recognizes specific structures on the hepatic cell surface and that the CS protein plays a role in this recognition, since antibodies directed against the CS protein block hepatoma cell invasion in vitro. No specific hepatic receptor has been identified, however.

The strict species specificity characteristic of the merozoite invasion of erythrocytes is not apparently applicable to sporozoite entry of hepatocytes. For example, *P. berghei* sporozoites can invade human hepatoma cell lines in vitro, whereas *P. berghei* merozoites cannot enter human erythrocytes.

Currently, investigators are working under the assumption that sporozoites do bind to specific hepatic surface molecules and are considering that these may be the same for all species of *Plasmodium*. Although we know the complete gene sequence for several CS proteins, we understand little of the biochemical events that regulate sporozoite invasion.

The gaps in our understanding are revealed by several questions:

How does the sporozoite recognize the hepatocyte cell surface, or does it recognize the Kupffer or endothelial cells first? What triggers the nonphagocytic cells to apparently endocytose the parasites? Do any plasma components contribute to the invasion process? How efficient is the invasion process (how many sporozoites enter and survive)'?

Are rhoptry contents involved in entry, and what then is their fate? What is the fate of the CS protein during invasion? The limited availability of sporozoites has hindered efforts addressing these questions. Recently, however, several in vitro systems have been developed which may be suitable to examine some of these basic questions.

In Vitro Hepatocyte Culture System

In vitro systems have been developed to examine *P. berghei* sporozoite entry with a cultured human lung fibroblast cell line (W138) and a hepatoma cell line (HepG2A 16). The fact that sporozoites enter fibroblasts at all suggests that receptor specificity is not particularly rigid, although it is unclear if the same receptors are employed by the two cell types.

Attachment and entry occur more efficiently in the hepatoma cell line and appear to be active processes on the part of the parasite, since entry is not inhibited by antiphagocytic drugs such as cytochalasins. It has been observed that the sporozoite sheds its surface coat during invasion. Antibody directed against the CS antigen dramatically inhibited invasion in vitro, suggesting that the protein is directly responsible for recognizing certain receptors on the hepatic cell.

Recently it has been found that antibodies raised against the repeat sequence of the *P. falciparuin* CS protein, Asn-Ala Asn-Pro-, significantly block sporozoite attachment and invasion of primary hepatocytes in culture. Furthermore, sporozoites that do invade in the presence of antibody develop abnormally and in some cases fail to mature. *P. falciparum* and *P. vivax* sporozoites also infect the hepatoma cell line HepG2-A16.

Although the hepatoma cell line system is suitable for in vitro invasion studies, a drawback is that after invasion, sporozoites of these two species develop only as far as intrahepatic trophozoites; mature schizonts and invasive merozoites cannot be obtained from this culture. More recently, the complete development of hepatic stages of *P. falciparum* and *P. vivax* in vitro has been reported. With the use of primary cultures of human hepatocytes, it was possible to obtain mature and infective merozoites released spontaneously from the cultured cells.

Primary cultures were inoculated with sporozoites obtained from mosquitoes fed on gametocytes. After a 20-hour incubation with sporozoites, intracellular forms could be seen. After 64 hours, intracellular schizonts were observed, and they developed to maturity after 6-7 days in culture.

Erythrocytes were added to hepatocyte cultures on day 7, and erythrocytic ring stages were subsequently identified. Although the infectivity rate was low (1 ring per 3×10^5 erythrocytes) such a system permits the examination of liver-derived merozoites. Because of the small number of parasites obtained in these cultures, the techniques to examine these stages in greater detail must be very sensitive.

Immunofluorescence is a moderately sensitive technique that would allow one to discern when certain proteins of the sporozoite are lost and when blood-stage antigens begin to be synthesized. This in vitro system to examine sporozoite entry obviously has great potential and will be suitable for studies on schizont development and stage-specific gene regulation.

THE ERYTHROCYTIC CYCLE

Ultrastructure

The erythrocytic cycle is initiated after merozoites leave the ruptured hepatic cell. The extracellular existence of merozoites in the plasma is transitory, and immediately on the invasion of erythrocytes, it is transformed to the ring stage. The merozoite is oval in shape, about I um in diameter, has a nucleus and various cytoplasmic organelles, and is surrounded by a double lipid bilayer membrane and thick surface coat.

Beneath the inner plasma membrane is a row of microtubules that may function as a cytoskeleton responsible for maintaining cell shape. The apical end of the merozoite is distinguished by a cone-shaped structure called the conoid. The underlying inner membrane is discontinuous at this end.

During invasion, the rhoptries and associated micronemes move to the apical end, and a ductule extending from each rhoptry forms a common duct that extends to the lip of the conoid structure. (Similarities with the ultrastructure of Toxoplasma *gondii* are described elsewhere in this book) Many merozoite proteins have been identified, and their probable location is shown in the diagram in Figure elsewhere in this chapter.

In addition to several organelles common to the Apicomplexa, merozoites contain mitochondria. Their mitochondria have poorly

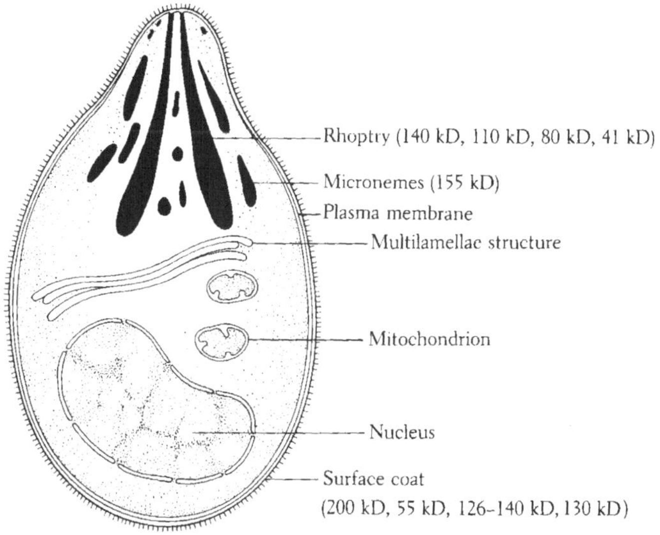

Figure 1.1: Localization of P. falciparum antigens. Major proteins of the merozoite stage that have been identified by monoclonal antibodies or bio-chemical properties. The surface-coat protein of 200 kD is processed to proteins of 90 kD and 50 kD at the merozoite stage.

developed cristae, and it is therefore assumed that certain biochemical components of the respiratory chain are not functional, although this has not been investigated in any detail. The major metabolic end product of the organism is lactate, indicating that glycolysis is the important pathway to energy production.

Another structure, known as the multilamellae structure, is an organelle bounded by layered membranes and usually located close to the mitochondrion. This location has prompted speculations that the multilamellae structure serves as an energy reservoir. The remainder of the cytoplasm is filled with ribosomes apparently unbound to endoplasmic reticulum. The merozoite undergoes many changes after invading erythrocytes.

It loses its surface coat and appears to discharge contents from the rhoptries during invasion. It comes to reside inside an endosomal compartment called the parasitophorous vacuole (PVM) that is formed by the invagination of the erythrocyte plasma membrane. The transformation of *P. falciparum* merozoites to rings, but not their further development, has been observed in a cell-free system.

The structures of the merozoite break down inside the erythrocytes; apical organelles and microtubules disappear. The rings are *biosynthe-*

tically quiescent stages, although ring stage—specific proteins are synthesized. Certain proteins that are present on other stages are absent on ring stages. The uninucleate trophozoite is characterized by the loss of the regular shape of the ring and the appearance of large food vacuoles.

At the trophozoite (feeding) stage, ingestion of the host cell cytoplasm occurs through a structure known as the cytostome. The cytostome invaginates into the parasite and is pinched off, fusing to form a food vacuole. The process of intracellular pinocytosis is found only in Plasmodia and a few other intracellular parasites. The contents of the food vacuole, principally hemoglobin, are digested by lysozymelike enzymes, the end product of hemoglobin being crystals of hemozoin.

The antimalarial drug chloroquine appears somehow to disrupt the digestion of hemoglobin, or interferes with sequestration of one of the toxic end products, ferriprotophorphyrin (hemin). Parasites resistant to chloroquine may have developed an alternate pathway to process digested hemoglobin.

More recent studies suggest that chloroquine-resistant strains of *P. falciparum* are more efficient in exporting chloroquine from the food vacuole. The proteases that regulate hemoglobin digestion have been studied with interest since their active sites could represent important targets for chemotherapeutic attack.

The intracellular schizont, by definition, has more than one nucleus. Schizogony (formation of the schizont) is the process of asexual nuclear division and is accompanied by considerable ultrastructural differentiation. The process of de novo formation of subcellular organelles such as the rhoptries and micronemes is uncommon in mammalian cells and therefore may be of particular interest to cell biologists.

The mitochondria enlarge and bud, and the submembrane microtubules and rhoptries reappear, at first randomly, in the cytoplasm. The schizont membrane begins to invaginate and eventually pinches off, forming individual merozoites. The numerous nuclei, rhoptries, micronemes, and other organelles migrate into the developing merozoite.

The only identified material remaining outside the merozoite is the hemozoin pigment, surrounded by its own membrane. Recently it has been possible to induce *P. knowlesi* trophozoites, stripped of the outer erythrocyte membrane, to divide to form multinucleated schizonts. At the time merozoites are ready for release, the host cell cytoplasm is fully digested and the parasitophorous vacuole membrane (PVM) has expanded to enclose the growing schizont.

The mature merozoites are surrounded by their own double membranes in addition to the PVM and the erythrocyte membrane. Biological membranes do not readily disassemble; therefore, the nature of the signal that induces these outer two membranes to rupture, allowing the individual merozoites to be released, is of exceptional basic biological interest.

It is known that the rupture of *P. knowlesi* schizonts is inhibited by chymostatin, suggesting that chymotrypsinlike enzymes may be involved in the release. Structural differences that exist between different species may be noteworthy for future investigation. The most notable are structural differences in the modification of the cytoplasm and membranes of the infected erythrocyte.

In erythrocytes infected with vivax-type parasites (for example, *P. vivax* and *P. cynomolgi*) caveolae-vesicle complexes located adjacent to the erythrocyte membrane have been observed. These complexes may correspond to Schuffner dots seen on Giemsa-stained blood films. The caveolae are typified by electron-dense clefts in the erythrocyte plasma membrane and closely associated vesicles in the host cytoplasm.

In *falciparum-type* parasites (e.g., *P. falciparum*, *P. fragile*, and *P. malariae)*, electron-dense excrescences or knob structures are observed and appear to be on the cytoplasmic face of the erythrocyte membrane. For *P. knowlesi*, electron-dense invagination or caveolae of the erythrocyte membrane of infected cells are observed.

Since *P. vivax* and *P. falciparum* both infect human cells, the differences in cytoplasmic and membrane structures presumably are not related to the host red cell but appear to be dictated by the parasite. In cells infected with all types of primate malaria parasites, membrane-bound clefts in the erythrocyte cytoplasm are seen.

These have been termed Maurer's clefts and appear under transmission electron microscopy as elongated vesicles. A parasite-synthesized protein of 50 kD has been identified as a component of the cleft membrane. The various cytoplasmic vesicles may be involved in intracellular transport from the intravacuolar schizont to the infected erythrocyte membrane.

It has been proposed that knob structures in *P. falciparum*infected cells are involved in the binding of infected erythrocytes to the endothelial cells of postcapillary venules during late schizogony. This sequestration process appears to be a protective measure against filtration of the cell by the spleen, and might provide a milieu of low oxygen tension favourable to terminal schizont development.

However, *P. malariae*-infected erythrocytes also have knobs but do not sequester in deep vascular beds; it therefore is unlikely that promotion of sequestration is the only function served by these excrescences. Once adapted to culture, *P. falciparum* rapidly looses the knob structures without consequence to its in vitro development. The chromosomal rearrangement of the gene for one of the knob-associated proteins has been shown to account for the loss of synthesis of this protein. How may we investigate the function of some of the erythrocyte *cytoplasmic membrane* structures, for instance, the intracytoplasmic vesicles and clefts that may be involved in cellular transport in the infected cell?

Since certain parasite-synthesized proteins are known to be localized in the infected-erythrocyte membrane, it may be possible to follow their transport from the schizont to the outer membrane by *immunocytochemistry*, a technique that can localize proteins in imbedded sections of the cell. The visualization depends on binding of an antibody directed against the specific protein of interest, tagged with an electron-dense marker such as gold or ferritin.

An example shown in Figure elsewhere in this chapter uses a monoclonal antibody directed against a *P. falciparum* rhoptry protein. This brief description of morphology indicates that many novel processes of the parasite would be interesting to study at the molecular level. How does the merozoite invade the small, rigid erythrocyte? How is development in an intracellular environment regulated?

What is the biochemical basis of the radical modification of the erythrocyte cytoskeleton? We shall discuss some of the processes in the following section.

Merozoite Invasion

Merozoite invasion of erythrocytes has long been a major interest of malaria biologists because it represents a process potentially vulnerable to inhibition by antibodies or drugs and because it is a unique event in terms of erythrocyte endocytosis. Its study can be traced to the early 1950s, when the species specificity of this interaction was first observed.

Although the mechanism of merozoite entry appears to be similar in most species, considerable evidence suggests that different plasmodial species recognize different erythrocyte surface proteins as receptors. A consequence of this specificity is that for the most part merozoites in vitro invade only erythrocytes of their natural vertebrate host.

For instance, *P. falciparum*, which infects humans and higher primates in vivo, invades only erythrocytes of humans, chimpanzees, and Aotus and Saimiri monkeys. *P. falciparum* merozoites do not invade erythrocytes of the rhesus monkey or avian erythrocytes. *P. berghei*, which causes natural infections in rodents, does not invade human erythrocytes. Such differences in host specificity must be very subtle, because many of the major erythrocyte surface proteins are highly conserved among mammals, although there are some interesting differences. Invasion requires at least two discrete steps: (1) receptor recognition and binding and (2) erythrocyte membrane deformation.

Receptor recognition: P. falciparum, P. knowlesi, and P. vivax

Initial attachment between the merozoite and the erythrocyte can involve any area of the parasite's surface, but entry proceeds only after alignment of the apical end onto the erythrocyte surface. Attachment between the apical end and the erythrocyte is through fibrils of the merozoite surface coat.

Whether the protein composition of the parasite's surface coat at the apical end differs from the rest of the surface coat is unknown. Attachment results in the formation of a tight junction between the two cells and subsequent invagination of the erythrocyte membrane. The tight junction formed moves back over the merozoite as the parasite proceeds to enter the forming parasitophorous vacuole created by the invaginating erythrocyte membrane.

The thick surface coat does not enter with the merozoite; it is sloughed off during entry and may be deposited on the erythrocyte surface. It is possible that the shedding of the surface coat is an active process, and its accumulation at the neck of the vacuole might theoretically be associated with modification in the organization of erythrocyte surface receptors. Early studies on merozoite invasion benefited from the extensive information available on the organization of the protein components of the erythrocyte membrane.

The two major surface proteins of the human erythrocyte are an anion transporter designated band 3 and glycophorin A, the most abundant in a family of related sialic acid-rich glycoproteins. The glycophorin family also consists of glycophorin B, C, and D. Glycophorin A and C, like band 3, span the lipid bilayer and therefore are said to be transmembrane.

The unique feature of the sialo-glycoproteins, which accounts for their name, is their high (30 percent) content of sialic acid. All three glycophorins are highly substituted with the O-linked tetrasaccharide of the following structure: NeuNAc 2 - 3 Gal β1- 3 (NeuNAc 2,6) GalNAc. In addition, *glycophorin* A and C contain a single N-linked *oligosacch-aride*. Considerable evidence has accumulated that *P. falciparum* merozoites depend on the glycophorins for invasion into human erythrocytes. Evidence comes from studies with abnormal erythrocytes having modified glycophorins and with enzyme-treated erythrocytes.

The N-terminal tryptic fragment of glycophorin (containing 11 O-linked tetrasaccharides) has been found to inhibit invasion, as do Fab fragments of monoclonal antibodies to glycophorin, which provides additional evidence. En(-a) erythrocytes lack glycophorin A, S-s-U cells lack glycophorin B, and Mk⁻Mk⁻ cells lack glycophorin A, B.

Tn cells lack the terminal (2 – 3) linked NeuNAc and Gal residues of the tetrasaccharide, and Cad cells contain an extra Ga1NAc residue in the tetrasaccharide. Invasion of *P. falciparum* merozoites into all these abnormal cells is considerably reduced, although it is entirely blocked only in the case of the Tn and Cad cells (in which all three glycophorins are altered).

This finding illustrates that all three glycophorins can act as receptors independently. The feature common to all glycophorins is the O-linked tetrasaccharide, and other recent data suggest that this is the critical site recognized by the merozoites. Neuraminidase and O-glycanase-treated erythrocytes are also resistant to invasion, further supporting the model for direct involvement of the carbohydrates in the binding site.

Invasion by *P. knowlesi* and *P.* vivax is normal in the glycophorin modified erythrocytes, underscoring the specificity of the interaction. Recently it has been found that variability in receptor recognition exists between different geographic isolates or strains. This finding is based on studies of invasion of seven isolates into neuraminidase- and endoglycosidase-treated erythrocytes.

Although some strains were found to be fully dependent on NeuNAc and glycophorin, in that invasion into neuraminidase and O-glycanase-treated cells was inhibited almost completely (5 percent invasion), other strains still invaded these same erythrocytes partially (25%-50%). It has been suggested that NeuNAc-independent invasion may reflect the ability of the merozoite to interact with a secondary low-affinity receptor other than glycophorin.

This receptor appears to be a trypsin-sensitive component of the erythrocyte surface and therefore could not be band 3, which is trypsin- and neuraminidase-resistant. Soon after receptor binding, a tight junction forms between the merozoite and erythrocyte. In contrast to the considerable detail known about the receptors for *P. falciparum*, information on the receptors for other species of *Plasmodium* has been elusive due in part to the difficulty in culture of these species in vitro.

The Duffy blood group antigen, a 35 – 45 kD glycoprotein, has been proposed as the receptor for both *P. knowlesi* and *P.* vivax. Neither species invades Duffy negative erythrocytes, analogous to the situation with *P. falciparum* and En(-a) erythrocytes. However, trypsin treatment of Duffy negative cells renders them susceptible to invasion by *P. knowlesi*, indicating the parasite is able to interact with a secondary receptor made available in these cells. Monoclonal antibody directed against the Duffy glycoprotein also blocks invasion by *P.* vivax.

Erythrocyte Membrane Deformation

The events that induce deformation of the erythrocyte, resulting in its invagination and ultimately in the formation of the endocytotic vacuole membrane (PVM), have not been defined. Given the rigid nature of the erythrocyte membrane and the absence of any phagocytic ability of the cell, certain key processes are thought to occur.

To appreciate these, a consideration of certain properties and components of the erythrocyte membrane is helpful. Measurements on the deformability of erythrocytes indicate that the membrane exhibits properties similar to a semisolid with considerable elastic properties. The structural components responsible for the rigid-elastic property are the proteins of the membrane-cytoskeleton network.

The major proteins of the cytoskeleton are the heterodimers of spectrin, ankyrin, band 4.1, erythrocyte actin, and band 4.9. Spectrin is linked to the major transmembrane protein band 3 by ankyrin and to the second major transmembrane protein, glycophorin A by band 4.1. These proteins form a highly ordered uninterrupted network that is extremely difficult to disrupt.

Even in erythrocyte ghosts, (hypotonically lysed cells devoid of hemoglobin) the superstructure of the membrane-cytoskeletal network is maintained. Evidence that spectrin and its interactions with the other membrane proteins are central to the control of cell shape and rigidity comes from experiments in which the organization of spectrin is modified and from studies of abnormal erythrocytes with cytoskeletal defects.

For instance, in hereditary elliptocytosis (a condition in which afflicted individuals have elliptical shaped erythrocytes) the biochemical alteration has been traced to an imbalance in the normal ratio of spectrin dimer-tetramer; more of the spectrin dimer is present in abnormal than in normal cells.

In other abnormal cells, spherocytes, there is an absolute reduction in the amount of spectrin. In still other cells, the binding of spectrin to ankyrin may be impaired. Such abnormal erythrocytes are not uncommon and could be of considerable use in elucidating the role of spectrin and other cytoskeletal proteins in merozoite invasion.

After merozoite receptor binding and junction formation, the erythrocyte membrane invaginates and forms an endocytotic cup or space while the merozoite remains attached to the neck of the forming vacuole by the tight junction.

The vacuolar membrane appears to expand rapidly until it is large enough to surround the invading merozoite. The expansion of the host membrane implies that there is probably a dramatic reorganization of the major *transmembrane* and cytoskeletal proteins spectrin and hand 3. Indeed, freeze-fracture studies of the vacuolar membrane suggest that it is free of the transmembrane proteins, indicating that proteins may migrate to the tight junction at the entrance of the vacuole, creating the protein-poor, lipid-rich region.

The critical question, however, is how this movement or *redistribution* of *erythrocyte* protein is regulated. Presumably the transmembrane proteins dissociate from the *cytoskeletal* proteins, and the individual components of the cytoskeleton are modified. We are left with no understanding of how the parasite may initiate these events. Two of several mechanisms that could account for erythrocyte membrane deformation appear the most accessible to investigate. One mechanism, similar to that described for the receptor-mediated endocytosis of virus and certain ligands, could be that binding of the merozoite to the erythrocyte receptors results in their cross-linking or capping.

The redistribution could result in disruption or uncoupling of the interactions of the transmembrane proteins with proteins of the cytoskeletal network. Capping of surface receptors in mammalian cells has been shown to be accompanied by rearrangements of the components of the cytoskeletal, which, by some unknown mechanism, regroup around the developing endocytotic vacuole and draw it into the cell cytoplasm.

Studies on merozoite invasion with abnormally shaped erythrocytes (ovalocytes) supports a model in which dissociation of cytoskeletal components is essential for invasion. The ovalocytes are resistant to invasion by *P. falciparum* and *P.* vivax. This abnormal cell is at least one-tenth as deformable as normal erythrocytes.

Specific alterations in biochemical associations between cytoskeletal membrane proteins contribute to this low deformability. Resistance to invasion may be due to an inability of the erythrocyte membrane proteins to dissociate and reorganize. Merozoites also do not invade erythrocytes fixed in low (1 percent) concentrations of glutaraldehyde.

If receptor binding induces membrane-protein reorganization, there must be proteins on the surface of the merozoite that bind with high affinity to the erythrocyte receptor. Parasite proteins that bind to the correct receptor have been identified for *P. falciparum*, *P. knowlesi*, and *P.* vivax. A second model to explain erythrocyte deformation involves the two organelles known as rhoptries and micronemes.

Since these organelles are only found in the invasive stages of the parasite, the sporozoite and merozoite, it has been assumed that they are involved in invasion. Electron micrographs and immunofluorescence micrographs can be interpreted to suggest that some material is secreted from the rhoptries into or onto the erythrocyte membrane.

The rhoptry proteins could be hydrophobic and thereby contribute to enhanced fluidity of the erythrocyte membrane. As a result, redistribution or destabilization of erythrocyte transmembrane proteins could occur. A diagram depicting a possible model of the various merozoite surface and rhoptry proteins during invasion is shown in Figure elsewhere in this chapter.

How may we examine the role of the proteins of the rhoptries and micronemes in merozoite invasion? During the course of production of monoclonal antibodies to *P. falciparum* merozoite antigens, common monoclonal antibodies that were selected in many laboratories were those directed against five proteins of the rhoptries; the proteins were 140 kD, 130 kD, 110 kD, 83 kD, and 41 kD.

The antibodies gave a characteristic immunofluorescent pattern of two punctate dots in each merozoite. By immunoelectron microscopy they have been localized to the electron-dense rhoptry organelle, as shown for the 110-kD protein in Figure elsewhere in this chapter. With use of the antibodies it should be possible to purify the rhoptry proteins by immunoaffinity chromatography.

It would then be necessary to devise a system to examine the insertion of such proteins in the erythrocyte membrane or in synthetic biomembranes containing erythrocyte-membrane proteins. Important questions should be addressed: Are the rhoptry proteins incorporated into the lipid bilayer?

Do erythrocyte-membrane proteins-band 3 and glycophorin -alter their distribution or specific interaction with each other and with cytoskeletal proteins upon incorporation of the parasite proteins? This question could be examined by assessing changes in patterns of cross-linking with chemical crosslinkers. Biochemical analysis of protein organization could also include studies of phosphorylation patterns, since

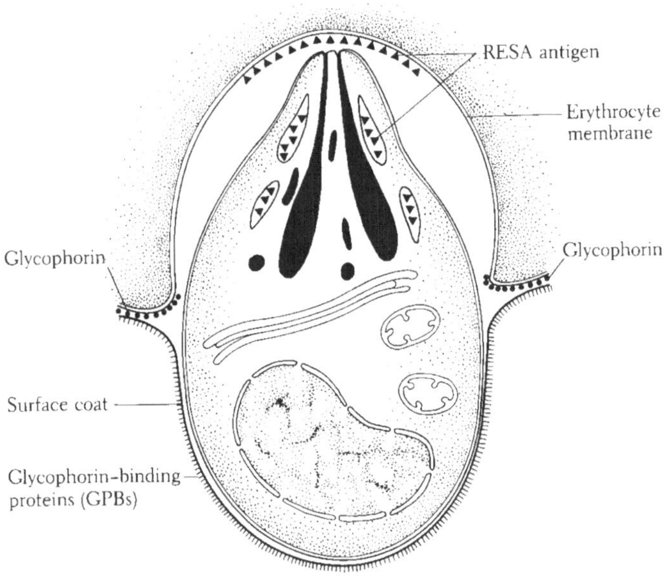

Figure 1.2: Model of merozoite protein localization during erythrocyte invasion. The glycophorin binding proteins bind to the erythrocyte receptor and remain external to the cell during invasion.

phosphokinase and phosphorylase reactions regulate interactions between spectrin and other cytoskeletal proteins. Resealed erythrocyte ghosts provide a system that may be useful in studies of invasion.

Ghosts are erythrocytes that have been hypotonically lysed and resealed. Red ghosts still contain some hemoglobin; white ghosts are devoid of hemoglobin. The amount of hemoglobin remaining after lysis depends on the procedure for lysis and resealing. During the resealing step, it is possible to include reagents that alter the internal (or cytoplasmic) face of the erythrocyte membrane.

The resealed ghosts are susceptible to merozoite invasion. Preparation and properties of erythrocyte ghosts, susceptible to invasion by the malarial parasites, have been described in detail. How may the system be used to study cytoplasmic events involved in invasion? The intraerythrocytic levels of ATP, inorganic phosphate, and intracellular CA^{++} alter the association between spectrin, actin, and other red-cell proteins.

In ghosts, it is possible to immobilize these states, whereas in intact erythrocytes, equilibrium is rapidly reestablished. In fact, reducing ATP levels in resealed ghosts was found to reduce merozoite invasion, suggesting that phosphorylation of certain membrane proteins was important to invasion. Interactions between cytoskeletal proteins and transmembrane proteins also can be modified with specific antibodies that could be included in the resealing step.

Such modifications may result in organizational changes in the external domains of transmembrane proteins (band 3 and glycophorin) that may affect merozoite invasion. Understanding merozoite invasion will eventually give us greater insight into the structural -functional relationship of erythrocyte membrane proteins.

Protein Trafficking in the Infected Erythrocyte

In all eukaryotic cells, proteins are synthesized on ribosomes present randomly in the cell cytoplasm. Shortly thereafter proteins find their way to specific subcellular organelles, the plasma membrane, or a secretory structure. Although the exact mechanisms of intracellular trafficking are not yet known, there is good evidence to suggest that coded in the protein sequence are certain peptides or other components that are specifically recognized by membranes of the organelles to which the proteins are destined to travel.

The mechanism for sorting of secretory proteins is known in considerable detail. A signal peptide on the N-terminus is recognized by a signal-recognition molecule that binds to a receptor or docking protein on the surface of the endoplasmic reticulum (ER). The emerging protein is then secreted into the lumen of the ER and eventually secreted when the ER fuses with the plasma membrane.

A consensus-signal sequence, seemingly contained in all secreted proteins, has been established, and no doubt other consensus sequences or domains that define transport to other organelles such as mitochondria and lysozomes will also be found. In the erythrocyte infected with a developing malarial parasite, parasite proteins are inserted into the developing membranes of the schizont.

It is not difficult to imagine the information needed for export to this membrane, because the route would be similar to that in a free-living eukaryotic cell. However, proteins are located in the space between the schizont membrane and the PVM, and as the PVM expands, parasite proteins are no doubt inserted into this membrane as well.

Such a protein may have two signal peptides, one to export it to the outside of the schizont and one to recognize the PVM, or it may have a hybrid signal that is sufficient to direct it to the second membrane. When a protein is translocated through the PVM, through the erythrocyte cytoplasm, and then inserted into the erythrocyte membrane or secreted, the signal sequences must be much more complex.

Do such proteins have three or more signal peptides, with each one recognized at each membrane for translocation, or is there a single hybrid signal sequence that guarantees its final destination? Clearly these are questions of interest to scientists working on intracellular trafficking.

In very few systems is there such complex trafficking as in the plasmodium-infected erythrocyte, and through study of this system we may learn some important principles governing protein recognition with respect to organelle and membrane biogenesis. As yet only a few specific parasite proteins have been unequivocally localized by microscopy to the erythrocyte membrane and none have been identified in the PVM.

These are the knob-associated proteins of 80-100 kD and a protein called MESA (merozoite-infected erythrocyte surface antigen) of 300 kD. However, there is indirect evidence that many parasite proteins probably exist in both membranes.

By comparing sequences or tertiary structures of such proteins, we may be able to identify peptides or domains responsible for their export from the schizont and translocation across the vacuole space or erythrocyte cytoplasm.

Modification of Erythrocyte Structure and Function

Few alterations in the host-cell ultrastructure or function that occurs after the merozoite invades the erythrocyte have been identified. The density of the ring-infected erythrocyte, its morphology, and its deformability are almost indistinguishable from that of the uninfected cell. About 12 to 16 hours after invasion, when the ring stage begins to transform to the trophozoite stage, certain events occur.

Parasite enzymes that specifically degrade hemoglobin are present. Since hemoglobin is the main source of amino acids for the developing schizont, it is very important to understand this pathway in detail. At the end of the intraerythrocytic stage, almost all the host hemoglobin has been digested. Major changes have been described in the activity of ion transporters of the erythrocyte membrane as the parasite develops from a trophozoite to a schizont. Ca^{++} levels are increased 25-fold in *P.* chabaudi-infected cells, possibly the result of an altered Ca^{++}-ATPase in the erythrocyte membrane.

There also may be newly synthesized Ca^{++} transporters inserted into the PVM. The presence of parasite-coded or -dependent transporters for monosaccharides and transferrin has also been reported. No new or modified transporters have been isolated or their protein structure analyzed in any detail, although they could represent model systems to examine membrane protein topogenesis. Theoretically, some might be targets for novel approaches to *chemotherapy*. Probably the most dramatic change in the infected erythrocyte is the change in cell shape and deformability.

The regular discoid shape and smooth surface of the normal erythrocyte is lost and the cell assumes an irregular shape with large protrusions, not unlike a sack of potatoes. It is assumed that the rigid erythrocyte cytoskeletal membrane network is radically altered. This is true of cells infected with all species of *Plasmodia* regardless of whether they do or do not synthesize knob structures or caveolae.

One consequence of the decreased deformability is enhanced filtration in the splenic red pulp. What is the origin of these modifications? Does the parasite secrete proteases that cleave the cytoskeleton proteins? Does the parasite synthesize proteins that bind to erythrocyte membrane proteins and disrupt their organization?

Perhaps only in virus-transformed mammalian cells are such dramatic reorganizations of the existing cell structures observed. The molecular explanation of the modifications may be relevant to general questions of maintenance of cell shape and morphology. How may we study these interactions?

It may be possible to mimic the morphological changes by treating erythrocytes with reagents known to alter cytoskeletal or membrane protein interactions. Alternatively, the cytoskeleton from infected cells can be extracted with minimum perturbations, and the altered associations can be characterized by classical methodologies.

In *P. falciparum* - infected erythrocytes a major modification of the erythrocyte membrane is the appearance of knob structures, electron dense plaques on the cytoplasmic side of the membrane. Two parasite-synthesized proteins have been localized to the knobs.

Sequestration of infected erythrocytes in the postcapillary venules is mediated by adherence of the erythrocyte surface located over the knob. The cell-cell adhesion appears to involve specific proteins on both the surface of the infected erythrocyte and the endothelial cell. An 88 kD glycoprotein recognized by the monoclonal antibody OKM5 has been suggested as possible endothelial cell surface receptor involved in adherence.

A corresponding protein on the infected erythrocyte surface, a so-called cytoadherence antigen, has been somewhat elusive to define, although antibody inhibition of endothelial cell adhesion by immune serum was found to be strain-specific, suggesting such a molecule is antigenically variant. Antibodies against the 80 kD and 300 kD proteins of knobs do not inhibit cytoadherence, suggesting they are not directly involved in binding.

In Vitro Cultivation of P. falciparum Asexual Stages

Many of the experiments proposed earlier can be performed with *P. falciparum* cultured in vitro. The practicality of using in vitro-cultured parasites rather than parasites taken from infected animals is becoming increasingly clear. The successful cultivation of *P. falciparum* in vitro was first reported in 1976, and most laboratories now use this method with minor modifications.

Low oxygen tension is an important condition for cultivation. The parasite is cultured in human erythrocytes in a simple medium with 10 percent human serum. It is possible to culture 20 - 30 ml of erythrocytes at a time, generally 8% -15 % of which are parasite-infected, so that after concentration with gelatin, approximately 1 ml (5×10^9 cells) of schizont-infected erythrocytes can be obtained.

For some unknown reason, a parasite density greater than 20 percent in in vitro cultures is difficult to maintain. Parasite proteins or lipids can readily be labeled with radioactive amino acids or other metabolites by including these in the medium. Erythrocytes, which have no proteinsynthesizing machinery, will not incorporate the label.

There have been reports on the culture of other species of *Plasmodium*, *P. berghei* and *P. knowlesi*, although *P. falciparum* is still the most popular culture system. To date there has been no successful long-term culture of *P.* vivax, another important species that infects humans. This has retarded aspects of research on the cell biology of *P.* vivax, but with the availability of cDNA libraries, it has been possible to sequence some of the important antigens of this species.

It is not understood why other species, such as *P.* vivax, do not grow in vitro under the conditions established for *P. falciparum.* This problem may be interesting to investigate, although past failures by other workers should be thoroughly sorted out before an attempt is made to initiate such a project.

Another advantage of in vitro cultivation is that it is possible to synchronize the various stages, for example, rings, trophozoites, and schizonts, and identify when specific proteins are expressed.

Isolation of P. falciparum Merozoites

The in vitro culture technique has also made possible the collection of viable *P. falciparum* merozoites. Although it was relatively easy to obtain infectious *P.* knowlesi merozoites from short-term cultures of parasites taken from an infected monkey, the shorter viability time of the *P. falciparum* merozoite (estimated to be 60 minutes) made similar studies with this species difficult. The *isolation* of viable *P. falciparum* merozoites was dependent on the ability to obtain synchronous cultures in which a high percentage of *schizont-infected* cells burst simultaneously.

In the first such method reported, highly synchronous cultures were produced by repeated cycles of concentrations of schizont-infected cells with gelatin, then the most mature population were allowed to reinvade in a short period (4-6 hours), and nonreleased schizonts were lysed with sorbitol. When merozoite release began, mature schizont-infected erythrocytes and uninfected erythrocytes were removed by low-speed centrifugation (600 g) and merozoites in the supernatant were collected by centrifugation at 2000 g.

It was estimated that 25 percent of the schizont population released merozoites in a 2-hour period. A maximum of 2-5 $\times$ 10^9 merozoites could be obtained in 1 hour from 2 ml of parasitized blood, although only 10 percent of these were infective. Several methods now exist for the isolation of spontaneously released *P. falciparum* merozoites from culture, and the modifications have resulted in greatly increased yields.

One method for collecting spontaneously released merozoites over a long period involves the use of a nylon membrane seive to remove debris and schizontinfected cell membranes. Merozoites were collected in the supernatant from concentrated cultures over a 6-hour period. Schizonts were removed from culture by lowspeed centrifugation (200 g).

The supernatant, containing merozoites, broken membranes, and *hemoglobin*, was filtered through an acrylic nylon membrane sieve (3 μm pore size) and then a membrane of 1.2 μm pore size. The effluent containing the *merozoites* was centrifuged at 3000 g for 10 minutes. From cultures containing 5 $\times$ 10^9 schizont-infected erythrocytes, 10^{10} merozoites were released and over 70 percent were recovered. The infectivity of the merozoites was estimated to be 80 percent.

For certain types of studies on invasion, it has been and will continue to be preferable to start with isolated merozoites rather than mature schizonts. In studies with free merozoites, problems that arise because of the toxic effects of reagents on the mature schizont are eliminated. It is anticipated that any biophysical studies on the erythrocyte membrane during merozoite invasion will require merozoites, since it is only with merozoites that one can obtain a tightly synchronous invasion.

However, if we want to detect biochemical and biophysical changes in the erythrocyte membrane during invasion, it will be necessary to have highly efficient invasion rates to permit measurement of subtle parameters of invasion.

This will require large-scale production of invasive merozoites. The rapid loss of viability is the major obstacle to overcome, and establishing procedures to stabilize or preserve released merozoites will be helpful.

THE SEXUAL CYCLE

Gametocyte Development and Culture

The gametocyte is the stage that links the asexual blood stages of the vertebrate host to the sexual stages of the mosquito. For reasons that are not understood, during the course of an infection, a certain percentage of asexual ring stages will not develop to form *schizonts* but will form *mature* male or female gametocytes that are infectious to the mosquito.

First observed in vitro in 1976, the process of gametocytogenesis occurs in in vitro cultures; development from rings to mature infective gametocytes requires 12-14 days. A small proportion of parasites develop into gametocytes at any given time. Strains differ in their propensity for gametocytogenesis in vitro; some strains rarely produce *gametocytes* in culture. *Supplementation* of the media for cultivation of the asexual blood stages with cyclic AMP or hypoxanthine promotes *gametocytogenesis* to variable degrees in different strains.

Gametocytes produced in vitro are capable of completing the sexual cycle; mosquitoes fed on gametocyte-containing cultures produce sporozoites infectious to chimpanzees and Aotus monkeys. Various attempts have been made to improve the efficiency of the in vitro culture of gametocytes, to produce sufficient numbers of cells for biochemical and *immunological* studies.

Two problems exist. One is to induce asexual stages to switch to gametocytes; the second is to promote gametocyte maturation. Once mature gametocytes have been produced, it is a relatively straightforward process to induce *gamete*, *zygote*, and *ookinete* formation.

A recent development using a semiautomated static culture may prove to be the most dependable system yet for the production of gametocytes. This system relies on propagation under prolonged uninterrupted periods of growth in the appropriate gas levels and temperature: 3 percent O_2, 4 percent CO_2, 93 percent N_2 at 37°C.

In this system, the number of gametocyte-infected erythrocytes can reach about 1 percent, or about 50 percent of the total parasite (sexual and asexual stage) -infected cells. It is possible that exposure to ambient temperatures and gases inhibits transformation.

Some isolates are better gametocyte producers than others, a fact that may be related to the density of the asexual stages from which they are derived; high densities of asexual stages appear to be correlated with low levels of gametocyte production. It is possible that conditions favourable to the asexual stages are unfavourable to gametocytes or that adverse conditions unfavourable to the blood stage induce gametocyte formation.

When human serum is replaced with fetal bovine serum, an increase in infective oocyst formation or gametocyte formation is observed. Clearly the development of a dependable system for the production of large numbers of gametocytes in culture will be of great value. Major questions to be studied concern signals that regulate gene expression during gametocytogenesis and expression of male and female specific genes.

Gamete Development

While still in the bloodstream of the infected host, the gametocyte will not develop further. After reaching maturity, 10-14 days after invasion of the erythrocyte, it is fully infectious to mosquitoes. If not ingested it probably disintegrates, which may be the reason antibodies directed against gamete antigens are sometimes found in infected individuals.

Gametocyte production in the host is thought to be staggered, which would increase the chances of a mosquito being infected at the appropriate stage for further development. Immediately upon being ingested by the mosquito, the gametocyte undergoes rapid transformation. In a process known as exflagellation, the mature gametocyte sheds the red cell membrane, and the macrogamete (female) and microgametocyte (male) are liberated in the mosquito midgut.

The *microgametocyte* completes exflagellation by dividing into eight motile microgametes. The microgamete then fuses with a macrogamete to form the zygote. Exflagellation and fertilization can be controlled in vitro: by the regulation of the temperature and the pH of medium to between 7.7 and 8.0, it was possible to ensure complete exflagellation production in *P. gallinaceum.*

The media used for transformation contained 10 millimole (mM) Tris, 15 5 mM NaCl, 10 mM glucose, and 25 mM $NaHCO_3$ pH 8.0.

Gamete production was reduced if $NaHCO_3$ was not included in the buffer. Similar conditions induced gametogenesis in *P. falciparum.* Fertilization to form the zygote takes place immediately (10-20 min) after exflagellation.

Fertilization has been described in detail in many electron microscopic studies, but little is known of the biochemical events governing fusion. Several methods exist for the separation of the large macrogametes and zygotes from the smaller microgametes. One method involves layering the blood on a Hypaque-Ficoll gradient and centrifuging for 10 minutes at 10,000g. Others have used metrizamide gradients or wheat germ agglutinin (lectin) chromatography to select macrogametes.

Ookinete Development

Conditions supporting the in vitro transformation of the fertilized zygote to the ookinete have been established for *P. gallinaceum.* Zygotes were incubated in Medium 199 supplemented with 17 mM dextran, 25 mM $NaHCO_3$, and 0.7 mM L-glutamine, plus antibiotics. After 24 hours, fully mature ookinetes were observed. These could be separated from unfertilized female gametes by centrifugation on a Hypaque/Ficoll gradient; mature *ookinetes*, being more dense, were collected in the pellet fraction.

However, this step represents the end of the line for the in vitro cultivation of plasmodia. The last remaining link in the cycle, that of the development of the ookinete to the oocyst to the sporozoite, has not been established yet in culture. As a consequence, little is known of the biochemical steps involved.

As the zygote develops it becomes a motile ookinete, which penetrates the intestinal wall of the mosquito. This interaction has been studied morphologically but not biochemically. The ookinete develops into an oocyst when it reaches the outer layer of the wall, the basement membrane.

The factors triggering ookinesis are unknown. The ookinete is similar in structure to the merozoites and sporozoite, having a double plasma membrane with a truncated cone-shaped apical end, except that it does not have rhoptries. The ookinete migrates through the epithelial cell layer, possibly between cells.

There is no biochemical description of migration of the ookinete through the gut wall to the basement membrane and development to an oocyst. Initially the oocyst is a single cell surrounded by a double membrane, with a single nucleus. Nuclear division occurs, and as the oocyst grows, vacuoles appear to form large clefts.

The clefts subdivide the cytoplasm to form sporoblasts, which give rise to sporozoites, in a manner morphologically similar to the development of merozoites from schizonts.

Identification of Surface Antigens of Sexual Stages

The availability of the in vitro system for production of *P. gallinaceum* gametes in culture has made possible the identification of their surface proteins and that of the fertilized zygote and ookinete. By immunizing rabbits with gametes and zygotes, antibodies against the surface antigens were obtained and found to block zygote formation, principally by binding to the gamete surface.

Monoclonal antibodies blocking development of *P. gallinaceum* midgut stages were produced and found to immunoprecipitate antigens of 240 kD, 56 kD, and 54 kD present on both male and female gametes and zygotes. Other proteins of 48 kD, 19 kD, and 17 kD were on female gametes only, and a protein of 28 kD was on male gametes only.

As zygotes undergo transformation to ookinetes, these proteins are shed from the parasite surface. Two new proteins of 28 kD and 26 kD appear on the ookinete surface; the 26 kD protein is immunoprecipitated by monoclonal antibodies that block ookinesis. The molecular events that regulate gametocytogenesis and fertilization of the micro- and macrogamete are of considerable importance but little understood.

Now that reliable in vitro culture systems are available, this question should be more accessible to investigate. Another problem that has received little attention is the migration of the ookinete through the mosquito gut mucosal cells. This could be examined by devising the appropriate endothelial-cell culture system and examining migration in vitro. Since each of these steps represents a stage for blocking parasite development, they all would be worthwhile for further study.

2

ENTAMOEBA HISTOLYTICA

Entamoeba histolytica is an enteric protozoan infecting 10 percent of the world's population, resulting in approximately 50 million cases of invasive colitis or liver abscess and 50,000 to 100,000 deaths per year. Considering that *E. histolytica* is the third leading parasitic cause of death, behind malaria and schistosomiasis, most scientists focus their efforts on the aspects of cell biology, biochemistry, and host immune response most relevant to understanding how this organism causes disease and the development of strategies to prevent it. This chapter will do the same.

EPIDEMIOLOGY AND CLINICAL DISEASE SYNDROMES

Infection with *E. histolytica* is acquired by ingestion of the acid-resistant cyst form, with a single cyst being a potentially infective dose. Transmission of amebic infection occurs by any means that allows fecal-oral *contamination*. Examples are fecal contamination of water supplies or food, poor levels of hygiene in the *institutionalized* mentally retarded population, oral-anal sexual practices, or infected food preparers with poor hygienic standards.

In the vast majority of individuals, infection of the large bowel by *E. histolytica* does not result in invasive disease as manifested by symptomatic colonic ulceration, a serum *antiamebic* antibody response, or liver abscess. The fraction of infected individuals who suffer from amebiasis is not uniform throughodut the world. In Mexico City up to

25 percent of infected individuals have symptomatic invasive disease, a figure probably 25 times greater than the incidence of colitis or liver abscess in infected sexually active male homosexuals in New York City, San Francisco, or London.

The parasite and host factors that determine the occurrence of amebic invasion are unclear and an area of great interest and controversy. Apparently, most individuals spontaneously eradicate noninvasive *E. histolytica* infection over a period of 6 to 12 months.

It is unknown if clearance of asymptomatic amebic infection is followed by host resistance to rechallenge; it probably is not, as there is an increasing prevalence of intestinal infection with increasing age, in contrast to infection with *Giardia lamblia*, where prevalence peaks at age 1- 5 years and then declines. Invasive colonic disease usually presents with bloody diarrhea and abdominal pain, and less often with fever. The parasite is found in flask-shaped ulcerations penetrating down to muscle tissue.

Amebae can form localized chronic lesions (amebomas) or can present in a fulminant form with total colonic involvement. An indolent presentation of amebiasis is very difficult to diagnose and can persist for years. Amebic liver *abscess* is actually a misnomer, as the so-called abscess is filled with proteinaceous debris rather than pus (*polymorphonuclear* cells). The *amebae* are found at the periphery of the lesion; multiple lesions are frequently seen. Patients who develop liver abscess usually do so within 3 months of acquisition of intestinal infection.

Interestingly, less than 20 percent of individuals have *E. histolytica* within their intestine when they manifest symptoms of a liver abscess, and they usually do not develop antiamebic serum antibodies until they have had symptoms for 7 days. How the parasite penetrates the gut and gains access to the portal venous system and the liver without immediately causing symptoms or eliciting a host humoral response is a mystery.

Life Cycle and Phylogeny

In the life cycle of *E. histolytica*, the infective cyst form can reside outside the host for weeks to months, depending on environmental conditions. After ingestion, excystation occurs in the small bowel. The factors that induce *excystation* are not totally defined; in vitro excystation requires low oxygen tension, inorganic salts, and appropriate osmotic conditions for culture of trophozoites.

A mature *quadranucleate* cyst forms a metacystic stage, and eight trophozoites result after cytoplasmic division. The *trophozoite* resides exclusively in the large bowel; again, apparently most often as a *comme-*

nsal organism. Invasion is limited to the *trophozoite* form; alternatively, the parasite can encyst with excretion of up to 45 million cysts per day per individual. The cyst wall contains chitin (a glucosamine and N-acetyl-D-glucosamine polymer) as shown by intense staining with the fluorescent dye Calcofluor M_2R and binding by glucosamine-recognizing plant lectins, such as wheat germ agglutinin.

A potential strategy for interrupting the life cycle of E. *histolytica* is use of chitin synthase inhibitors such as Polyoxin D and Nikomycin, which are structural analogs of the chitin precursor UDP-N-*acetylglucosamine*. Entamoeba *histolytica* belongs to the family *Entamoebidae* of the order Amoebida in the subphylum Sarcodina of the pseudopod-forming protozoan superclass Rhizopoda. Within the genus *Entamoeba* are two recognized species that infect the large bowel of humans, *E. histolytica* and *Entamoeba hartmanni;* other *Entamoeba* include *E. moshkovskii*, E. *invadens, E. terrapinae, E. knowlesi, E. aulostomi, and* E. *gingivalis*.

At present, taxonomy of *Entamoebae* is based on morphology, in vitro growth characteristics, virulence, antigenic distinctness, amino acid content, drug susceptibility, and host specificity. The degree of DNA hybridization or sequence homology between species has not been determined. A presently controversial area is the use of isoenzyme analysis to identify *E. histolytica* strains with distinct pathogenic abilities. Starch gel electrophoresis of *E. histolytica* of clinical isolates, with associated bacterial flora, from patients with invasive amebiasis has been found to have characteristic mobility patterns for hexokinase, *phosphoglucomutase*, L-malate, $NADP^+$ oxidoreductase, and glucose phosphate isomerase when compared to amebae cultured from asymptomatic individuals who have noninvasive intestinal infection.

Some investigators interpret this data to indicate distinct pathogenic and nonpathogenic strains of *E. histolytica* and to indicate that individuals infected with nonpathogenic strains are not at future risk for invasive amebiasis and do not pose a risk to others. I believe there are insufficient data to support this assumption.

The long-term follow-up of individuals with "nonpathogenic" infection has been inadequate, cross-infection with stability of zymodeme pattern has not been evaluated, and recent studies with a closed nonpathogenic isolate demonstrated changes in zymodeme to a pathogenic pattern during in vitro association of the ameba with irradiated bacterial flora obtained from a patient who had *amebic colitis*.

The utility of zymodeme analysis and designation of strain

specificity awaits rigorous studies of DNA homology and a more complete understanding of the molecular regulation of parasite pathogenicity.

Structure

E. histolytica trophozoites are 10 to 60 micrometers (μm) long and contain a single nucleus of 3 - 5 μm; cysts average 12 μm with one to four nuclei, which are morphologically identical to the nucleus of the trophozoite. The nuclei contain chromatin granules that are evenly distributed on the interior of the nuclear membrane.

Trophozoite cytoplasm contains numerous vacuoles; amebae that are highly virulent in vivo or cytopathogenic in vitro have a greater degree of vacuolization. Cysts contain glycogen granules or aggregates that stain with iodine and chromatoidal bars, rounded rod-shaped masses of ribosomes.

Scanning and transmission electron microscopy reveal that E. *histolytica* trophozoites have a surface glycocalyx that binds Concanavalin A and ruthenium red. At the uroid area extension of multiple filopodia is noted. The cell ribosomes within exist in a free or aggregated form; the typical Golgi apparatus is absent, and it is unclear how the parasite processes proteins.

Microfilament cytoskeletal structures have been identified; the gene for actin is the first and presently the only gene cloned from *E. histolytica*. Trophozoites rapidly aggregate and "*cap*" attached Concanavalin A or antiamebic antibodies; *microfilament* inhibitors such as cytochalasin D prevent surface "capping." Mitosis has not been observed in *E. histolytica* despite numerous studies of in vitro cultivated organisms.

Pathogenicity

Pathogenesis can be defined as the origination and development of a disease. The concepts of disease causation by *E. histolytica* include (1) colonization of the gut by a virulent amebic strain with adherence to the intestinal mucus layer, (2) disruption of intestinal barriers by enzymes or toxic products, and (3) lysis of intestinal cells and host inflammatory cells, leading to mucosal interruption, colonic ulcers, and deep-tissue and/or distant-organ (liver) invasion.

INTESTINAL COLONIZATION AND *E. HISTOLYTICA* ADHERENCE MECHANISMS

Intestinal infection with *E. histolytica* is species specific, with humans and Old World primates the only reservoir for natural infection. Although various animal models have been studied, including those of

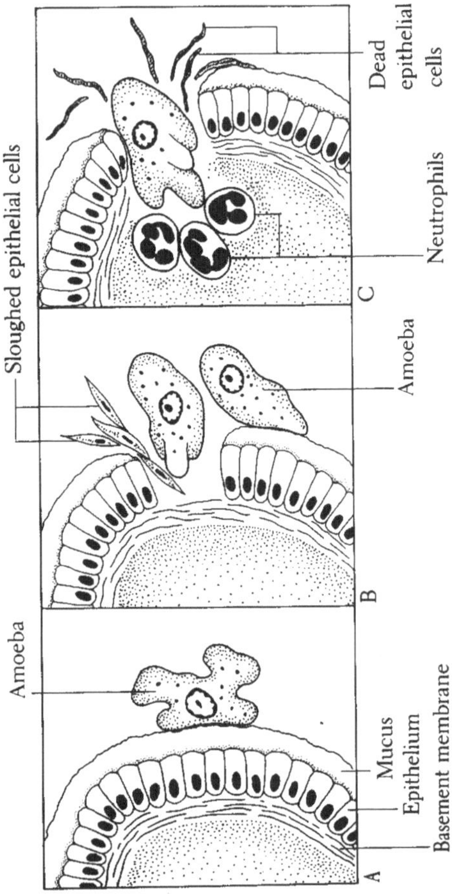

Figure 2.1: Pathogenesis of invasive amebiasis. Discrete steps in the disease pathogenesis include adherence to the intestinal mucus barrier (A), depletion of the mucus layer and disruption of the integrity of the intestinal mucosa (B), penetration of the trophozoite with lysis of adherent epithelial cells and responding host inflammatory cells (C).

dogs, cats, rats, guinea pigs, and gerbils, no model of intestinal disease directly parallels the course of human disease, that is, ingestion of trophozoites, followed by colonic disease, encystation, and transmission.

Host species specificity may be related to intrinsic *amebic* properties (i.e., *adherence proteins*) or to such host factors as intestinal microflora and colonic redox potential. Younger age increases susceptibility of animals to infection with axenic trophozoites, a finding that is consistent with the rapidly fatal invasive *amebiasis* reported in infants.

The mechanisms underlying increased pathogenicity in younger animals are unclear; perhaps host factors (e.g., secretory antibody, intestinal mucosal changes) are important. During *intraluminal* intestinal infection there is a close association and probable nutritional dependence of *E. histolytica* on the gut bacterial *flora*.

In models of intestinal disease the in vivo virulence of *E. histolytica* depends on the presence of viable bacteria. As previously summarized, recent experiments suggest that in vitro association of *E. histolytica* trophozoites with bacteria from a human host with invasive colonic amebiasis results in a change of pathogenic phenotype.

The mechanisms by which bacteria alter parasite pathogenicity are unclear. Bacteria with mannose-binding substances on their cell surface adhere to and are ingested by trophozoites; amebae also adhere to non-mannose-binding bacterial species opsonized with specific antibacterial antibody.

In addition, *E. histolytica* trophozoites adhere to and ingest nonopsonized bacteria that contain galactose or N-acetyl-D-galactosamine (GalNAc) residues on their surface, such as *Escherichia coli* 055 or *Salmonella greenside* 050. An increase in the in vitro virulence of axenic *E. histolytica trophozoites* follows their brief (30-minute) incubation with live adherent bacteria.

Bacteria inactivated by heating, fixed in glutaraldehyde, or exposed to inhibitors of protein synthesis do not augment parasite cytopathogenicity or in vivo virulence; in addition, metronidazole inhibits bacterium-mediated augmentation of virulence. One possible explanation for this *phenomenon* is that bacteria function as scavengers of *oxidized* molecules and stimulate the *parasite's* electron transport system.

Whether bacteria induce gene switching or alter mRNA transcription or translation in *E. histolytica* is unknown. Bacteria may also lower the oxidation-reduction potential in the gut lumen, thereby facilitating amebic growth and pathogenicity. In sequentially studied animal models, *E. histolytica* trophozoites adhere to the colonic mucosa before invasion. Colonic biopsies of patients have demonstrated amebae in the bowel lumen or adherent to the mucus layer.

Depletion of the colonic mucus layer is apparently necessary for amebic penetration to the epithelial barrier. In vitro studies of adherence of *E. histolytica* trophozoites to target cells, colonic mucosal-organ culture preparations, and purified colonic mucins have identified the relevant parasite adherence molecule.

A galactose or N-acetyl-D-galactosamine (Gal/GaINAc)-inhibitable E. *histolytica* lectin mediates in vitro adherence. Millimolar concentrations of galactose or GalNAc, but not numerous other monosaccharides, inhibit adherence of axenic trophozoites to Chinese hamster ovary (CHO) cells. The galactose terminal glycoprotein, asialoorosomucoid (ASOR), is more effective than asialofetuin and 1000-fold more effective than

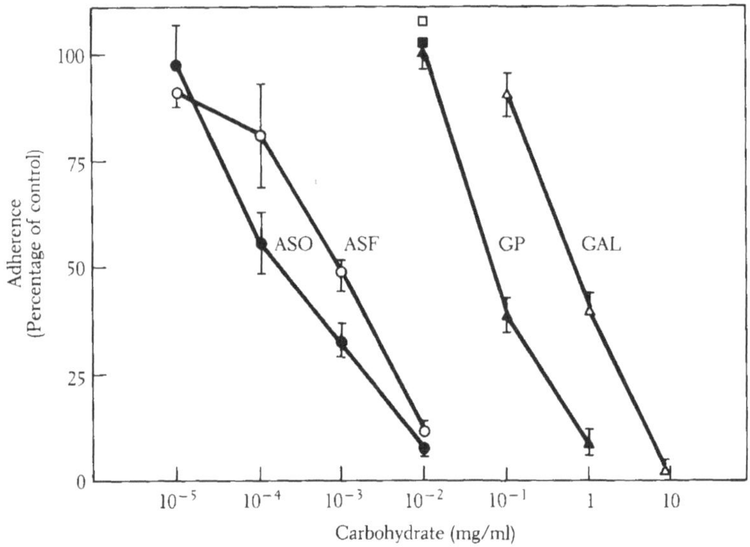

Figure 2.2: Carbohydrate inhibition of amebic adherence to target cells. Adherence was expressed as percentage of adherence in paired studies performed in control medium (where 60 percent of amebae had at least three adherent CHO cells upon suspension of the pellet by vortexing).

galactose in inhibiting amebic adherence to CHO cells. The amebic Gal/GalNAc lectin also mediates parasite adherence to erythrocytes, mononuclear cells, and numerous other mammalian cells in tissue culture and to opsonized bacteria or bacteria with galactose-containing lipopolysaccharide.

Adherence of [^{3}H]thymidine-labeled axenic *E. histolytica* trophozoites to fixed rat and human colonic mucosa in vitro is specifically inhibited by GalNAc, galactose, and asialofetuin and human (10%) and rabbit (5%) immune sera, but not control sera. GalNAc also inhibits adherence of amebae to unfixed rat submucosa.

Therefore, the amebic Gal/GalNAc lectin mediates adherence to the colonic mucosa and submucosa; antiam-ebic antibodies are inhibitory, suggesting that gut antiamebic sIgA could have a protective role. The isolation of the *E. histolytica* Gal/GalNAc-inhibitable adherence protein was accomplished by producing adherence inhibitory monoclonal antibodies and taking advantage of the protein's carbohydrate-binding properties.

When ^{35}S-methionine metabolically labeled amebic proteins from a culture filtrate or detergent-solubilized (octylglucoside) trophozoites are applied to an ASOR affinity column and the column is washed, a peak of ^{35}S activity can be eluted with galactose. SDS-PAGE of the eluate under reducing conditions with autoradiography demonstrates 35- and 170-kilodalton (kD) metabolically labeled amebic proteins.

The purifed galactose binding protein was confirmed to be the *E. histolytica* Gal/GaINAc adherence lectin by three procedures: (1) application of ^{35}S methionine metabolically labeled amebic proteins to an adherence inhibitory monoclonal antibody-affinity column results in elution of the same amebic proteins, (2) the most adherence-inhibitory monoclonal antibody, F- 14, exclusively recognizes by immunoblotting the 170-kD protein purified by ASO affinity chromatography, and lastly, (3) the Gal/GaINAc lectin purified by H8-5 immunoaffinity chromatography binds to CHO cells in a galactose-specific manner and competitively inhibits subsequent adherence by viable amebae.

In addition, polyclonal antibodies produced by immunization with immunoaffinity-purified lectin specifically recognize the 170-kD lectin subunit on immunoblotting and completely inhibit parasite in vitro adherence to CHO cells. As will be discussed, the Gal/GaINAc lectin is the major antigen recognized by human immune serum, further supporting its central role in pathogenicity.

Surface expression of the Gal/GaINAc adherence lectin depends on parasite protein synthesis rather than on recirculation through an acid pH endocytic vesicle system. The lectin is also the major protein released from viable trophozoites in vitro.

The secreted and membrane-associated forms of the Gal/GaINAc lectin account for 26 percent of secreted and 6 percent of total metabolically labeled amebic proteins, as determined by SDS-PAGE, autoradiography, and laser densitometry. A lectin subunit structure has been identified: 3 5- and 170-kD metabolically labeled proteins are present only when immunoaffinity-purifed lectin is subject to SDS-PAGE under reducing conditions (BME); under nonreducing conditions the lectin has an approximate mobility on SDS-PAGE of 260 kD.

The 170-kD heavy subunit mediates attachment, as indicated by its exclusive recognition by adherence inhibitory monoclonal and polyclonal antibodies; the function of the nonimmunogenic 35-kD light subunit is unknown. The relevant high-affinity receptors for the *E. histolytica* Gal/Ga1NAc lectin are human colonic mucins. Colonic mucins are rich in galactose and Ga1NAc; purified human and rat colonic mucins have been found to inhibit amebic adherence to CHO cells and to homologous rat colonic epithelial cells.

Oxidation and enzymatic cleavage of the mucins' galactose and GalNAc residues abrogate its inhibitory activity. The binding of iodinated rat colonic mucins to axenic *E. histolytica* trophozoites is galactose-specific, saturable, reversible, and pH-dependent. Analysis of ^{125}Imucins binding to *E. histolytica* trophozoites by the nonlinear least-square technique, assuming a mucin molecular weight of 9×10^5 daltons (D), reveals 2.8×10^3 binding sites per ameba with a dissociation constant (kD) of 8.2×10^{-11}.

The low number of apparent binding sites is undoubtedly due to cross-linking of multiple lectin molecules by the large mucin species. A monoclonal antibody (F-14) specific for the 170-kD heavy subunit of the Gal/GalNAc adherence lectin completely inhibits the binding of rat ^{125}1-mucins to amebae. Finally, rat mucins bound to a solid support can affinity-purify the amebic lectin from parasite-conditioned medium.

Therefore, colonic mucin glycoproteins act as an important host defense by binding to the *E. histolytica* Gal/GalNAc adherence lectin, thereby preventing amebic attachment to and cytolysis of host epithelial cells. However, adherence to colonic mucins may facilitate intestinal colonization by amebae; inhibition by antilectin secretory IgA antibody could be a potent host defense against *E. histolytica* luminal infection.

An additional amebic lectin has also been described, but its role in pathogenesis is less well defined. Hemagglutinating activity in sonicates of E. *histolytica* is active at acid pH (5.7 and not 7.2) and best inhibited

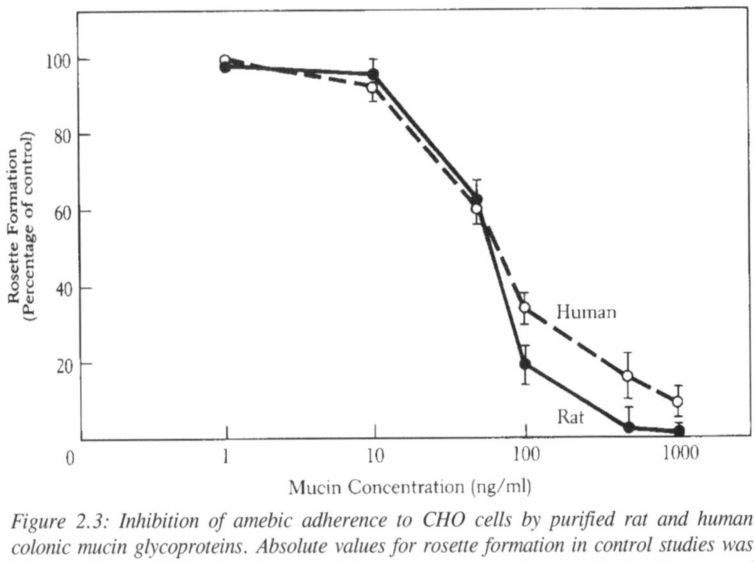

Figure 2.3: Inhibition of amebic adherence to CHO cells by purified rat and human colonic mucin glycoproteins. Absolute values for rosette formation in control studies was 77 ± 5.55%. At ? 50 ng/ml, there was inhibition of amebae adherence, P <.001 compared with control for each.

by the trimer or tetramer of N-acetyl-D-glucosamine (chitotriose). This chitotriose-inhibitable lectin was recently isolated by sepharose 4B chromatography and electroelution from SDS-PAGE. The purified 220-kD protein agglutinates human erythrocytes in a chitotriose-inhibitable manner and competes with binding of trophozoites to monolayers of MDCK cells.

Monoclonal and polyclonal antibodies raised to the purified chitotriose lectin bind to the surface of viable trophozoites, but only partially inhibit amebic adherence to erythrocytes or MDCK cells. It is important to note that although galactose or GalNAc can completely inhibit amebic adherence to CHO cells at 4°C, these monosaccharides do not prevent parasite phagocytosis of viable target cells.

The possibility that additional parasite surface molecules are involved in phagocytosis is strongly supported by studies of monoclonal antibodies selected by their ability to inhibit *E. histolytica* erythrophagocytosis. These antibodies recognize a 112-kD amebic protein on immunoblotting; this putative *E. histolytica* adherence protein has not been further characterized.

E. HISTOLYTICA SECRETORY ENZYMES AND TOXINS

Numerous proteolytic enzymes have been isolated from E. *histolytica*, all of which are inhibited by serum and may require direct parasite contact for release onto host tissue. Hyaluronidase activity has been demonstrated in multiple strains of *E. histolytica*; however, enzyme activity is not correlated with pathogenicity. Other enzyme activities of both pathogenic and nonpathogenic invasive strains include trypsin, pepsin, gelatinase, and hydrolytic enzymes for casein, fibrin, and hemoglobin, all of which are seruminhibited.

E. histolytica has a cathepsin B proteinase of 16 kD, pH 5.0 optimum, which is inhibited by serum f-2 macroglobulin, and has a reversible cell-releasing cytopathic effect on tissue culture cells. As is typical of cysteine proteinases, its activity for specific substrates is inhibited by p-chloromercuribenzoate.

Two axenic strains (HMI and Rahman) were found to have more proteinase activity per milligram of amebic protein than three other less virulent strains (HK-9 and Entamoeba-like Laredo and Huff strains). *E. histolytica* contains a serum-inhibitable collagenase activity with greater specificity for type I than type III collagen. Collagenase activity can be demonstrated only when amebae make direct contact with collagen substrate.

Collagen-lytic activity has correlated with reported virulence in three strains of axenic amebae (HM1, H-200NIH, and HK-9). A -N-acetyl-glucosaminidase has been purified from two axenic strains of *E. histolytica* (HK-9 and H-200-NIH) with the use of culture supernatant. This enzyme could have a role in the breakdown of phagocytized erythrocytes or disruption of glycoprotein bonds between adjacent intestinal mucosal epithelial cells.

A 56-kD-secreted neutral thiol proteinase has been isolated from *E. histolytica by* FPLC anion exchange and chromatofocusing chromatography. In vitro, this enzyme degrades connective-tissue extracellular matrix and specifically fibronectin, laminin, and type I collagen. The 56-kD proteinase is also cytopathic for culture monolayers, probably by degrading cellular anchoring proteins; it is also a plasmogen activator.

Parasite proteinases probably contribute to amebic invasive activities and also complicate attempts by scientists to purify nondegraded *E. histolytica* proteins. Amebic secretion of a cytotoxin or enterotoxin has been postulated as a mechanism contributing to human disease. Although human pathology and experimental animal studies indicate that colonic mucosal damage occurs only at the site of adherent amebae, such studies do not exclude an enterotoxin effect.

Soluble fractions of *E. histolytica* sonicate have been demonstrated to have enterotoxic activity in indomethacin, 0.1 milligrams per microgram (mg/11g), -treated rats and rabbits. Enterotoxigenic activity is inhibited by fetuin or high concentrations of indomethacin.

An *E. histolytica* enterotoxin was recently partially purified and found to be heat labile; to be inhibited by sialoglycoproteins (fetuin and mucin) and by p-chloromercuribenzoate; and to have a molecular weight on SDS-PAGE of 30,000. Lysates of *E. histolytica* applied to the serosal side of rabbit ileum in a Ussing chamber induce a transient increase in short circuit current, a finding suggestive of a secretory effect.

This effect can be inhibited with the calcium channel blocker verapamil; amebic lysates contain serotonin, at 4.0 nanograms per milligram (ng/mg), which is at least partly responsible for secretory effects. Whether viable amebae elaborate an enterotoxin or produce an intestinal secretory response upon adherence to or invasion of the submucosa remains to be determined.

E. HISTOLYTICA CYTOLYTIC ACTIVITY

The characteristic pathology of invasive amebiasis consists of trophozoites surrounded by a necrotic eosinophilic debris (Figure 8-8), presumably the result of amebic lysis of surrounding tissues. In vitro studies of parasite cytolytic activity have contributed to our understanding of this event. By cinemicroscopy, kinetic analysis, and suspension of cells in dextran, studies a number of years ago demonstrated that the in vitro cytolethal effect of *E. histolytica* occurs on contact with target cells.

The sequence of events in the interaction of axenic trophozoites with target cells has been established: amebic adherence is followed by cytolysis of the adherent target cell, which in turn is followed by parasite phagocytosis of the dead target cell. In vivo and in vitro studies demonstrate that *E. histolytica* provides a chemoattractant signal for polymorphonuclear neutrophils.

Light microscopy studies of the early events in the formation of experimental amebic liver abscess in the hamster suggested that parasite contact-dependent lysis of neutrophils has a deleterious effect on distant hepatocytes. The in vitro interaction of trophozoites with human neutrophils reveals that amebae lyse neutrophils on contact and that release of toxic nonoxidative neutrophil constituents enhances the parasite-mediated destruction of Chang liver cell monolayers.

Soluble *E. histolytica* proteins inhibit human neutrophil baseline and stimulated oxidative activities; this finding may account for the parasite's relative immunity to neutrophil oxidative effector activity. Therefore, attraction and contact-dependent cytolysis of neutrophils is an important component in the pathogenesis of invasive amebiasis.

Lysis of target cells in vitro requires the establishment of adherence by the parasite's Gal/GaINAc-inhibitable surface lectin. Galactose or GaINAc (10-40 mg/ml) completely inhibits amebic lysis of target CHO cells, as quantified by release of "Indium oxine or counting in a cell sorter.

Purified rat colonic mucins, which specifically bind to the Gal/GaINAc lectin, totally inhibit amebic cytolysis of isolated rat colonic epithelial cells. GaINAc, 45 millimolar (mM) concentration, inhibits the killing of neutrophils by axenic trophozoites, allowing the neutrophils to turn table and kill the amebae. Amebic killing of activated human monocyte-derived macrophages, T lymphocytes, and BHK cell monolayers has also been found to be galactoseinhibitable.

The Gal/Ga1NAc lectin molecule may be a cytotoxin and thus directly contribute to target cell death. As discussed later, purified lectin induces a rise in target cell free intracellular calcium concentration. The Gal/GalNAc lectin is also found to be mitogenie for human

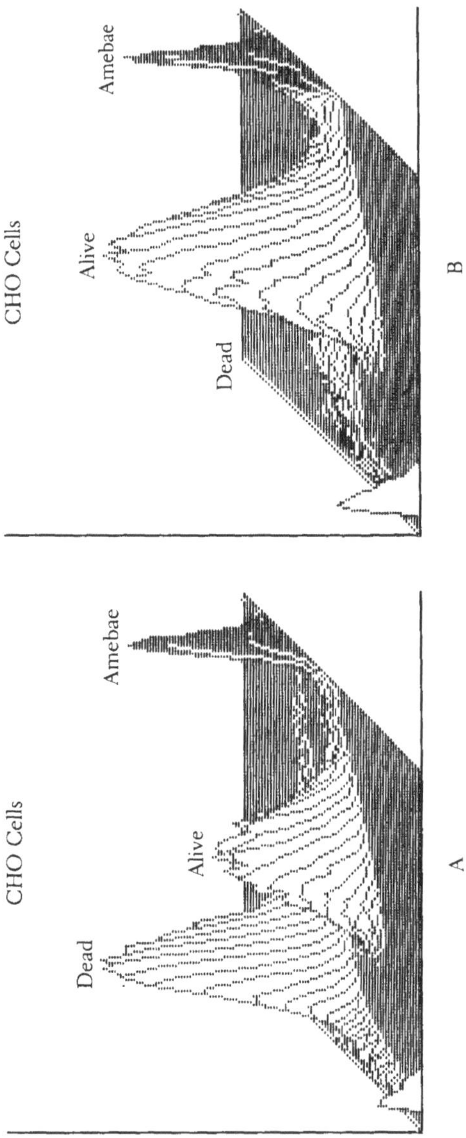

Figure 2.4: Galactose inhibitable extracellular cytolysis of target CHO cells by E. histolytica trophozoites, as determined by cell sorting. Target CHO cells (2 × 10^5) with or without amebae (10°) were centrifuged and incubated for 2 hours at 37°C with (B) or without (A) galactose (20 mg/ml). After incubation, cells were placed on ice, galactose (10 mg/ml) was added to all tubes, and the cells were vortexed to elute adherent CHO cells from amebae.

lymphocytes, as shown by specific inhibition with asialofetuin, coelution of mitogenic and CHO-cell agglutinating activity from a gel filtration column, correlation of mitogenicity with lectin activity in different *E. histolytica* strains, and asialofetuin-inhibitable mitogenicity of immuno affinity-purified Gal/GalNAc lectin.

Further studies on the subunit structure and cytolytic activities of the lectin are necessary. The relationship of the Gal/GalNAc lectin to virulence was further studied by using axenic strains which express different levels of in vivo virulence and in vitro cytopathogenicity. In vitro virulence for target CHO cells and human neutrophils (PMNs) in four strains is HM1-IMSS > H303-NIH = 200-NIH > nonvirulent Laredo.

Gel filtration chromatography of a soluble fraction of amebic sonicate demonstrates a GalNAc-inhibitable lectin that agglutinates CHO cells, erythrocytes, and PMNs. HMI amebae contained greater specific lectin activity (agglutinating activity per milligram of protein) and lymphocyte mitogenic activity than did 303, 200, and Laredo amebae. Mutagenized E. histolytica clones (L_6, C93, C919), selected by their inability to ingest bacteria, are avirulent in vivo, and adhere to and kill fewer CHO cells than do the parent HM 1:IMSS strain.

Galactose (10 mg/ml) completely inhibits adherence of all mutants to CHO cells. Avirulent mutants are more susceptible to being killed by human neutrophils; their soluble protein preparations are also markedly less mitogenic for human lymphocytes and have lower CHO cell -agglutinating activity.

Indirect immunofluorescence or immunoprecipitation with Gal/GalNAc lectin-specific monoclonal antibodies (F-14 and H8-5) reveals 170-kD Gal/GalNAc lectin heavy subunit in all clones studied. ^{125}1-mucins bind in a saturable and galactose-specific manner to avirulent amebic clones, and the number of mucin binding sites and dissociation constants was comparable to HM 1:IMSS.

However, all the avirulent clones studied are markedly deficient in internalization and subsequent exocytosis of '^{25}1-mucins. They also exhibit a lower turnover rate of surface lectin molecules, as indicated by studies with cyclohexamide exposure and ^{125}1-mucin binding. Therefore, amebic in vivo virulence and in vitro adherence and cytolytic activities depend not only on the presence of functional surface Gal/GalNAc lectin molecules, but also on their organization on the surface membrane and rate of parasite membrane turnover.

Cytolysis of adherent target cells by *E. histolytica* depends on parasite microfilament function, phospholipase A (PLA) enzyme activity, and maintenance of an acid pH in endocytic vesicles. Parasitic cytolytic activity can be stimulated by phorbol esters and is preceded by a rapid rise in target cell but not amebic free intracellular calcium concentration ($[Ca^{++}]_i$).

E. histolytica trophozoites have been found to contain two PLA enzymes: a Ca^{++}-dependent pH 7.5 optimal and a Ca^{++}-independent pH 4.5 optimal enzyme. The Ca^{++}-dependent enzyme is highly associated with the surface plasma membrane. The molecular weight of both PLA enzymes has been estimated to be 38 kD by gel filtration chromatography and immunoblotting with PLA-specific antibodies.

Isoelectric focusing with transfer to nitrocellulose and immunoblotting with anti-PLA antibodies revealed two distinct bands with isoelectric points of 4.5 and 5.5. Known PLA inhibitors, such as Quinacrine, phosphatidylcholine, and Rosenthal's inhibitor, inhibit parasite cytolysis of CHO cells and the in vitro enzymatic activity of the *E. histolytica* Ca^{++}-dependent PLA.

Production of lysophospholipids in amebae (end products of the PLA-mediated hydrolysis of diacylphospholipids), as quantified by thin-layer chromatography of ^{32}P incorporation into diacylphospholipid, is increased during parasite adherence to and lysis of target CHO cells. Addition of anti-PLA serum to amebae and CHO cells at 4°C has no effect on adherence.

However, exposure of amebae to heat-inactivated anti-PLA serum for 1 hour at 37°C inhibits subsequent amebic adherence at 4°C; control horse sera has no effect. AntiPLA inhibited amebic killing of CHO cells. These studies indicate that amebic PLA has a role in promoting parasite adherence and a central role in amebic cytolysis of target cells. *E. histolytica* vesicle pH has been measured with fluorescein isothiocyanate linked to dextran; endocytic vesicle pH is 5.1 ± 0.2 by spectrofluorimetry. Concentrations of NH_4Cl sufficient to increase vesicle pH to ? 5.7 inhibit amebic killing of target CHO cells.

A similar inhibitory effect is observed with the weak bases primaquine and chloroquine. Ammonium chloride affects neither amebic adherence to CHO cells at 4°C nor binding and ingestion of ^{3}H-leucine-labeled bacteria by the parasite. Exposure to NH_4Cl for 48 hours (which has no effect on amebic protein synthesis) or to the protein-synthesis inhibitor cyclohexamide for 3 hours produces persistent inhibition of amebic cytolytic activity.

Therefore, an uninterrupted acid pH in amebic intracellular endocytic vesicles is necessary for the delivery and activity of lysosomal proteins that participate in parasite cytolytic activity. Exocytosis of acid pH vesicles may be required for *E. histolytica* cytolytic activity. Vesicle exocytosis has been studied with the use of release of endocytosed ^{125}Iodine (^{125}I)-labeled tyrosine-conjugated dextran. ^{125}I-dextran enters

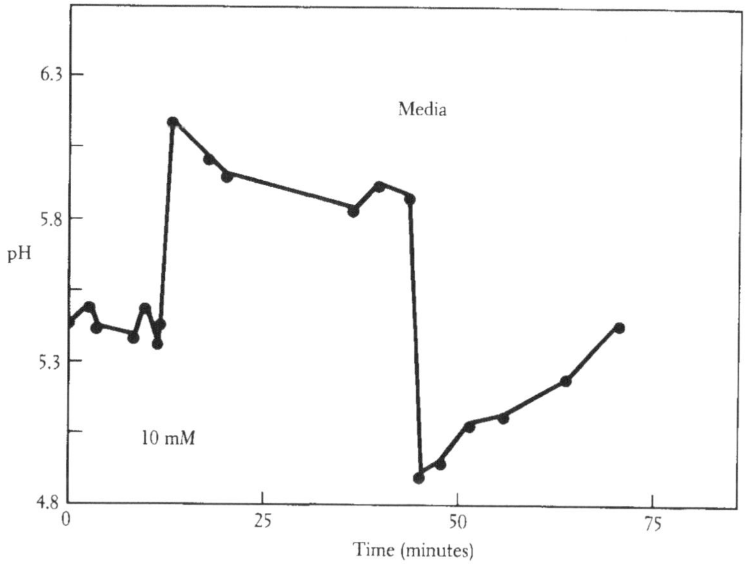

Figure 2.5: Effect of NH_4Cl on E. histolytica vesicle pH. In this preparation with a baseline vesicle pH of 5.4, NH_4Cl (20 mM) produced a rapid rise in vesicle pH of 6.1. When NH_4Cl was removed from the medium by washing, the vesicle rapidly reacidified (hyperacidified) to pH 4.9 and slowly returned to baseline over the next 20-30 minutes.

the acid pH vesicles of HM 1 amebae and is not degraded. Exocytosis is temperature-dependent and inhibited at 37°C by cytochalasin D, EDTA, or the putative *intracellular* calcium antagonist TMB-8. Calcium ionophore A23187 and phorbol myristate acetate enhance amebic exocytosis; elevation of vesicle pH with NH_4Cl has no effect.

Centrifugation of amebae with target CHO cells results in decreased ^{125}I-dextran release into the supernatant after 30 or 60 minutes at 37°C; interestingly, ^{125}I-dextran release is at control values when galactose or GalNAc is added, but remains decreased in the presence of mannose and N-acetyl-D-glucosamine (which have no effect on amebic adherence and cytolysis).

Phagocytosis of inert particles such as serum-exposed latex beads also has no effect on dextran release from acid pH vesicles. In summary, exocytosis of E. *histolytica* acid pH vesicles is temperature-, microfilament-, and calcium-dependent, stimulated by *phorbol* esters, and apparently down-regulated or directed into target cells during parasite adherence and cytolytic events.

Phorbol esters are specific activators of protein kinase C (PKC) enzymes, which are important in the intracellular transduction of many receptor-mediated calcium-dependent signals. Addition of phorbol 12-

myristate, 13-acetate (PMA) at 10^{-6} or 10^{-7} M results in a greater than twofold enhancement in amebic killing of target CHO cells over the next 30 minutes. Prior exposure of only the amebae, but not the CHO cells, to PMA for 5 minutes produces a similar effect; the inactive analogue, 4-α-phorbol, has no effect.

PMA does not promote amebic adherence but does enhance amebic cytolysis of previously adherent target cells. *Sphingosine*, a specific inhibitor of PKC, totally blocks PMA stimulated or basal amebic cytolytic activity. These studies indicate that an *E. histolytica* PKC is involved in regulation of parasite cytolytic activities; the mechanisms responsible for the natural in vivo activation of amebic PKC are unknown but should relate to the binding to the target cell by the Gal/GaINAc adherence lectin.

The role of Ca^{++} ions in E. *histolytica* cytolytic activity has been recently investigated. The calcium chelator EDTA and the putative intracellular calcium antagonist TMB-8 inhibit amebic cytolytic activity. In addition, calcium channel blockers verapamil and bepridil inhibit amebic *cytolytic* activity and increase parasite surface *membrane* impedance.

Hypotheses recently tested were that Ca^{++} functions as a second messenger stimulating amebic cytolytic activity and that entry of Ca^{++} from the extracellular compartment is the final mechanism responsible for target cell death. $[Ca^{++}]$; was measured in individual amebae and target cells (CHO cells and human PMN) utilizing the Ca^{++} probe Fura-2 and computer-enhanced digitized microscopy.

Motile *E. histolytica* trophozoites demonstrate random cyclic increases in $[Ca^{++}]$; at the leading edge or tail regions of cell cytoplasm. There is no increase in regional or total amebic $[Ca^{++}]$; upon contact with a target CHO cell. Target CHO cells and PMN exhibit a marked irreversible rise in $[Ca^{++}]$; within 30-300 seconds after contact by an ameba.

This increase in $[Ca^{++}]$; precedes the development of nonspecific target cell membrane permeability, as determined by leakage of Fura-2. Target CHO cells contiguous on a monolayer to a cell contacted by an ameba demonstrate a rapid but reversible rise in $[Ca^{++}]$; and do not die. Galactose totally abrogates the rise in target CHO cell $[Ca^{++}]$; that occurs upon contact by amebae. Purified Gal/GaINAc lectin (0.25 μg/ml) induces a galactose sensitive rise in CHO cell $[Ca^{++}]$; that is comparable to the rise observed with viable amebae.

In summary, elevation of amebic $[Ca^{++}]$; does not appear to be required for initiation of parasite adherence and cytolytic activities. Adherence by *E. histolytica* induces a rapid and substantial rise in target cell $[Ca^{++}]_i$, which is mediated at least in part by the Gal/GalNAc lectin. Prolonged elevation of target cell $[Ca^{++}]_i$ directly contributes to, but may not be sufficient for, target cell death.

A putative mediator of target cell ion flux is the *E. histolytica* pore forming protein described a number of years ago. This 13-15 kD parasite protein induces rapid ion flux (Na^+, K^+, and to a lesser extent Ca^{++}) across lipid bilayers or vesicles and depolarizes J774 macrophages, erythrocytes, and mouse spleen lymphocytes.

The ionophore is normally not released from viable trophozoites; however, secretion can be induced by calcium ionophore A23187, Concanavalin A, and *E. coli lipopolysaccharide*. The pore-forming protein is packaged in dense intracellular aggregates within amehae. Unfortunately, there is no direct evidence as yet linking this cytolytic mediator to the in vitro killing of target cells by *E. histo-lytica* trophozoites. Potential intracellular functions and the mechanisms by which the parasite avoids harmful ion fluxes at its plasma membrane are unknown.

We do not yet have sufficient information to determine the exact sequence of events and the identification of all the parasite molecules responsible for lysis of target cells by *E. histolytica* trophozoites. A working model is as follows. Adherence initiated by the Gal/Ga1NAc lectin results in a cellular signal activating parasite protein kinase C, which stimulates amebic cytolytic activities.

Parasite phospholipase A activity promotes amebic target cell fusion and is also stimulated by contact with target cells. Disruption of the target cell membrane is preceded by a tremendous influx of extracellular Ca^{++} ions into the target cell, as a result of cytotoxin activities of the Gal/GalNAc lectin or possibly transfer of the amebic pore-forming protein to the target cell membrane.

Parasite molecules that are putative final mediators of target cell death include Gal/GalNAc lectin toxic subunits, the pore-forming protein, lysodiacyl-phospholipids that result from amebic PLA_2 activity, and an as yet undefined lysosomal constituent whose activity requires an acid pH.

HUMAN IMMUNE RESPONSE TO *E. HISTOLYTICA*

Nonspecific Defense Mechanisms

Barriers to infection by enteric parasites include low gastric pH, digestive enzymes, competition by normal intestinal bacterial flora, and the protective mucus blanket covering the entire length of the gut epithelium. Stomach acid is an effective defense agaisnt trophozoites but not the chitinous cyst form. Bile salts may interact with components of human breast milk to lyse *Giardia lamblia*, but this mechanism is unlikely to be relevant to *E. histolytica* infection.

Bacteria promote growth and virulence of *E. histolytica;* however, experiments directed at determining if intestinal species could reduce parasite pathogenicity or interfere with amebic growth have not been performed. Bacterial competition for iron, production of toxic metabolites such as shortchain fatty acids, and effects of bacterial enzymes on trophozoites are potential mechanisms contributing to host resistance.

There is sufficient information to state that colonic mucins serve as a major nonimmune host defense against invasion by E. *histolytica.* As discussed earlier, colonic mucins are the high-affinity receptor for the amebic Gal/GaINAc adherence lectin, and they prevent parasite attachment to and lysis of colonic epithelial cells.

Experimental models of invasive colonic amebiasis demonstrate depletion of the mucus blanket before parasite invasion. *E. histolytica* trophozoites show potent mucous secretagogue effects when injected into rat colonic loops, possibly a result of parasite proteolytic enzymes. Immobilization or trapping of trophozoites in colonic mucus may be augmented in immune individuals who experience reinfection, as has been observed in experimental nematode infections.

Complement-Mediated Resistance

E. histolytica trophozoites are susceptible in vitro to complement-mediated lysis through alternative or classical pathway activation. However, invasive amebiasis appears to result from a subpopulation of complement-resistant trophozoites, as shown by study of liver abscess isolates. In addition, one can select complement-resistant clones in vitro by long-term culture with increasing concentrations of serum.

The complement membrane attack complex apparently attaches to the ameba's plasma membrane; the mechanism of parasite resistance to complement-mediated lysis is undefined, but it may relate to the ability of trophozoites to rapidly turn over their surface membrane.

Acquired Resistance to Invasive Amebiasis

No adequate prospective controlled studies have yet determined the incidence of invasive amebiasis or intestinal colonization in patients previously cured of amebic colitis or liver abscess. Uncontrolled and anecdotal reports suggest that such individuals have substantial resistance to a recurrence of invasive amebiasis.

This is supported by experimental animal models in which cure of invasive infection or immunization with whole parasite proteins results in immunity to subsequent intestinal or intrahepatic challenge with *E. histolytica* trophozoites. There is sufficient data to conclude that both antibody and cell-mediated immune responses contribute to resistance in the immune individuals.

Serum and Intestinal Secretory Antibody Response

Within 1 to 2 weeks from the onset of invasive amebiasis, patients develop a high titer serum antiamebic antibody response, as determined by a variety of quantitative methods. The parasite antigens recognized by human immune sera have been recently defined by immunoblotting. The 170-kD heavy subunit of the Gal/GalNAc adherence lectin is the most prominently recognized antigen, as determined by immuno precipitation; in addition, virtually all patients studied who have been cured of well-documented invasive amebiasis have serum antibody to the lectin.

This finding is important because specific antilectin antibody inhibits both in vitro adherence of amebae to colonic mucins or target epithelial cells and parasite destruction of CHO cell monolayers at 37°C. The latter observation is important, as trophozoites have the ability to recurrently aggregate and shed attached antibodies.

Other major amebic antigens recognized by immune sera include 37- and 90-kD surface glycoproteins and a 59-kD cytoplasmic glycoprotein. Uncharacterized coproantibodies of the IgA class have been identified in patients with amebic colitis; it is unknown whether an sIgA secretory antibody response occurs in asymptomatic intestinal infection. Development of a serum antibody response does not result in spontaneous resolution of established amebic colitis or liver abscess, but it certainly may contribute to resistance to subsequent invasive disease.

Cell-Mediated Immune Responses

Patients cured of amebic liver abscess demonstrate an antigen-specific T-lymphocyte proliferative response with production of lymphokines, including gamma interferon, capable in vitro of activating monocyte-derived macrophage amebicidal activity. Axenic *E. histolytica* trophozoites kill human neutrophils, mononuclear cells, and monocytederived macrophages in vitro without loss of parasite viability.

However, activated macrophages are effective in killing trophozoites through both oxidative and nonoxidative effector mechanisms. In addition, cytotoxic T-cell activity can be elicited from patient cells in vitro by incubation with *E. histolytica* antigens. The mechanisms by which activated macrophages and cytotoxic T-cells overcome amebic cytolytic mechanisms, as opposed to polymorphonuclear neutrophils, remains undefined.

Cell-mediated immunity certainly plays an important role in preventing or limiting invasive amebiasis, but it is not relevant to the parasite's initial penetration through the colonic mucosal epithelium. This supposition is supported by an apparently low incidence of invasive amebiasis in individuals with the acquired immune deficiency syndrome (AIDS), despite a substantial prevalence of *E. histolytica* intestinal infection.

Some authorities believe this is due to a fortuitous infection by nonpathogenic strains in AIDS patients in developed countries; however, in such areas of the third world as Haiti or Zaire, there has not been an increased occurrence of severe invasive amebiasis in AIDS patients. As with other parasites, *E. histolytica* may specifically suppress the host's cell-mediated immune response during the pathogenesis of invasive disease. Serum from patients with liver abscess inhibits the in vitro antigen-specific T-cell proliferative response.

The mechanism has not been defined; in addition, the parasite could induce suppressive T-cell activities. A candidate for such effects is the released form of the Gal/GaINAc lectin, which is mitogenic in vitro and induces proliferation of a suppressor subset of T-lymphocytes. Further investigation of the effects of *E. histolytica* on host immunity is necessary, especially in regard to future design of an effective vaccine.

PROSPECTS FOR A VACCINE

There is tremendous need for a vaccine providing effective immunity for *E. histolytica* infection. The highest prevalence of infection and greatest disease burden are found in developing countries that are without the resources or stability to provide sanitary facilities to prevent the spread of amebic infection.

Therapy of amebiasis is complex, costly, and not without toxicity, and it certainly is not feasible for the large numbers of asymptomatically infected humans who apparently act as the reservoir for those who suffer invasive disease. Our best hope is that biomedical research will develop a vaccine to prevent the morbidity and mortality of invasive disease or, better yet, provide resistance to intestinal colonization by *E. histolytica*.

Animal models support the concept that immunization with *E. histolytica* proteins will provide protection against invasive amebiasis. However, we lack the epidemiologic studies to be certain that cure of natural human infection provides immunity.

Nevertheless, recent biochemical characterization of parasite adherence mechanisms, proteolytic enzymes, cytolytic activities, and antigenic proteins provide a large number of potential approaches for development of a vaccine.

We need to determine the genetic code for major parasite virulence factors and antigens in order to optimally identify nontoxic immunogenic parasite proteins and have maximum flexibility for choosing a vaccine delivery system. Work will be hampered by the lack of animal models that truly parallel human intestinal infection.

Despite these problems, this author is confident that in the next decade we will surpass the advances that followed development of axenic culture in 1978 and that numerous vaccines will be ready for testing in the field.

3

TRYPANOSOMA

Initially, cell biologists were attracted to African trypanosomes because of their fascinating antigenic variation-the process by which these protozoan parasites evade the immune response of their mammalian host by periodically changing their surface coat. As information about the structural and genetic aspects of this process became available, it revealed additional unexpected features of trypanosomes that were equally intriguing.

Experimental investigations of these additional features are now among the most active areas of trypanosome research and provide the best hope for identifying new drugs to combat these parasites. This chapter summarizes our present understanding of the biochemical basis of antigenic variation and discusses two other distinctive features of trypanosomes: the organization of their microtubules and the presence of a unique cytoplasmic organelle called the glycosome, which contains the enzymes catalyzing glycolysis and other metabolic pathways.

ANTIGENIC VARIATION

Antigenic variation is a consequence of changes in the chemical composition of the surface coat, which covers the entire surface of the *trypanosome*. This surface coat is visible in transmission electron microscopy as an electron-dense layer from 12 to 15 nanometers (nm) thick that lies outside of the lipid bilayer of the plasma membrane.

It is composed of a monolayer of about 10^7 closely packed copies of a glycoprotein molecule called the variant surface glycoprotein, or VSG. By sequentially expressing genes that encode different VSG sequences, a trypanosome population is able to change its antigenic profile and keep one step ahead of the immune response against it. The protein structure of VSGs, their arrangement on the cell surface, and their attachment to the plasma membrane have been subjects of much study in recent years, as has the *immunochemical* profile of the coat.

Fully processed VSGs have molecular sizes between 55 and 60 kilodaltons (kD). They contain about 450 amino acids and have 7 percent to 17 percent of their weight as carbohydrate distributed between two different classes of oligosaccharide side chain. One class is composed of asparaginelinked oligosaccharides which, in most respects, are similar to the N-linked oligosaccharides found in many other *eukaryotic* glycoproteins.

The number and positions of the asparagine residues to which these oligosaccharides are linked vary from one VSG to another. Curiously, although these carbohydrate moieties can be distributed throughout the polypeptide backbone, they are not accessible to plant lectins (which bind specifically to *carbohydrates*) when the VSG is on the parasite surface.

Instead, they are apparently buried within the matrix of tightly packed VSGs. The second class of oligosaccharide has a more unusual structure. Most membrane-bound glycoproteins of eukaryotes are anchored to the plasma membrane by a sequence of hydrophobic amino acids embedded in the membrane, which often completely spans the bilayer to link with a cytoplasmic domain.

The trypanosome eschews such a conventional mode of attachment for VSG, instead favouring a more exotic, although not unique, linkage to a glycolipid molecule. The C-terminal carboxyl group of the VSG is in an amide linkage to an ethanolamine, which, in turn, is coupled through a phosphodiester linkage to an *oligosaccharide* containing three mannose residues and a side chain with a variable number of galactose molecules.

At the reducing terminus of this glycan moiety is a molecule of glucosamine that is O-glycosidically linked to myo-inositol of phosphatidylinositol. In Trypanosoma *brucei* both acyl groups of the phosphatidylinositol are myristic acid ($C_{14:0}$), a relatively rare fatty acid in the trypanosome.

The trypanosome contains a phospholipase-C enzyme whose activity is specific for this glucosaminyl phosphatidylinositol. When activated, it cleaves the phosphate between the *diacylglycerol* and the *inositol*, resulting in the release of the surface coat from the plasma membrane. The role of this intriguing phospholipase in the life cycle of the trypano-

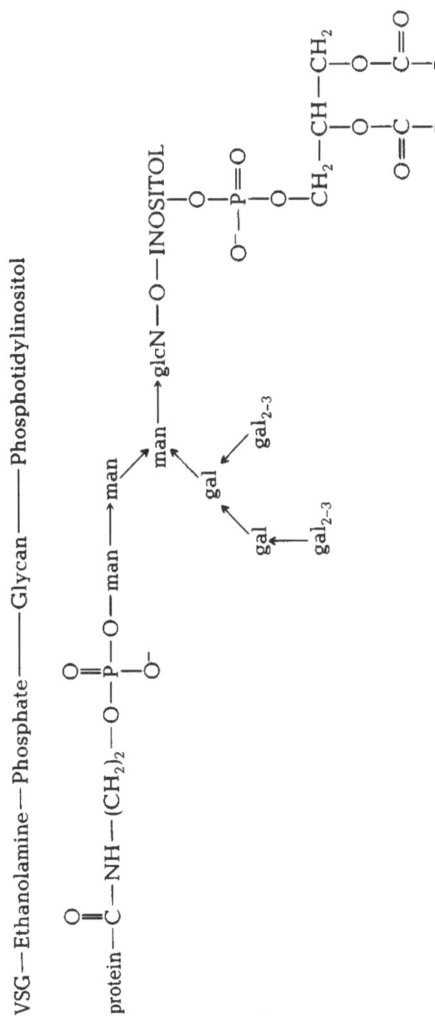

Figure 3.1: Structure of the glucosaminyl phosphatidylinositol anchor of a Trypanosoma brucei *VSG; man, mannose; gal, galactose; glcN, glucosamine; R, $(CH_2)_{12}CH_3$, the side chain of myristic acid. The positions of the carbon atoms in the various sugar linkages are known but, for brevity, are not shown here.*

some is not yet clear. Biochemists working on VSGs have used it unwittingly for many years, because its activation upon disruption of the plasma membrane leads to the release of the VSG in a water-soluble form that may be purified readily to homogeneity in tens of milligrams.

Although free VSG can be detected in the circulation of infected animals, most of it is probably released from dying trypanosomes rather than from trypanosomes undergoing a VSG switch. Whether the lipase also has a role in this switch from the expression of one surface coat to another is not known.

Antigenic variation of trypanosomes in the bloodstream is actually a rare event, occurring only about once in every 10^6-10^7 trypanosomes per generation. Thus, it has not been possible to study the switch directly; we have been able to look only at the biochemical footprints of this switch many generations after it has happened.

In contrast, when trypanosomes are ingested by a tsetse fly, they differentiate quickly to a form lacking the surface coat. This step can be mimicked in the laboratory by shifting a culture of trypanosomes from 37°C to 26°C in the appropriate media. This temperature shift is accompanied by activation of the phospholipase, and the subsequent release of the VSG also seems to involve loss of liberated diacylglycerol from the membrane.

The enzyme has recently been purified to homogeneity, and it will be interesting to see whether specific inhibitors of its activity can be identified, and if so, what effect they will have on the life cycle of the parasite. The VSG of trypanosomes is the best-characterized example of such a glycolipid linkage of a surface protein.

However, many proteins in other organisms are known to contain similar or identical linkages, including the P63 surface protease of *Leishmania*, acetylcholinesterase, and decay accelerating factor (DAF) of red blood cells, the Thy-1 lymphoid and neuronal differentiation antigen, and the placental alkaline phosphatase.

The malaria parasite, *Plasmodium falci parum*, contains a membrane protein linked to a similar glycolipid that contains no enzymatic activity when on the surface but becomes a protease when released in its soluble form. Many other membrane-associated proteins probably have similar *glycolipid* linkages, and their structures and biological significance will be an active area of investigation in the future. For the moment, however, trypanosomes stand out because of presence of the *phospholipase-C* activity that can quickly release the cell's entire surface coat.

The abundance of both the substrate and the enzyme makes the trypanosome the organism of choice in searching for the biochemical and biological basis for this release phenomenon. Because immunization of rabbits with released VSG molecules stimulates production of many antibodies (some of which are directed at the C-terminal oligosaccharide), antibodies are available for the detection of such protein-bound glycolipids in trypanosomes and other organisms.

This antigenic determinant on VSG that is also present on other eukaryotic cells is known as the cross-reacting determinant, or CRD. The combination of phospholipase treatment and detection with anti-

CRD antibodies has been used to identify CRD-like structures not only on trypanosomes but also on red blood cell acetylcholinesterase and DAF, on P63 of *Leishmania*, and on the surface antigen of *Paramecium aurelii*. Nevertheless, the full extent of the glycan similarities in different organisms is not known.

Some differences do occur because the Thy-1 anchor, in contrast to the VSG glycan anchor, contains no galactose and has one mole of N-acetylgalactosamine. The special properties imparted to a membrane protein through a glucosaminylphosphatidylinositol anchor, in contrast to a more conventional transmembrane hydrophobic sequence, have not as yet been established.

One obvious possibility is that the protein can be released rapidly when the anchor is enzymatically disrupted. Another possibility is that different membrane anchors affect the enzymatic activity of a surface protease (as has been shown for the surface protease of *Plasmodium)*. Alternatively, this anchor might provide some conservation of space in the lipid bilayer or perhaps permit greater lateral mobility of the protein within the membrane's lipid bilayer.

The amino acid sequence diversity within the entire family of VSG molecules is so great that the presence of the CRD on the VSG is responsible for virtually all the immunological cross-reactions among different VSG molecules. Side-by-side comparison of different VSG sequences shows a hypervariability far more pronounced than that found in immunoglobulin variable region domains.

This diversity is most pronounced within the N-terminal two-thirds of the molecule, which is believed to contain the parts of the VSG that are exposed on the surface of the living trypanosome. Within this portion of the molecule, the only significant sequence similarity among VSCs seems to be the occurrence of a cysteine residue between positions 14 and 17, although there is some tendency toward positional conservation of hydrophobic and small side groups.

In the last 50-100 residues at the C-terminus, some sequence similarities do emerge that are sufficient to allow classification of VSGs into two sequence families, class I and class II. Class I VSGs terminate with an aspartate or asparagine residue onto which the glycolipid is bound, whereas class II VSGs have a C-terminal serinc. In each class the positions of several cysteines and some charged residues are generally conserved, suggesting that they contribute to a common structure of the C-terminal similarity domain that is class-specific, because the two classes are different.

The VSG mRNA encodes a C-terminal tail of 23 (class I) or 17 (class II) amino acids that is absent from the mature glycoprotein. These additional amino acids are largely hydrophobic, except for one lysine, and probably function to temporarily anchor the VSG to a membrane until the glycolipid can be transferred onto the nascent polypeptide. The classification into class I and class II includes these additional amino acids and, indeed, the most sequence conservation occurs within this region.

At the extreme C-terminus, the class I and class II sequences converge, since all the C-terminal hydrophobic tails terminate in either leucyl-leucyl-phenylalanine or leucylleucyl-leucine. In addition to these C-terminal sequence similarities, further structural similarity is indicated by the fact that all VSGs can be cleaved into two domains by the limited action of trypsin or other proteolytic enzymes.

These enzymes produce an N-terminal fragment comprising two-thirds to three-quarters of the molecule, which is sometimes termed the hypervariable domain, and a C-terminal fragment containing one-third to one-quarter of the sequence, known as the similarity domain. VSGs associate to form homodimers both in solution and on the trypanosome surface.

In addition, it appears that each of the two proteolytic domains can also form a dimes Crystallization of two different N-terminal hypervariable domains, one isolated from a class I VSG and one from a class II VSG, has allowed a search for higher orders of structural similarity within VSGs that are only distantly related at the amino acid-sequence level.

Interestingly, these two VSGs were found to share a common structural motif. Each hypervariabledomain dimer contains a symmetrical bundle of alpha-helices distributed around the longitudinal axis of the molecule. The bundle, which is approximately nine nm long, compared with the 12 -15-nm thickness of the surface coat, has sixfold symmetry at the C-terminal end of the domain, fourfold symmetry in the central region, and sixfold symmetry again at the N-terminus.

Although the presence of large amounts of *alpha-helix* in VSGs has been inferred from spectroscopic measurements, secondary structure predictions failed to identify the locations of these alpha-helices in the VSG for which the most structural information is currently available.

This failure points to the inadequacy of the rules currently available for secondary structure prediction and highlights the fact that with a database of approximately 1000 VSG genes in the trypanosome genome, the VSG system offers an excellent opportunity for the generation of new and better rules for the correlation of sequence and structure. Clearly such correlations would be of interest to a much wider audience of protein biochemists than just trypanosome specialists.

The eventual elucidation of the three-dimensional structures of VSGs to high resolution should provide answers to some interesting questions. First, what are the locations of the antigenic determinants that are exposed on the surface of the living trypanosome? Surely, the changes in this portion of the molecule provide the effective limit to the size of the VSG repertoire.

Second, and of almost equal interest, what are the locations of the epitopes that are not exposed on the living trypanosome? Why do VSGs vary so much in these cryptic antigenic determinants, which would seem to have no survival value for the trypanosome?

If the trypanosome does have a system for shuffling segments of VSG genes to create entirely new VSG sequences, as seems increasingly probable, then it may be that selection by the immune system for antigenically distinct variants is a secondary event, and that the primary selection pressure is for the ability of such new sequences to form a particular structure for the surface coat, impermeable to complement and other components of the immune system.

Third, does the tendency of VSGs to form dimers suggest that packing compatibility of the new VSG with the old VSG is important in maintaining the integrity of the surface coat during the crucial switch period and plays a role in the order of VSG appearance? Other interesting questions include where the buried asparagine-linked carbohydrate moieties are positioned relative to the VSG peptide backbone, since these structures are not exposed on the surface of the living trypanosome.

The oligosaccharide component of the C-terminal glycolipid also is not exposed, because of its location underlying the surface coat. Furthermore, there is currently no information on the structures of the C-terminal similarity domains since, to date, only N-terminal hypervariable domains have been crystallized.

The intact VSG molecule has proved refractory to crystallization, and no successful attempt to crystallize the C-terminal domain independently has yet been reported. Finally, the successful determination of the three-dimensional structure of an entire VSG structure should provide information about how individual VSG molecules are packed onto the trypanosome's surface.

From this consideration of antigenic variation and the properties of the surface coat, it seems likely that attempts to produce a vaccine for trypanosomiasis are doomed. Therefore, most current studies on VSG focus on its synthesis, membrane integration, and membrane release as potential targets for chemotherapy.

Of obvious interest is the role of the VSG-specific phospholipase C in antigenic variation, and the extent to which interference with correct functioning of this enzyme could assist the infected host. The biosynthetic pathway of the precursors for the glycolipid tail is another potential chemotherapeutic target, even though such glycolipids are not confined to the trypanosome.

The glycan structure shown in Figure 3-2 suggests that its synthesis involves several novel enzymes not yet described whose inhibition would prevent VSG attachment to the membrane. Another consideration is the unusual and absolute specificity for myristic acid as the acyl groups in the phosphatidylinositol of T. brucei VSGs.

Perhaps furthest in the future, if VSGs of different sequences do share a common structural motif, then this structure may reflect a common protein-folding pathway. Agents that interfere with this pathway could prevent proper assembly of the surface coat, with fatal consequences for the trypanosome.

THE MICROTUBULES

All eukaryotic cells contain tubular protein structures known as microtubules. Microtubules have many roles within the cell, including chromosome *segregation*, *motility*, and maintenance of shape. *Microtubules* are formed by polymerization of heterodimers of α- and β-tubulin. Tubulins have been purified from many organisms and have been extensively studied.

However, the microtubules of the trypanosomes have received less attention than they deserve, probably because of the overwhelming interest in the VSG. The *hemoflagellates*, of which trypanosomes are an example, have a unique arrangement of *microtubules* in the cell body. Underlying the *plasma* membrane, and in close contact with it, is a helical array of singlet microtubules.

This subpellicular array is responsible for the characteristic shape of the parasite. The microtubules are laterally interconnected and form tight membrane contacts, the precise nature of which is not understood. In addition, the *flagellum* of the organism contains the conventional axoneme, which in cross section contains a circle of nine microtubules with an additional central pair.

This arrangement is common to all *flagellated* organisms and the axoneme is responsible for cell locomotion. Finally, trypanosomes contain a transient intranuclear spindle, present only during nuclear division.

Tubulins are very abundant proteins in trypanosomes, second only to the VSG. Comparatively little work has been done on these proteins despite their ready availability. Tubulins are generally a heterogeneous group of proteins. Although both α- and β-tubulins have molecular weights of about 50,000, expression of different tubulin genes produces proteins that differ slightly in amino acid sequence.

Differences in posttranslational modification also can lead to some heterogeneity. In trypanosomes, pellicular and flagellar microtubules may be distinct because a monoclonal antibody has been found that recognizes tubulin only in the flagellum. In addition, evidence for heterogeneity within the subpellicular microtubules comes from the related kinetoplastid organism Crithidia fasciculata.

Three different forms of α-tubulin are found in the pellicular microtubules, only two of which occur in the *cytoplasmic pool*, whereas the third form appears in the axoneme only. Some of this heterogeneity is generated by posttranslational modification of a tyrosine residue. In all eukaryotes, this reaction occurs only on the α-tubulin chain.

Heterogeneity in the β-tubulins of trypanosomes has not yet been detected. Trypanosoma b. rhodesiense contains about 15 α-tubulin and 15 β-tubulin genes arranged predominantly as tandem arrays of α-β-tubulin gene repeats. One of these repeat units has been cloned and sequenced, allowing a comparison of the trypanosomal tubulins with those of their vertebrate hosts.

The β-tubulin gene encodes a protein of 442 amino acids; the a-tubulin gene specifies a protein of 451 amino acids. Both contain a tyrosine as the C-terminal amino acid. Thus, it seems likely that the posttranslational modification of α-tubulin involves both a tubulin tyrosine carboxypeptidase, which removes this terminal tyrosine, and a tyrosine transpeptidase, which adds it back on.

This apparently redundant action seems to occur in other organisms as well, since C-terminal tyrosines are encoded by both the rat and human α-tubulin genes. However, in contrast to higher eukaryotes, the trypanosome β-tubulin gene also encodes a C-terminal tyrosine, and yet there is no evidence for posttranslational tyrosinolation of β-tubulin in trypanosomes. This difference indicates that trypanosomes must have a highly specific system for tyrosinolation and detyrosinolation.

About 40 percent sequence identity is present in the genes for trypanosome α-tubulin and β-tubulin, indicating that they have diverged from each other to an extent similar to that found in tubulins of other organisms. More interesting is the extent to which these α- and β-tubulin sequences have diverged from the α- and β-tubulin sequences of other species.

Comparison of the predicted sequences of T. b. rhodesiense α- and β-tubulin with those of rats, pigs, and humans shows about 84%-85% amino acid sequence identity, compared with 70%-71% identity with the corresponding tubulins of yeasts. The sequence differences are not evenly distributed throughout the molecules. For β-tubulin, the most variable regions are between positions 1 and 80, 340 and 390, and 430 and the C-terminus.

For the α-tubulins, the corresponding variable regions are between positions 128 and 154, 168 and 204, and 437 and the C-terminus. In both the α- and β-tubulins there are also strongly conserved regions in which amino acid substitutions are generally conservative. What is the significance of such differences? Microtubules have proved to be very good targets for drugs.

In particular, the benzimidazole antihelmintics probably act by depolymerizing microtubules in nematodes. The benzimidazoles, however, have no effect on protozoan parasites such as the trypanosomes. Similarly, other drugs such as colchicine are potent inhibitors of microtubule formation in higher eukaryotes, but have no effect on protozoan parasites or, indeed, on other lower eukaryotes.

In studies with isolated tubulins, benzimidazoles have a much higher affinity for nematode tubulin, whereas colchicine is more specific for tubulins of higher eukaryotes. As yet, there are no agents that hind selectively to microtubules of protozoan parasites. A careful sequence comparison of tubulins from the protozoa, from nematodes, and from vertebrates might aid both in the identification of the residues involved in drug binding and in the development of a new generation of compounds selective for protozoa.

In addition to the a- and,8-tubulins, microtubules contain other proteins called microtubule-associated proteins (MAPs). The best-characterized MAPS have molecular weights of about 300,000 daltons and about 55,000-65,000 daltons. These latter proteins are generally known as the Tau MAPs. MAPs probably mediate the associations of *microtubules* with other cellular organelles and the interactions among different microtubules.

The high-molecular-weight MAPs also seem to promote the polymerization of tubulins into *microtubules*. One study using porcine brain α-

and β-tubulins concluded that amino acid residues 434 - 440 of β-tubulins are crucial for the binding of both classes of MAPs. This region corresponds to one of the variable portions in the comparison of different β-tubulin sequences.

Should this conclusion be correct, then the interaction between MAPs and tubulins in protozoa may offer another advantage for selectivity in the development of novel drugs. Although no work has been performed directly on MAPs in trypanosomes or any other protozoan parasite, some indirect evidence exists for the presence of still other proteins that perturb microtubule function. A number of tricyclic antidepressants, most notably the *phenothiazines*, have been shown to disrupt the contact between the *subpellicular microtubules* of *trypanosomes* and the plasma membrane, which leads to a loss of cell motility and death.

A phenothiazine binding protein of 60,000 daltons has been purified from *T. brucei* and has been shown to be unique to trypanosomatids. Indeed, monoclonal antibody binding studies show that the protein is not well conserved even among different trypanosome *subgenera*.

The function of this protein is unknown, but one possibility is that it is a microtubule-associated protein whose function is to connect the subpellicular microtubules to the plasma membrane. This region of the trypanosome cytoskeleton will be interesting to investigate further.

The Glycosome

In the vertebrate bloodstream, where they have ample access to glucose, trypanosomes derive ATP *predominantly* from anaerobic glycolysis through the Embden-Myerhoff pathway. Indeed, trypanosomes have the highest known glycolytic rate of any eukaryote. Most of the enzymes of the *glycolytic* pathway are confined to an organelle unique to the *trypanosome*, called the *glycosome*.

The glycosome contains the first seven enzymes of the glycolytic pathway and two additional enzymes involved in *glycerol metabolism*. These enzymes are *hexokinase*, glucose phosphate *isomerase*, phosphofructokinase, fructose 1,6-bis-phosphate aldolase, triosephosphate isomerase, D-glyceraldehyde-3-phosphate dehydrogenase, phosphoglycerate kinase, glycerol 3-phosphate dehydrogenase, and glycerol kinase.

These enzymes differ in interesting ways from those found in the mammalian host of the parasite. In particular, their properties in solution, following disruption of the glycosome, indicate that they associate with each other to form multienzyme complexes.

One attractive suggestion to account for such associations is that the substrate, glucose, is channeled through a chain of enzyme-active sites to provide the impetus for the observed rapid rates of glycolysis. Recent experiments, however, indicate that this is not the case, and the advantage to the parasite of compartmentalization of the glycolytic pathway remains uncertain.

It is intriguing to ask how the glycosome itself is assembled. The organelle contains no DNA and no ribosomes; therefore, the enzymes must be synthesized elsewhere in the cytoplasm and transported into, or assembled simultaneously with, the basic glycosome structure.

Translation of the mRNAs for several of the enzymes has been shown to occur on free, rather than membrane-bound, cytosolic ribosomes, indicating that the nascent polypeptides are imported into the glycosome. It is likely, therefore, that each polypeptide found in the glycosome contains a unique signal to facilitate transport into the glycosome, and this signal is likely to be common to all proteins of the glycosome but absent from proteins found exclusively in the cytoplasm or elsewhere in the parasite.

Much recent work centers on the search for such a signal; if identified, it could provide a target for the rational design of new trypanocidal drugs. Comparison of the physical properties and amino acid sequences of glycosomal enzymes with their counterparts in the cytosol of both trypanosomes and their mammalian hosts has revealed a few differences.

In general, the trypanosomal enzymes are more basic and are slightly larger in size. The three-dimensional structures of several of the *mammalian* enzymes are known, and the sequences of the *trypanosome* enzymes are sufficiently similar to suggest that they adopt similar folding patterns.

When the sequences of the *glycosomal phosphoglycerate* kinase, triosephosphate isomerase, or glyceraldehyde-3-phosphate dehydrogenase are compared with the known structures of their vertebrate counterparts, the additional positive charges found on the trypanosomal enzymes are clustered at two spots on the surface of the enzyme.

It has been suggested that these positively charged "hot spots" may function as the postulated glycosome recognition sequences. The distance between the two hot spots is about 12 angstroms (A), which is about the distance between the two negatively charged groups on a well-known trypanocidal drug, *suramin*, whose mode of action is uncertain. It will indeed be fascinating to determine if an interaction between the suramin molecule and the glycosomal enzymes is responsible for this drug's activity.

Eventually, a knowledge of the three-dimensional structures of each of the enzymes of the glycosome will be necessary to allow comparison with the homologous enzymes of the vertebrate host. This information should be extremely helpful in devising trypanosome-specific inhibitors of glycolysis.

OTHER SIGNIFICANT FEATURES

Other features of the trypanosome interest the cell biologist and biochemist. When in the vertebrate host, all trypanosomes obtain their ATP entirely from anaerobic glycolysis, although some trypanosomes in the bloodstream population prudently preadapt to aerobic life in the tsetse fly midgut by switching on some of the enzymes involved in mitochondrial respiration.

These trypanosome forms, when ingested, probably propagate the population in the tsetse fly. The environmental signals controlling these changes in the trypanosome's metabolism have not yet been identified, nor have the mechanisms by which such signals are transduced to the mitochondrion. As discussed in other chapter of this book, the trypanosome's mitochondrial DNA is remarkably complex, and although much is known, many questions remain to be answered about the functioning of this organelle in the trypanosome.

Other interesting puzzles are posed by the innate resistance of humans to several trypanosome species that readily infect domestic and wild animals. For example, Try*panosoma brucei brucei* infects cattle but not humans because it is lysed by normal human serum. On the other hand, *Trypanosoma brucei rhodesiense* and *T. brucei gambiense*, both of which are morphologically indistinguishable from *T. b. brucei*, grow well in the human bloodstream and are the main causes of human trypanosomiasis.

The mechanism by which *T. b. brucei* is killed by human serum is not completely understood, nor is the mechanism of the acquired resistance trait to *T. b. rhodesiense* or *gambiense*. The high-density-lipoprotein (HDL) fraction of human serum has been implicated in the killing, which seems to involve ion leakage leading to osmotic death. Intriguingly, although it was thought that *T. b. brucei* and *T. b. rhodesiense* were distinct subspecies, it now appears that *T. b. brucei* can, itself, occasionally switch to a form resistant to the action of human serum and is therefore infective to human beings, behaving in all respects like T. *b. rhodesiense*. Again, the nature of this switch and the signal that triggers it are unknown.

Trypanosomes lack one feature that would otherwise make them an ideal system for study by molecular or cellular biologists: the absence of a clearly defined sexual stage in the life cycle. The corollary is an absence of literature on the genetics of trypanosomes, which has hindered progress in other areas, such as in the study of the molecular biology of antigenic variation.

This deficiency might be remedied if a system could be developed for transfection of trypanosomes by exogenous DNA whose expression was properly regulated. However, to date the trypanosome has proved refractory to transfection in which the introduced DNA is transcribed with fidelity.

By looking at the frequency of homozygous and heterozygous forms of different isoenzyme markers, it has been established that bloodstream trypomastigotes are diploid for housekeeping genes and that the frequency distribution for homozygotes and heterozygotes is consistent with the occurrence of a sexual stage in the life cycle.

This stage probably occurs in the tsetse fly, perhaps within the salivary glands, and it has been possible to genetically cross different strains of trypanosomes. Such experiments should provide the foundation for the study of trypanosome genetics. Rapid developments in this area will likely occur over the next few years.

4

LEISHMANIA

Many species of *trypanosomatid* protozoa of the genus Leishmania are parasites of man. They are transmitted by blood-sucking female *phlebotomine* sandflies. Figure elsewhere in this chapter presents schematically various forms of *leishmanias* reported in the insect and mammalian hosts. The parasite lives extracellularly in the alimentary tract of the fly, largely as motile *promastigotes*, or cells each with a flagellum at their anterior end.

When delivered into the mammalian host by the vector, they infect macrophages of the reticuloendothelial system and therein transform into nonmotile amastigotes. Subsequent multiplication of amastigotes is believed to lyse the infected macrophages, and the released amastigotes infect additional macrophages, resulting in the chronic diseases collectively known as leishmaniasis.

There are simple cutaneous, diffuse *cutaneous*, *mucocutaneous*, and *visceral* forms of the disease, the last being often fatal in untreated cases. The variations in the clinical manifestations of leishmaniasis are due largely to the different species of parasites involved and partly the status of host immunity.

Leishmaniasis was first recognized as an important disease of humans at the turn of the century. It remains widespread in all continents except Australia. The epidemiological perspective on Leishmania organisms and leishmaniasis is in a state of flux; several endemic foci have been discovered frequently in recent years-especially in Africa and South and Central America, where different species of parasites, sandfly vectors, and reservoir animals are involved in transmission.

There also have been epidemic outbreaks, resulting in part from inadequate vector control programs and the emergence of drug-resistant parasites. Today, hundreds of millions of people in new and old endemic foci are at risk of contracting leishmaniasis.

Leishmanias are a parasite of paradox. The evolutionary adaptation of organisms such as leishmanias to a parasite's way of life presumably proceeds from an extracellular to an intracellular mode. Intracellular parasitism in such cases is viewed generally as an evolutionary strategy of parasites to escape from humoral immunity of the host.

Yet, the pathogenicity of leishmanias hinges completely on their ability to infect macrophages, an archetype of phagocytes important in the cellular defense of the host against invading microorganisms. How leishmanias manage not only to escape from destruction by these cells but to survive, differentiate, and multiply *intracellularly* is a question of academic and practical importance, relevant to the pathogenic mechanism of leishmanias as well as to the immunobiology and cytopathology of leishmaniasis.

Like all cases of intracellular parasitism, leishmanial infection of macrophages follows multiple steps of host-parasite cellular interactions. The sequential events of such cell - cell interactions are (1) attachment of leishmanias to macrophages; (2) entry of Icishinanias into macrophages; (3) intracellular survival of leishmanias; (4) intracellular differentiation of leishmanias from promastigotes into amastigotes; and (5) intracellular multiplication of amastigotes.

How do these events occur at the cellular level? What is the biochemical or molecular basis of such cell-cell interactions? These questions have been studied more intensively during the last decade, following the advent of technical improvement for the isolation and cultivation of macrophages and both stages of leishmanias in vitro. Leishmanial infection of macrophages is studied in vitro to facilitate the analysis of the sequential steps involved.

The macrophages used are largely derived from the peritoneal cavity of rodents and, to some extent, from human peripheral blood monocytes. Leishmanias used are amastigotes isolated from infected animals or macrophages in culture and promastigotes grown in cell-free media. Promastigotes are grown to late-log or stationary phase when infective cells corresponding to those in the vector become more abundant.

This chapter summarizes and discusses pertinent points in the sequence of five events, emphasizing recent developments in cell biology in this area.

ATTACHMENT OF LEISHMANIAS TO MACROPHAGES

The adhesion of leishmanias to the macrophage surface is a prerequisite for gaining intracellular entry. Binding must occur for both stages of the parasite during evolution of the disease, in the initial primary infection by promastigotes deposited by the sandfly into animal skin and in the subsequent infection at a later stage by the amastigotes released from heavily parasitized macrophages.

In vitro study of *leishmania-macrophage* binding indicates molecular compatibility at the host-parasite membrane interface. Leishmanias are clearly predisposed to bind to macrophages: promastigotes bind avidly to these phagocytes, less well to fibroblasts, poorly to lymphocytes, and hardly, if at all, to erythrocytes.

The existence of specific membrane-binding sites during leishmania-macrophage interactions is suggested by ultrastructural observations of points of attachment separated by gaps of nonadhesion. Moreover, promastigote-macrophage binding follows a saturation kinetics suggestive of ligand -receptor interactions.

This proposal has gained increasing support by recent findings that such binding can be blocked by presumed ligands of low. molecular weight or complex molecules purified from the parasite surface and by the antibodies or their Fab fragments specific to either macrophage surface receptors or to leishmania membrane molecules.

The list of *macrophage* surface molecules involved includes their receptors for antibody, complement, mannose, and fibronectin. All these receptors are known to have biological importance in cell - cell interactions. The surface molecules of leishmanias implicated in their binding to the macrophages appear to be *glycoconjugates*.

Leishmanias possess antigenic molecules on their surface. It has long been noted by a number of investigators that opsonization of living promastigotes with antisera prepared against them in laboratory animals or those from infected animals increases their uptake by macrophages. For example, prior treatment of *Leishmania donovani* promastigotes with rabbit antisera doubles the rate of their subsequent binding to hamster macrophages.

Phagocytosis of *L. donovani* by mouse macrophages is increased when the host cells are pretreated with sera from infected mice. Similar findings in other systems leave no doubt that this binding is mediated by opsonic or cytophilic antileishmania antibodies, which bridge Fe receptors of macrophages and the surface antigens of leishmanias.

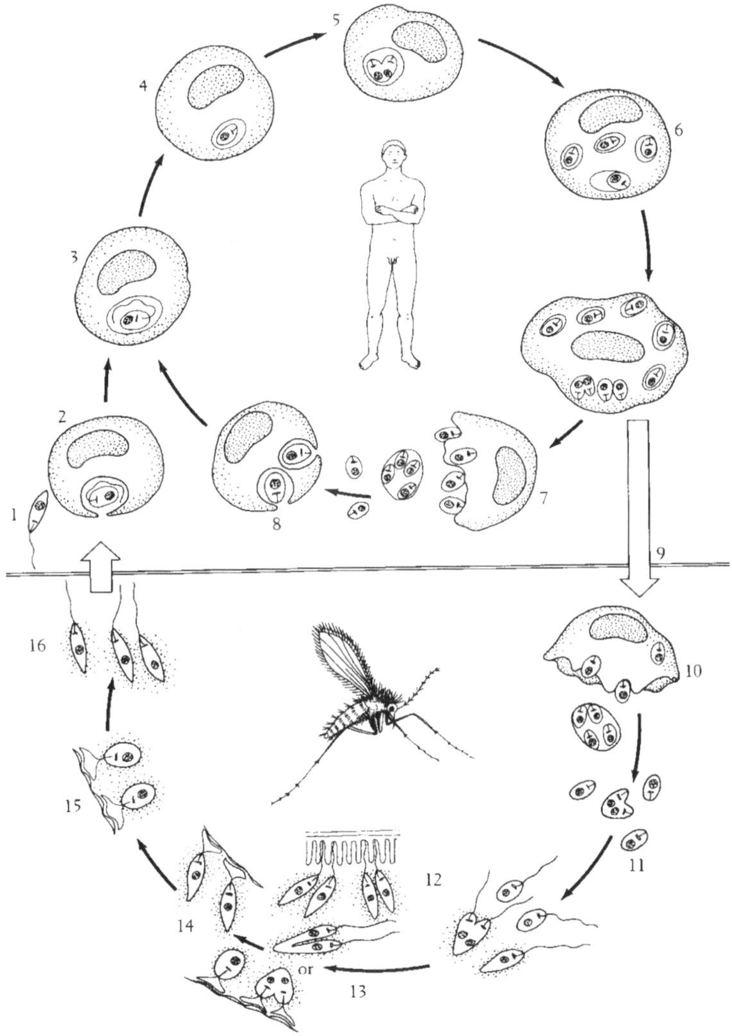

Figure 4.1: Leishmanial infection in sandfly and in mammalian hosts. (1) Delivery of promastigotes (proboscis form) into human skin by the bite of sandfly vector; (2) attachment and engulfment by phagocytosis of promastigotes by a macrophage; (3) fusion of phagosome containing a promastigote with lysosome in a macrophage; (4) differentiation of promastigote into amastigote in the phagolysosome of the infected macrophage; (5) multiplication of an amastigote in a parasite-containing or parasitophorous vacuole; (6) formation of large parasitophorous vacuole and continuing replication of intravacuolar amastigotes; (7) rupture of heavily parasitized macrophage and release of amastigotes; (8) phagocytosis of released amastigotes by a macrophage; (9) ingestion of parasitized macrophage by sandfly after a blood meal taken from infected person or reservoir animal; (10-16) development of promastigotes in the sandfly vector.

Leishmanial promastigotes of different species have been shown to fix complement. Evidence indicates the adsorption of C3 to and its conversion into Cab and iC3b by protease (gp63) on the surface of promastigotes. Their phagocytosis by macrophages is increased several times after complement fixation, and this is significantly inhibited by monoclonal antibodies or their Fab fragments specific to the iC3b receptor (CR3) of the macrophages.

This iC3b receptor-dependent uptake of promastigotes also occurs under serum-free conditions, suggesting that it is mediated by the complement endogenously produced by the macrophages. That complement activation may be a means employed by promastigotes to facilitate their entry into phagocytes is thus suggested.

Monosaccharides, such as mannose, N-acetylglucosamine, N-galactosamine, galactose and/or sialic acid have been detected by specific probes (e.g., plant lectins) as terminal residues of glycoconjugates on the surface of various leishmania species. The possible participation of mannose residues on the surface of *promastigotes* as one of the determinants in their binding to macrophages was first proposed on the basis of competition-inhibition types of experiments under serum-free conditions using zymosan and mannose.

Recent work provides strong support for this notion. The binding of *promastigotes* to *macrophages* is greatly reduced when the latter cells are cultured on mannancoated glass coverslips to sequester their mannose receptors, thereby making them unavailable for binding. Promastigote-macrophage binding through other monosaccharide-specific pathways is also possible, but remains to be explored. Such monosaccharide specificity of host-parasite interactions at the cellular level may bear on the well known tissue tropism of *Leishmania* species.

There are indeed quantitative and qualitative differences on the externally disposed sugar residues detected in different *Leishmania* species. Other known receptors of macrophages that may be involved in their binding of leishmanias include those for fibronectin. This molecule has been well characterized biochemically and is instrumental in several cell-cell adhesion interactions between different host cells on the one hand, and host cells and microbes on the other.

There is evidence for the adhesion of serum fibronectin to leishmanias, leading to their increased binding to macrophages. Host fibronectin may serve simply as a bridge to enhance adhesion or also facilitate *phagocytosis* of *Leishmania* by cooperation with the macrophage complement receptor.

Which endogenous surface molecules of leishmanias are responsible for their binding to the receptors of macrophages? All leishmania surface antigens that react to natural antibodies or that can elicit opsonic and cytophilic antibodies are potentially involved as participants in the Fc receptor-dependent binding.

The two species of surface glycoconjugates that have been identified recently as candidates for the macrophage-binding molecules of promastigotes function apparently independently of the mechanism mediated by Fe receptors. A surface antigenic glycoprotein of 63 kD (gp63) has been purified from *Leishmania amazonensis* to homogeneity by monoclonal antibody affinity chromatography. Preadsorption of these molecules to macrophages inhibits their binding of promastigotes by 50 percent. Since this antigen contains terminal mannose residues, the mannose receptors on the surface of macrophages may well be those that bind this saccharide.

A glycoprotein of similar molecular mass was also isolated from *Leishmania mexicana* by concanavalin A and anionic exchange column chromatography. The Fab fragments of a polyvalent antibody prepared against this antigen inhibit promastigote-macrophage binding. The purified antigen incorporated into liposomes binds complement and competes with mannan for binding to macrophages.

It is suggested that gp63 is the leishmania ligand responsible for binding of promastigotes to both mannose receptors and iC3b receptors of the macrophages. It has been shown that gp63 is a surface protease present in all pathogenic species of *Leishmania* examined. Conservation of gp63 and its enzymatic activity indicate a universal importance for this molecule in the cleavage of complement by leishmanias for binding to macrophage receptors.

Recently, analysis of the gene encoding gp63 revealed the presence of an RGD sequence, a known ligand for a family of receptors including CR3 of macrophages. An RGD-containing peptide was subsequently synthesized on the basis of the gp63 gene sequence and found to inhibit significantly the binding of promastigotes to macrophages.

This finding, coupled with the inhibitory activity of the antibodies specific to either CR3 or the synthetic peptide, suggests that the binding of promastigotes to macrophages may be mediated also directly by the interaction of the RGD sequence in the gp63 to the receptor of concern. Another parasite surface molecule of interest is a species of glycolipid, which has been purified from *L. major* by monoclonal antibody affinity chromatography and from *L. donovani* biochemically, known as *lipophosph-*

oglycan. The Fab fragments of the antibody inhibit promastigote-macrophage binding by 80 percent. The receptors of macrophages for this leishmanial antigen are not CR3 but do belong to the integrin family. Recent work outlined in the foregoing paragraph lends credence to the proposal that leishmanias use preexisting receptors of macrophages for binding, probably through multiple pathways.

The binding of cells in this host-parasite system may occur through the direct interactions of their native surface molecules or through the intervention of soluble mediators released by the host cells, for example, antibodies, complement, and fibronectin. It is possible that there are binding mechanisms that do not use specific macrophage receptors.

Different leishmanias may also use different binding mechanisms. These are additional areas that require investigation. Topics of interest concerning receptor-mediated mechanisms are the cooperation or competition among different binding pathways identified and their relative importance in the natural infection.

Under serum-free conditions, there appears to be cooperation among different receptors described earlier. Of interest is the possibility that the binding mechanism may change completely or partly, involving other pathways mediated, for example, by Fc receptors in the presence of antibodies generated against leishmania surface antigens.

The macrophage-binding ligands of leishmanias can also be "masked" by other molecules derived either from the host or from the vector and "denuded" or clustered by the capping phenomenon of membrane molecules mediated, for example, by antibodies and lectins.

Conceivably, all these events may affect the leishmania-macrophage binding under natural conditions and possibly alter the intracellular fate of leishmanias. This hypothesis is supported by a recent finding indicating that the entry of leishmanias into macrophages through iC3b receptors results in only a minimal respiratory burst in the host cell.

Since promastigotes are susceptible to the toxic effects of oxygen radicals, the reduced burst may favour parasite survival. Detailed analysis of leishmania surface molecules and their interactions with macrophage receptors may yield useful information on the relative importance of the different binding pathways.

INTRACELLULAR ENTRY OF LEISHMANIAS INTO MACROPHAGES

Leishmanias bound to the surface of the host cells must be interiorized to achieve intracellular parasitism. Phagocytic activity of macrophages plays a major role in this process. As noted, blocking phagocytosis with cytochalasins prevents parasite entry. Under scanning and transmission electron microscopes, the cytological events have been well described for the uptake of leishmanial promastigotes by macrophages.

The attachment of leishmanias through either their anterior or posterior end induces an extensive membrane ruffling formation of the macrophage surface. The parasites are subsequently engulfed by cellular pseudopodia, as found during phagocytosis of other microorganisms or particles by macrophages.

The process requires the expenditure of energy on the part of the macrophages and the participation of their cytokinetic elements, such as actin. The attachment of leishmanias to the surface of macrophages presumably triggers phagocytosis by mechanisms similar to those under investigation in other systems, including a sequential binding of molecules on host cell and parasite surfaces, in a zipperlike mechanism.

Intracellular Survival of Leishmanias in Macrophages

Afteegaining entry into macrophages, leishmanias must find ways to defend themselves against a battery of powerful microbicidal mechanisms known to exist in these phagocytes. How leishmanias survive intracellularly is a matter of considerable interest, given our understanding of the major roles played by these phagocytes in host defense generally. Discussion here will be limited to the cellular and molecular aspects of this event. After entry into macrophages, leishmanias are lodged in phagosomes to which lysosomes of the macrophages fuse, creating phagolysosomes.

Surprisingly, leishmanias survive in this hostile environment, which normally destroys most microorganisms ingested by macrophages. Leishmanias share this capability with few other species of intracellular parasites, *Mycobacterium leprae* and *Coxiella burnettii* being the other exceptional pathogens that survive in this subcellular compartment. How do leishmanias resist microbicidal factors in the lysosomal compartments of macrophages? Since many potential microbicidal properties have been reported for macrophages but have not been systematically studied for leishmania specifically, this question is not easily answered.

Phagocytosis of many microorganisms triggers a respiratory burst by mononuclear phagocytes, resulting in the generation of microbicidal oxygen radicals such as *hydrogen peroxide*, *hydroxyl radicals*, and singlet oxygen. There has been report of an unusual iron-containing superoxide dismutase of trypanosomatid protozoa, including leishmanias, that allows them to dismutate superoxide anions into hydrogen peroxide and molecular oxygen. More recently "trypanothione," similar to glutathione of mammalian cells, has been discovered in these parasites.

In contrast to mammalian glutathione "trypanothione" possesses additional molecules of spermidine. Leishmanias have little or no catalase and may rely on trypanothione peroxidase as the major scavenger for the detoxification of hydrogen peroxide. It is possible that these and similar enzyme systems of leishmanias work in concert to dispose of the oxidative metabolites generated not only from their own aerobic respiration but also from the respiratory burst of the mononuclear phagocytes.

Of interest is the finding that an acid phosphatase purified from the plasma membrane of *L.* donovani diminishes the respiratory burst of neutrophils induced by zymosan. The implication of this finding is that the binding of leishmanias to phagocytes may result in the generation of oxygen metabolites in amounts less than usual, thereby relieving the burden of detoxification for the parasites. Mononuclear phagocytes possess a number of "nonoxidative" microbicidal factors, such as channel or pore-forming molecules (polyperforins) that might result in perforation of microbial cell walls or membranes, and lysosomal hydrolytic enzymes.

Surface membrane glycoproteins of *L. m. amazonensis* are refractory to degradation at pH 5.0 by lysosomal preparations purified from rat liver. Leishmanias may be protected by a surface layer of molecules resistant to acid hydrolases, enabling them to survive in the acidic environment of the macrophage's ***phagolysosome***.

Leishmania surface molecules may also play an active role in detoxification of microbicidal factors in this environment; gp63 has been identified as a protease active at pH 4.0 and conceivably could destroy host enzymes that normally have microbicidal properties. Additional protection against lysosomal enzymes might be conferred on leishmania by their metabolites, which are released into their immediate surroundings.

It has been suggested that ammonium ions and proteases released by *L. m. mexicana* might interfere with lysosomal functions by raising the intralysosomal pH and by directly interacting with lysosomal enzymes, respectively\ Soluble factors excreted by *L. major* (called "excreted factors") are reported to inhibit the activity of beta-galactosidase and to partially protect *erythrocytes* from degradation by macrophages; other lysosomal enzymes tested are not affected. The "*excreted factors*" appear to contain glycolipids and glycopeptides possibly shed from the leishmania cell surface, but their precise composition and chemical structure have not been well characterized. There may be multiple factors at the disposal of leishmanias to disarm the degradative actions of lysosomes.

"*Molecular mimicry*" has been proposed as a means of intralysosomal survival of leishmania, on the assumptions that mechanisms must exist whereby hydrolytic enzymes in the lysosome avoid mutual digestion and that leishmania surface or secreted molecules, by virtue of their resemblance to lysosomal enzymes, may somehow fit into such a "scheme of protection."

The acid phosphatase (a usual lysosomal marker enzyme) and protease found on leishmania surface may represent examples involved in this phenomenon. Additional possibilities have been suggested. Surface glycoconjugates of leishmanias are anchored to their plasma membrane via glycosyl phosphotidylinositol, analogous to that reported for the variant-specific glycoproteins of African trypanosomes.

Furthermore, a promastigote surface glycoprotein is released on their entry into *macrophages* and becomes demonstrable on the macrophage surface. The release of the leishmania surface glycoproteins may be triggered by activation of a phosphotidylinositol-specific phospholipase C endogenous to the parasites or to the lysosomes of macrophages.

Do one or more of these molecules released from leishmanias inhibit lysosomal enzymes directly or shut off their "trigger" and "activator" of respiratory burst, if they indeed work in sequence as a cascade of reactions? Further investigation into the molecular structure of leishmania membrane molecules (e.g., gp63) and their interactions or the interactions of their components after release with macrophages will undoubtedly provide insight into questions relating to the intracellular survival mechanisms of leishmanias.

Of relevance is the recent finding that leishmania surface *lipophosphoglycan* inhibits *proteinkinase C*, which may be involved in the activation of microbicidal mechanisms during phagocytosis by macrophages.

Cellular Differentiation of Leishmanias

In the *phagolysosome* of macrophages, leishmanias differentiate from promastigotes into amastigotes, an adaptation necessary for their survival during the transition from an extracellular to an intracellular environment. Which factors trigger this differentiation? Some leishmania species differentiate from promastigotes into forms resembling *amastig-*

otes in *nonlysosomal* compartments of human *fibroblasts*. This finding suggests that transformation probably is not triggered by events dependent on the activation of lysosomal enzymes. The body temperature of the mammalian host and as yet undefined factors in the intracellular milieu are involved, but may not be absolutely required. Forms that resemble amastigotes morphologically have been observed in aged cultures of promastigotes grown continuously at 27°C.

It has been possible to obtain such "amastigote forms" of leishmanias from promastigotes of some species incubated in a serum-containing medium at 33-35°C in the absence of macrophages or other mammalian cells. These forms have some morphologic, antigenic, and metabolic similarities to intracellular amastigotes but nonetheless may not be identical to tissue-derived amastigotes.

Profound morphological and biochemical changes accompany leishmanial differentiation from promastigotes into amastigotes. Regression of external flagella occurs, as does shortening of the body length and reduction in the number of pellicular microtubules and other organelles.

There is a substantial reduction in the biosynthesis of macromolecules and in oxygen consumption. The diminution of leishmanias in size, growth rates, and metabolic activities during this differentiation may represent a generalized biological "attenuation," perhaps occurring in the face of a very hostile microenvironment.

This notion may be incorrect, however, because cyclic nucleotides, certain nucleoside metabolic enzymes, sterol and fatty acid biosynthetic enzymes, membrane antigenic molecules, and heat-shock proteins appear to be synthesized by amastigotes either as new products or at a level higher than those in promastigotes.

Indeed, cross hybridization between genomic and eDNA libraries prepared from amastigotes and promnastigotes provides evidence for the selective expression of genes specific to these different leishmanial stages. The regulatory mechanisms of gene expression for biosynthesis of specific proteins during leishmanial differentiation may vary with different species.

For example, tubulin biosynthesis occurs at a higher rate in promastigotes than in amastigotes. This is regulated under either post transcriptional control (*L. m. ama*zonensis) or transcriptional control (*L. enriettii*).

The regulatory mechanisms of gene expression during interstage transformation of leishmania are clearly a fertile area for research, one that could divulge unique biological control mechanisms.

INTRACELLULAR MULTIPLICATION OF LEISHMANIAS

Leishmanias must multiply to cause all the sequelae of leishmaniasis, as only a very small number of promastigotes are delivered into the mammalian host by the sandfly vector. Shortly after the differentiation from promastigotes into amastigotes, leishmanias have been seen to divide in cultured macrophages.

Cell division of leishmanias and other trypanosomatid protozoa is akin to binary fission of bacteria. In general, division of the flagella, flagellar pockets, kinetoplasts, and nuclei precedes that of the cell; a division furrow forms usually at the anterior end and extends posteriorly, splitting each cells lengthwise into two daughter cells. Where do leishmanial amastigotes multiply intracellularly in macrophages? They do so in the parasite-containing vacuoles, which have properties of secondary lysosomes.

Leishmania residence in this site is not unexpected since lysosome-phagosome fusion occurs shortly after parasite entry into macrophages. Gentirmous residence of leishmanias in this cellular compartment is indicated by the following evidence: (1) electron microscopy and UV fluorescent microscopy have shown that the tracer labels (e.g., thorotrast or FITC-dextran) added to the culture medium of infected cells accumulate in the parasite-containing vacuole, and (2) this vacuole has an acidic pH of 5.0 to 5.5, as determined by fluorometric assays of FITC-dextran-labeled macrophages infected with leishmanias.

This compartment represents a portion of the lysosome-phagosome vacuolar system of the macrophages and is accessible to the molecules present in the immediate environment of the infected cells. Amastigotes may occupy only a portion of the vacuolar space, and some adhere to the vacuolar membrane; the remaining portion of the vacuole is fluid-filled.

The nutritional implications of the intraphagolysosomal residence for leishmanias in macrophages are that they must be acid-tolerant in their metabolism and that they might use nutrients that are lysosomotropic or are taken into the phagosome-lysosome vacuolar system by endocytic or other transport activity of the macrophages.

Oxygen consumption and utilization of energy substrates for respiration by L. donovani proceed optimally for amastigotes at an ambient pH of 5.0 and for promastigotes at neutral pH, respectively. A proton pump system reported in their plasma membrane presumably assists in compensating for the proton concentration gradient that exists between their intracellular milieu and extracellular environment. The transport of certain substrates required for macromolecular biosynthesis appears to be driven by this proton pump.

Macrophages may not supply all the essential substrates needed by the leishmania. There is evidence that intracellular amastigotes acquire heme from the culture medium instead of from that synthesized by macrophages; leishmanias cannot synthesize this compound de novo.

Furthermore, success has been reported in growing some leishmania species as amastigotelike forms at 34°C in cell-free medium containing additional factors, especially water soluble vitamins and nucleosides. It is not known if these are nutrients normally supplied to the parasites by macrophages, enabling them to grow intracellularly.

Ectoenzymes of leishmanias, such as acid phosphatase and nucleotidases, have been postulated as serving a nutritional role in scavenging purine nucleotides by leishmanias, since these and related protozoa lack the pathway for de novo purine synthesis.

The major surface glycoprotein (gp63) of leishmanias as a protease may function similarly by breaking down proteins into peptides and amino acids that can then be used by the parasite. Lysosomes have long been considered the "*digestive bag*" of mammalian cells.

Whether leishmanias exploit the degradative capacity of the lysosomal enzymes for their own nutritional gains (much like some parasitic helminths do in the intestinal tract of their host) is an interesting question that awaits further assessment.

5

TOXOPLASMA

Toxoplasma gondii, an obligate intracellular protozoan parasite, was first described by Charles Nicolle in 1908, one year before he did the work on typhus that earned him the Nobel Prize in Medicine. Nicolle and a colleague found *T. gondii* in the African rodent *Ctenodactylus gondi,* which supplied the parasite's species name.

The genus name does not refer to any toxic property of the parasite but instead is derived from the Greek *toxon,* bow (as in bow and arrow), in reference to the crescent shape of the organism. Although *T. gondii* has been known for eight decades, it is the most recent of the major human parasites to have its life cycle understood. Not until 1970 did several laboratories independently establish the critical role of felines as the definitive host.

Infection of humans with *T. gondii* is common but generally asymptomatic. Toxoplasmosis poses a major clinical problem in two contexts. If a woman has a primary infection during pregnancy, her developing fetus may also become infected and suffer severe congenital defects. Recrudescent or primary toxoplasmosis in patients with a defect in cell-mediated immunity, as in AIDS, can result in fatal encephalitis.

TAXONOMY AND LIFE CYCLE

Toxoplasma gondii has been assigned to the phylum Apicomplexa and class Sporozoa, which also includes the malaria parasites (genus Plasmodium). However, in contrast to the narrow vertebrate host ranges of the Plasmodia, *T. gondii* is a cosmopolitan parasite that infects a wide variety of birds and mammals. Acute toxoplasmosis in these hosts

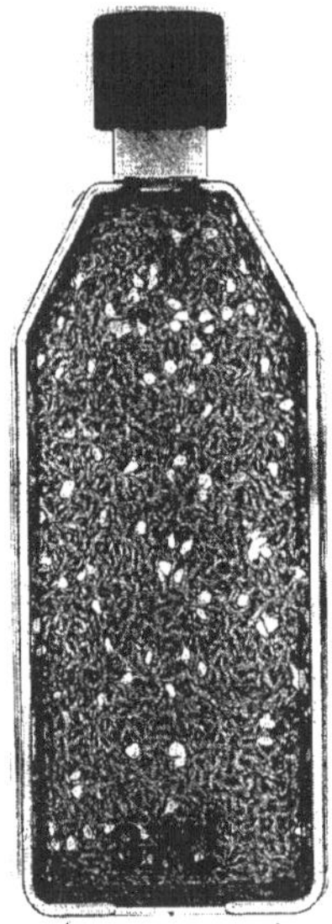

Figure 5.1: Plaques formed by T. gondii 7 *days after infection of a confluent monolayer culture of human fibroblasts. The fibroblasts have been stained for photography. The plaques are the small, completely clear areas.*

is characterized by intracellular growth in many tissues of the rapidly dividing tachyzoite stage. As the immune response controls the acute infection, some of the tachyzoites become encysted, particularly in muscle and brain, in an essentially dormant stage termed the bradyzoite.

These cysts contain hundreds of bradyzoites within a wall that is contributed, at least in part, by the host cell, and they are retained for years and possibly for the lifetime of the vertebrate host. If the tissue that contains these cysts is eaten by a nonfeline carnivore, the bradyzoites are released in the intestine and again yield an infection characterized initially by rapid growth of tachyzoites and ultimately by the persistence of encysted bradyzoites.

However, when encysted bradyzoites are eaten by a member of the cat family, a different scenario ensues. In addition to yielding tachyzoites, the bradyzoites also differentiate within intestinal epithelial cells through several stages of schizogony to yield male and female gametes.

These gametes fuse to form a zygote, which synthesizes an impervious protective wall for itself and is excreted in the feces as a unicellular unsporulated oocyst. At ambient temperatures the excreted oocyst sporulates and becomes infectious through three cell divisions yielding eight sporozoites, all contained within the oocyst wall.

When a sporulated oocyst is ingested by a mammal or bird, the sporozoites are released and infect the intestinal epithelial cells. They become rapidly multiplying tachyzoites that produce first an acute and then a chronic infection with encysted bradyzoites, thereby completing the natural life cycle.

Since only the tachyzoite stage of *T. gondii* can be conveniently grown in cultured cells, most knowledge of the cell biology of *T. gondii* is drawn from studies of this rapidly growing asexual form. This stage offers an excellent model for the cell biologist interested in the complex system of one eukaryotic cell parasitizing another.

Principal among the advantages of this parasite are the ability of the tachyzoite to grow in practically any cultured mammalian cell and the availability of a plaque assay for infectivity that allows precise titrations, easy cloning, and simple selection of mutants. Although a good deal has been learned about the cell biology of *T. gondii*, major gaps in our knowledge remain.

Fortunately, some of these gaps can be filled by reference to data from studies of *Eimeria tenella*, a related parasite of chickens that belongs to the same subclass, the Coccidia, as does *T. gondii*. Although extrapolation of data from this closely related organism may not always be reliable, potentially useful new experimental approaches to the study of *T. gondii* may be suggested by data from *E. tenella*.

MORPHOLOGY AND COMPOSITION

Tachyzoites of *T. gondii* are crescent-shaped cells, about 6 μm long and 2 μm wide. They share many cytological features with other eukaryotic cells, including a nucleus, mitochondria, Golgi apparatus, and endoplasmic reticulum. Only a few studies of the RNA of *T. gondii* have been reported. The ribosomal RNA consists of the usual large and small molecules that are presumably associated with their respective ribosomal subunits.

Recent reports demonstrate conclusively that the mRNA of *T. gondii* resembles that of other eukaryotic cells in bearing a 3'-polyadenylated tail. This mRNA has been translated in heterologous systems to yield polypeptide products serologically identifiable as *T. gondii* proteins.

The DNA content of the sporozoite stage of *T. gondii* has been determined to be about 0.1 μg/cell through direct microfluorometric analysis of single cells. This value is the haploid DNA content of the parasite because all stages except the zygote are haploid. Several

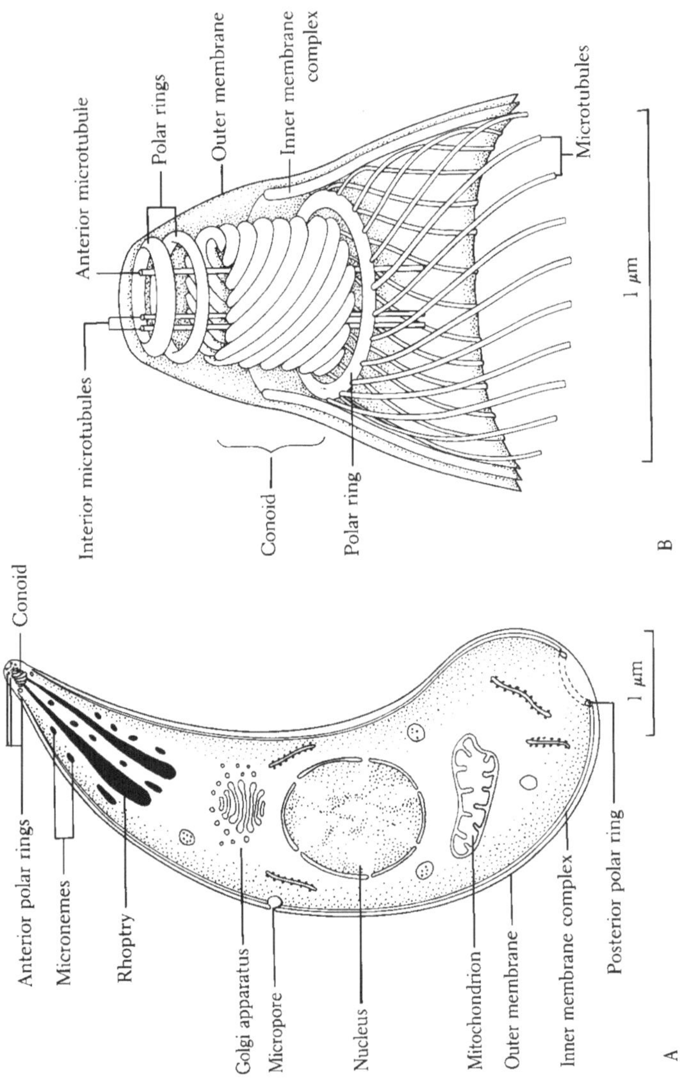

Figure 5.2: A. The ultrastructure of the tachyzoite of T. gondii (based on various electron microscopic studies). B. Detailed view of the structure of the anterior end of T. gondii.

laboratories have prepared genomic and eDNA libraries for *T. gondii*. As might be expected from the size of its genome, the tachyzoite contains a vast array of proteins.

At least 1000 proteins have been observed by autoradiography of two-dimensional electrophoresis of biosynthetically labeled parasites, a value that *undoubtedly* underestimates the complexity of the organism. In contrast, cell surface specific *radioiodination* followed by SDS acrylamide gel electrophoresis reveals only a limited array of five to seven major radioactive bands with relative molecular weights (M_r) that range from 14,000 to 60,000.

The most prominent protein (M_r 30,000) may represent as much as 3 percent of the total parasite protein. Like some surface proteins of the Plasmodia, this protein contains an immunodominant repetitive epitope. The relative simplicity of the tachyzoite surface is reflected in the humoral immune response, which primarily recognizes four major surface antigens of M_r 14,000 to 43,000.

Unlike most eukaryotic cells, the *T. gondii* tachyzoite is reportedly unable to bind any of the fluorescently labeled lectins that are generally used to identify surface glycoproteins. This difference from other eukaryotes is likely to be more apparent than real, for recent studies have detected low levels of concanavalin A binding both to the intact organism and to isolated proteins.

It may simply be that for steric reasons, the glycosyl residues of the surface proteins of *T. gondii* are not readily accessible to lectins. In addition to the general characteristics that define *T. gondii* as a eukaryotic cell, the tachyzoite also has a number of structures that mark it as a member of the *Apicomplexa*, and within that phylum as one of the subclass Coccidia. Many of these ultrastructural features were, in fact, first observed in *T. gondii*.

The tachyzoites are coated with not one but three unit membranes that together make up the pellicle. The outer membrane is continuous. The two closely apposed innermost membranes are discontinuous, ending at structures called polar rings, which are located at both the anterior and the posterior ends of the parasites.

The innermost membranes also have small circular gaps called micropores that may be involved in the uptake of nutrients. The subpellicular cytoskeleton is composed of 22 microtubules that stretch from the anterior polar ring through most of the length of the parasite.

The anterior end of the *T. gondii* tachyzoite is marked by the presence of the conoid, a hollow, truncated cone of spirally wound fibers that are also likely to be microtubules. Protrusion of this structure during the early stages of entry into a host cell can be detected by both light and electron microscopy.

Two intracellular organelles peculiar to the Apicomplexa are also thought to play a role in the penetration of host cells. The rhoptries are club-shaped, densely osrophilic structures whose narrow ends terminate in the conoid. Their structure suggests a secretory function that is probably carried out in the early stages of host-cell entry. Each parasite has only a small number of rhoptries, perhaps only two. Packed between the rhoptries are a large number of smaller osmophilic vesicles called micronemes. The relationship between these two types of anterior organelles remains unclear although the micronemes may also play a role in penetration.

Infection of Host Cells

A critical event in the life of any obligate intracellular parasite is the infection of its host cell. This process can conveniently be considered to occur in two steps, attachment and penetration, or invasion; unfortunately, practically nothing is known of the first, and the precise events of the second are disputed.

The conventional view of the attachment of an intracellular protozoan parasite to its host cell requires recognition by the parasite of some specific macromolecule on the host cell surface. For certain Plasmodium species, substantial progress has been made in identification of the host cell receptor.

The only clue as to the nature of the host cell receptor for *T. gondii* is the remarkably broad range of cells that can be infected, namely cells of a wide variety of histological types from all mammals, probably from all birds, and from at least one reptile. Such a broad host range all but rules out any specific protein as the receptor and forces the consideration of components that are common to the plasma membranes of most cells.

The only two likely possibilities are lipids and the glycosyl residues that are present on both glycoproteins and glycolipids. Existing evidence argues against glycosyl residues because addition of a wide variety of sugars to the extracellular medium fails to block the infection of cultured cells by *T. gondii*. However, it may be that these sugars would have mimicked the true receptor more effectively had they been linked to a carrier protein.

An alternative possibility, that *T. gondii* recognizes cellular membranes by attachment to some lipid component, should be considered. Cholesterol, a component of all animal cell plasma membranes, has been implicated as the receptor for certain rickettsia, which are obligate intracellular bacteria.

However it occurs, attachment of *T. gondii* serves to orient the parasite with its anterior end, which bears the conoid and rhoptries, in contact with the plasma membrane of the host cell. At this time the *conoid* is extended and the tachyzoites proceed rapidly to invade and soon come to lie within a *cytoplasmic vacuole* called the *parasitophorous* vacuole. Many ultrastructural studies of invasion by *T. gondii* have used mouse peritoneal macrophages as the host cell, probably because of the long-standing tradition of maintaining the parasite in vivo by serial intraperitoneal passage.

In retrospect, however, this use of macrophages was probably unfortunate. The macrophage is capable of *phagocytosing* dead *T. gondii* through a mechanism unrelated to the active invasion that results in a productive infection. The two processes, phagocytosis and invasion, initially yield a superficially similar outcome, a parasite within a cytoplasmic vacuole.

However, when dead parasites or even live parasites coated with antibody are phagocytosed, they are doomed to destruction by an assortment of agents, including lysosomal enzymes and active oxygen metabolites. The complications of studying a culture in which both phagocytosis and invasion are taking place can be avoided by using one of the many nonphagocytic cultured cells that allow penetration and growth of the parasite.

The penetration of a host cell by *T. gondii* probably requires the interplay of biochemical and biomechanical events, although their relative importance is uncertain. The anterior *organelles*, *rhoptries* and micronemes, are generally regarded as secretory in nature and are thought to produce substances that promote the penetration of *T. gondii* into its host cell.

Both biochemical and ultrastructural evidence support this contention. A fraction of lysed *T. gondii* that increases the ability of the parasite to invade cultured cells has been partially purified. This material, termed "penetrationenhancing factor," is active at 1 μg protein/ml and seems not to be lysosomal in origin.

Instead, immunofluorescence using antibody made against partially purified penetration-enhancing factor showed it to be preferentially located within the *rhoptry* region of intact parasites, suggesting that this factor is a secretory product.

This conclusion is supported by ultrastructural studies showing that during the invasion of host cells, the membranes of the rhoptries fuse with the plasma membrane of the parasite in a manner that would release the contents of the rhoptries close to the host cell membrane. The biochemical role of the *penetration*-enhancing factor, or rhoptry secretion (if indeed they are *synonymous*), remains to be determined. It is likely to alter the properties of the host cell membrane, perhaps by increasing its fluidity, in such a way as to promote penetration of the parasite. At concentrations significantly higher than those required to promote invasion, the penetration-enhancing factor is actually lytic to cultured cells.

The significance of these observations and elucidation of the precise role of the penetration-enhancing factor must await further study. The recent preparation of a *monoclonal* antibody against penetration-enhancing factor provides a promising direction for the future study of this factor. Once attachment has occurred, secretion from the rhoptries and invasion by the parasite are remarkably rapid. Several investigators have noted that invasion is complete in less than 15 seconds.

Various mechanisms have been proposed to explain this process, some claiming the major role for the host cell and others favoring active penetration by the parasite. The truth lies somewhere between the two extremes, although the parasite probably plays the *predominant* role.

Before the model presented below can be considered, the related topics of capping and motility in the tachyzoite must be considered. Capping is the process by which polyclonal antibodies attached to the surface of *T. gondii* are transported to its posterior end and then shed into the medium.

This process presumably reflects the action of an actin-based contractile system coupled to pellicular proteins and perhaps microtubules. Capping of antibodylinked pellicular proteins is thought to be closely related to the motility of *T. gondii* tachyzoites. Anyone who observes extracellular parasites in cell cultures is immediately struck by their rapid twisting motions, particularly just after an infected cell has lysed.

Although it has no flagella or any of the other specialized organelles associated with motility, the *T. gondii tachyzoite* is capable of rapid twisting and gliding motions, provided that it is attached to some substratum, such as a *monolayer* of cultured cells or a plastic tissue-culture plate.

This motility is likely to be related to the phenomenon of capping. In a reasonable model for *motility*, *pellicle* proteins attached to the *substratum* are transported to the rear of the organism, resulting in forward motion. The direction is determined by the subpellicular microtubules acting through linear arrays of intramembranous proteins.

How are these phenomena related to penetration of the parasite into a host cell? The hypothesis described below depends heavily on a model originally developed for *E. tenella*, in which the processes of

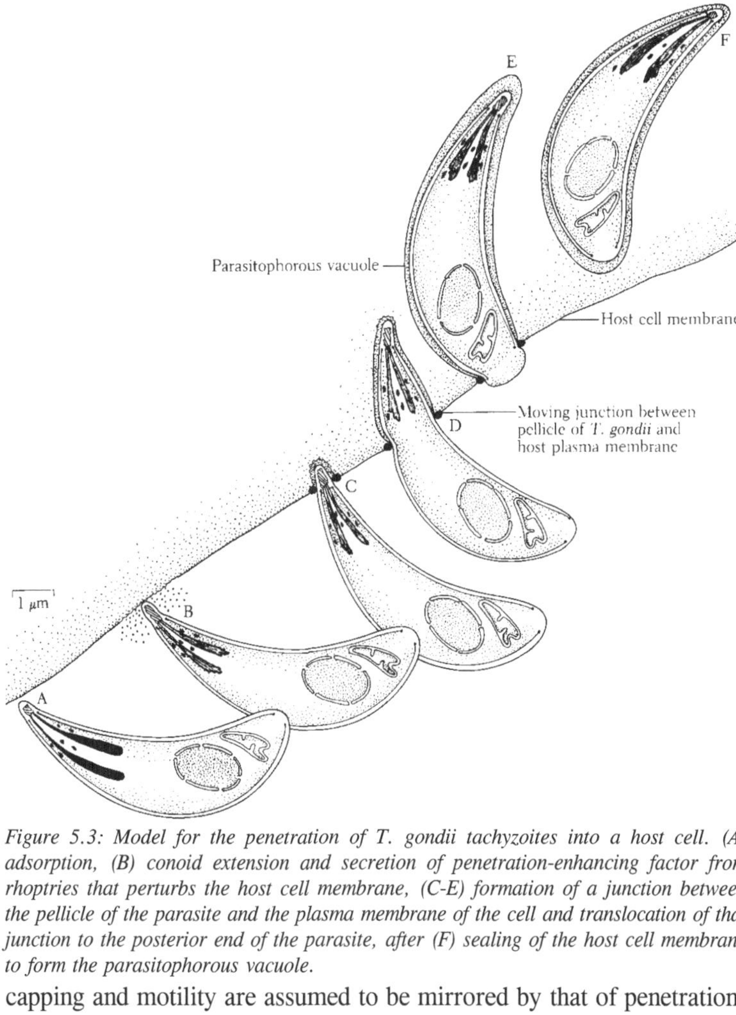

Figure 5.3: Model for the penetration of T. gondii tachyzoites into a host cell. (A) adsorption, (B) conoid extension and secretion of penetration-enhancing factor from rhoptries that perturbs the host cell membrane, (C-E) formation of a junction between the pellicle of the parasite and the plasma membrane of the cell and translocation of that junction to the posterior end of the parasite, after (F) sealing of the host cell membrane to form the parasitophorous vacuole.

capping and motility are assumed to be mirrored by that of penetration. In this model, the parasite first attaches through an unidentified receptor and immediately perturbs the host plasma membrane by secretion from its rhoptries. A close apposition of the parasite pellicle and the perturbed host cell membrane ensues.

This junction is then "capped" (that is, transported away from the anterior end), which drives the parasite into the cell and at the same time generates the *parasitophorous vacuolar* membrane from the plasma membrane of the host cell.

Finally, as the *capping* process reaches the posterior end of the parasite, the junction between the parasite and the host cell membrane is broken and the host cell plasma membrane fuses to yield a tachyzoite lying free within a cytoplasmic vacuole.

Although the role of the host cell during this process is secondary to that of the parasite, the host cell is *probably* not wholly passive. For example, its cytoskeleton must somehow *accommodate* the intrusion of the parasite. The evidence supporting the foregoing model is largely circumstantial. *T. gondii* will invade certain erythrocytes and indeed multiply within *immature nucleated erythroid* precursor cells.

The invasion of mature erythrocytes provides a useful model system because these cells are incapable of *phagocytosis*. During their invasion the close apposition of the host cell and parasite membranes is readily observed. Further evidence for this apposition comes from a striking study of the invasion of cells by *T. gondii* that have been coated with monoclonal antibody directed against the principal surface protein (M_r 30,000) of the tachyzoite.

Fortunately, this particular antibody is not capped and therefore serves as a marker for the entire surface of an extracellular parasite that has been treated with *monoclonal antibody*. Uniform coating of the surface of extracellular parasites can be demonstrated in electron micrographs with the immunoperoxidase method.

As these surface-labeled parasites invade host cells, the attached antibody is stripped off at the point of the moving junction between host and parasite membranes, testifying to its tightness. At present it is not known if only the attached antibody is shed during entry or if its antigen is lost as well. The role of actin in the biomechanical events associated with the penetration of *T. gondii is* supported by the observation that cytochalasin D blocks penetration but not attachment.

This observation does not exclude a role of actin in the host. Penetration of host cells by *T. gondii* also depends on energy metabolism by the parasite and possibly also by the host cell (compare the penetration of *Plasmodia* described elsewhere in this book). If this model for penetration is accepted, the principal unresolved issue becomes the severity of the effect on the host cell membrane at the site of entry.

Several ultrastructural studies suggest that the host cell membrane is physically disrupted and that the newly intracellular parasite lies within torn membrane *fragments* but partially exposed to the cytoplasm of its host cell. The vacuolar membrane is then thought to be quickly knit together, perhaps through the addition of membrane *components* supplied by the parasite.

In the *alternative*, simpler *model* adopted in Figure 2-4, the host cell membrane is assumed to remain intact during the entire process of penetration, and the breaks in this membrane observed during entry are considered artifacts ascribed to fragility induced by the secretion from the rhoptries.

The Role of the Parasitophorous Vacuole in the Intracellular Growth of *T. gondii*

However it is formed, the parasitophorous vacuole is a safe haven for the growth of *T. gondii*. In sharp contrast to the fate of a cytoplasmic phagosomal vacuole, the parasitophorous vacuole avoids both fusion with lysosomes and acidification. Instead, the outside of the parasitophorous vacuole becomes covered with host-cell mitochondria.

How these two seemingly similar vacuoles come to have totally different fates remains a mystery that is central to our understanding the intracellular growth of *T. gondii*. The absence of lysosomal fusion and acidification of the parasitophorous vacuole does not reflect a global defect in the host cell.

If a phagocytic cell infected with *T. gondii* also contains a phagosome, the phagosome is acidified and fuses normally with lysosomes. Thus, the inhibition of these functions is peculiar to the parasitophorous vacuole. The only likely way in which such a vacuole can communicate with the host cell is through the domains of vacuolar membrane proteins that are exposed to host cell cytoplasm.

T. gondii could determine the fate of its parasitophorous vacuole in several ways: (a) host proteins that signal lysosomal fusion and acidification could be systematically excluded during formation of the vacuole, (b) host cell proteins that signal these cellular functions could be altered allosterically or in some other manner to negate the signal, or (c) parasite-specific proteins that override the cellular signals could be incorporated into the vacuolar membrane.

One of the major difficulties in distinguishing among these explanations is that the vacuolar membrane has never been purified because of its fragility and lack of obvious identifying characteristics.

MULTIPLICATION OF THE TACHYZOITE

Secure within its parasitophorous vacuole, the tachyzoite begins to multiply; the division time of 5 to 9 hours is characteristic of whichever strain one is studying. As might be expected, greater virulence in vivo is associated with more rapid growth in vitro. Within any one vacuole,

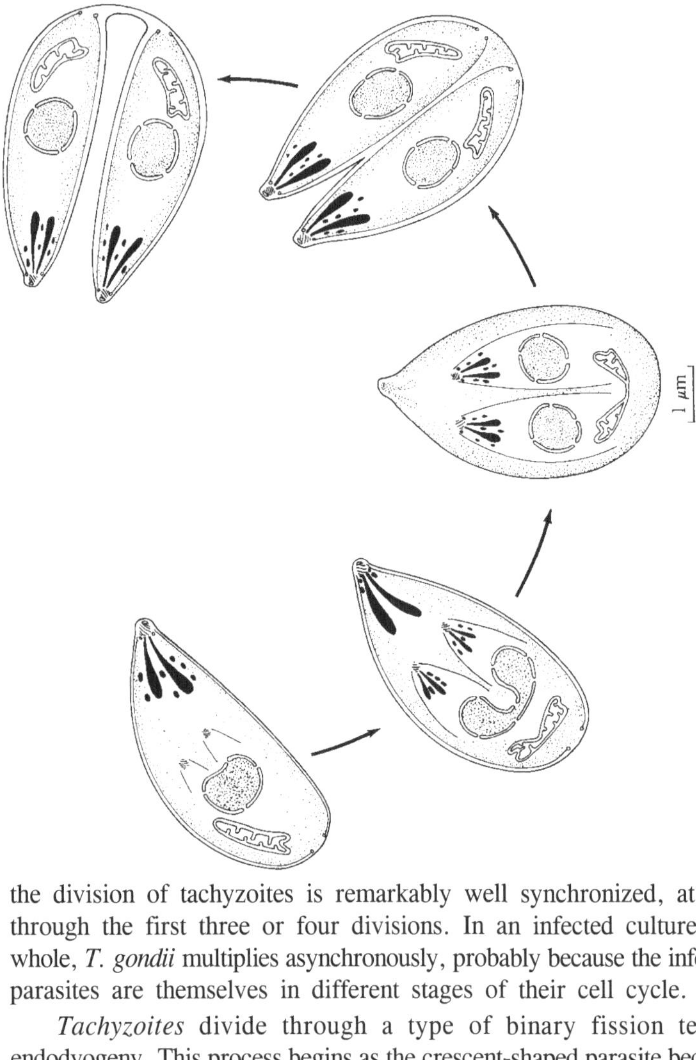

Figure 5.4: Stages in the division of tachyzoites of T. gondii by endodyogeny (based on various electron microscopic studies).

the division of tachyzoites is remarkably well synchronized, at least through the first three or four divisions. In an infected culture as a whole, *T. gondii* multiplies asynchronously, probably because the infecting parasites are themselves in different stages of their cell cycle.

Tachyzoites divide through a type of binary fission termed endodyogeny. This process begins as the crescent-shaped parasite becomes more spherical. Below the anterior pole in the cytoplasm of the mother cell, the two internal pellicular membranes of the *daughter* cells begin to be organized and soon acquire their own *rudimentary rhoptries*, micronemes, and conoids.

As the internal membranes grow posteriorly, the nucleus of the mother cell divides and the daughter nuclei become enclosed within the new inner *membranes* as they extend to the posterior pole. In contrast to mitosis in higher eukaryotes, the nuclear membrane of *T. gondii* remains intact and its chromosomes do not condense at metaphase. The mitochondria of the mother cell are also divided between the daughter cells.

As the daughter cells, now virtually complete, enlarge to fill the mother cell, the inner membrane complex of the mother cell disappears while the outer membrane is reused as the outer layer of the pellicle of the daughter cells. The daughter cells may remain temporarily attached at their posterior ends through a residual body of mother-cell cytoplasm.

The tachyzoites produced by synchronous endodyogeny in individual cultured cells usually lie in the same plane and form the rosettes that are characteristic of *T. gondii*. As the multiplication of tachyzoites progresses, the parasitophorous vacuole expands to fill more and more of the host cell cytoplasmic volume. The origin of the additional membrane required for the expansion of the vacuole is unknown.

It is likely to be supplied by the host but a contribution by the parasite cannot be ruled out. Remarkably, the growth of tachyzoites has little apparent effect upon the host cell until it lyses to release a new crop of parasites. Autoradiography detects no marked diminution of incorporation of amino acids into host cell proteins or of nucleosides into host cell nucleic acids.

Even the entry of cells into S phase, as detected by extensive nuclear incorporation of thymidine, or into mitosis—probably the most sensitive measure of the host cell's sense of well being—does not seem to be markedly affected by infection with *T. gondii*.

Perhaps the fact that the growing parasites are insulated from the host cell cytoplasm by the *parasitophorous* vacuole diminishes their impact on host cell metabolism. Roughly 2 days after infection, both the vacuolar membrane and the host cell lyse to release 64 to 256 *tachyzoites*. As observed by phase-contrast microscopy, this release is rapid and the newly emerging parasites are highly motile.

BIOCHEMICAL COMMUNICATION BETWEEN HOST CELL AND PARASITE

Understanding the biochemistry of the host-parasite relationship in cells infected with tachyzoites of *T. gondii* depends to a large extent on our knowledge of the function of the parasitophorous vacuolar membrane. All biochemical traffic between host cell and parasite must, of necessity, cross this membrane. There is no evidence that pyrimidine nucleotides or deoxynucleotides are exchanged between host cell and parasite. The experiments designed to detect any flow of uridine triphosphate (UTP) or thymidine triphosphate (TTP) from the host cell to *T. gondii* used a mutant parasite that is resistant to fluorodeoxyuridine (FUDR), as will be discussed. This mutant lacks an enzyme that plays the central role in pyrimidine salvage by *T. gondii*.

Autoradiography shows that this mutant is incapable of incorporating either [^{3}H]uridine or [^{3}H]deoxyuridine. However, the host cell, as expected, incorporates these precursors efficiently. Thus, the infected host cell labeled with [^{3}H]uridine must contain an ample amount of [^{3}H]UTP, the immediate precursor for RNA synthesis.

Since there is no doubt that the intracellular mutant parasites could use this [^{3}H]UTP if it were present in their own cytoplasm, the fact that they are unlabeled in autoradiography experiments proves that *T. gondii* has no direct access to the pyrimidine nucleotide pool of its host cell. The same argument can be applied to prove that the TTP pool of the host cell, which is efficiently labeled by [^{3}H)deoxyuridine, is unavailable to the parasite.

To examine the reverse possibility, that pyrimidine nucleotides of the parasite were available to the host cell, wild-type parasites could be used because human fibroblast host cells lack the salvage enzyme uracil phosphoribosyltransferase. When these cells are infected with wild-type *T. gondii* that are capable of incorporating uracil, autoradiography shows that incorporation of [^{3}H]uracil is confined to the intracellular parasites.

Since this precursor is used to make UTP and TTP for use in nucleic acid synthesis, these nucleotides synthesized by the parasite must be unavailable to the host cell. If they were available, the cytoplasm and nuclei of infected host cells would be labeled while the uninfected cells would remain unlabeled.

The purine nucleotide pool of the parasite is also unavailable to its host cell. This conclusion is based upon autoradiography of infected Lesch-Nyhan fibroblasts labeled with [^{3}H]hypoxanthine. Although these mutant cells are incapable of incorporating [^{3}H]hypoxanthine, their intracellular parasites are efficiently labeled and must contain labeled ATP and GTP to which the host cell has no access.

This series of experiments on nucleotide exchange leaves only the traffic of purine nucleotides from host cell to parasite unexamined. As described later, access to host cell purines is critical for the growth of *T. gondii*. The energy (ATP) required to support the intracellular growth of *T. gondii is* undoubtedly produced by the parasite itself.

Extracellular tachyzoites can incorporate label from exogenous ATP that contains [^{3}H]adenine, but only after the phosphate groups are removed. All stages of *T. gondii* contain cristate mitochondria that closely resemble those found in most eukaryotic cells. Since extracellular parasites have been shown to respire and to contain enzymes of the tricarboxylic acid (TCA) cycle, there is good reason to believe that these mitochondria are fully functional, in that the production of ATP is coupled to this respiration.

However, there is no direct evidence that this is the case. It is clear that something unexplained happens to the mitochondria of *T. gondii* after the tachyzoite enters host cells. A fluorescent rhodamine dye, R123, is specifically taken up by the mitochondria of extracellular *T. gondii.* This mitochondrial staining is sensitive to agents that disrupt the mitochondrial membrane potential and presumably reflects this potential.

Remarkably, the mitochondria of intracellular parasites fail to take up the rhodamine dye even when it is injected directly into the parasitophorous vacuole. Dye injected in this manner even crosses the vacuolar membrane and stains the mitochondria of the host cell. These important observations suggest a reduced mitochondrial membrane potential in intracellular parasites.

Thus, the relative importance of oxidative phosphorylation and glycolysis in ATP production by actively growing intracellular parasites remains unknown. The fact that the host cell itself is actively engaged in both modes of ATP production makes this a particularly difficult problem to attack.

One reasonable approach would be to study the respiration of intracellular tachyzoites growing in a mutant host cell that is incapable of oxidative phosphorylation. Such mutant cells are known to support the growth of *T. gondii*.

The Biochemical Role of the Host Cell

Perhaps the most fundamental cell-biological question that can be asked about *T. gondii,* and indeed about all obligate intracellular parasites, is why the host cell is required at all. Current knowledge allows no decisive answer. For the most part, all that we can do is to deprive the parasite of certain host cell functions, thereby narrowing the range of explanations for obligate intracellular parasitism that we need to consider.

The most decisive experiment in this vein is the demonstration that *T. gondii* grows quite normally in enucleated cells. In a single stroke, de novo RNA and DNA synthesis by the host cell are excluded as essential for the parasite. This conclusion is supported by experiments with drugs. Blocking host cell DNA synthesis with fluorodeoxyuridine (FUDR), an inhibitor of thymidylic acid synthetase, has no effect on the growth of an FUDR-resistant mutant of *T. gondii.*

Similarly, a specific inhibitor of host cell mRNA synthesis, alpha-amanitin, allows normal growth of wild-type *T. gondii,* whose mRNA synthesis is relatively insensitive to this drug. The possible dependence of *T. gondii* on ongoing host-cell protein synthesis is more difficult to study because all drugs that inhibit host protein synthesis also block the growth of the parasite.

Studies with enucleated cells cannot exclude a role for host cell protein synthesis because of the presence of long-lived cytoplasmic mRNA. Two lines of evidence argue against host cell protein synthesis as a significant factor in the intracellular growth of *T. gondii.* The first approach takes advantage of the fact that the *mycotoxin muconomycin* A is a very poorly reversible inhibitor of protein synthesis: human fibroblasts treated with muconomycin A and washed free of the drug remain incapable of incorporating amino acids when incubated in drug-free medium.

When cells treated in this way are infected with *T. gondii,* the parasites grow normally, and *autoradiography* demonstrates that [^{3}H]leucine is incorporated by the growing parasites but not by the host cell. The second approach to examining a requirement for host cell protein synthesis used a mutant host cell in which protein synthesis is temperature-sensitive because of a thermolabile leucyl-tRNA synthetase.

Mutant Chinese *hamster ovary* (CHO) cells with this therinolabile enzyme are incapable of protein synthesis at 40°C, yet support normal growth of *T. gondii* at this temperature. Another biosynthetic activity of the host cell that may be important to *T. gondii is* lipid synthesis. Nothing is known of this aspect of the host-parasite relationship for *T. gondii.* However, because two other Apicomplexan parasites, *Plasmodium berghei* and *E. tenella* are thought to be incapable of cholesterol synthesis, *T. gondii* probably also depends on its host cell for cholesterol.

Nothing is known of how host cell lipids might be transferred to intracellular parasites. As noted earlier, the synthesis of nucleic acids and proteins by the host cell is not essential for the intracellular growth of *T. gondii.* Yet the host cell must contribute something critical to the parasite in order to account for its obligate intracellular growth. Only one such contribution has been conclusively identified: *T. gondii* is absolutely dependent upon its host cell for a supply of purines.

The demonstration of this requirement illustrates the difficulty of studying the biosynthetic capability of an *intracellular protozoan* parasite and offers one useful solution. The nutritional requirements and the biosynthetic capabilities of a free-living protozoan are relatively easily defined: the requirement for a given nutrient can be detected by observing the lack of growth in a medium deficient in that nutrient.

Alternatively, the ability to carry out a given sequence of biosynthetic steps can be demonstrated unequivocally by supplying an isotopically labeled precursor in the medium and tracing its radioactivity to the final product in the free-living organism.

Neither of these simple *strategies* can be used to define the *biosynthetic* capabilities of an intracellular protozoan parasite because it is impossible to distinguish true biosynthesis on the part of the parasite from biosynthesis by the host cell followed by export across the parasitophorous vacuole to the intracellular parasite. One easy way to make this distinction is to use a mutant host cell with a biochemical defect in a specific pathway. When such a host is infected, any *biosynthetic* activity that is observed must be ascribed to the *intracellular* parasite.

This approach is illustrated by the demonstration that *T. gondii is* incapable of de novo purine synthesis. In these experiments, the mutant host cell is a CHO cell that is completely deficient in 5-amino-4-imidazolecarboxamide ribonucleotide formyltransferase.

This mutant is incapable of growth in the absence of exogenous purines and cannot incorporate [^{14}C]formate into the purine ring. *T. gondii* grows normally in these cells even though the medium contains no purines. Two explanations could account for this growth. The parasite could be growing at the expense of preformed host-cell purines or could be synthesizing the purine ring *de novo*.

To distinguish between these alternatives, infected mutant cultures are labeled with [^{14}C] formate, and the parasite nucleic acid bases are examined for radioactivity. None is found in the parasite's purines, although the methyl group of their thymine is labeled, showing that the parasites have access to the labeled precursor. *T. gondii,* like other parasitic protozoa, is therefore incapable of purine synthesis.

The reason for this widespread biosynthetic deficiency among *phylogenetically* diverse organisms remains to be established. Since *T. gondii* grows normally within cultured cells in medium that supplies no purines, the host cell is the only possible source for this essential nutrient. The forms in which the host purines enter the *parasitophorous* vacuole and are taken up by the parasite are unknown.

A glimpse of purine salvage by *T. gondii* can be obtained because tachyzoites, freshly released from infected cells, are briefly capable of limited RNA synthesis. Under these conditions, the parasite can *incorporate* a variety of *purine nucleotides*, *nucleosides*, and free bases. Of particular interest is the ability of the extracellular parasites to incorporate *exogenous* ATP into their nucleic acids.

This observation suggests that host cell ATP might be directly used by the parasite, provided that it could enter the parasitophorous vacuole. However, when doubly labeled ATP that contains ^{3}H in the purine ring and ^{32}P in the alpha phosphate is supplied, only the purine ring is incorporated into the RNA of the parasite. Thus the ATP must be extensively degraded before or as it enters the parasite.

Two purine salvage enzymes have been demonstrated in *T. gondii,* adenosine kinase and hypoxanthine-guanine phosphoribosyltransferase. The relative roles played by these two enzymes are not completely resolved. However, adenosine kinase-less mutants, as will be seen later, grow entirely normally; therefore, *hypoxanthine-guanine* phosphoribosyl *transferase*, acting alone, can provide adequate purine salvage.

Conversely, parasite mutants lacking hypoxanthine-guanine phosphoribosyl transferase have never been isolated. Such a mutant should be readily selected through its resistance to azaguanine in cultures of Lesch-Nyhan fibroblasts, which themselves lack this enzyme. This failure to select such a parasite mutant suggests that hypoxanthine-guanine *phosphoribosyl* transferase may be an essential enzyme for *T. gondii.*

The frequent observation that the parasitophorous vacuole, in which *T. gondii* grows, is lined on the host cytoplasmic side with host cell mitochondria has led to the reasonable suggestion that these mitochondria migrate there to supply ATP to the vacuole and thence to the parasite.

Although this sequence of events may happen, it is by no means essential for the parasite: *T. gondii* grows entirely normally in a mutant host cell in which the mitochondria are incapable of oxidative phosphorylation and ATP synthesis. The ability of intracellular *T. gondii* to synthesize pyrimidines can be studied in experiments analogous to those that demonstrated a requirement for purines.

However, quite the opposite conclusion is obtained. The parasite is entirely capable of pyrimidine synthesis. This ability is demonstrated with a mutant CHO host cell with three defects in the pyrimidine pathway, the most profound being a complete absence of dihydro-orotase. Uninfected cultures depend on exogenous uridine for growth. These host cells are almost totally incapable of incorporating labeled aspartic acid,

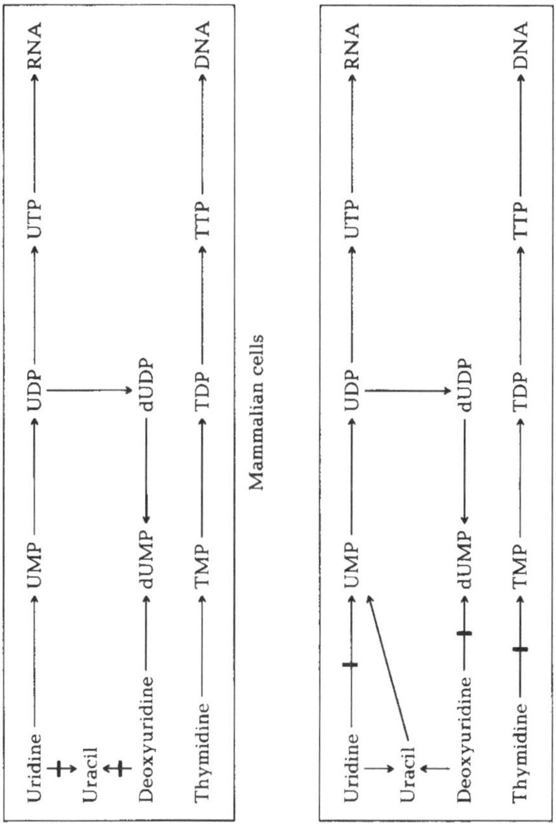

Figure 5.5: Comparison of pyrimidine salvage and nucleotide interconversion by T. gondii and by its mammalian host cell. Cytidine nucleotides are omitted for clarity. An arrow with a block indicates a reaction that is absent or biochemically unimportant. Abbreviations: UMP, UDP, UTP: uridine mono-, di-, and triphosphates, respectively; dUMP, dUDP, dUTP: deoxyuridine mono-, di-, and triphosphates, respectively; TMP, TDP, TTP: thymidine mono-, di-, and triphosphates, respectively.

a pyrimidine precursor, into nucleic acid pyrimidines. However, when these mutant CHO cells are infected with *T. gondii,* the cultures show efficient incorporation of [^{14}C]aspartate into the pyrimidines of the intracellular parasites.

This circumstantial proof that *T. gondii is* capable of pyrimidine synthesis was definitively confirmed by the systematic demonstration of each of the enzymes of the synthetic pathway. Although *T. gondii is* capable of de novo synthesis of pyrimidines, it probably can, at least under certain circumstances, also employ salvage pathways to supply its needs.

The *physiologically* important pyrimidine salvage pathways have been shown to converge on one enzyme, uracil phosphoribosyltransferase. Mutants lacking this enzyme are readily selected through their resistance to FUDR, as discussed later. These mutants are incapable of incorporating not only uracil but also uridine and *deoxyuridine.*

Thus both of these nucleosides must be cleaved to produce uracil before the pyrimidine base can be salvaged by the parasite. Although uridine kinase has been demonstrated in *T. gondii,* it must play a minor role since the FUDR-resistant mutant described earlier is also resistant to fluorouridine, which is known to be a substrate of this kinase.

The salvage pathways for *pyrimidines* in *T. gondii* and in human cells are compared in Figure elsewhere in this chapter. The relative roles of de novo synthesis and salvage of pyrimidines in the growth of wild-type *T. gondii* remain to be established. Apparently either can suffice to support growth. The FUDR-resistant mutant that is incapable of salvage grows normally, presumably through de novo synthesis.

Conversely, the wild type grows well when de novo synthesis is blocked by pyrazofurin or by CO_2 starvation, both of which suppress growth of a mutant defective in pyrimidine salvage. In summary, because *T. gondii* is an obligate intracellular parasite, the host cell must supply something that is not available in rich media that do not support parasite growth.

What the host cell supplies remains a mystery. The synthesis of pyrimidines, proteins, and nucleic acids by the host cell is not essential; lipid synthesis remains to be examined. Although the host cell must supply purines to *T. gondii,* this explanation is clearly not complete, since rich media that contain *purines* fail to support extracellular growth of *T. gondii.*

OTHER STAGES OF *T. GONDII*

In contrast to the substantial body of knowledge of the cell biology of the tachyzoite of *T. gondii,* much less is known about the other stages of the parasite, because they can be studied only in vivo. However, we have some evidence of *bradyzoite* formation in cultured cells.

These "bradyziotes" appear to be encased in cystlike structures; more important, they share two important biological properties with bradyzoites produced in vivo: resistance to pepsin and the induction of oocyst formation within 1 week after ingestion by cats.

However, the in vitro production of encysted bradyzoites is seldom a consistent phenomenon, and the conditions that promote it are poorly understood. Bradyzoites produced in vivo are antigenically distinct from tachyzoites and also can be distinguished by their *cytoplasmic* granules, which probably represent stored carbohydrates that may serve as a source of energy during their long dormant phase and during their entry into intestinal cells when the dormant bradyzoite phase is interrupted as a carnivore eats tissue that contains cysts. With the possible exception of the production of first-generation schizonts, none of the steps that lead to the formation of gametes in the feline intestine has been observed in vitro.

The gametogeny of *T. gondii* therefore has been inaccessible to most of the tools of cell biology, with the exception of light and electron microscopy and Mendelian genetics. It should be noted that the problem of accomplishing in vitro gametogeny and oocyst formation by *T. gondii* may not be intractable since it has been accomplished with *E. tenella.*

The process leading to the formation of male and female gametes in the feline intestine is relatively rapid, in that oocysts, the ultimate product of gamete fusion, begin to be excreted only 3 to 5 days after a cat ingests encysted bradyzoites. Nonetheless, it is a complex process in which the parasite population is expanded by extensive multiplication through five distinct steps of *schizogony*, which are distinguishable by light microscopy. The basis for sexual differentiation in *T. gondii is* poorly understood, as it is for all *Apicomplexans*.

However, it is well established that sex is not genetically determined in the sense that parasites in the asexual tachyzoite or sporozoite stages are not committed to make gametes of only one sex. This conclusion is based on the *observations* that *tachyzoites* cloned by plaque formation and sporozoites cloned by *micromanipulation* can be grown to populations capable of normal oocyst formation when their bradyzoites are fed to cats.

Thus sexual differentiation in *T. gondii* gametogenesis is probably determined physiologically by some unidentified *microenvironmental* influence in the cat intestinal epithelium. At some point during the series of schizogonies that lead to the formation of *gametocytes*, the parasites must become committed to production of gametes of only one sex. *Microspectrophotometric* determination of DNA content suggests that this commitment is made at or before the third generation of *schizogony*, since the merozoites of this generation show the first evidence of the increased DNA content that is characteristic of the microgametocytes, which give rise to microgametes.

The mature microgamete (male gamete) of *T. gondii* is the only stage whose motility depends upon flagella. Its cytoplasm contains little more than a nucleus and a mitochondrion that undoubtedly supplies the energy to drive its two flagella. Although there is no evidence on this point, analogy with the well-studied *Plasmodia* suggests that the male gamete is likely to bear surface antigens, both on the flagella and on the plasma membrane, that are different from those characterized in the tachyzoite. The chemical signals, if indeed there are any, that allow a male gamete to seek and find a mature female gamete are unknown and cannot be readily studied until gametogenesis can be accomplished in vitro.

The macrogamete (female gamete) of *T. gondii is* a relatively large spherical cell that is also likely to be antigenically distinct from the various asexual stages. The macrogamete is distinguished primarily by the presence of two kinds of peripheral cytoplasmic granules. Because of their role in the construction of the oocyst wall, they, are termed wall-forming bodies I and II.

Shortly after gametes fuse to form a zygote, particulate material from these bodies, together with proliferating membranes, combines to form the outer and inner layers, respectively, of the rigid and impervious wall of the oocyst. The latter stages of this process, the final formation of the inner layer of the wall, become increasingly difficult for ultrastructural study because the impermeability of the developing oocyst wall prevents penetration of the usual fixatives.

The mature unsporulated oocyst of *T. gondii* can be purified from cat feces by a combination of velocity and equilibrium sucrose gradient centrifugation. Sporulation, which requires adequate aeration for 1 to 3 days at room temperature, results in the production of eight progeny sporozoites, packed four each into two sporocysts, all retained within the original oocyst wall.

Both the sporozoites and the interior face of the oocyst wall bear stage-specific antigens. Since the oocyst wall is remarkably impermeable, sporulation can conveniently be carried out in 0.5 N H2SO4, which serves to kill any residual fecal bacteria. The oocyst wall is also impervious to NaOH and sodium hypochlorite. No analyses of the oocyst wall of *T. gondii* are available to explain this remarkable resistance to various harsh chemical treatments.

However, studies of the oocyst wall of E. tenella offer data that are probably relevant to *T. gondii*. The outer layer of this oocyst wall is composed primarily of fatty alcohols in which a C26 compound predominates. The inner layer is composed almost entirely of a single glycoprotein of M, 10,000 with substantial sulfhydryl cross-linking.

In summary, although we know a good deal about the tachyzoite of *T. gondii*, the stimuli for gametogenesis and the antigenicity and metabolism of the gametes remain complete mysteries. The reason for this difference is clear: the tachyzoite multiplies readily in cultured cells, but the sexual stages are found only in the feline intestine. One of the current challenges in the research with *T. gondii* is to accomplish gametogenesis in cell or organ cultures.

GENETICS OF *T. GONDII*

Although the study of Mendelian genetics is no simple task with any parasitic protozoan, *T. gondii* offers a reasonably useful system for several reasons. Most important, because the asexual forms are haploid, any potentially recessive mutation will be expressed. In addition, the ability of the tachyzoites to form plaques in cultured cells allows mutants to be cloned easily.

Growth of parasites in cultured cells also allows application of the various methods for chemical mutagenesis that have become routine in the production of mammalian cell mutants. Since *T. gondii* grows well over the relatively broad temperature range of 33 ° to 40°C, it has been possible to isolate a large number of temperature-sensitive mutants that grow normally at the lower temperature but are incapable of plaque formation at 40°C.

The principal advantage of temperature-sensitive mutations is that they can be found, at least in theory, in any gene that has an essential protein product. However, the disadvantage of this potentially wide array of mutations is that precise biochemical characterization of the defect is generally difficult.

None of the temperature-sensitive mutants of *T. gondii* has been so characterized. However, these mutants, all isolated from the hypervirulent RH strain of *T. gondii,* are often remarkably avirulent for mice, and one of them has some potential as a vaccine.

The mutants that have been most useful in the study of *T. gondii* are drug-resistant. Two advantages of these mutants are that they can be directly selected by the drug and that their biochemical characterization is often relatively simple. One important constraint in the selection of drug-resistant mutants of *T. gondii is* that the drug used must not compromise the ability of the host cell to support the growth of the intracellular parasite during the week-long incubation required for the formation of plaques.

The simplest way to avoid these complications is to use drugs that affect a host cell function that is not essential for the growth of *T. gondii.* Since DNA synthesis by the host cell is not essential for the parasite, drugs that inhibit eukaryotic DNA synthesis have proved to be of particular value in selecting mutants of *T. gondii.* An alternative approach is essential when using drugs that are incompatible with the long-term survival of cultured cells, such as inhibitors of protein synthesis. In this case the most useful tactic is to use host cell mutants that are themselves resistant to the drug in question, provided that resistance is not the result of impermeability to the drug.

Several of the *T. gondii* mutants resistant to inhibitors of DNA synthesis have been characterized biochemically. Adenine arabinoside (araA) is an analogue of deoxyadenosine. When incorporated into the nucleotide pool in the form of the nucleoside triphosphate, araA inhibits DNA synthesis by blocking the incorporation of deoxyATP.

Two independently isolated araA-resistant mutants of *T. gondii* lack the salvage enzyme adenosine kinase, which catalyzes the first step in the incorporation of araA into the nucleotide pool of the parasite. This mutation is not lethal to the parasite, because its hypoxanthine-guanine phosphoribosyltransferase is sufficient for purine salvage.

Fluorodeoxyuridine (FUDR) is an analogue of deoxyuridine. Its mononucleotide is a potent noncompetitive inhibitor of thymidylic acid synthetase and thus of DNA synthesis. A mutant of *T. gondii* that is 100-fold more resistant to FUDR lacks the salvage enzyme uracil phosphoribosyl transferase. This mutation is not lethal, because de novo synthesis can supply the parasite's need for pyrimidines.

Uracil phosphoribosyl transferase catalyzes the incorporation of fluorouracil into the nucleotide pool of the wild-type parasite after fluorouracil is produced from FUDR by the action of a nucleoside phosphorylase. What is probably the same enzyme produces fluorouracil from fluorouridine. Thus the FUDR-resistant mutant is also resistant to fluorouridine and fluorouracil.

As noted above, this mutant has been useful in excluding pyrimidine nucleotide exchange between host cell and parasite and in elucidating the physiologically significant pathways for pyrimidine salvage by *T. gondii*. Two other mutants of *T. gondii* resistant to other inhibitors of DNA synthesis are less well characterized. Hydroxyurea blocks the synthesis of deoxynucleotides by inhibiting ribonucleotide reductase.

Because a resistant mutant does not have an enlarged pyrimidine deoxynucleotide pool, it is unlikely that it is resistant to hydroxyurea through the overproduction of ribonucleotide reductase. Hydroxyurea inhibits the incorporation of [^{3}H]uracil into the deoxynucleotide pool of the wild type but not of the mutant parasite. Thus the resistance of the mutant is probably a result of an altered ribonucleotide reductase that is less sensitive to the drug.

Aphidicolin inhibits DNA synthesis by binding to and inhibiting

DNA polymerase alpha at a site that is thought to overlap more or less completely with the binding site for dcoxyCTP. A mutant of *T. gondii* that is fourfold more resistant than the wild type to aphidicolin overproduces deoxyCTP approximately threefold. Since this deoxynucleotide is known to reverse the action of aphidicolin in a competitive manner, it is likely that its overproduction is the basis for resistance in this mutant.

The drug-resistant mutants of *T. gondii* described earlier have been used in a series of genetic crosses. At present these studies of the Mendelian genetics must use in vivo experiments in cats because of the inability to accomplish gametogenesis in vitro. Two potential pitfalls should be noted.

The most commonly used laboratory strain of *T. gondii,* called RH, has lost the ability to undergo gametogenesis in the feline intestine. This strain has been maintained by serial intraperitoneal passage in mice over many decades. Under these conditions, there is no selective advantage for the retention of genes that are uniquely expressed during gametogenesis.

Indeed, if these genes represent a significant fraction of the genome, their continued maintenance during prolonged passage of the asexual form may be a sufficient burden to provide a small selective advantage to mutants in which they are deleted. This situation is not unique to *T. gondii*. Prolonged "syringe passage" of murine plasmodia has also been shown to yield strains incapable of gametogenesis.

Even if a strain capable of gametogenesis is used to select mutants for use in genetic crosses, the possibility of inadvertently introducing a secondary mutation that blocks gametogenesis must be borne in mind. Such a secondary mutation could be introduced during the chemical mutagenesis required to induce the desired mutation or could be selected inadvertently during the prolonged asexual growth required during the mutant selection.

Several drug-resistant mutants selected from a strain of *T. gondii* known to make gametes have been found to be incapable of forming oocysts. When the mutants that have lost the ability to make oocysts are crossed with a different mutant resistant to another drug and of proved fertility, no recombinants are obtained.

This negative result suggests that the inability to make oocysts results from a defect in the production of both male and female gametes, because making either one alone should be sufficient for a successful cross with another mutant that can make both kinds of gametes.

Provided that both drug-resistant clones are by themselves able to make oocysts, recombination between them can easily be detected. The usual procedure is to produce encysted bradyzoites in chronically infected mice, using separate mice for each clone. Mouse brains, examined microscopically for cysts, are fed to seronegative kittens so that they ingest approximately equal numbers of cysts of each genotype.

Oocysts purified from the cat feces are allowed to sporulate. Finally, sporozoites released from the oocysts are examined in cultured cells for recombinants resistant to both drugs. Such recombination is readily demonstrated in experiments in which the two parental strains were resistant to FUDR and to araA, respectively.

The greatest frequency of doubly resistant recombinants observed is about 12 percent. The reciprocal doubly sensitive recombinant can also be detected. In considering the results from genetic crosses with *T. gondii,* it should be noted that the term *recombinant is* used in its most general sense, to designate progeny parasites that have inherited genetic markers from two different parental strains; the term therefore does not imply crossing over between two genetic loci on the same chromosome.

Recombinants could easily arise from the independent assortment of chromosomes at meiosis and, as will be noted, this may be the only way in which they can be formed. In order to interpret the results of genetic crosses done with *T. gondii* and other coccidial parasites, it is necessary to speculate upon the possibility of a peculiarity in their meiosis.

The meiotic reduction to the characteristic haploidy of *T. gondii* certainly occurs during sporulation of the oocyst. In contrast to their behavior in the mitotic divisions that take place during endodyogeny of the tachyzoite, the chromosomes of *T. gondii* and of other coccidia condense during the first division of sporulation. In most eukaryotic organisms the meiotic reduction to a haploid state requires two cell divisions.

During metaphase of the first division the homologous chromosomes are found in the form of tetrads with each chromosome split into two chromatids. This is the stage at which meiotic crossing-over takes place and its morphological manifestations, the chiasmata, are observed. In contrast the coccidia are thought, on cytological grounds, to accomplish meiosis in a single cell division that immediately yields haploid progeny.

Consistent with this model, there are no indications of chiasmata. Although these conclusions are based primarily on the cytology of the *Eimeria,* if correct, they are probably also valid for *T. gondii.* This model of single-step meiosis has important implications for an interpretation of recombination in the coccidia. If the meiotic reduction to haploidy is accomplished in a single step without the formation of tetrads and the opportunity that they afford for crossing over, genetic markers are locked into the chromosomes that bear them.

Linkage therefore should be absolute for genetic markers on the same chromosome, whereas markers on different chromosomes should be randomly distributed among the progeny by independent assortment of homologous chromosomes during the single-step meiosis. Likewise, each oocyst resulting from a genetic cross should contain sporozoites of only two genotypes.

Tests for recombination with four drug-resistance markers in *T. gondii* show only independent assortment, with the exception of two mutants-one resistant to hydroxyurea and the other to FUDR-that yield no doubly resistant recombinants and thus appear to exhibit the absolute linkage predicted by the model described here.

In this case, however, linkage is effectively ruled out because crosses between these two mutants yield the expected numbers of reciprocal recombinants that are sensitive to both drugs. The doubly resistant recombinants are not detected because the FUDR-resistance gene phenotypically suppresses the hydroxyurea-resistance gene, possibly by altering the deoxynucleotide pools of the parasite.

However, in accord with the model of single-step ineiosis, some genetic crosses between two mutants of *E. tenella* show evidence of absolute linkage. In interpreting quantitative data from crosses involving unlinked markers in *T. gondii*, one feature of gametogenesis must be borne in mind.

Since sexual differentiation in *T. gondii* is not genetically determined, each of the two parental strains used in a binary cross will produce both male and female gametes in the intestine of the infected cat. If both parents in the cross are used in exactly equal numbers, half of the matings will be self-crosses between gametes of the same strain.

Thus, only half of the zygotes that are formed will be capable of giving rise to recombinants. These zygotes will yield 25 percent doubly drug—resistant recombinant sporozoites by independent assortment of genetic markers on different chromosomes. However, the apparent frequency of these recombinants will be halved, because an equal number of progeny will be produced from the self-crosses.

Thus the highest possible frequency of recombinants that can be achieved is 12.5 percent, which is just larger than the greatest value

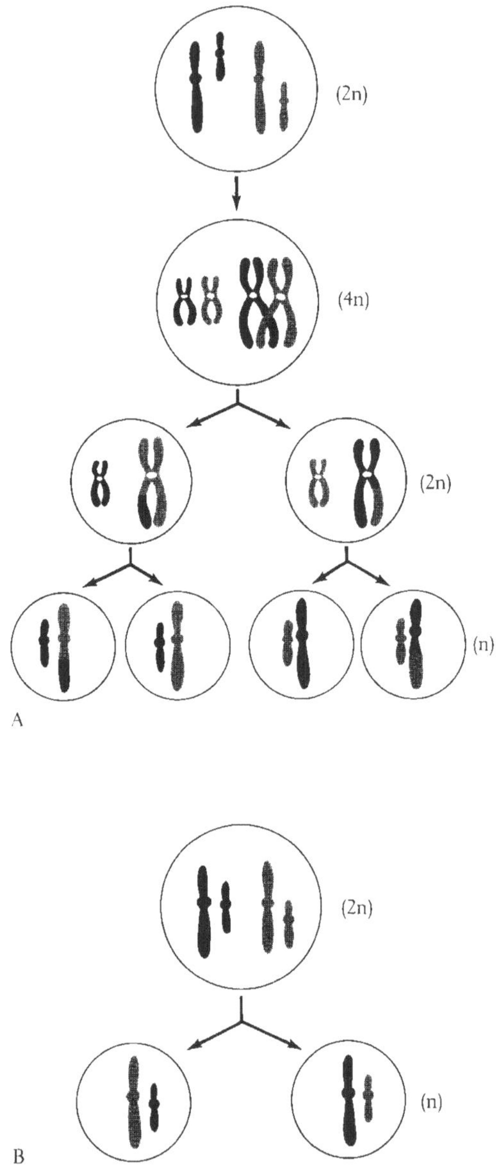

Figure 5.6: Comparison of (A) conventional meiosis and (B) the single step meiosis thought to be characteristic of the Coccidia. Only two different chromosomes are shown for clarity. The chromosomes donated by the male are shown in black; those donated by the females are shown in gray. The conventional meiosis shows a chiasma and a single meiotic crossover.

actually observed with *T. gondii* and with *E. tenella*. The maximal recombination frequency of 12.5 percent can be achieved only when the parental strains are present in exactly equal numbers.

As the ratio of infecting parents deviates from 1 : 1, the expected maximal frequency of recombination between unlinked markers falls because self-crosses between gametes of the majority parent come to predominate. Thus, when genetic crosses with *T. gondii* are analyzed it is important to know the parental ratios that are actually involved.

In theory, this ratio can he measured either at the input of encysted bradyzoites in the brains of mice fed to the kittens or in the output of sporozoites in the sporulated oocysts recovered from the kitten's feces. Although bradyzoites can be readily titrated in a plaque assay, their measurement may not reliably reflect the number of gametes produced in the cat intestine.

Various strains of *T. gondii* and even individual preparations of encysted bradyzoites may not be uniform in their quantitative abilities to produce gametes. The most desirable measurement would be a determination of the numbers of gametes of each genotype in the feline intestine, but such assays are impossible.

However, a close approximation of this measurement can be obtained, given the assumption that the gametes of each genotype have the same efficiency of mating and ultimately of producing sporulated oocysts. Under these assumptions, the ratio of sporozoites resistant to the two different drugs used as genetic markers should equal the ratio of the functional gametes of the parental genotypes actually present in the intestine of the infected kitten.

This ratio then allows a simple calculation of the expected frequency of recombination between unlinked markers as one-half of the product of the frequencies of the two parental genotypes in the progeny sporozoites.

Note that in a binary cross, if the parental genotypes are equal (each = 0.5), this equation predicts the maximal frequency of recombination noted above, 0.125. An advantage of understanding the relationship between parental genotypes measured in the progeny sporozoites and expected frequency of recombinants is that a single kitten can be used for a large number of simultaneous crosses between various drug-resistant mutants.

The only assumption required is that mating is random. This approach has been used in analyzing the data by infecting the same kitten with four different drug-resistant mutants, and the results were consistent with theory. A good many more mutants of *T. gondii* will have to be used in crosses to make any inroads into the problem of defining linkage groups that presumably define the chromosomes of *T. gondii*. In resolving this problem Mendelian crosses are likely to be overtaken by molecular genetic techniques that can easily be coupled with the separation of parasite chromosomes by pulsed field electrophoresis.

6

SCHISTOSOMA

As trematodes, schistosomes share the phylum of flatworms (*Platyhelminthes*) with such organisms as tapeworms and planaria. Although these are generally considered among the "lowest" bilaterally symmetrical animals, they are *profoundly* complex creatures and provide an exceptional challenge to the cell biologist.

Each stage of their life cycle consists of numerous cell types arranged into tissues, organs, and organ systems showing great diversity in cell size, structure, and function. Analysis of the membrane biology and the physiology of transformation between stages of schistosomes has been carried out in recent years and has revealed some exciting new information. This chapter is devoted primarily to interstage transformation and other general aspects of cell biology.

LIFE CYCLE OF THE PARASITE

Humans are hosts to about a half dozen species of *schistosomes* although other *mammals*, such as cattle, horses, and dogs, may carry these parasites in endemic regions. The intermediate hosts are various species of freshwater snails. *Cercariae*, the stage infectious to man, are released from the snail into fresh water, penetrate the host skin, and become schistosomulae.

After a few days, schistosomulae enter the systemic *venous* return, pass to the lungs, and in most species migrate to the portal system between the intestine and liver. There the parasites mature as adult male and female *schistosomes*, and the latter produce thousands of eggs, which lodge in the liver and cause *granulomas* and *fibrosis*. Other eggs rupture through the bowel wall and are passed with stool, which may contaminate lakes or rivers. *Miracidia* hatch from eggs deposited in fresh water and penetrate snail vectors where they transform into sporocysts. The sporocysts subsequently give rise to the cercariae, which are released into the water and are capable of infecting other susceptible hosts.

THE MIRACIDIUM AND INTRAMOLLUSCAN STAGES

The miracidium, which infects the snail intermediate host, is 200 micrometers (μm) in length and 40 μm in diameter and is passed in the feces within an ovoid egg made of chitin, measuring about 300 *μm* by 100 μm. On the miracidial surface are 21 ciliated and anucleate epithelial plates, attached by septate junctions to narrow syncytial ridges connected to cell bodies deep within the parasite.

Ciliated *sensory* nerve cells lie within the *syncytial ridges* and connect to a central nerve plexus. There is a basement membrane overlying two concentric layers of smooth muscle that envelop internal structures, which include secretory glands involved in penetrating the snail; an excretory system marked by flame cells; and primitive germ cells that will develop into daughter sporocysts.

Within the snail, the *miracidium* sheds the epithelial plates, expands the syncitial ridges to cover the entire parasite surface, and transforms into a mother sporocyst. Mother sporocysts reproduce asexually, making daughter sporocysts which migrate to the hepatopancreas of the snail where they produce cercariae, completing the cycle.

For a miracidium to infect the snail it must hatch from the egg, swim through fresh water, find and penetrate the snail, and shed the epithelium and remodel its surface. Manipulation of the environmental conditions that might trigger these events and observation of the parasites by video microscopy have revealed some of the stimuli and processes involved in miracidial infectivity.

Miracidia swim at about 2 millimeters (mm) per second by the synchronous beating of the cilia on the epithelial plates. The ciliary beating stops when the miracidium is placed in *physiological* saline but continues when the miracidium is placed in fresh water. This finding indicates that when the miracidium is in the egg within the body of the mammalian host, the cilia do not beat and the parasite remains within the egg.

However, when the eggs are passed into fresh water, the miracidium "swims" by the beating of the cilia within the egg. When the shell

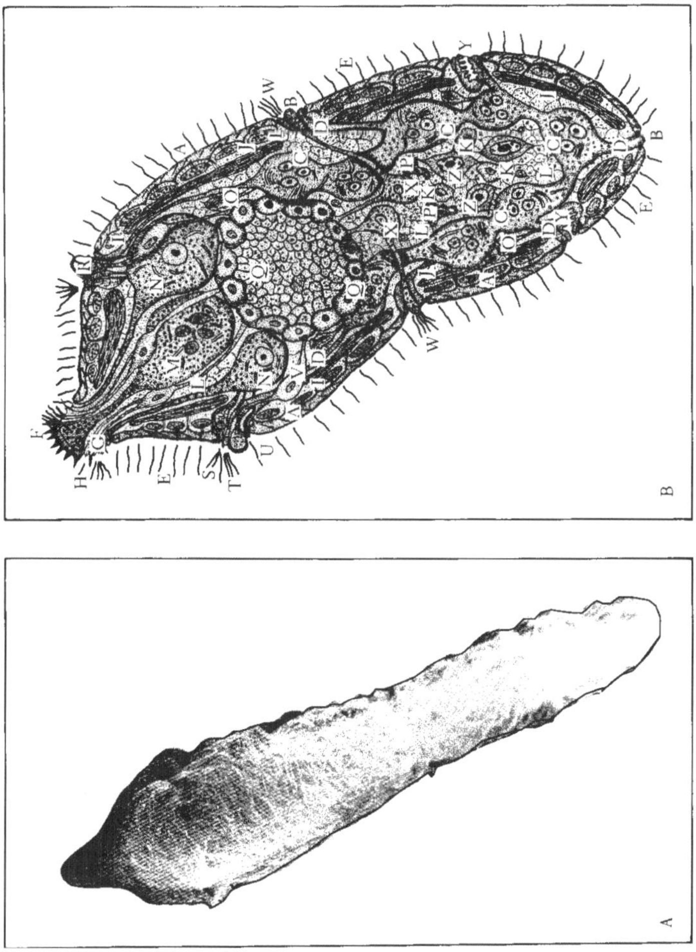

Figure 6.1: Miracidium of Schistosoma mansoni. A. Scanning electron micrograph of miracidium showing cilia (original X975). B. Schematic representation of miracidium based on electron micrographs. A, epidermal plate; B, epidermal ridge; C, ridge cyton; D, cytoplasmic bridge; E, cilium and its rootlet; F, terebratorium and the profile of cytoplasmic expansion; G, multiciliated, deep-pit sensory papilla; H, uniciliated sensory papills; I, outer circular muscle fiber; J, inner longitudinal muscle fiber; K, interstitial cyton; L, processes of interstitial cells; M, apical gland and secretory duct; N, lateral gland and secretory duct; O, flame cell with excretory tubule; P, cyton of common excretory tubule; Q, neural mass with peripheral ganglia; R, internal papilla; S, multiciliated saccular sensory organelle; T, multiciliated shallow-pit sensory papilla; U, uniciliated sensory papilla; V, perikaryon of the neuron to internal papilla; W, multiciliated sensory papilla; X, perikaryon of the multiciliated sensory papilla; Y, execretory vesicle; Z, germ cell.

fractures, the miricidium can escape. A swimming miracidium turns not by an asymmetric heating of the cilia as does *a Paramecium*, but, rather by angling the body (like a rudder) and using the musculature beneath the epithelial plates.

Miracidia accumulate around the snail or in a drop of snail-conditioned water (water in which snails have been placed for a period of time) by turning more frequently and swimming around in circles. The accumulation of miracidia within a drop of snail-conditioned water can be inhibited by eserine sulfate (*physostigmine*).

This acetylcholinesterase inhibitor paralyzes the muscles of miracidia (and all other stages of the parasite) so that they cannot turn. Conversely, miracidia accumulate in a drop of serotonin, which transiently increases the muscular activity of miracidia. Miracidia stop swimming and may shed their epithelial plates when saline is added to fresh water.

In the presence of serotonin, miracidia transferred from fresh water to saline stop swimming but do not transform, suggesting that the nervous system of the parasite is involved in sensing or transducing the osmotic signal for transformation. Within 2 hours after penetration into a snail host, the ciliated plates are shed from the miracidium.

The epidermal ridges gradually broaden until by the second day a continuous new surface layer appears around the newly formed mother sporocyst. At the outer surface of this layer numerous microvillus-like folds appear, covered by a fuzzy electron-dense coat which constitutes the actual interface for metabolic exchange with the hemolymph and for challenge by amebocytes of the snail host.

The new syncytial tegument contains mitochondria, ribosomes, endoplasmic reticulum, glycogen, lipid, and other normal constituents of eukaryotic cells, and it remains connected with the nucleated cell bodies further beneath the surface. This arrangement is retained in the tegument of the mother sporocyst.

During subsequent development the muscular layers and parenchymal cells degenerate, the scattered germinal cells become more prominent, and the central portion of the sporocyst differentiates into a brood chamber. Now a remarkably rapid and efficient round of asexual reproduction occurs.

Less than a week after infection, daughter sporocyst embryos begin to form by subdivision and differentiation from germinal cells that bud from the inner wall of the saccular mother sporocyst. Starting 5 to 6 days later, they escape, and proceed rapidly through hemolymph vessels and sinuses to the hepatopancreas and ovotestis of the snail. These active vermiform daughter sporocysts, up to a quarter of a millimeter long, contain muscle fibers, protonephridial and nervous systems, and a complement of their own germinal cells to make the next generation.

As in other stages, the tegument is typically syncytial and anucleate, resting on a basement membrane, with connections to the nucleated cell bodies below the muscle fibers. Production by germinal cells of early cercarial embryos ("germ balls") normally begins around the time that the daughter sporocysts exit from the mother.

By 3 weeks after infection, the first cercariae are almost fully formed within the daughter sporocysts of *Schistosoma mansoni*. They begin to escape a few days later, first into the hemolymph of the snail, and then through the snail's integument into the surrounding water, where they swim away to find their definitive host.

In *S. japonicum* the process is much slower, with cercarial embryos developing some 2 months after infection of the Onco*melania* snail. All cercariae arising from a single miracidium are presumably identical and will produce adults of the same sex.

Therefore, a snail releasing both male and female cercariae had been penetrated by at least two separate miracidia. It has been shown recently that daughter sporocysts transplanted surgically into new snails will give rise to additional daughter sporocysts and that this process can be repeated through numerous passages.

It is not yet clear whether the transplanted daughter sporocysts merely proliferate by growing and budding in the plenitude of their new environment or if the contained germ balls become diverted from production of cercariae and actually produce a further generation of sporocysts.

What is apparent is that the extent of development of sporocysts is naturally limited by the volume and nutritive resources within the original snail host, and when artificially freed from such constraints, the amount of sporocyst tissue potentially arising from a single miracidium is essentially limitless.

We can take advantage of this capability to maintain genetically constant clones of schistosomes by repeated surgical implantation from a single unimiracidially infected donor into generations of fresh snails.

THE CERCARIA

Cercariae are composed of a body about 125 μm long and 25 um in diameter, to which is attached a 200-μm-long tail. Video microscopy has revealed that a cercaria swims from the snail to the mammalian host by alternating side-to-side rhythmic contractions (at 20 cycles per second) of the musculature of the body and tail.

The swimming cercariae are covered by a single continuous syncytial tegument about 0.5 um thick on the body and 0.2 ,um thick on the tail. The tegument is virtually devoid of ribosomes, secretory structures, and other organelles that, along with the nuclei of the syncytium, are found in cellular extensions into the subtegumentary region.

A trilaminate plasma membrane over a trilaminate basement membrane forms the outer surface of the tegument, which is covered by a dense, labile glycocalyx about 1 to 2 μm thick. This material, probably a complex carbohydrate, consists of numerous fibrils, each about 8 to 15 nanometers (nm) thick, which may protect the cercaria.

It is shed once the cercaria has penetrated the skin of its vertebrate host. The highly antigenic glycocalyx can combine with antibody to produce the "*cerkarienhtillen reaktion*" (CHR), sometimes used as a serological test for schistosomiasis. In this procedure, cercariae are incubated with serum from a suspected case of schistosomiasis.

If antischistosomal antibodies are present, the cercarial surface undergoes a blebbing reaction. The cercarial glycocalyx also activates complement by the alternative pathway, so that fresh human serum (even from an individual never exposed to schistosomes) kills cercariae in vitro. The cercarial body contains unicellular glands whose secretion products are probably involved in facilitating penetration into the skin of the host.

Several proteinases produced by these glands can digest elastin, gelatin, laminin, fibronectin, keratin, type I (interstitial) collagen and types IV and VII (basement membrane) collagen. Presumably degradation of these extracellular proteins of the host destroy a potential barrier to penetration.

Other elements within the cercaria include a primitive "*brain*" anlage, a well-developed flame-cell (osmoregulatory) system, and primordial digestive and reproductive systems that are destined to function only in later stages. Reproductive structures are not developed in the cercarial body, and it is impossible to tell males from females *morphologically* until perhaps 3 weeks after host penetration (in the *schistosomulum* stage).

DEVELOPMENT FROM THE CERCARIA TO THE SCHISTOSOMULUM

At the moment of cercarial penetration, the tail is cast off and the body enters the skin of the definitive host. Sometimes penetration is attempted into a host that cannot support further parasite maturation. Cercarial dermatitis ("swimmer's itch") of humans represents an example of such an aborted infection.

When nonhuman schistosomes (commonly, schistosomes of birds) enter the skin of human bathers, they die in the subdermal connective tissue and there elicit a hypersensitivity reaction that gives rise to the dermatitis. A cercaria penetrates the host skin and transforms to a schistosomulum by losing the tail, emptying the secretory glands, shedding the glycocalyx, and forming a new, double-unit membrane on the syncytial surface.

These changes occur in vitro when cercariae (1) penetrate through an excised skin into physiological medium or (2) have their tails removed mechanically and are incubated in saline. The environmental trigger for surface transformation appears to be a step increase in the saline concentration rather than the absolute saline concentration, because cercariae transform to schistosomula when they go from fresh water to 120 mOsm saline (the osmolarity of the snail) or to 300 mOsm saline (the mammalian osmolarity).

Similarly, cercariae dissected from the snail hepatopancreas and placed into 120 mOsm saline transform when they are shifted to 300 mOsm saline, indicating also that immediate prior experience in fresh water is not necessary for triggering transformation. The nervous system is apparently involved in sensing or effecting transformation, because the acetylcholinesterase inhibitor, eserine sulfate, inhibits in a reversible manner cercarial surface transformation to schistosomula.

Eserine sulfate also inhibits cercarial swimming, glandular secretion, and skin penetration. This inhibition permits investigators to radiolabel the surface of eserine sulfate -treated cercariae and study its fate with subsequent transformation under permissive conditions.

In addition, cercariae, which are prevented from transforming into schistomula, can be assessed for their interaction with antibodies, complement, or host effector cells. Such studies can shed light on the nature of the tegument of transformed schistosomula, particularly as it relates to a target of host defense.

Because cercariae transform to schistosomula and live for days in completely defined medium, it is possible to study changes in parasite antigenicity and susceptibility to immune killing in the absence of host antigen acquisition. Scanning electron microscopy has revealed the appearance-within 5 minutes of transformation of a single set of microvilli over the entire tegumental surface. These microvilli elongate to 3-5μm and fall off into the medium within 40-60 minutes. With the microvilli, some two-thirds of the fibrillar glycocalyx is shed, but much of the glycocalyx remains on the surface of schistosomula.

This residual glycocalyx on recently transformed schistosomula may account for the binding of antibody or of alternative pathway complement components to these organisms. Preformed multilaminate membranous vesicles, which are secreted onto the parasite surface from cell bodies below the muscle layer, provide the membrane that is added onto the tegument surface of the transforming parasite to replace the shed *microvilli*.

These membranous vesicles change the outer tegumental membrane from the single-unit membrane of the cercariae to the new, double-unit membrane found on the surface of schistosomula and adult schistosomes. The outer and inner components of the double-unit membrane are different (as shown by freeze-fracture microscopy).

The parasite membrane has been the focus of much study because it can fuse with the plasma membranes of adherent effector cells in vitro, presenting an intriguing biological phenomenon. Radiolabeling of the schistosomular surface shows at least 12 new *glycoproteins* not identified on the surface of cercariae. In addition, schistosomula bind the lectin *concanavalin* A, a lectin that does not bind to the cercarial surface.

An interesting consequence of events that occur during the period when the cercarial glycocalyx is lost and the double-unit membrane is formed is the loss of resistance of schistosomula to the hypoosmolar stress of fresh water. After 3 to 4 days in the subdermal layers of an appropriate host, the young schistosomula enter the bloodstream where they transit the circulation briefly, passing through the right side of the heart into the pulmonary artery.

They arrive in the pulmonary capillaries on or soon after the fourth day and remain at least 2 or 3 days. By then, subtle and poorly understood surface changes have rendered the schistosomula resistant to the lethal action of the humoral or cellular mechanisms of immune attack. In the pulmonary capillaries, the fibrous interstitial layer beneath the tegument, as well as some of the anterior musculature, disintegrates and disappears.

This process may be a prerequisite for the extreme changes in shape necessary for the *schistosomula* to traverse the narrow vessels. The parasites elongate and lose much of their fine body *spination*, except for broad bands at either end, which seem to help them in crawling through the capillaries. The young schistosomula now measure only 8 μm in diameter, the approximate size of the smallest pulmonary capillaries through which the schistosomula must crawl.

After passing through the lungs, schistosomula of most species come to rest in the hepatic and portal venous plexus. Exceptions are S. *haematobium*, which migrates to the venules surrounding the bladder, and the Indian cattle parasite *S. nasalis*, which migrates to the nasal mucosa. In *S. mansoni*, the *schistosomula* are first observed in the portal system 6 days after infection in mice (7 days in hamsters) but they may take up to 40 days to wander to this site. In *S. japonicum* they arrive in the rodent liver within 3 days of infection.

Subsequent development is best understood in the species parasitizing humans. In *S. mansoni* and *S. japonicum* (and presumably in most others) immature schistosomula find partners of the opposite sex (when available) within the portal vein, where pairing occurs. The young pairs migrate against the portal blood flow into the venous branches, where maturation is completed and egg laying commences about 5 weeks after infection.

Worms may live for 10 years or more, although shorter life spans are the rule. The mechanism by which male and female schistosomes recognize each other has been a topic of interest in recent years, since strategies to prevent pairing could represent a novel approach to disease control.

THE TEGUMENT OF THE SCHISTOSOMULUM AND ADULT SCHISTOSOME

The tegument of schistosomes consists of a syncytium having cytoplasmic connections with underlying nucleated cell bodies (cytons). The outer tegumentary surface is often marked by folds and is pitted with numerous openings of tubular canals readily seen with the scanning electron microscope.

These presumably provide added surface for absorption of nutrients. In mature male worms, the dorsal surface is marked by warty tubercles bearing many heavy spines which help to maintain the position of the worm pair against the blood flow. The surface of the male worm is characterized by thousands of spines in the suckers, throughout the gynecophoral canal and elsewhere.

All the spines are invested by the tegumental membranes. The female surface is generally wrinkled annularly, and is smooth except for dense spination in the posterior end surrounding the aperture of the osmoregulatory system (excretory pore).

A scattering of sensory organelles of various types is found on the surface of both sexes. There is some evidence for regional differentiation of the surface from one part of the worm to another, but this has not been well explored.

The tegumental syncytium itself, about 4 ,urn thick, is poor in organelles, having only scattered mitochondria and various types of membrane-bound inclusion bodies. Its outer plasma membrane has a unique heptalaminate structure that represents two fused lipid bilayers, each of which contains inner and outer leaflets.

Much attention has been given to the turnover of the adult surface. The rapid renewal of surface components is generally considered a crucial process in protecting schistosomes from immune damage. However, some early studies based on biosynthetic metabolic labeling or the binding of various materials to the surface apparently failed to distinguish between normal membrane renewal and shedding of tegument under adverse conditions, and some workers reported very rapid rates of surface turnover.

Recent evidence shows that adherent immunological markers, specifically antibodies to the human complement component Cab may remain for several weeks on the surface of worms maintained in vitro. It has been suggested also that different areas of the worm surface may turn over at different rates. Underlying the tegument is a basal lamina, from which microtubules extend into the tegumentary matrix.

The nucleated (sometimes multinucleated) tegumental cell bodies are found beneath the muscle fibers and are the source of the granular inclusions found in the overlying syncytium. These cells also contain mitochondria and the Golgi apparatus. The surface may be disrupted or released by freeze-thawing or by incubation in dilute digitonin, in similar detergents, or merely in phosphate buffered saline.

The component layers can be enriched or purified by gradient centrifugation and by confirmation that a particular subcellular component has been isolated, for example, by assessing specific enzyme markers, detecting radioactive surface label (commonly ^{125}lodine), or analyzing interaction with surface-binding ligands such as lectins or specific antibodies.

Some investigators perceive the outer surface of schistosomes as capable of unidirectional transport of solutes and water by virtue of morphological, enzymatic, and functional asymmetry. For example, if the two bilayers are removed by sequential incubations in 0.1 % digitonin, only the inner layer possesses alkaline phosphatase and a sodium and magnesium ATPase, analogous to the apical plasma membrane of other animal epithelia. In contrast, the outer bilayer, which is predominantly lipid, is thought to function primarily to maintain a permeability barrier to soluble proteins.

The adult schistosome tegument is rich in lipids, containing *sphingomyelin*, *phosphatidylcholine*, *phosphatidylserine*, *phosphatidylinositol* and *phosphatidylethanolamine*. There is a high content of eicosanoic acid (barely present in the mammalian host), synthesized by the worms from fatty acid precursors in the blood. Portions of the tegument contain specialized structures, particularly spines of various shapes and sizes, which are especially prominent on the ventral sucker.

Small bulbous nerve endings, with or without attached cilia, are scattered on the surface of both sexes. Presumably these are sensors to detect and transmit environmental messages to other parts of the organism. How these or other receptors may act in such life functions as migration and mate finding is still unknown. Continuous with the outer surface is the lining of the esophagus and intestinal ceca.

The transition from the tegument to the anterior esophagus is accompanied by increasing complexity and folding of the surface. In this region, esophageal glands produce and transport secretory granules (presumably containing proteolytic enzymes) to the lumen. The cecal lumen itself is similar in adults of both sexes. Its lining is thrown into complex, irregular projections that serve for pinocytosis of hemoglobin breakdown products.

A potent proteinase, whose activity is stimulated by sulfhydryl-containing compounds, acts in digestion of host blood. As *acoelomate* animals, *schistosomes* and other *Platyhelminthes* lack a body cavity and a circulatory system. The internal organs are embedded within a solid cellular parenchyma. This tissue is composed of several cell types, including the cell bodies of the syncytial tegument and at least two kinds of muscle cells.

One of these has large, electron-lucent nuclei, large cytoplasmic vacuoles containing a finely granular material, and abundant free ribosomes. The other, much smaller, has scanty cytoplasm but also gives rise to muscle fibers. In addition there are nerve cells, at least some of which contain electron-dense, membrane-bound vesicles reminiscent of neurosecretory granules.

The solid tissue is traversed by a network of osmoregulatory (or excretory) tubules emanating from flame cells and collecting through ducts into the excretory opening at the posterior tip. The *parenchyma*

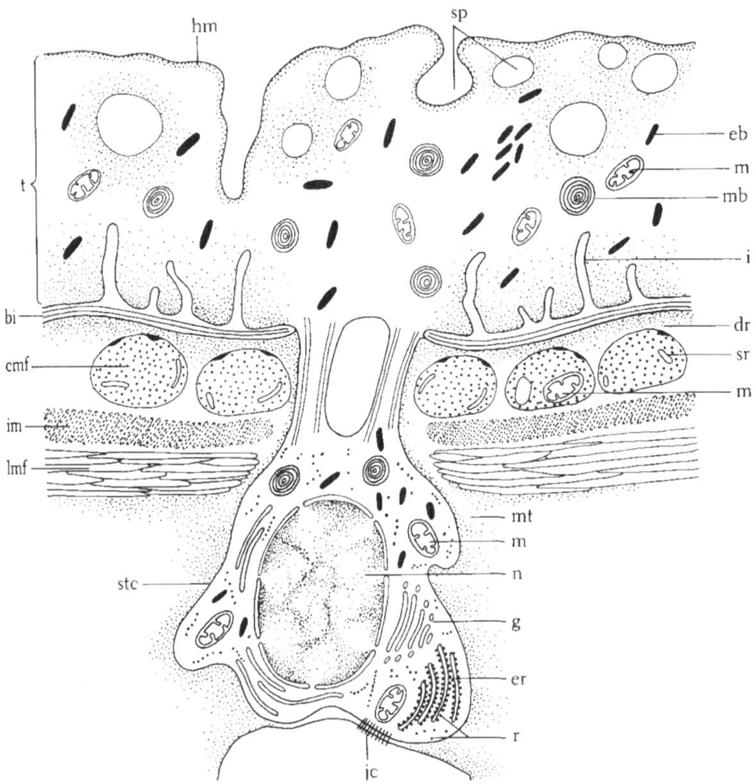

Figure 6.2: Representation of adult schistosome tegument and underlying structures: bi, basal lamina; cmf, circularly arranged muscle fibers; dr, peripheral dense region of muscle fibre; eb, elongate body; g, Golgi region; hm, heptalaminate outer membrane; i, invagination of basal membrane; im, interstitial material; jc, junctional complex with parenchymal cell; lmf, longitudinal muscle fibre; m, mitochondrion; mb, membraneous body; mt, microtubule; n, nucleus; r, ribosomes; sp, surface pits; sr, sarcoplasmic reticulum; stc, subtegumental cell; t, tegument.

occupies the bulk of male schistosomes from just behind the testes to the posterior end of the body. The long, slender females of the common schistosomes, filled to a large extent with reproductive structures, also have parenchyma filling the intervening space.

The Adult Male

The male reproductive system is far simpler than that of the female and is relatively uniform in the commonly considered *Schistosoma* species infecting humans and domestic animals. The system consists usually of about four to eight testes, located dorsal to the anterior part of the gynecophoral canal, with a collecting duct leading to the genital pore.

Around each testis is a dense heterogeneous basal lamina within a layer of circular muscle fibers. The germinal cells were examined during the heyday of descriptive cytology in the early decades of this century but have not been the subject of recent scrutiny.

They arise from the lining of the testicular wall, and after undergoing spermatogonial divisions, the daughter cells separate. Meiotic divisions lead to spermatids and eventually to mature sperm cells in a conventional manner. At least two types of nongerminal cells have been described within the testes, closely associated with spermatids and maturing sperm cells.

These may help regulate the production of spermatozoa, or may possess nutritive, supportive, or phagocytic functions. Some recent studies have followed the incorporation of tritiated thymidine into *S. mansoni*. In young worms, thymidine incorporation was found throughout the tissues. After about 3 5 days of age, when worms were sexually mature, incorporation occurred principally in the testes, indicating a continuing high degree of DNA synthesis in reproductive tissues with only isolated sites of activity in somatic tissues.

At 45 days after infection, autoradiography indicated that the densely labeled cells were always in a peripheral position in the testes, with the central area generally unlabeled. In late spermatocytes of *S. mansoni*, the Golgi complex may be absent, which perhaps is associated with the absence of an acrosome in the mature sperm.

In fine structure, the sperm of most schistosomes appear typical of animal sperm, although an acrosome is lacking. In *Schistosomatium douthitti*, sperm cells are biflagellated, with a thin head about 30 to 35 tm long, sometimes appearing ribbonlike, and two short flagella less than half the head length.

Sperm cell biology therefore suggests a phylogenetic split between these and other schistosomes. In *S. mansoni* the head measures 2 by 8 μm, rounded anteriorly and tapered posteriorly. A prominent anterior mass of undifferentiated mitochondria lies beneath the plasma membrane in a cuplike depression in the nucleus.

The nucleus itself is largely electron-opaque, but contains electron-lucent patches of Feulgen-negative material. A single layer of microtubules is found between the periphery of the large nucleus and the plasma membrane of the sperm head. The single flagellum, about 20 ,um long, may be of the 9 + 0 tubule configuration or some variant.

The Adult Female

Female schistosomes, particularly in the species that parasitize birds, demonstrate considerable variation in shape, from elongated and filiform to flattened and leaflike. Mammalian species in general are less variable but still exhibit a range of forms, from the familiar cylindrical females of *Schistosoma* to the broad, flat females in *Schistosomahum*.

The external surface of female schistosomes that have been observed by scanning electron microscopy is simpler and more uniform than that of the heavily spined male. For the most part, females have a relatively featureless tegument with delicate transverse ridges bearing both ciliated and nerve papillae. Under higher magnification, tegumental pores may be seen throughout.

Near the posterior end commonly lies the area of long, sharp spines previously mentioned. The schistosome female reproductive tract was described in general terms by Theodor Bilharz, the German physician who first saw adult schistosomes while performing autopsies in Cairo in the early 1850s. This reproductive tract is much more complex than the male system.

There is always a single ovary, filled with cells in various stages of development, neatly displayed in linear progression from the smaller and more *immature oogonia* in the blind anterior area to the more loosely packed oocytes ready for discharge into the oviduct. Sperm cells that have come upstream from the female gonopore congregate in the dilated proximal oviduct to *rendezvous* with and *penetrate* the newly discharged oocytes.

Oogonia have a large, irregularly shaped nucleus with clumped chromatin masses and a *nucleolus*, and a narrow rim of cytoplasm. Cytoplasmic organelles vary with the stage of maturation and degree of metabolic activity. In the mature oocyte, there is usually a well-defined nucleolus and little nuclear chromatin; ribosomes are often associated with the nuclear membrane.

The cytoplasm also contains ribosomes, granular endoplasmic reticulum, mitochondria, and abundant Golgi material. Dense cortical granules, formed from the Golgi complexes, are located under the peripheral membrane. In female *S. mansoni* from unisexual infections (in which no males are present) the ovary is small, often coiled, and relatively inconspicuous, and the entire reproductive system is greatly retarded in development.

Little is known in general about the control of cellular development and movement in the ovary of parasitic flatworms. When adults of *S. mansoni*, *S. japonicum*, and *S. haematobium* are incubated in tritiated thymidine and surgically implanted into the circulatory system of hamsters, nuclear label is taken up rapidly into oogonia at the anterior periphery of the ovary. After 3 days, labeled cells appear in the central anterior region of the ovary.

Label is seen in the nuclei of primary oocytes in S. *japonicum* in 6 days, and in the other species in 7 days. Electron microscope autoradiography shows extranuclear DNA associated with mitochondria in the oocytes of *S. mansoni*. Some investigators who have labeled *S. mansoni* females with tritiated thymidine find label only in the anterior oogonial cells.

The ovary has understandably been a favourite potential target of chemotherapy. Antimonials and miracil, for example, lead to complete destruction of ovarian tissues. Niridazole causes a massive extrusion of ovarian cells into the uterus, which are then passed out by the worms. Emetine, although very destructive to the vitelline gland, has little effect on the ovary.

The early egg consists of the oocyte (normally with contained sperm cell) plus mature vitelline cells. In *S. japonicum* the number of vitelline cells is usually about 20; in *S. mansoni*, about 30 to 40. As a general rule in trematodes, eggshell formation begins in the ootype, which contains a mucoid secretion that forms a thin coat over the cells destined to make up the egg.

Granules freed from the vitelline cells migrate to the exterior of the package. As the granules coalesce, the shell gradually thickens in a process that may involve a quinone tanning system. Then the cells may switch to production of lipid globules, which provide nourishment for the miracidial embryo within the eggshell.

The autofluorescence of vitelline material and eggshells is well known and readily demonstrable by fluorescence microscopy. The shell consists of sclerotin, a tanned protein derived from phenolic precursors present in the vitelline granules. Phenol oxidase activity, reported in *S. mansoni* and *S. japonicum*, is depressed by many drugs that inhibit protein tanning.

The resulting eggs are distorted and lack normal shell and contents. The *vitelline gland* occupies the posterior half to two-thirds of the body. Many follicles connect through ducts to the large vitelline duct, which opens into the oviduct. *Vitcllinc* cells arc haploid, suggesting a common origin of the vitelline gland and ovary.

In *S. mansoni* cultured in vitro from cercariae to adults, vitelline cells are essentially normal, demonstrating that specific host influences are not necessary for their development. The high demands of egg production dictate an active metabolic role for the vitelline gland.

The intimate relation between the nutrient-providing intestinal ceca and the vitelline gland is shown by the thin border between these organs. Assuming that each female S. mansoni produces 300 eggs per day and there are 38 vitelline cells per egg, the vitelline gland in this species must release about 11,000 mature cells daily.

In *S. japonicum* this figure is higher perhaps by a factor of 10. Various authors have estimated that a female S. mansoni converts from 10 percent to 100 percent of her own body weight into eggs every day.

Many workers have studied the effects of antischistosomal drugs on the vitelline gland because of its importance in egg production and its high biosynthetic turnover. Fuadin, Astiban, lucanthone, hycanthone, miracil, niridazole, and other drugs all have deleterious effects on vitelline cells.

CHROMOSOMES

We may wonder how it is that the peculiar sexual separation in this family developed from what were certainly hermaphroditic ancestors. What is known now is that male and female schistosomes have distinct chromosomal patterns. Sex chromosomes have been found in a dozen species of schistosomes, in which the female appears to be heterogametic. That is, sex is determined-as in birds-through the ovum, rather than through the sperm.

It is very difficult to obtain chromosome preparations from adult schistosomes, but relatively simple to find metaphase figures in sporocysts taken from the intermediate host snail. Therefore most karyology of schistosomes has been done from the larval stages. Studies have been conducted in 11 species from mammals and 5 from birds. Of the mammalian species, those from Africa, Asia, and North America are distinct.

Each genus and species has a different karyotype, distinguishable by C-banding if not by chromosome morphology. All of the African and Asian mammalian schistosomes have diploid numbers of 16, but the two species from North America, *Schistosomatium douthitti* and *Heterobilharzia americana*, have 14 and 20, respectively.

Information about schistosome cytogenetics, although still very crude, should be compatible with emerging knowledge about the molecular biology of this group, discussed in other chapter of this book.

7

FILARIA WORM

Filarial parasites have complex life cycles that include an obligatory maturation period in a hematophagous arthropod vector and a stage of further differentiation followed by reproductive activity in a vertebrate host. Like most species of filarial nematodes, those that cause onchocerciasis (*Onchocerca volvulus*) or *lymphatic* filariasis in humans (*Wuchereria bancrofti*, *Brugia malayi*, and *B. timori*) have a limited host range in nature.

However, some filarids develop normally in experimentally infected laboratory animals that are not their natural hosts. These experimental models of lymphatic filariasis differ from natural infections in three variables that are known to affect immune responses to defined antigens: the frequency of exposure, the initial route of presentation, and the amount of parasite antigen presented to the host.

Most experimental infections are induced by a single parenteral injection of a large number of infective larvae. In contrast, natural infections are acquired over a period of weeks to months through "*trickle infections*," or repeated penetrations of the skin by small numbers of larvae deposited by the vector.

Because of these differences, some immunologic phenomena observed in animal models may not be relevant to host-parasite interactions in naturally acquired lymphatic filariasis. In natural as well as in laboratory infections, several developmental stages of filarial worms can be present simultancously in the final host, and these are likely to interact with the immune system in different ways. For example, infective larvae, adult worms, and microfilariae reside in the skin, lymphatic vessels, and blood, respectively; their being in different tissues influences the way the host is sensitized to stage-specific parasite antigens and where immune effector mechanisms must operate.

Different filarial stages also present distinct target surfaces to the immune system: larval and adult worms are bounded by a typical nematode cuticle, whereas microfilariae of some species are enclosed in a multilayered sheath derived from the original eggshell and separated from the underlying cuticle by an electron-lucent space.

These distinct physical and chemical properties of the worms' surface are likely to influence the susceptibility of various developmental stages to different immune effector mechanisms. The simultaneous presence of multiple worm stages that share many common antigens also complicates analysis of host reactions to stage-specific antigens.

To circumvent some of these problems, increasing use is being made of the "proxy" method of infection. In this approach, a single developmental stage isolated from a suitable host is surgically transferred to a new host of the same or different animal species.

In this way, one can study reactions to one worm stage without interference from host responses elicited by earlier developmental stages. Studies of this nature indicate that adult worms or microfilariae can survive in some species of animals that are innately resistant to infection with filarial larvae.

Such studies reinforce the concept of the stage specificity of protective immune responses in filariasis. This chapter focuses on four major topics of the immunobiology of lymphatic filariasis: mechanisms of resistance to infection, immune reactions that control the number of microfilariae circulating in blood, mechanisms of immune evasion, and the pathogenesis of filarial disease syndromes.

It is not intended to be an exhaustive review of the subject; our aim is to illustrate general principles with selected examples. Where appropriate, nonimmunologic variables that affect the ultimate outcome of an individual's exposure to filarial helminths are briefly mentioned. The immunology of onchocerciasis is not considered here, because several excellent recent reviews of this topic are available.

Other aspects of the general biology of filarial helminths are the subject of recent reviews listed at the end of this chapter. Finally, some terms used in this chapter require definition. Prepatency is the interval between the onset of infection and the appearance of microfilariae in blood, patency is the period of microfilaremia, and latency is the period of postpatent infection. Latent infections often are referred to as "occult" filariasis, a term we will not use, because prepatency can also be

Table 7.1: Parasitological Characteristics of Filarial Worms.

Parasite species	*Natural hosts*	*Location*		*Sheathed microf-ilariae*
		Adult worms	*Microfi-lariae*	
Brugia malayi, *B. timori*	Humans, primates	Lymphatics	Blood	Yes
B. pahangi	Primates, cats, other	Lymphatics	Blood	Yes
Wucheria hancrofti	Humans	Lymphatics	Blood	Yes
Dipetalonema viteae	Jirds	Subcutaneous	Blood	No
Litomosoides carinii	Cotton rats	Pleura	Blood	No
Dirofilaria immitis	Dogs	Heart, lungs	Blood	No
Onchocerca volvulus	Humans	Subcutaneous	Skin, eyes	No

considered a period of occult filariasis, that is, one during which microfilariae are absent from the circulation. Filarial infections in animals often progress through these three stages in a timely fashion, and lymphatic filariasis in human beings probably follows a similar course.

IMMUNE EFFECTOR MECHANISMS

Innate and Acquired Resistance to Filarial Infections

Microfilaremia or clinical symptoms of lymphatic filariasis are absent in a variable but sizable proportion of long-term residents of endemic areas, but whether immune resistance develops during natural infections is a question that defies simple answers.

Filarial helminths complete several steps of their complex life cycle in the vertebrate host. Each one of these maturational stages constitutes a potential target of protective immune responses. However, not all stages can be readily quantified, and therein lies the difficulty of assessing immune resistance in filariasis.

Quantitative recovery of infective larvae, the most direct measurement of immune resistance, is difficult to achieve even under optimal experimental conditions because of the rapid migration of larvae from the infection site. It is relatively simple to monitor blood levels of microfilariac, but this measurement of host resistance is inadequate because the number of microfilariae in peripheral blood does not correlate with adult worm burdens, and, as is discussed later in this chapter, microfilaremia may be absent when fertile adult worms are present in host tissues.

Thus, quantitative recovery of adult worms is the most commonly used index of host resistance in filariasis. This indirect measurement should be interpreted with caution, however, because the number of adult worms that can be recovered from individual animals infected with the same number of infective larvae varies tremendously even among inbred animal strains.

Despite our inability to measure the phenomenon directly, several lines of evidence suggest that host immune responses to antigens on early larval stages confer some degree of resistance to primary infections with filarial helminths. Several species of filarids develop normally in naturally resistant hosts, provided the infection is initiated with larvae that have undergone partial development in a proxy host rather than with vector-derived larvae.

For example, increasing numbers of adult *Brugia pahangi* are recovered when progressively more mature larval stages are transplanted from jirds to naturally resistant mice. If such patterns of resistance are truly related to immune *phenomena*, rather than to differences in metabolic requirements of distinct parasite stages, then they would be an example of remarkable stage specificity of immune effector mechanisms in filariasis. Direct evidence for a role of immune reactions in innate resistance to filariasis comes from studies in animals with congenital or acquired immune deficiencies.

Such animals are more susceptible than their immunocompetent counterparts to filarial infections. Although adult mice resist *B. pahangi*, a proportion of mice inoculated shortly after birth with larvae of this parasite species go on to harbor patent infections. This has been attributed to the relative immune incompetence of mammals during the neonatal period.

Normally resistant rats that are immune suppressed before inoculation with *Litomosoides carinii* or *Dipetalonema viteae* infective larvae likewise develop patent infections and yield large numbers of adult worms. Models of selective *immuno-deficiencies* suggest that a thymus-dependent immune response contributes to innate resistance to filarial parasites.

Congenitally athymic rats are susceptible to infection with *D. viteae*, a parasite to which their euthymic litterrnates are resistant, and *B. pahangi* readily infects athymic animals of strains of rats that are innately resistant to this parasite. Similarly, athymic (nude) mice are fully susceptible to larval-initiated infection with *B. pahangi* and *B. malayi*.

However, implantation of a thymic graft several weeks before inoculation of infective larvae not only confers complete protection against infection but also enables the mice to produce cellular and humoral immune responses to larval antigens. It should be emphasized that host immunity most likely is only one of the factors that determine primary resistance to filarial infections. Some of the variability in adult worm recovery from inbred animals can be explained by such nonimmunological factors as the age and sex of the experimental host.

Genetic differences between strains, mostly unrelated to major histocompatibility loci, also influence to some extent the susceptibility of experimental animals to filarial infections. Furthermore, innate or immune-mediated resistance appears highly target-specific: nude mice that are susceptible to *Brugia spp.* remain resistant to *Wuchereria bancrofti*.

These examples of natural immune-mediated resistance to larval infection suggest that susceptible populations might be rendered resistant through vaccination. This idea prompts two major questions: (1) What is the precise mechanism of larval killing in naturally resistant animals, and (2) how can the components of the larvicidal mechanisms be elicited in otherwise susceptible hosts?

In vitro studies reveal that infective larvae can be killed by antibody-dependent cell-mediated cytotoxic (ADCC) immune reactions similar to those that act on microfilariae; they are described below. These studies led to the widespread belief that ADCC reactions mediate resistance to filarial worms, as has been postulated for several other helminth infections.

However, the presence of antibodies that mediate this reaction correlates poorly with resistance to infection. Sera from virtually all residents of areas endemic for brugian or bancroftian filariasis contain such antibodies, even though many of these individuals remain susceptible to infection. Some cats repeatedly infected with third stage larvae of *B. pahangi* become amicrofilaremic and develop partial resistance to reinfection.

Yet antibodies to larvae and adult worms are present in both "resistant" as well as in susceptible (microfilaremic) cats. Similarly, mice, jirds, and hamsters differ widely in their susceptibility to *D. viteae*, but resistance is not correlated with the development of antibodies to the cuticle of infective third-stage larvae of this parasite species.

Thus, it is clear that the in vitro ADCC assay does not adequately reflect the process that kills larvae in vivo. Recent studies in two animal models nevertheless indicate that cooperation between humoral and cellular components of the immune system can lead to some degree of resistance to filarial infections. Adoptive transfer of cells and sera from jirds infected with *L. carinii* retards the development of larvae injected into the recipient; neither immune cells nor immune serum alone is effective.

Likewise, nude mice given immune serum or B cells from donors immunized with *B. pahangi* larvae are not protected against a larval challenge. However, transfer of primed B and T lymphocytes from similarly immunized donors confers complete protection on the recipients, which promptly produce high titers of antibodies and delayed hypersensitivity reactions to larval antigens.

The success of such adoptive transfers in conferring resistance indicates that protective immunity might be elicited by direct immunization. Conventional mice, which kill larvae of *B. pahangi* within 3 to 4 weeks after inoculation and are therefore considered resistant to infection, eliminate subsequent larval inocula within 10 days and exhibit greatly potentiated humoral and cellular immune responses to larval antigens after rechallenge. This suggests that reexposure to parasite antigens augments immune responses that may contribute to the "natural resistance" of refractory hosts.

Unfortunately, the opposite may be true in "naturally susceptible" hosts of filariasis. For example, jirds infected with *B. pahangi* manifest increased rather than decreased susceptibility to reinfection. In already infected jirds, recovery rates of adult worms resulting from challenge infections are twice those in previously uninfected jirds, although worms developing in the previously parasitized animals are smaller than in the naive recipients.

As will be discussed later, this intriguing result has been attributed to immune suppression induced by the primary infection. Thus, a primary infection in a susceptible host may not elicit immunologic resistance to reinfection. On the other hand, while hyporesponsiveness to filarial antigens is a characteristic of filariasis in humans and in animal models, repeatedly infected animals, like residents of highly filariasis-endemic areas, seldom suffer from overwhelming parasitemias. The number of adult worms increases with each administration of larvae during most experimental trickle infections, but the proportional increment in parasite load decreases with time, and the development of larvae in later challenges appears to be delayed.

This result has been observed even in natural host-parasite combinations such as *L. carinii* infections in cotton rats and *D. viteae* infections in jirds. In most cases, direct evidence that these phenomena are immune-mediated is lacking. Although it is uncertain whether natural hosts develop immune resistance through previous infections, it is clear that resistance to infection can be induced by several manipulations that enhance host immune responses to filarial antigens.

Soluble parasite materials, whether they are somatic extracts or excretory-secretory products, are generally inefficient in conferring protection against larval challenge, but they protect when combined with an adjuvant. For example, homogenates of *L. carinii* larvae produce a high degree of resistance to infection in albino rats when administered as an emulsion in Freund's adjuvant, but not when used alone. Irradiated larvae have been more successful than parasite extracts to vaccinate animals against several filarial species.

For example, dogs can be protected against *Diro filaria* immitis, albino rats against *L. carinii*, and cats and jirds against *B. pahangi*. The rationale for using such vaccines is that by inhibiting the development of the larvae, the host will be exposed to antigens on early larval stages for a longer period than during natural infections, but experimental evidence to support this assumption is not available.

In at least one model, irradiated larvae induce a moderate degree of lymphatic pathology that may not be acceptable in human beings. Termination of filarial infections with drugs before the parasite matures and causes lymphatic pathology is a promising variant of the attenuated larval vaccine approach. This protocol induces resistance to *D. immitis* in ferrets, and to *B. pahangi* in jirds.

However, resistance of monkeys to reinfection with *B. malayi* apparently does not occur after successful drug treatment of patent infections. Nor is it clear whether elimination of microfilaremia with diethylcarbamazine, which reverses the state of immune unresponsiveness to parasite antigens associated with patent brugian filariasis in humans, leads to increased resistance to reinfection.

Epidemiologic studies of previously treated populations suggest it does not. In contrast, immune reconstitution of nude mice parasitized by *B. pahangi* or *B. malayi* induces resistance to reinfection and kills adult worms but levels of circulating microfilariae are not affected.

Thus, immune effector mechanisms that mediate protection against reinfection appear to be highly stage-specific, being both elicited by and directed against antigens on larval stages. Much remains to be learned about the nature of protective immune responses and the antigens that elicit these reactions.

Control of Microfilaremia

Microfilaremia is essential for the transmission of lymph-dwelling filarial helminths. Their survival as a species depends on the presence of microfilariae in peripheral blood of the vertebrate host in numbers adequate to infect the appropriate vector. In most natural hosts, the duration of patent filariasis far exceeds the estimated life span of individual microfilariae, even when reinfection is known not to take place.

In contrast, patency lasts only for a relatively brief period in many experimental models of filariasis. Infections with this characteristic, such as L. *carinii* in albino rats and *D. viteae* in hamsters, have been used extensively to study the nature of host immune responses that lead to latent filariasis. Some observations made in these models undoubtedly reflect the uniqueness of the "unnatural" host-parasite combination, but studies of natural hosts that develop latent filariasis, while differing in detail, generally support the broad concepts derived from these model infections.

Foremost is the notion that microfilariae themselves are the primary target of immune reactions that lead to latency. This idea is based on the observation that fecund adult worms can be recovered from animals with latent infections; these worms continue to produce microfilariae in vitro and upon transfer to naive recipients in vivo.

Three lines of evidence indicate that host immune responses control microfilaremia in animals with latent filariasis. First, immune suppression of primary hosts with postpatent infections results in the reappearance of microfilariae in blood. Second, adoptive transfer of sera from animals with latent filariasis reduces microfilaremia in the recipients.

Third, immunization with microfilarial antigens prevents the development or reduces the level and duration of microfilaremia but usually has no effect on adult worm recovery. These observations indicate a remarkable stage specificity of host immune reactions that control microfilaremia. Three mechanisms by which immune sera can reduce levels of circulating microfilariae have been identified.

Inhibition of Embryogenesis

Sera from hamsters with latent *D. viteae* infections inhibit embryogenesis and prevent the release of microfilariae in vitro by affecting the fecundity, but not the fertility, of female worms. Whether this phenomenon occurs in vivo is not easy to ascertain, because it is technically difficult to distinguish between inhibition of embryogenesis and subsequent destruction of microfilariae in intact infected animals.

In situ trapping of microfilariae Immune sera also participate in host reactions that prevent microfilariae from entering the bloodstream. After 3 to 4 months of infection, latency develops in albino rats infected with L. carinii. The disappearance of microfilariae from peripheral blood is caused by a localized immune process that traps the worms in the pleural cavity.

When adult worms are transplanted into the peritoneal cavity of rats with latent infections, microfilariae appear in recipients' blood. This does not happen when adult worms or microfilariae are transferred into the pleural cavity of such animals. Microfilariae released in the pleural cavity of rats with latent L. carinii infections become covered with leukocytes and, one presumes, are killed in situ before they are able to enter the circulation.

Similar selective trapping of microfilariae also occurs in the pleural cavity of cotton rats (the natural host of L. carinii) immunized with microfilarial antigens before infection. This adherence phenomenon can be reproduced in vitro. Antiparasite IgE present in sera from rats with latent infections promotes cellular adherence to L. carinii microfilariae; another heat-labile serum component, probably complement, augments this reaction.

Neutrophils, eosinophils, and macrophages adhere to microfilariae in vitro, but only neutrophils and macrophages kill the parasite, whereas peripheral blood lymphocytes or peritoneal mast cells neither adhere to nor kill L. carinii microfilariae. In this in vitro model, the worms appear to be killed by an antibody-dependent cell-mediated cytotoxic (ADCC) reaction.

These in vitro observations fail to represent the in vivo situation in two respects. Examination of the pleural content of rats with latent L. carinii infections often reveals cells, mostly lymphocytes and macrophages, attached to living microfilariae. Hence, the in vitro model evidently does not identify the type of cell that kills the worms in vivo. Second, sera from rats with latent infections readily promote cellular adherence to *L. carinii* in vitro, but adoptive transfer of such sera often fails to reduce microfilaremia. Furthermore, microfilariae are not retained and killed in the peritoneal cavity of rats with latent infections, even though the required constituents of the in vitro killing system should be present at this site as they are in the pleural cavity.

Table 7.2: Compartmentalization of Immune Responses to Litomosoides Carinii Microfilariae.

Worm stage transplanted	*Recipient status*	*Transplant site*	*Microfilaremia*
Adult	Normal	Pleura	Yes
Latent	Pleura	No	
Adult	Normal	Peritoneum	Yes
Latent	Peritoneum	Yes	
Microfilariae	Normal	Pleura	Yes
Latent	Pleura	No	

Thus, anatomical compartmentalization of host immune mechanisms may influence the in vivo killing of microfilariae in ways which cannot be adequately reproduced in vitro.

Such compartmentalization of immune effector mechanisms could explain several clinical features of lymphatic filariasis in natural hosts. For example, the absence of microfilaremia in patients with elephantiasis could be due to the development of local immunity at sites that harbor adult worms, thereby preventing microfilariae from reaching the peripheral circulation.

The appearance of microfilariae in the blood of arnicrofilaremic patients with elephantiasis treated with corticosteroids, and the induction of localized acute adenitis with microfilaricidal drugs such as diethylcarbamazine support this hypothesis. A similar phenomenon of immune compartmentalization can be invoked to explain the pathogenesis of the tropical pulmonary eosinophilia (TPE) syndrome, discussed in a later section.

Removal of Microfilariae from the Circulation

A third antibody-dependent mechanism that leads to latent filariasis is the clearance of microfilariae from blood. In many animal models, adoptive transfer of immune sera or monoclonal antibodies induces a rapid decline in the number of circulating microfilariae due to sequestration of worms in host tissues.

This result has also been observed in natural infections such as those caused *by W. banerofti* in humans and *D. immitis* in dogs. Other particulate antigens such as antibody-coated or malaria-infected red cells are cleared mostly by the reticuloendothelial system of the spleen and liver, but microfilariae are retained predominantly in the lungs of dogs infected with *D. immitis* or mice infected with *B. malayi.*

Table 7.3: ADCC Reactions Kill Microfilariae In Vivo.

	Fate of microfilariae implanted in chambers (pore size)	
Host status and response	0.4	4
In host with latent infection		
Antibodies on cuticle	Yes	Yes
Cells attached to worms	No	Yes
Microfilariae killed	No	Yes
In naive host		
Antibodies on cuticle	No	No
Cells attached to worms	No	No
Microfilariae killed	No	No
In recipient of immune serum		
Antibodies on cuticle	Yes	Yes
Cells attached to worms	No	Yes
Microfilariae killed	No	Yes

The same process probably occurs in humans with lymphatic filariasis, although in some patients with brugian filariasis the spleen appears to be the major organ that traps microfilariae. Microfilariae cleared from blood are believed to be killed by an ADCC reaction similar to that observed in the pleural cavity of *L. carinii* -infected rats, as described earlier.

That such a reaction can kill microfilariae in vivo is supported by studies on the fate of *D. viteae* microfilariae contained within diffusion chambers implanted into hamsters with latent infections. The relative ease with which ADCC reactions can be produced in vitro has prompted numerous investigators to study which antibody-cell combinations can "kill" filarial worms.

In most of these studies, loss of microfilarial motility is equated with parasite death. It should be emphasized that the true measure of microfilariae damage or death should be the parasite's ability to infect and develop in the appropriate vector. Nonmotile parasites conceivably could recover function when suspended in the blood ingested by mosquitoes.

Conversely, parasites that remain motile may in fact be sufficiently damaged to prevent their subsequent development in the vector. Nevertheless, such studies have yielded interesting results. The isotype of antibodies and the nature of cells that participate in ADCC reactions to microfilariae greatly differ among various host-parasite combinations.

This may reflect differences in the ability of distinct filarial species to resist potentially toxic molecules released by some types of cells attached to the worms' surface. Alternatively, various host species may use distinct effector mechanisms to control microfilaremia caused by the same parasite. Current evidence is consistent with either interpretation.

Table 7.4: In Vitro Killing of Microfilariae by ADCC Reactions.

Parasite	*Host*	*Antibody class*	*Effector cell*
Dipetalonema viteae	hamster	19S (IgM)	M/multiple
D. viteae	rat	IgE	M/Eo
Litomosoides carinii	rat	IgE	Eo/M
Wucheria bancrofti	man	IgG	multiple
Brugia malayi	man	IgG	M/multiples
Onchocerca volvulus	man	IgG	Eo/neutro
B. pahangi	cat	IgG	Eo/neutro
Dirofilaria immitis	dog	IgM	Neutro

Whether in vitro ADCC reactions adequately represent the mechanisms that kill microfilariae in vivo remains a matter of considerable debate. Critics of this concept point out that, at least in the *L. carinii-albino* rat and the *D. viteae*-hamster models, the predominant types of cells that adhere to and "kill" microfilariae in vitro are different from those that appear to operate in vivo.

This difference may simply reflect the limitations of in vitro assays. Some cells may not be able to kill microfilariae in vitro because they must be activated by factors secreted by other cell types that are underrepresented in the populations used for in vitro assays.

Conversely, in vitro effector cells may not kill parasites in vivo because they are not attracted to their worm target or because other factors, for example, immune complexes, interfere with cell-parasite interactions. Most likely, microfilariae are killed in vivo by the combined effects of several cell types that act sequentially or in concert, although it is not always possible to determine which cells kill the worms and which ones scavenge the dead carcass.

No direct evidence exists to support the popular notion that ADCC-mediated clearance of microfilariae is a process that controls the level of microfilaremia in natural hosts. A proportion of microfilariae isolated from patients with brugian filariasis have immunoglobulin (possibly antibody) on their surface. That these worms are destined to be removed from the circulation is a plausible, but unproven, assumption.

On the other hand, the pace at which 19S (IgM) antibodies to the cuticle of *D. viteae* microfilariae become detectable correlates with the duration of microfilaremia in various strains of hamsters. Thus, it appears probable, albeit unproved, that the relatively stable levels of microfilaremia characteristic of natural infections are maintained to a certain extent by the same types of host immune reactions to *microfilariae* as those that lead to latent filariasis in experimental infections.

Which microfilarial antigens act as targets of such "protective" immune responses remains unknown. Clear-cut associations between the absence of microfilaremia and detectable serum levels of antibodies to surface antigens of microfilariae have been described in many natural and experimental filarial infections.

Formal proof is still lacking, however, that surface-directed antibodies mediate microfilarial clearance. In fact, immune sera that reduce microfilaremia in the *B. malayi*-mouse model react with many constituents of microfilariae but appear devoid of antibodies to surface antigens.

Other possible target antigens for clearance-mediating antibodies include proteases secreted by the worms (particularly those that might inactivate ADCC-mediating antibodies) and worm-derived modulators of immune effector cells or inhibitors of inflammatory reactions. Experiments to determine which parasite antigens are specifically recognized by sera from amicrofilaremic donors are in progress in many laboratories.

So far, differential recognition of microfilarial antigens with relative molecular weights (M_r) of 25 kilodaltons (kD), 70 kD, and 75 kD has been reported. In addition, two monoclonal antibodies that reduce microfilaremia upon adoptive transfer have been described.

These react with microfilarial antigens of 70 and 75 kD, and 110 kD, respectively, and should provide invaluable reagents to isolate microfilarial antigens that act as targets of immune responses resulting in the clearance of this parasite stage from the circulation.

IMMUNE EVASION

The mere fact that filarial parasites develop and survive in immunocompetent hosts indicates that they are able to evade or resist host immune responses, either by hampering immune effector mechanisms or by preventing the development of immune responses with protective potential. Several mechanisms by which filarids may evade host immune responses have been identified.

Immune Evasion by Disguise, or the Invisible Parasite

It would seem natural that microfilariae might blend into their environment by acquiring a surface coat of natural constituents of blood that would shield parasite antigens from host reactions and thereby enhance the worms' survival. Several types of host molecules have been found on the surface of microfilariae.

Albumin can be detected on blood- or tissue-derived microfilariae of some filarial species, but not on microfilariae shed in vitro. The biological role of this molecule in terms of parasite survival is unclear. Host albumin often prevents the radiolabeling of parasite surface antigens, but it does not appear to inhibit the killing of microfilariae by ADCC reactions to these antigens.

Table 7.5: Possible Mechanisms of Immune Evasion by Filarial Worms.

Disquise of parasite antigens by host molecules (albumin, blood group substances, immunoglobulin)
Polyclonal activation of host immune system Immune suppression
Inactivation of immune effector mechanisms (complement, antibody, other)
Other mechanisms (surface turnover, innate resistance)

The protective role of host blood group substances remains equally in doubt. Isohemagglutinins promote the mixed agglutination of *W. bancrofti* microfilariae with erythrocytes, and blood group A and B determinants have been detected on these parasites (but not on microfilariae of some other species).

One report suggests that blood group antigens may not contribute to the survival of filarial worms: immunization of jirds with cat antigens does not alter the recovery or longevity of *B. pahangi* transferred from cats into these jirds.

However, these experiments did not rule out the possibility of rapid exchange of cat-derived blood-group determinants for jird determinants once the microfilariae were in the latter's bloodstream. Such exchange can occur in vitro: when microfilariae of *W. bancrofti* are incubated in heterologous sera, blood group determinants present on the worms are rapidly replaced with those present in the serum.

Regardless of their role in immune evasion, blood group substances or other host-derived molecules may insure the continual recirculation of microfilariae by masking surface determinants of the parasite that lack sialic acid, which might otherwise trigger clearance of the worms by the reticuloendothelial system.

Immunoglobulin also can be present on microfilariae recovered from blood or tissues of infected donors but is absent from microfilariae produced in vitro by gravid female worms. In contrast to blood group determinants, immunoglobulins are not adsorbed by microfilariae incubated in vitro in normal human serum. This finding suggests that "adsorbed" immunoglobulin constitutes anti microfilaria] antibody.

These antibodies could favor parasite survival if they do not themselves kill the worms but instead prevent a protective type of immune effector mechanism from reacting with its target antigen. Such "blocking" antibodies have been identified in other parasitic infections and in tumor models.

Thus, although several types of host molecules at times can be present on filarial 3 worms, it is far from evident that they contribute to the survival of parasites in vivo. In fact, the true origin of these putative host molecules remains in doubt, because many studies performed so far fail to prove that fllariae themselves lack the ability to produce the "adsorbed" host material.

Polyclonal Activation of the Host's Immune System

Many parasitic infections are associated with some degree of polyclonal activation of the host's immune system. This pattern is also true for filariasis: elevated titers of antifilarial antibodies per se account for only a proportion of the increased levels of serum *immunoglobulins* observed in patients with lymphatic filariasis.

Filaria-specific T cell clones augment the in vitro production of specific antibody and of "*nonspecific*" immunoglobulin by sensitized human B cells. *B. malayi* microfilariae also contain a mitogen that stimulates the B cell helper activity of T lymphocytes from uninfected donors. Thus, both specific parasite antigens and nonspecific mitogenic *stimuli* may contribute to the *hypergammaglobulinemia* of *lymphatic* filariasis. Polyclonal activation could favor parasite survival in several ways. It could engage the host's immune system in the production of antibodies or the expansion of T cell clones reacting with worm antigens that are irrelevant to the host-parasite relationship to the detriment of immune responses with protective potential.

It could generate antibodies that react with "relevant" antigens, yet are unable to mediate effects that benefit the host, for example, blocking antibodies. It could also produce large amounts of immune complexes that could interfere with both the afferent and efferent arms of immune responses to worm antigens.

Immune complexes containing parasite antigen can be readily detected in sera from infected patients or animals and inhibit, for example, the in vitro killing of microfilariae by ADCC reactions.

Immune Suppression

Cellular and humoral immune responses to parasite antigens are more vigorous in amicrofilaremic hosts than in those with patent filarial infections. This results in part from the activation of immunosuppressive regulatory circuits of the host's immune system by parasite molecules. Active suppressor T lymphocytes and phagocytic cells presumed to be suppressor macrophages are present in the blood of microfilaremic patients and in the spleen and lymph nodes of infected animals.

Sera from microfilaremic donors contain substances that inhibit proliferation of T cells induced by parasite antigens. Cells from microfilaremic donors also produce less interleukin-2 and gamma interferon than lymphocytes from amicrofilaremic individuals upon stimulation with parasite antigens.

These interrelated but evidently independent mechanisms suppress immune responses to filarial antigens without affecting the response to antigens from other sources. In addition to this type of antigen-specific suppression, parasite extracts also inhibit mitogen-induced proliferation of lymphocytes from infected as well as uninfected donors, a form of nonspecific immune suppression.

In animal models, antigenspecific and nonspecific modes of immune suppression appear to be mediated by distinct cell types that are differentially distributed among organs and tissues of the immune system. Precisely what activates suppressor cells in microfilaremic hosts remains unclear. Termination of microfilaremia with drugs restores the ability of treated individuals to react to filarial antigens.

It is therefore not surprising that antigenic extracts of microfilariae can induce suppressor T lymphocytes. Such extracts contain proteins of high molecular weight that suppress mitogen-induced lymphocyte proliferation; whether the same parasite materials also inhibit T cell responses to filarial antigens remains to be determined.

Immuno suppressive worm products of similar high molecular weight are present in peritoneal exudates of jirds and in sera and lymph of nude mice infected with *B. malayi*, suggesting that such molecules could be active in vivo. Microfilariae are not the only worm stage that contains immunosuppressive molecules: extracts of adult *B. malayi* also suppress the in vitro reactivity of sensitized T cells to microfilarial antigens.

This finding suggests that immune responses to later worm stages may be modulated by cross-reactive determinants present in early developmental stages of filarial helminths. Although immune suppression is most pronounced in microfilaremic hosts, the phenomenon may occur much earlier after the onset of infection than is generally recognized and predate the onset of patency.

For example, in the *B. malayi* jird model, immune suppression can first be demonstrated 2 to 3 weeks after infection, when third stage larvae first moult in the mammalian host. The onset of immune suppression in human filariasis is difficult to date, but it appears to start soon after previously unexposed individuals immigrate into an endemic area.

Comparison of immune responses to filarial antigens in children and adult natives of endemic areas further suggests that the phenomenon increases with prolonged exposure. In addition, pre- or perinatal exposure to circulating worm antigens may induce neonatal tolerance to filarial antigens in offspring of infected mothers.

This possibility might explain the marked differences in the clinical course of lymphatic filariasis in native and immigrant residents of endemic areas, a concept supported by studies in animal models. Filaria-induced suppression of host immunity could benefit the parasite in several ways.

One can speculate that the first few larvae of natural trickle infections suppress their host's immune system in order to allow the development of larvae that subsequently invade the same host. This notion is supported by experimental observations. Immune suppression induced by an established infection could also decrease the host's resistance to reinfection and thereby increase worm burdens.

This result has been observed in experimental filariasis. For example, adult *L. carinii* transferred to naive cotton rats are rejected, but they survive in previously infected rats. One must recall, however, that infected individuals rarely display overwhelming parasitemias, so this aspect of immune suppression may be balanced by active sensitization to parasite antigens in the repeatedly infected host.

On the other hand, although immune suppression would favor parasite survival, it may also be beneficial to the host by reducing the intensity of immune-mediated components of lymphatic pathology. This has been well documented in the *B. pahangi-jird* model, and will be described later in the chapter.

The role of the nonspecific type of immune suppression in the pathogenesis of lymphatic filariasis is difficult to assess. A priori, this suppression should increase the host's susceptibility to environmental pathogens. In contrast to malaria, a disease in which nonspecific immune suppression is prominent, lymphatic filariasis appears not to be associated with increased morbidity or mortality from common infections.

In fact, the severity of malaria is said to be reduced by concomitant filariasis. On the other hand, it has been suggested that streptococcal infections contribute to the pathogenesis of elephantiasis by exacerbating preexisting lymphatic lesions. Whether filaria-induced immune suppression weakens resistance to this pathogen and predisposes to the *poly-parasitism* commonly observed in endemic areas is unknown.

Poor responses to some types of vaccines have been described, but these were noted in both infected and apparently healthy residents of the endemic area.

Inactivation of Immune Effector Mechanisms

Microfilariae of various species activate complement through the alternative pathway, a finding that is consistent with the relatively low amount of sialic acid on their surface. Several types of host cells possess receptors for complement, but these cells might not be able to interact with microfilariae covered with C3 fragments that lack the appropriate polypeptide sequences for recognition.

Whether this property is a mechanism of immune evasion could be confirmed by detailed biochemical analysis of the complement fragments generated during the activation of C3 by filarial helminths. Antibodies that promote the adherence of cells to the sheath of *B. malayi* microfilariae are inactivated when added to the worms in vitro.

This process leads to a progressive decline in antibody levels in the supernatant of these cultures and reduces the adherence of cells to microfilariae pretreated with antibody. The Fc portion of such antibody is functionally and/or physically destroyed, perhaps by one of the numerous proteases present in and secreted by microfilariae, while the antigen-binding part of the molecule remains attached to the parasite. This process could be an extremely effective mechanism by which microfilariae resist ADCC reactions to antigens on their surface.

It might explain, for example, why microfilariae covered with "immunoglobulin" continue to circulate in natural hosts. Reexamination of this finding with antisera to defined portions of antibody molecules might very well confirm that the phenomenon of antibody inactivation occurs in vivo as well as in vitro.

Table 7.6: Functional Inactivation of Antibodies by *B. malayi* Microfilariae.

Duration of preincubation with antibody (hours)	*Antibody portion detectable*	
	F(ab′)$_2$	*Fc*
2	Yes	Yes
24	Yes	No

Recent studies indicate that filariae contain enzymes that convert arachidonic acid into pharmacologically active products. These results raise the possibility that these parasites might be able to inactivate host-derived mediators of inflammation. A similar mechanism may explain the relative resistance of *B. malayi* microfilariae to oxygen-derived products generated by host cells that are toxic to other parasites and kill mammalian target cells.

Finally, parasite-mediated induction of isotype-specific helper T cells, such as those that contribute to the high levels of nonspecific IgE present in sera from individuals with helminth infections, might contribute to the survival of filarial worms.

Saturation of cell surface receptors with polyclonal IgE directed against nonparasite antigens could effectively prevent the triggering of mast cells by filarial antigens and thereby avert the possible damage to the parasite that would otherwise be caused by the crosslinking of filaria-specific IgE on mast cells by parasite antigens.

Other Mechanisms of Immune Evasion

Several other mechanisms of immune evasion have been suggested, but they remain to be evaluated experimentally. Filariae probably do not show the sort of antigenic variation described for some protozoa, but third- and fourth-stage larvae of *D. immitis*, for example, differ greatly in the structure, charge, and antigenic makeup of their respective cuticles. Thus, the moulting process renders obsolete immune reactions to third stage larval antigens and exposes the host to previously hidden antigenic determinants. Whether rapid turnover of the surface of other parasite stages contributes to their survival is not known.

Developmental changes in the properties of microfilarial sheaths have been detected, but there is no conclusive evidence for turnover of the epicuticular surface of filarial helminths between the larval moults and in the adult stage. In addition to developmental changes in the surface properties of filarial worms, the complex structure of filarial surfaces per se undoubtedly provides a certain degree of innate resistance of these worms to certain types of immune effector mechanisms.

Cytolytic T cells are believed to kill by "puncturing" the lipid bilayer membrane of their targets. Controversy exists as to whether filariae are bounded by a "true" membrane, but it is difficult to imagine that T cells would be able to invaginate the filarial cuticle. Similarly, the microfilarial sheath, which is rich in chitinlike material, may confer upon microfilariae an additional degree of innate resistance to immune effector mechanisms.

Finally, an individual's ability to recognize stage-specific antigens must influence the outcome of exposure to filarial worms. So far, none of the genetic factors that influence an individual's ability to control filarial infections has been definitively linked to immune response genes or to genes encoded in the major histocompatibility complex.

However, the duration of microfilaremia in animals with subtle defects of the immune system generally exceeds that in their immunocompetent counterparts and varies among genetically different strains of the same animal species. This difference suggests that filarial parasites are able to exploit to their advantage some as yet poorly defined characteristics of immune responses to parasite antigens that differ among members of genetically heterogeneous populations.

IMMUNOPATHOLOGY OF LYMPHATIC FILARIASIS

W, bancrofti, *B. malayi*, and B. *timori* cause a broad spectrum of acute and chronic disease manifestations in human beings. Signs of acute filariasis include recurrent episodes of fever accompanied by acute lymphadenitis, retrograde lymphangitis, and transient lymphedema; orchitis, epididymitis, and funiculitis; and acute asthmalike attacks characteristic of the tropical eosinophilia syndrome.

Chronic manifestations of lymphatic filariasis consist of persistent *lymphedema*, *elephantiasis*, *hydroceles*, and *chyluria*. Immune complex

-mediated *glomerulonephritis*, *endomyocardial fibrosis*, and multijoint arthritis are uncommon sequelae of filarial infections.

Pathogenesis of Lymphatic Lesions

The lymphatic pathology resulting from experimental filarial infections in animal models has been described in detail and appears to be similar to that noted in the surprisingly few available human biopsy and autopsy materials. These descriptive studies have popularized several concepts of the pathogenesis of lymphatic filariasis. First, it is generally believed that adult worms are the primary cause of lymphatic pathology.

Gross lymphatic lesions generally are associated with adult parasites; microfilariae appear to induce little, if any, lymphatic pathology. Viable adult worms in dilated lymphatics are usually not surrounded by inflammatory infiltrates, but tissues containing dead and degenerating worms characteristically show a granulomatous inflammation with partial or complete occlusion of the lymphatic lumen.

The lymphatic wall may be thickened; interstitial and intraluminal fibrosis are frequently seen in what are considered to be longstanding lesions. However, other parasite stages may contribute to the lymphatic pathology of filarial infections.

Minor alterations in lymphatics occur as early as 3 days after injection of infective larvae of B. *pahangi* into cats, and continued heavy exposure to infective larvae may exacerbate symptomatic lesions. Studies in other animal models further suggest that moulting fluids, products of preadult worm stages, or substances released by female worms may initiate the observed pathological changes, but this possibility has not yet been tested experimentally.

Concurrent bacterial or fungal infections can exacerbate worm-induced lesions in experimental animals, a finding that may be relevant to the situation in endemic areas where individuals at risk often are poorly shod. Precisely what triggers the recurrent episodes of acute adenitis and lymphangitis in human filariasis remains to be determined.

It also is unknown if the pathogenesis of these acute events is the same as that of lesions associated with chronic elephantiasis. In marked contrast to the pathogenesis in lymphatic filariasis, most pathological changes in the skin and eyes of individuals infected with 0. volvulus, the cause of river blindness in humans, appear to be triggered by the microfilarial stage of this parasite.

These lesions have been attributed to immediate type hypersensitivity responses, to immune complex reactions, or to direct “toxic” effects elicited by O. volvulus microfilariae. Adult O. volvulus induce the formation of subcutaneous onchocercomata. These circumscribed fibrous nodules contain most female worms and consist of variable granulomatous reactions containing macrophages, T lymphocytes, plasma cells, fibroblasts and blood vessels, and a fibrous capsule.

A second concept is that the location of adult filariae determines which anatomical sites are affected. This criterion would explain, for example, why urogenital lesions are common in bancroftian but rare in brugian filariasis.

Different species of filarial larvae evidently manifest characteristic tropisms for certain body sites that influence the ultimate localization of the adult worms. It is also thought that the lymphatic lesions caused by any of the three human filariae have the same pathogenesis, irrespective of the clinical manifestations they elicit.

Observations in traditional models of lymphatic filariasis have also led to the widely accepted idea that lymphatic damage and the resulting clinical manifestations of filariasis are caused by host immune responses to antigens released from degenerating adult worms. For example, treatment with immunosuppressive agents reduces the degree of lymphatic pathology.

Furthermore, cell-mediated and humoral responses to antigenic extracts of adult worms are generally much higher in symptomatic individuals than in those with asymptomatic microfilaremia. Such descriptive studies provide no direct proof, however, that host reactions to parasite antigens cause the acute or chronic disease manifestations of lymphatic filariasis.

The traditional view that the lymphatic pathology of filariasis is caused almost entirely by host immune responses to dead or dying adult worms is challenged by recent findings in the *B. malayi*- nude mouse model, which indicate that dilation of lymphatics and chronic lymphedema can develop in the absence of detectable host immune responses to filarial antigens.

The pathologic changes in nude mice parasitized with adult *B. malayi* are similar to those observed in other host species, except that cellular infiltrates into interstitial tissues and parasitized lymphatics are notably absent. Lymphatics of nude mice harboring adult worms become massively dilated and tortuous, a process that resembles early lymphatic changes in human filariasis and that is reversed by surgical removal of the worms.

A minority of these mice develop chronic lymphedema of limbs drained by the affected lymphatics. Lesions of comparable severity are not induced by infections with *B. pahangi* or *B. patei*, an observation reminiscent of the marked geographic differences in the prevalence or severity of chronic lymphatic filariasis in various endemic areas.

These findings suggest that adult *B. malayi* trigger lymphatic pathology by the direct action of as-yet-unidentified worm products on host tissues in the absence of filaria-specific immune responses. With the exception of inflammatory reactions to the parasite, most clinical and pathological manifestations of chronic filariasis-even the secondary hyperkeratotic and fibrotic changes in the skin-also occur in nonfilarial lymphatic disease and lymphedema from any cause.

Studies in nonfilarial models of lymphedema suggest that chronic dermal backflow of high-protein lymph is sufficient to cause these lesions. The protein content in dermal lymph obtained from *B. malayi* - infected nude mice is high. If the protein concentration of lymph or hydrocoele fluid were similarly elevated in human filariasis, this concept would provide an attractive alternative to the traditional views on the pathogenesis of chronic lymphatic filariasis.

The idea that lymphostasis may be the pathogenic mechanism that leads to lymphedema and elephantiasis in filarial infections is also supported by clinical observations: the creation of lymphovenous shunts to drain lymph accumulated in affected limbs results in a rapid, dramatic regression of advanced filarial elephantiasis, a condition once assumed to be irreversible.

Lymphedema and dermal backflow in nonfilarial conditions can occur without mechanical blockage of lymph channels. The same is true in the *B. malayi-nude* mouse model of filariasis. Most likely, dilatation of lymphatic vessels with concomitant loss of valvular function and flaccid paralysis greatly reduce the ability of lymphatics to drain interstitial fluids.

This process might particularly affect tissues in close proximity to adult worms. These tissues appear to be subjected to the activity of enzymes released by the parasites, as indicated, for example, by the increased rate of collagen turnover in tissues of cats parasitized with *B. malayi*.

These studies suggest that adult worms can initiate some components of lymphatic pathology by acting directly on host tissues, but it is clear that host immune responses to parasite antigens aggravate the pathological consequences of filarial infections.

Immune reconstitution of nude mice by administration of cells from mice that have rejected a larval inoculum results in an episode of acute lymphangitis and in the death of a proportion of adult *B. malayi* present in the lymphatics of the recipient. These worms become surrounded by inflammatory cells, and lymphatics harboring parasites become partially or completely obstructed by granulomas in which the worms now are embedded, by aggregates of as yet unidentified cells, or by ill-defined lymph thrombi.

Such reconstituted mice also display humoral and cell-mediated immune responses to worm antigens. Additional evidence for a role of host immune responses in the pathogenesis of lymphatic filariasis comes from studies in the *B. pahangi*-jird model. Lymphatic lesions in jirds infected several times by the subcutaneous route are more severe than in singly infected animals.

Presensitization of jirds to soluble parasite extracts increases the severity of lymphatic lesions, which are most marked in animals with latent infections and high antibody titers. In this study, presensitization of jirds did not affect adult worm development; hence, the death of larvae or adult *B.* pahangi or the differences in parasite burdens cannot be invoked to account for the increased severity of lesions in the treated animals.

On the other hand, a single subcutaneous challenge inoculum causes less severe lymphatic pathology in jirds already carrying an intraperitoneal infection than in previously uninfected jirds. These experiments strongly support the idea that even though immune responses to filarial antigens may not actually initiate the pathologic process, they almost certainly contribute to the lymphatic pathology.

They also suggest that the way in which parasite antigens are presented to the host's immune system may have a dramatic impact on the pathological consequences of filarial infections. These concepts are of critical importance to the future development of vaccines or other forms of immunoprophylaxis.

Pathogenesis of the Tropical Pulmonary Eosinophilia (TPE) Syndrome

The pathogenesis of the filaria-induced syndrome of tropical pulmonary eosinophilia (TPE) markedly differs from that of the lymphatic pathology. Microfilariae play virtually no role in inducing lymphatic inflammation, and the continual clearance of microfilariae in the lungs and other organs is generally not associated with definable clinical symptoms or marked tissue reactions.

Perhaps this pattern reflects the ability of this parasite stage to suppress its host's immune system, as described earlier. However, microfilariae appear to be the main cause of the TPE syndrome, which consists of recurrent episodes of asthmalike attacks that often occur at night, elevated serum levels of total and filaria-specific IgE, a marked increase in the number of eosinophilic granulocytes in blood and tissues, and nonspecific but characteristic radiographic changes in the lungs.

The syndrome occurs in individuals who appear to be hyperreactive to many filarial antigens, but especially to those derived from microfilariae. In particular, levels of IgG and IgE antibodies to microfilarial antigens are much higher in patients with TPE than in those with other filarial disease syndromes.

TPE most likely results from the orderly succession of two types of immune responses to microfilarial antigens. According to this concept, the syndrome starts when microfilariae are trapped in the lungs and are killed in situ. This first step is believed to be mediated by ADCC reactions that require IgG antibodies to surface antigens on the worms, as described earlier.

Dying microfilariae then would release internal antigens and allergens that elicit no obvious adverse reactions in the majority of patients with filariasis. In allergic individuals, however, these parasite molecules would combine with filaria-specific IgE antibody. Antigen-induced cross-linking of IgE on pulmonary mast cells would then trigger the release of these cells' wide array of soluble mediators of immediate hypersensitivity reactions.

This process results in the clinical symptoms of recurrent bouts of asthmatic attacks. Thus, TPE is believed to be a form of latent filariasis in an allergically sensitized hyperimmune individual. Why do only some patients with lymphatic filariasis develop TPE? Serum levels of filaria-specific IgE antibodies are much lower in individuals with lymphatic forms of filariasis than in patients with TPE.

This finding suggests that IgE responses to parasite allergens are subjected to immunoregulatory control, as has been described for other types of antifilarial immune responses. In addition, sera from patients with lymphatic filariasis contain blocking IgG (mostly IgG4) antibodies that react with the same parasite molecules as those recognized by IgE antibodies.

Reaction of IgG blocking antibodies with microfilarial allergens in the fluid phase most likely prevents the interaction of worm products with cell-bound IgE. Although patients with and without TPE can be segregated on the basis of in vitro reactions to microfilarial antigens, studies performed so far fail to explain the apparent inability of patients with TPE to generate adequate levels of blocking antibodies, and why only a minority of patients with filarial infections develop this syndrome. Perhaps the syndrome occurs only in patients who are superinfected with or exposed to filarial parasites of animals.

Filariae of various species share many antigenic determinants; release of common allergens when animal parasites are killed in a nonpermissive host could conceivably trigger the symptoms of TPE in individuals allergically sensitized by prior infection with human parasites. This idea remains unproved, but at least one human volunteer experimentally infected with *B. pahangi* developed symptoms consistent with the TPE syndrome.

8

Liver Fluke

FASCIOLA GIGANTICA

This is a parasite of the liver and bile ducts of cattle, sheep, goats, and wild ruminants in Africa and Asia. It is of great veterinary importance, causing the disease fascioliasis or liver rot in cattle, accounting for considerable economic loss annually.

Its better known relative, *Fasciola hepatica,* the common liver fluke of sheep, is parasitic in the liver and bile ducts of sheep and other ruminants as well as man all over the world, but mainly in temperate regions. Because of its great economic importance it has been the subject of intensive research and is the type usually described in textbooks of parasitology.

Comparatively less is known about *F. gigantica* although it is now receiving increasing attention. What information is available in West Africa has been reviewed by Schillhorn van Veen. Fortunately, there is great similarity in the morphology, life cycle, and pathogenicity between the two species. A generalized account will therefore be given here, stressing some of the information available about *F. gigantica* since it is of greater importance in tropical Africa.

Family. FASCIOLIDAE

Major diagnostic features of the family include:

1. Large, flattened leaf-like forms.
2. Most organs digestive and reproductive—are complicated by extensive branching (digitating).
3. Usually parasitic in the liver and bile ducts of vertebrates, but one species, *Fasciolopsis buski*, is found in the intestine.

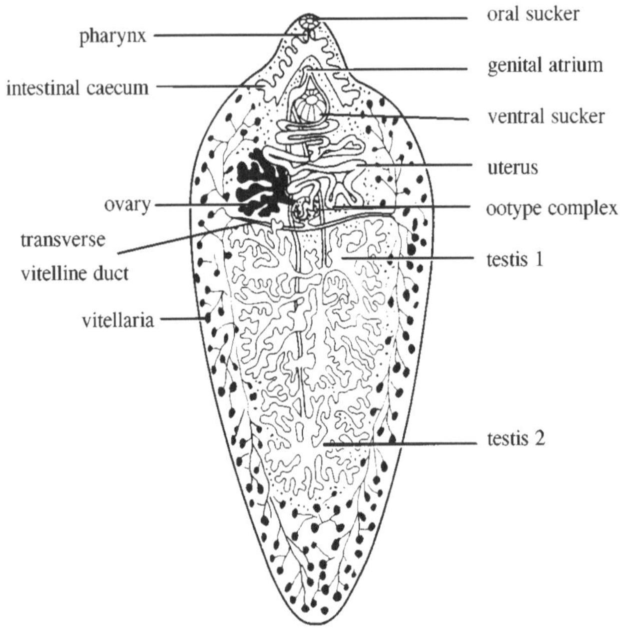

Figure 8.1: Fasciola gigantica adult.

4. Cercariae are gymnocephalous.
5. Metacercaria encyst on vegetation thus establishing a two-host cycle.

Striking features of adult

1. Large leaf-like forms.
2. Oral cone and 'shoulder' at anterior end.
3. Branched intestinal caeca.
4. Branched testes and ovary.
5. Uterus relatively short, tightly coiled, and limited to the side opposite the ovary at the anterior end.
6. Vitellaria extensive, occupying the whole of the lateral fields.

Physical Differences between F. Gigantica and F. Hepatica

It is hard to distinguish one from the other. Generally, *F. gigantica* is larger (25 to 75 × 12 mm) and oblong in shape with a greatly prolonged posterior portion, while *F. hepatica* is smaller (up to 30 x 13 mm) and more or less triangular in shape. Also, the eggs of *F. gigantica* are substantially larger than those of *F. hepatica*.

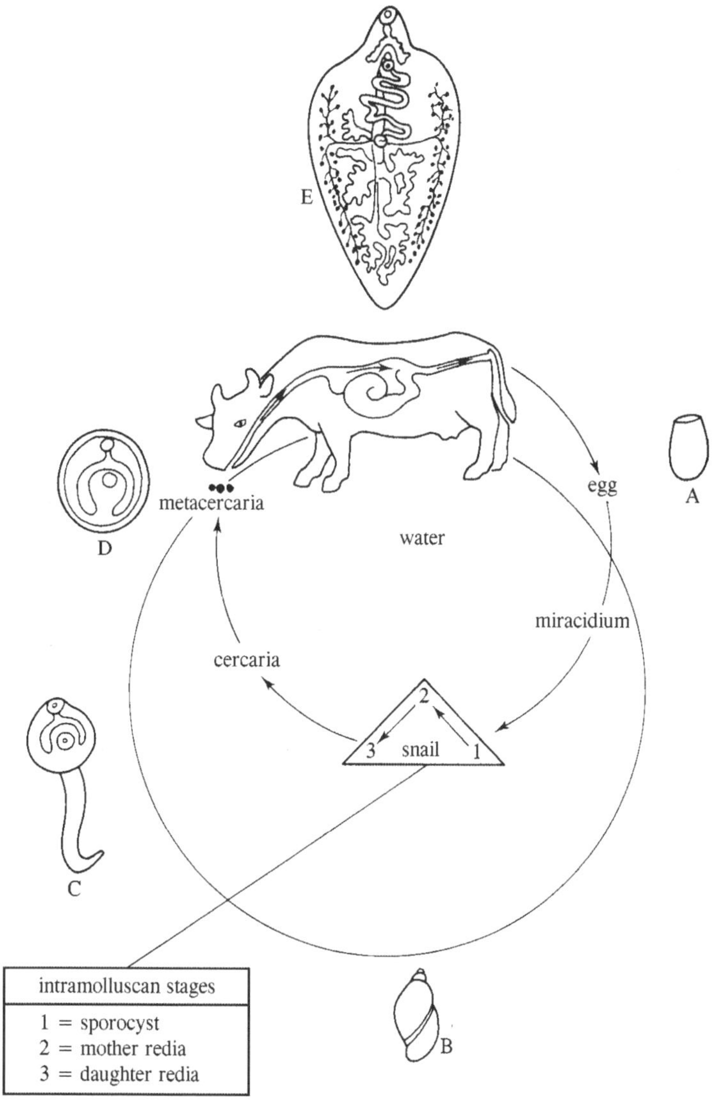

Figure 8.2: Life cycle of Fasciola hepatica : A. egg, B. Lymnaea sp., C. cercaria, D. metacercaria, E. adult

Highlights of life cycle

1. The life cycle of *Fasciola hepatica* was the first trematode life cycle to be unravelled and this was accomplished independently by the Englishman Thomas and the German

Leukhart. Their results were published within 10 days of each other in 1882. This is regarded as one of the landmarks in parasitology.

2. Eggs hatch with light stimulus.
3. Miracidia locate snails by chemotaxis.
4. Sporocyst produces rediae and rediae may produce second-generation rediae. According to Smyth, a single miracidium of F *hepatica* can give rise to up to forty rediae and ultimately about six hundred cercariae.
5. Gymnocephalous cercariae with cystogenous glands.
6. Encystment of cercariae on vegetation occurs at the edge of water. Detailed accounts of the process of encystment and the structure of the cyst have been given by Dixon, Dixon and Mercer, and Mercer and Dixon.
7. Sheep and cattle become infected by ingesting metacercariae while grazing.
8. Metacercariae excyst in the duodenum. According to Dixon this is an active process triggered off by the right conditions in the small intestine. The larva then digests a hole in the ventral side of the cyst wall through which it emerges.
9. The young adult punctures its way into the body cavity and wanders around until it locates the liver capsule which it then penetrates. It burrows through the liver tissue, feeding on cells until it gets to the bile duct which it then enters. This stage of development has been extensively studied by Dawes.
10. Adults may live for up to 8 years.

The life cycles of both *F. hepatica* and *F. gigantica* are similar in the essential stages outlined above, but there are important differences to be outlined below.

Differences in life cycles between *F. gigantica* and *F. hepatica*

1. *Snail intermediate hosts. Fasciola hepatica* is specific to the amphibious snail *Lymnaea truncatula* which thrives very well in marshy ground and the muddy banks of slow-flowing streams and ponds.

   Though experiments have shown that its miracidia can penetrate a wide variety of lymnaeids, they can only develop and produce cercariae in *L. truncatula* and three other species (Pantalouris). However, polymorphism occurs in different populations of *L. truncatula* so there is considerable difficulty and controversy about the identification of these species.

Fasciola gigantica, on the other hand, infects snails of the superspecies *Lymnaea auricularia,* the representative of which is *L. natalensis* in tropical Africa. The only lymnaeid snail encountered in Nigeria by Ukoli and his colleagues is *L. natalensis,* implying that *F. gigantica* is the predominant liver fluke in Nigeria.

2. The habitats of both species of lymnaeids are different, and this has profound consequences on their life cycles. First, *L. truncatula* is an amphibious, mud-dwelling species which is constantly liable to exposure when its habitat dries up.

   Thus, all stages (eggs, young, and adult snails) can withstand desiccation for considerable periods. *Lynznaea natalensis,* on the other hand, is fully aquatic.
3. The eggs of *F. gigantica* do not survive well at low temperatures.
4. The behaviour of the miracidia is influenced by the habitats of the snail intermediate hosts. Thus, the miracidia of F. *hepatica* show positive phototactic responses, bringing them to the surface, while those of *F. gigantica* are exactly the opposite (negative responses), keeping them in deeper water where their snail hosts are found.
5. While it has been established that the intramolluscan stages of FF *hepatica* are produced as follows:

   Miracidium → mother sporocyst → first generation rediae → daughter rediae → cercariae

   Ogambo-Ongoma and Goodman have shown that in *F. gigantica* there is no pre-redial sporocyst generation, the miracidium metamorphosing directly into a mother redia. They also showed that there are four redial generations, the first batch of cercariae being produced by the third generation. Thus the intramolluscan stages can be represented as follows:

Miracidium → mother rediae → second generation rediae → third generation rediae → fourth generation rediae → cerariae

However, Palmieri, Sullivan and Ow-Yang in an investigation to confirm this finding showed that a sporocyst stage is unmistakably involved in the intramolluscan development of *F. gigantica,* as has previously been established for *F. gigantica* and other members of the family Fasciolidae.

6. *Fasciola gigantica is* better adapted as a parasite of cattle than *F. hepatica* and develops relatively poorly in rabbits. Infectivity of *F. gigantica* in cattle is greater than that of *F. hepatica* and infections tend to be more prolonged. It normally does not infect man, unlike *F. hepatica*, but Hammond maintains that human infection with *F. gigantica* may be more common than the records indicate.

FASCIOLIASIS

PATHOLOGY

The pathology of fascioliasis caused by *Fasciola hepatica* in sheep has been the subject of intensive research and much is known about it. Taylor and Pantalouris have given detailed reviews of the subject.

Comparatively less research has been done on fascioliasis caused by *F. gigantica,* although, according to Sewell from results of his experiments in Nigeria, the pathogenesis of the disease in both cases is essentially similar. Bitakaramire and Haroun and Hussein have described the clinico-pathology of fascioliasis from *F. gigantica* in cattle in Kenya and Sudan respectively.

Basically, two stages are recognized:

1. *The acute stage* in which the young adults, which have just penetrated the liver, wander about feeding on cells and blood in the liver tissue.

   They form burrows and tunnels through the liver parenchyma leaving tracks of detritus behind. Eventually, these tracts are healed by deposition of fibrous tissue.

   Sometimes when there is massive invasion, there may be general inflammation of the liver resulting in acute hepatitis.

2. *The chronic stage.* After about 6 to 8 weeks, the adults enter the bile ducts, causing inflammation which leads to their thickening and hardening as a result of production of fibrous tissues in their walls.

   In cattle, the ducts may even undergo calcification. Some of the branches of the bile duct are obstructed both by the eggs or by the worms themselves, causing jaundice. Also, their epithelium may be ruptured so that some of the worms re-enter the liver parenchyma causing large abscesses.

In summary, the clinical syndrome of chronic fascioliasis is that the liver is small, hard, with rough and uneven surfaces with a lot of fibrous tissues (generalized coarse cirrhosis). The most characteristic feature is the thickened bile duct and its branches running through the liver substance in all directions.

One of the features, of fascioliasis is anaemia which most likely results from a combination of the blood-feeding activity oI the worms from the mucous lining of the bile ducts (cf. the blood-sucking activity of hookworms from the small intestine in Taylor) and the action of toxins secreted by the worms.

Finally migrating flukes may reach ectopic locations like the eye, brain, skin (where they produce ulcers), qjlungs (where they cause acute pneumonia and peribronchial inflammation) or even the uterus (ca usin sterility with the possibility of re-natal infection of the foetus *in utero).*

Acute fascioliasis which results from direct damage of the liver has a rapid course. There is rapid weight loss, rapidly progressive anaemia, and jaundice and death occurs suddenly and is not anticipated. However, Sewell has shown that massive dosage of metacercariae of *F. gigantica* is required to cause death in cattle.

Animals which survive the acute phase then go into the chronic phase in which there is a marked decrease of meat production (in sheep, infected animals produce 30 per cent less meat than healthy ones, and meat of poorer quality at that). There is also a great reduction in milk production (up to 50 per cent in cattle) and milk of poorer quality too. The chronic phase is less dramatic but its effect is more protracted, affected animals becoming more anaemic, emaciated and weak.

They finally die of exhaustion after many months or years. Lighter infections may show no clear symptoms of the disease beyond poor oductivity. It m !Inoted however-that under natural conditions animals are exposed to repeated infections; hence it common to find cases with mixed effects of acute and chronic fascioliasis.

Fasciola gigantica is better adapted as a parasite of cattle than *F. hepatica*. On the other hand, *F. gigantica* infection is more acute and causes more death in sheep than in cattle. There is also evidence that local breeds of cattle have lower prevalence rates and fluke burdens of *F. gigantica* than exotic breeds and crosses of local and exotic breeds. *Fasciola hepatica,* in association with the bacterium *Clostridium oedematiens,* causes the notorious *black disease* of sheep which is rapidly fatal.

FASCIOLIASIS ECONOMIC IMPORTANCE

It has proved very difficult to make reliable estimates of the economic losses due to fascioliasis. In the acute cases which result in death, the loss can be determined by estimating the value of the dead cow or sheep. But most cases are chronic and even though it is possible to observe a general loss of condition and failure to develop the full productive capacity of the stock, it is difficult to put a price on this.

Thus, even for *F. hepatica,* estimates have been mainly derived from slaughter house records of condemned livers judged unfit for human consumption. The carcasses of such animals have usually been passed as good and sold to consumers, but to what extent the 'bad' livers have affected the productivity and quality of the meat and milk in the affected animals has not been fully determined.

For example, Taylor (1964) cites the example of the condemnation of 12 000 tons of liver of cattle per annum in the United Kingdom while Chengpresents an estimate of an annual loss of $1 million due to condemnation of cattle liver as a result of fascioliasis in the United States over an eleven year period.

If it has been difficult to assign reliable figures to economic losses due to fascioliasis in the temperate countries where sheep and cattle husbandry is controlled in farms and ranches, and slaughtering and selling of meat and milk is strictly supervised, the situation in many parts of tropical Africa is virtually impossible to assess.

This is because cattle rearing is done mainly by nomadic herdsmen who drive their cattle through vast distances (across the country in the case of Nigeria) in response to the seasons and in search of pastures and water. Slaughtering and selling of meat is still largely done privately by individual owners with very limited supervision from health authorities.

Then there is the possibility that the full effect of fascioliasis is masked by the practice of cattle owners culling their infected animals prematurely, before the full effect of the disease becomes apparent. Furthermore, the general condition of the animals is not enhanced by multiple infection with other helminths like strongyles and amphistomes, general underand malnutrition, and loss of weight due to extensive wandering in search of food.

Above all, the threat of trypanosomiasis is always there, and many of these cattle are afflicted by the disease. Thus it is extremely difficult to estimate what losses are specifically due to fascioliasis. Finally, very little research has been done in this area and there are few reliable statistics; those that are available provide a very tenuous basis for comparison.

However, there have been reports in the literature of slaughter-house surveys from different parts of Africa. This reveals the magnitude of the problem as far as the liver condition is concerned. Both McCullough and Sequin have expressed the view that fascioliasis is not considered an important disease of livestock in Ghana and Togo respectively, and the recent low percentages of condemned livers recorded by Uzoukwu and Ikeme at Nsukka in Nigeria would tend to support this view.

However, much higher prevalences have been recorded from other parts of West Africa-parts of Chad with up to 97 per cent and certain districts in Zaria, Nigeria, with from 26 to 52 per cent. Nevertheless, Sewell has given an estimate of a loss of £l .3 million sterling per annum in Nigeria, and Preston and Castelino have estimated a loss of £160 000 sterling per annum in Kenya arising from condemnation of cattle liver due to fascioliasis from *F. gigantica.*

FASCIOLIASIS—DIAGNOSIS AND TREATMENT

Diagnosis is by demonstration of the eggs in the faeces. Also, the presence of antibodies can be detected by a number of immunodiagnostic tests including: precipitin reaction, complement fixation tests, fluorescent antibody tests, and skin tests (based on' hypersensitivity).

However, these techniques and the interpretation of the results so obtained are often too complicated to be of use under field conditions, especially where the chances of cross-reaction with other helminth infections are high. Many antihelminthic drugs have been developed, the most widely used being carbon tetrachloride. It has some disadvantages in that, to be effective, near-toxic doses have to be administered.

It does not act on young migratory flukes, so treatment has to be repeated at intervals to catch the worms as they enter the bile ducts. Hexachloi·ethane 'is also widely used but is ineffective against young migrating worms as well. It also has toxic side-effects, but these seem to be reversed in a week.

Other drugs commonly in use are hexachlorophene, bithionolsul-phoxyde, bromphenophos, nichlopholon, nitroxynil, and rafoxanide all with varying degrees of efficacy. Although all these drugs have fasciolicidal properties, rigorous tests about their safety are still in progress. One important practical note in the treatment of chroiic wasting disease in tsetse-infested areas,of West Africa isthat a trypanocide is first administered, but if the animal's condition fails to improve, a fasciolicide is then given.

FASCIOLIASIS EPIZOOTIOLOGY AND CONTROL

Fascioliasis is prevalent where cattle or sheep graze in areas in which the appropriate lymnaeid snail hosts thrive. Many wild animals are reported to serve as reservoirs, although Hammond, from his survey of sixteen species of African wildlife to assess their importance in the epizootiology of the disease, concluded tentatively that fascioliasis is not very prevalent in African wildlife. Control measures for *F. hepatica* have taken the form of a two-pronged attack

1. Chemotherapy of animals to improve their general condition and reduce egg output.
2. Prevention of new infections, either by reducing snail populations or by modifying the grazing management to keep away the herd from potentially dangerous locations.

In spite of the tremendous efforts put into the study of the biology and ecology of *Lymnaea truncatula* and the various methods devised for controlling the snails, success has not come easily. Two major approaches have been adopted: the use of molluscicides and drainage of the habitats.

Though they have reduced incidence, none has achieved complete eradication. The introduction by Ollarenshaw and his associates of the use of weather forecasting to predict infection and hence determine when to apply control measures has been a useful strategy.

Progress has been slow, mainly because of the amphibious nature of the snails which makes it difficult to delimit their territory. On the other hand, *L. natalensis is* a truly aquatic snail which is suited to life in lakes and ponds where the water is deep enough and clean enough to allow for adequate oxygenation.

Thus, even though the extent of the habitats can be more precisely defined, they present a different set of problems altogether which knowledge of the ecology of *L. truncatula* cannot help to solve. Unfortunately, knowledge of the epidemiology and methods and regimens of control of fascioliasis in tropical Africa is scanty.

Surveys of the distribution of *L. natalensis* have been carried out in Uganda by Coyle, in Ghana by McCullough, in south-western Nigeria by Adeleke, Asumu, Ndifon, Okwuosa, and Ukoli and Asumu, and in

Zaria, Nigeria, by Schilihorn van Veen. There have also been reports of a few restricted surveys in East Africa, the most significant being the one by Preston and Castelino who reported the successful application of a molluscicide, N-tritylmorpholine, in a dam in Kenya to control fascioliasis.

It is apparent from these accounts that *L. natalensis* prefers slow-flowing or standing water in lakes, ponds, sluggish streams, etc., to fast-flowing streams and large rivers. Also, the adult snails and egg masses are unable to withstand desiccation, and are capable of surviving drought for only a limited period.

However, Preston and Castelino speculated that they are capable of aestivating in dried mud and Vassiliades recorded a survival time of 1 to 3 months, but under humid conditions. The pH level of the water is critical to the survival of the snails in the habitat, lowering of the pH being associated with large-scale mortality.

In the savanna of West Africa, the snail population density increases towards the end of the rainy season and reaches a peak in the early dry sesson. Thus the application of molluscicides would be most effective if done during this period, knowledge which was exploited in one of the few successful control attempts in which Preston and Castelino found that the optimal time for applying molluscicide is when the water is at its maximum level.

The first step necessary for effective snail control is to survey the area to map out the distribution of snails and determine transmission and potential transmission foci. Admittedly, with the few reports mentioned above, there is a dearth of information about this in most parts of tropical Africa.

Secondly, the ecological profile of the snail habitats must be characterized. Thus physicochemical factors like temperature, pH, oxygen concentration, conductivity, salinity, nature of the substratum, etc., as well as biotic factors like the type of vegetation, plant and animal associations, and climatic factors have to be investigated.

As in the case of schistosomiasis, information on all these areas are indispensable when planning control programmes. Such information is, however, virtually non-existent in tropical Africa. The snail vector research programme being undertaken in the Department of Zoology, University of Ibadan, Nigeria, by Ukoli and his associates was initiated precisely to provide such information.

Nevertheless, McCullough concludes, on purely snail ecological grounds, that *F. gigantica* is not likely to be a great threat in Ghana because the sites where the snails are found have no special significance as grazing grounds.

He predicts, however, that the development of the Volta Dam is likely to increase the dissemination of the snails and hence the transmission of *F. gignatica* in the future. Even if it were to be a major threat, any control strategies adopted will still present special problems.

In Nigeria, for example, the snails have a focal distribution, their habitats being scattered over a wide area, and molluscicidal control over such a wide area could present nearly insurmountable problems. The ultimate in control measures, if indeed fascioliasis due to *F. gigantica* becomes a major disease, is to radically alter the husbandry method to that of ranching and confining the cattle to well-defined areas. In this way the potential transmission foci can be readily identified and various control procedures applied; e.g.

1. The snail habitats could be fenced off to keep away the grazing animals.
2. A frequent change of pastures would reduce infection of young animals.
3. The services of trained manpower would need to be obtained and the cooperation of the cattle owners and herdsmen elicited.
4. Floodplain grazing could be limited to just before the rainy season and this could help to prevent outbreaks in the savanna.

If chemical control of snails were to be attempted, then molluscicides would have to be applied. The most widely used molluscicide for the control of snail hosts of trematodes is copper sulphate. It has, however, to be applied at high concentrations (with the risk of copper poisoning of the cattle or sheep) and it does not kill snail eggs.

Other molluscicides which have yielded satisfactory results are sodium pentachlorophenate and, of course, N-tritylmorpholine. However, much groundwork still has to be done to develop a strategy which will produce the greatest benefits from its application from the economic, ecological, and animal health points of view.

That these are effective snail-killing agents is no longer in doubt, but experience with *L. truncatula* has shown that sufficient numbers of snails escape and repopulate the habitat again when the effect of the molluscicide has worn off. Thus, other measures must be developed to supplement mollusciciding.

As in the control of schistosomiasis, integrated control is now being advocated as the answer, involving chemotherapy, effective diagnostic tests, *pasture management*, *drainage of habitats*, biological control methods, and mollusciciding.

Biological Control

Taylor lists as predators of *L. truncatula* the following birds: plovers, snipes and other wading birds, curlews, ducks, starlings, etc. Although they feed on snails, the practical value of their activities from the point of view of disease control is doubtful.

Nevertheless, cases in which birds have reduced snail populations in some habitats are known, e.g. the case of ducks clearing away almost all the *L. natalensis* in a series of ponds in Uganda. Frogs also eat snails. The larvae of sciomyzid flies feed entirely on living tissues of snails, although there is no conclusive evidence about the extent of the destruction these larvae can cause in a snail population.

It is appropriate to end this account with the words of Pantalouris, who says this parasite has 'so far avoided radical control by man ; drugs fail to kill the younger migratory stages, vaccines are ineffective, neither ecological measures nor grazing management eliminate all risk to stock (although they greatly reduce it), and many wild animals provide a reservoir of infection. The clue to the solution of the problem is contained in this statement, and it is only research which will provide the answers.

9

TAPE WORM

The cestodes show most of the characteristics of the platyhelminths. They possess, however, three very important features which set them apart from all other classes, namely

1. Elongated ribbon-like body usually divided into a number of segments called proglottids, giving a tape-like appearance (hence the name tapeworms).
2. Complete lack of alimentary canal.
3. A characteristic embryo stage called *hexacanth* embryo with three pairs of claw-like hooks with a thick outer covering of keratinous material called *embryophore*.

Other important characteristics include:

4. The body is distinguishable into an anterior *scolex* bearing some form of holdfast organ and the rest of the body called the *strobila*, both parts being separated by a short narrow

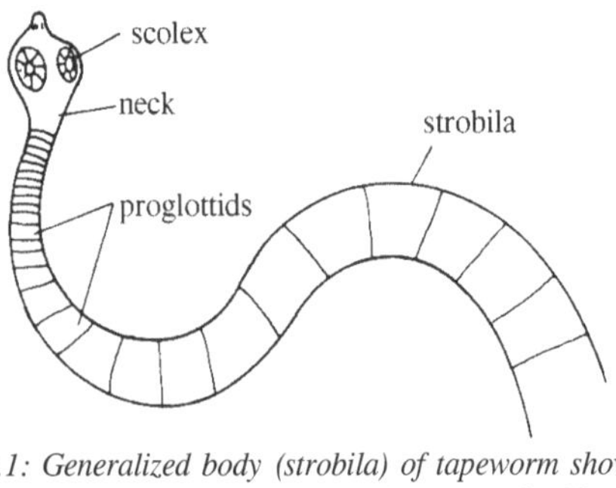

Figure 9.1: Generalized body (strobila) of tapeworm showing scolex, neck, and body segmented into proglottids.

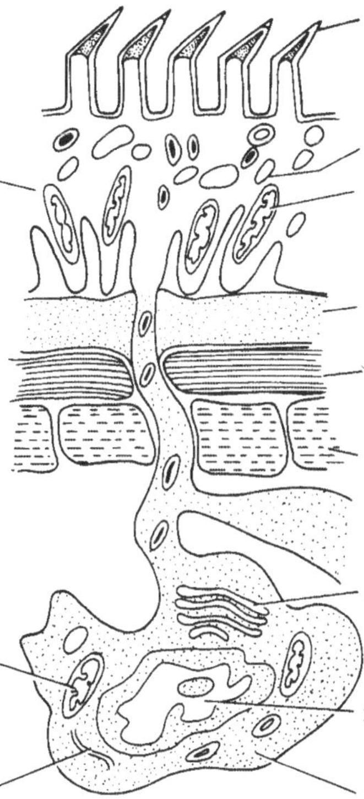

Figure 9.2: Structure of tegument of cestode as revealed by the electron microscope.

neck region from which new segments are budded or proliferated. Thus the youngest segments are near the neck and the oldest located towards the posterior end of the strobila.

5. Each segment bears a complete set of reproductive organs. It follows from feature 4 above that the gonads are in progressive stages of sexual maturity antero-posteriorly.

   Thus anteriorly, we find mostly immature segments, followed by mature segments around the mid-region of the body with fully developed gonads, and finally, at the posterior end, ripe or gravid segments whose uteri are filled with eggs or embryos.

6. Among members of one order, the Caryophyllaeidea, however, there is no budding, the body is not divided into segments, and there is only one set of reproductive organs. These are called *monozoic* cestodes while those with several proglottids are *polyzoic*.

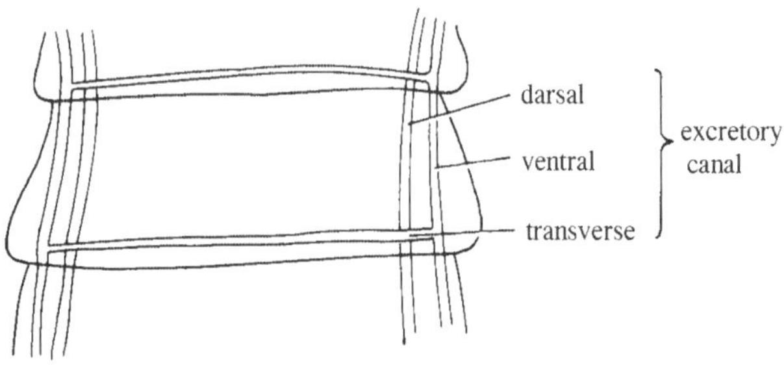

Figure 9.3: A proglottid showing the excretory canals.

7. The life cycle is indirect, involving one or more intermediate hosts which are either invertebrates (mainly arthropods) or vertebrates.
8. The adults are endoparasitic, living exclusively in the alimentary canal of vertebrate hosts.

Morphological Features

Tegument

The body surface is covered by a tegument which, as in the Digenea, is a cytoplasmic extension of the tegumental cells lying underneath the muscle layers. A peculiarity of the cestode tegument revealed by electron microscope studies is the possession of *microtriches*.

These are long spine-like processes which, in greatly increasing the surface area of the tegument, increase its digestive-absorptive capacity enormously of great importance since cestodes lack a gut.

The tegument also shows metabolic activity, possessing mitochondria, cytoplasmic organelles, Golgi bodies, etc. For useful accounts of the structure and function of the tegument, see the reviews of Lee and Smyth.

Nervous System

There is a pair of nerve ganglia in the scolex from which run a total of ten longitudinal nerve cords posteriorly, the most prominent of which are the dorsal and ventral cords. From these, peripheral nerves supply the musculature and tegument.

Excretory System

The excretory units are the flame cells scattered all over the parenchyma and connected by tubules to longitudinal excretory canals on each side of the body, of which the dorsal and ventral canals are the most prominent. At the posterior margin of each segment, a transverse excretory canal connects the ventral longitudinal canals. The longitudinal canals unite in the scolex and in mature strobila they open out independently at the posterior end of the strobila.

Scolex

The type of holdfast organ in the scolex is a useful diagnostic feature for the classification of the cestodes into orders. There are three basic forms of organs of attachment

(a) *Bothria:* long narrow grooves of weak muscularity.

(b) *Bothridia* or *Phyllidea:* broad, leaf-like structures with thin flexible margins. They are extremely variable in appearance.

Acetabula or Suckers

Muscular, cup-shaped sucking organs essentially the same as those of the Digenea.

In addition, all these organs may be supplemented with hooks or spines which, in scoleces with acetabula, are borne on an anterior projection of the scolex called the *rostellum* which is usually protrusible.

Classification

There is controversy about the classification of the class Cestoda into orders. Although up to ten to twelve orders have been recognized

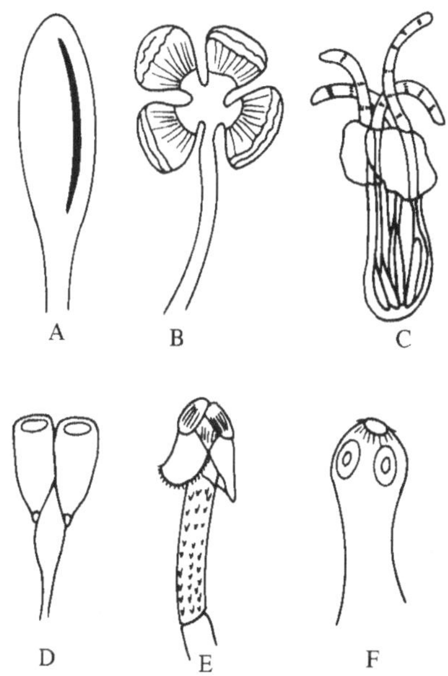

Figure 9.4: Types of scolex in the cestodes;A. scolex with bnothrium, B.C.D.E. scoleces with different types of bothridia (phyllidea), F. scolex with muscular cup-shaped suckers (acetabula).

by various authors, only four are widely accepted as valid. The major features used include

1. The type of scolex and holdfast organ.
2. The degree of strobilization or segmentation.
3. The structure and location, or distribution, of vitellaria.
4. The location of the genital pores.

Although cestodes *of* medical and economic importance in tropical Africa are found exclusively in the two orders Cyclophyllidea and Pseudophyllidea, the major diagnostic features of the following orders are presented to give a fair idea of the diversity among the cestodes. For more detailed classification, the reader is referred to the authoritative works by Schmidt, Voge, Wardle and McLeod, and Yamaguti.

Order 1. PSEUDOPHYLLIDEA

1. Scolex with two bothria with or without hooks.
2. Genital pores are lateral or median.
3. Vitellaria are follicular mainly in lateral fields.
4. Uterus opens out through a median uterine pore.
5. Eggs are operculate with ciliated larva called *coracidium.*
6. Parasites of fish and fish-eating vertebrates.

Order 2. CYCLOPHYLLIDEA

1. Scolex with four acetabula, with or without rostellum which may or may not be armed.
2. Genital pores are lateral.
3. Vitellarium is a single compact gland posterior to the ovary.
4. No uterine pore.
5. Mainly parasites of birds and mammals.

Order 3. CARYOPHYLLIDEA

1. Monozoic, i.e. no segmentation, with a single set of reproductive organs.
2. Scolex is unspecialized or with bothria.
3. Genital pore is median.
4. Vitellaria are follicular, scattered or lateral.
5. Uterine pore is present.
6. Some workers include this group among the pseudophyllideans.
7. Parasites of teleost fishes.

Order 4. PROTEOCEPHALIDEA

1. Scolex with four acetabula and occasionally with an additional

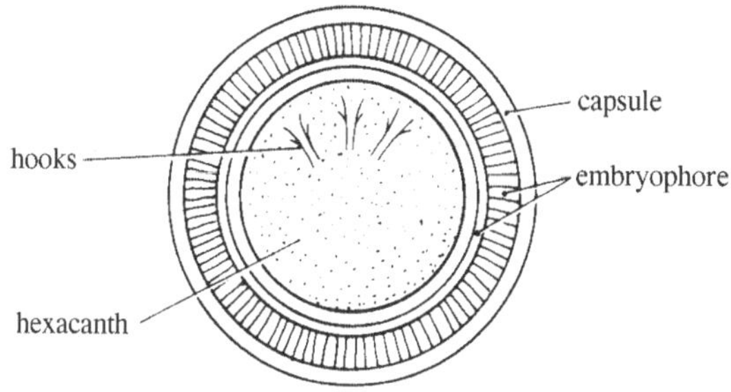

Figure 9.5: The structure of the cestode hexacanth embryo with the three pairs of hooks and surrounded by a number of envelopes.

fifth apical sucker.

2. Vitellaria are follicular, in lateral margins.
3. Parasites of cold-blooded vertebrates.

Order 5. TETRAPHYLLIDEA

1. Scolex with four bothridia.
2. Parasites of elasmobranchs.

Order 6. TRYPANORHYNCHA

1. Scolex with two or four bothridia and four eversible tentacles *(proboscoides)* armed with spines or hooks.
2. Vitellaria are follicular, cortical and encircling other reproductive organs.
3. Parasites of elasmobranchs.

Cestode Development

Both cross- and self-fertilization have been observed in cestodes. In some cestodes, self-fertilization involves different proglottids of the same individual, while in others it actually involves sperm and ova of the same proglottid.

The zygote develops by cell division into a characteristic embryo called an *oncosphere* or *hexacanth embryo* because it possesses three pairs of hooks. Basically the embryo is surrounded by a number of envelopes developed to varying degrees, thereby producing different types of eggs. These are:

1. The egg *capsule* on the outside
2. A thick protective *embryophore*, and
3. The *oncospheral membrane*, thin and covering the embryo.

Smyth (1969a) recognized two groups of cestodes based on

1. The structure and type of development of the eggs.

2. The disposition of the vitellaria.
3. Hatching process.
4. Life cycle.

Group I Cestodes

This group includes all cestode orders except the order *Cyclophyllidea*.

1. They possess many features in common with digenetic trematodes, e.g.
   (a) Extensive vitellaria are disposed in lateral fields.
   (b) The egg capsule is well-developed, operculate, made of sclerotin formed from secretions of the vitelline cells, several of which surround the ovum.
   (c) Embryonation takes place outside in the presence of oxygen and water.
   (d) The hatching process is similar to that of the digenetic trematodes; it is triggered by light and the coracidium escapes through the operculum into water. Further development takes place after ingestion by the aquatic intermediate host.

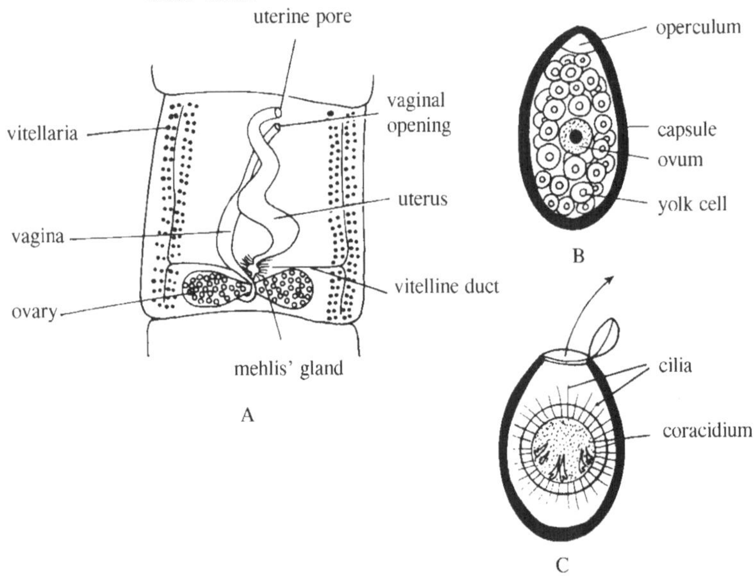

Figure 9.6: Essential features of Group I Cestodes: A. mature proglottid, B. operculate egg with many vitelline cells surrounding ovum. C. egg shell containing mature ciliated hexacanth embryo (coracidium).

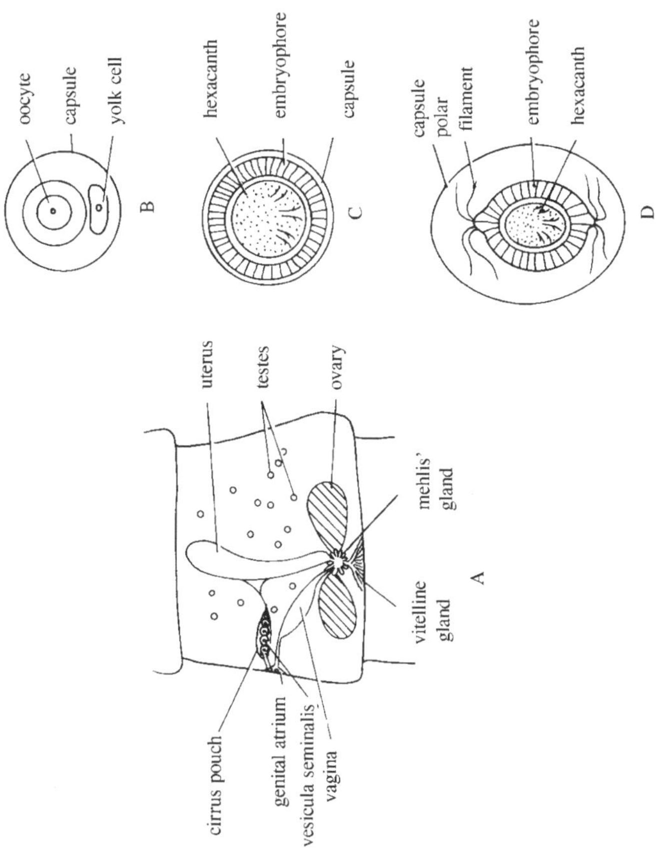

Figure 9.7: Essential features of Group 11 Cestodes: A. mature proglottid, B. egg with one vitelline cell, C. mature hexacanth embryo of Taeniid with embryophore covered by thin capsule, D. hexacanth embryo of Hymenolepis nana with polar filaments.

2. The hexacanth has a ciliated embryophore, hence it is called a coracidium.
3. In this group, the Pseudophyllidea have been most studied.

Group II Cestodes

This group comprises the order Cyclophyllidea.

1. The vitelline gland is single, compact, post-ovarian.
2. The egg shell encloses a single vitelline cell which plays no part in its formation.
3. The uterus has no uterine pore.
4. The hexacanth embryo has a thick embryophore made of keratin and the capsule when present is a thin membrane not made of sclerotin.
5. Eggs are usually embryonated when laid, with no aquatic stage.

6. Hatching occurs inside the intermediate host after ingestion and involves mechanical as well as digestive action of the enzymes on the envelopes surrounding the embryo.

   Also the released embryo needs to be activated after hatching in a similar manner to the process of excystment of the trematode metacercariae. Physico-chemical factors such as pH, Eh, and pCO_2 as well as the nature of bile are likely to play a part in this.
7. In this group, eggs of the family Taeniidae have been most studied.

Cestode Life Cycles

The cyclophyllidean *Hymenolepis nana* is capable of completing its entire life cycle in the intestine of the definitive host (rat or man), i.e. direct life cycle. All other cestodes have an indirect life cycle. A wide variety of vertebrates and invertebrates, both aquatic and terrestrial, serve as intermediate hosts. Group I Cestodes by and large using aquatic hosts while Group 11 Cestodes favouring terrestrial hosts.

On the whole, only comparatively few cestode life cycles are known and these seem to fall broadly into two basic patterns corresponding to the Group I and Group II classification above. However, as will become apparent, there is great variation within these patterns as well as in the types of larval forms encountered among the cestodes.

Group I life cycles (Order Pseudophyllidea)

1. Coracidium hatches out in water.
2. Coracidium is ingested by first intermediate host, usually an aquatic arthropod.
3. Coracidium sheds the ciliated embryophore and using its six hooks penetrates through the gut wall into the haemocoel.
4. It metamorphoses into *procercoid larva* which is elongated with six hooks confined to a posterior bulb called *cercomer*, marked off from the rest of the body by a constriction.
5. When the first intermediate host is eaten by the second intermediate host (usually a fish) the procercoid penetrates through the gut wall and eventually reaches the skeletal muscle (flesh) of the fish.
6. It metamorphoses gradually into the third larval stage, the *plerocercoid larva*, losing the cercomer and hooks, becoming more elongated, ribbon-like but not segmented, with the scolex partially formed.

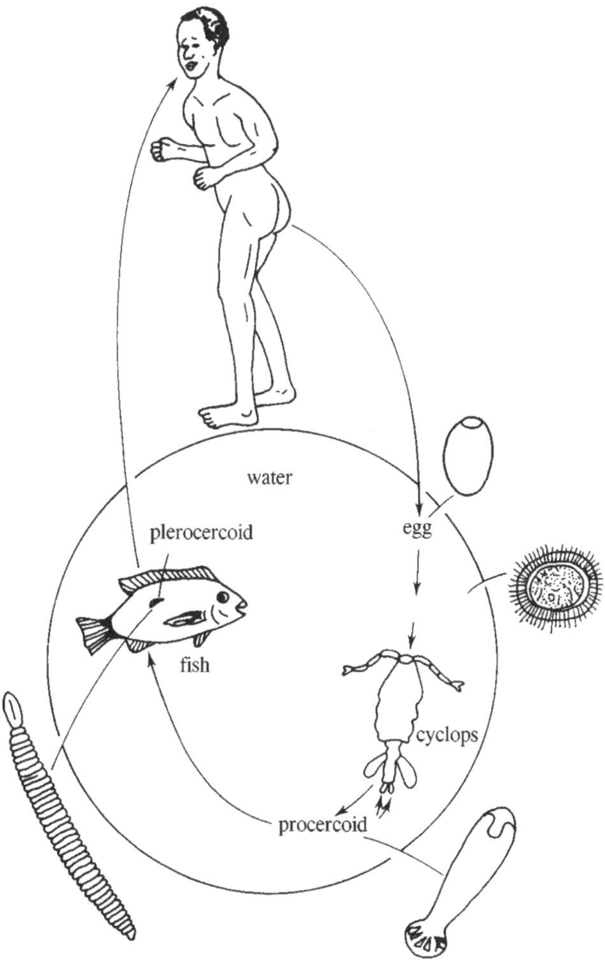

Figure 9.8: Life cycle of Group I Cestodes.

7. The definitive host becomes infected when it ingests the second intermediate host and the plerocercoid attaches to the intestinal wall with the scolex and develops into an adult sexually mature worm.

Group II life cycles (Order Cyclophyllidea)

1. Larva does not hatch until ingested by the intermediate host.

2. The hatched larva penetrates through the gut wall using hooks and is carried to a suitable site where it metamorphoses into one of a number of larval stages collectively known as *metacestodes*.

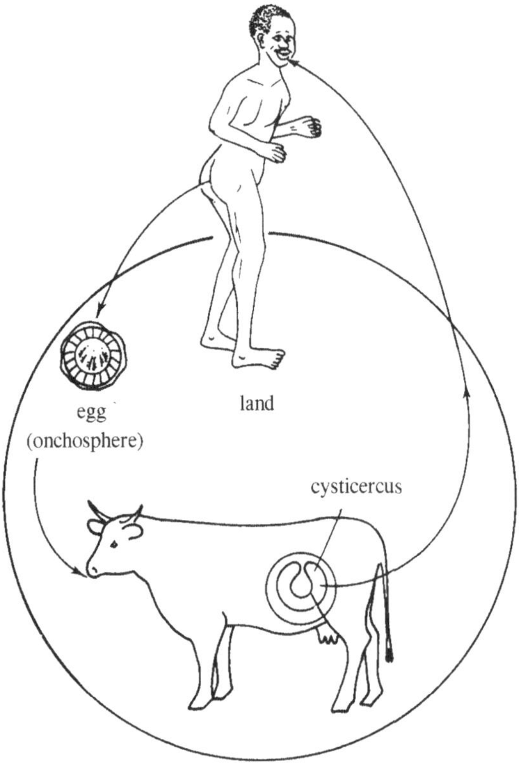

Figure 9.9: Life cycle of Group II Cestodes.

3. The definitive host becomes infected by eating an intermediate host harbouring a metacestode which then metamorphoses, attaches to the intestinal wall, and develops into a sexually mature adult worm.

The following are some of the more common metacestodes of Cyclophyllidea of importance in tropical Africa:

1. *Cysticercoid* is a solid-bodied larva with an anterior vesicle bearing the scolex which is not invaginated and a posterior tail (= cercomer) containing the larval hooks.
2. *Cysticercus* is a fluid-filled bladder from whose wall (the germinative layer) arises a single scolex which is invaginated and retracted. Among the Taeniidae the cysticercus (or bladderworm) undergoes asexual reproduction by budding to produce:

   (a) *Coenurus*, with a number of scoleces budded off from the

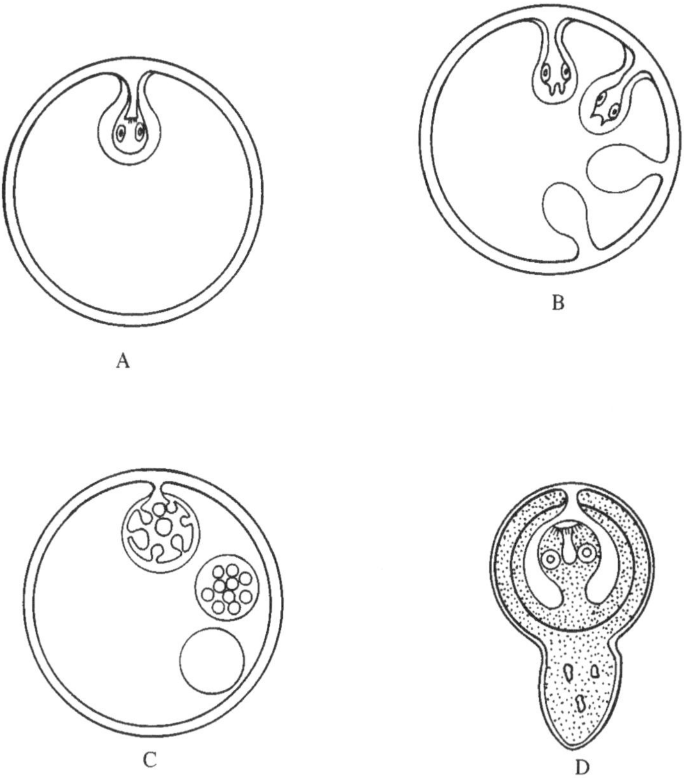

Figure 9.10: Common metacestodes of Cyclophyllidea in tropical Africa: A. cysticercus, B. coenurus, C. hydatid, D. cysticercoid

germinative layer of the bladder, but still attached to it.

(*b*) *Hydatid, a* bladderworm in which scoleces do not arise directly from the germinative layer but from the walls of *brood capsules* which are budded off from the bladder wall. Each hydatid contains several scoleces sometimes numbering in millions, and can reach a diameter of 10 cm or over, holding up to a quart of hydatid fluid. There are two types of hydatid

(*i*) *Zinilocular hydatid*, showing endogenous budding to produce brood capsules with scoleces, as described above.

(*ii*) *Multilocular or alveolar hydatid*, in which exogenous budding occurs to produce *daughter cysts* which then bud off brood capsules from which arise scoleces.

The hydatid fluid is replaced by a jelly-like mass or fibrous tissue which simulates some form of malignant growth like cancer, invading and ramifying through host tissues.

Yamaguti gives a more detailed classification of metacestodes.

TAENIA SANINATA AND *T. SOLIUM*—GENERAL BIOLOGY

Some of the features of the order Cyclophyllidea are contained in the description of Group II Cestodes, but the chief diagnostic features are outlined as follows:

1. Scolex is small, with four well-developed muscular acetabula.
2. Scolex can be with or without a rostellum which may be armed or unarmed.
3. Vitellarium is single, compact, post-ovarian.
4. Genital opening is lateral.
5. No uterine opening.
6. Strobila apolytic, i.e. the posterior mature proglottids are shed when ripe.
7. Egg shell encloses only a single vitelline cell together with a fertilized ovum.
8. Egg capsule, when present, is usually thin and not made of sclerotin, but the embryophore surrounding the embryo is thick and made of keratin.
9. Eggs are fully embryonated and infective to the intermediate host when laid.
10. Intermediate hosts are usually terrestrial animals.
11. Adults are usually parasitic in the intestines of birds and mammals.
12. The order contains most of the cestodes of medical, veterinary, and economic importance, the most important belonging to the family Taeniidae.

Family. TAENIIDAE

The major diagnostic features are shown in Figure elsewhere in this chapter:

1. Medium to large size.
2. Rostellum, when present, is armed and non-retractable.
3. Ovary is bilobed, located near the posterior margin of the proglottid.

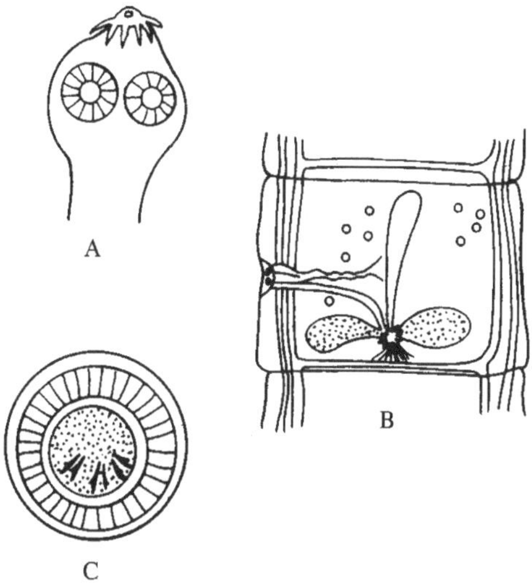

Figure 9.11: Morphology of Taeniid: A. scolex, B. mature proglottid, C. hexacanth embryo

4. Testes are numerous.
5. Gravid uterus with central stem and a number of lateral branches.
6. Egg capsule is a very thin membrane which is usually lost in most eggs found in faeces.
7. Metacestodes are bladderworms of various types.
8. The intermediate hosts are usually mammals, mainly herbivores, rodents, and even man.
9. Contains most of the cestodes of medical and veterinary importance in tropical Africa.

Taenia saginata (= *Taeniarhynchus saginatus*, the beef tapeworm of man) and *T. solium* (the pork tapeworm of man) are the two most common tapeworm species of man, occurring in different parts of the world. *Taenia saginata* is the most widely distributed, being cosmopolitan, especially in beef-eating countries, while *T. solium* is more restricted in distribution to pork-eating countries.

There are important morphological and biological differences between the two species which will be considered later, but of great significance is differences in the pathogenicity and economic consequences of their larval stages. While the adults of the two species rarely produce more than mild pathogenic effects or symptoms in man, the larval stage of TT *solium* known as *Cysticercus cellulosae* can be highly pathogenic in man causing the condition known as *cysticercosis*. On the other hand, the larva of *T. saginata* known as *C'vsticercus bovis* does not infect man, but when found in the flesh of cattle leads to large-scale condemnation of beef, resulting in serious economic loss.

Table 9.1: Major Differences Between *Taenia saginata* and *T. solium*.

F*eature*	*T. saginala*	*T. solium*
Size	3-7 m (sometimes up to 25 m) long	2-3 m (sometimes up to 10m) long
No. of proglottids	1000-2000 (sheds 3-10 daily)	800-1000 (sheds 8-10 daily)
No. of eggs per proglottid	100 000	40 000
Scolex	Cuboidal, up to 2.0 mm in diameter	Spheroid, about 1.0 mm in diameter
Rostellum	Absent	Present, armed with two circlets of 22—32 hooks
No. of testes	800—1200	300-500
Shape of ovary	Bilobed	Trilobed
Gravid uterus	15-25 lateral branches on each side	7-13 lateral branches on each side
Vaginal sphincter	Present	Absent
Gravid proglottid	When detached, active and creep out through anus and crawl about individually	When detached, passive
Intermediate hosts	Mostly domestic Bovidae, mainly cattle	Mostly pigs; also man

It is very difficult to differentiate specimens of the two species in the absence of the scolex. Although the number of lateral branches on each side of the gravid uterus is generally a good diagnostic feature the presence or absence of the vaginal sphincter is considered more reliable.

Highlights of life cycle

1. Proglottids are detached and passed out with faeces.
2. *Taenia saginata* proglottids disintegrate, scattering the eggs (oncospheres) in the soil, while the detached proglottids of *T. solium* do not disintegrate and are more likely to be swallowed whole by the intermediate host.

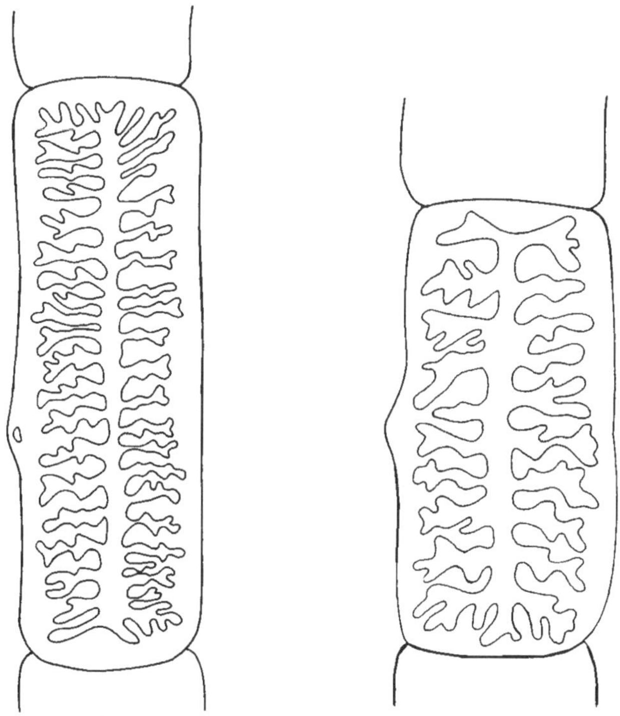

A B

Figure 9.12: Gravid proglottids of
A. Taenia saginata and B. T. solium.

3. Oncospheres hatch out in the duodenum after the actions of gastric and pancreatic secretions.
4. The oncosphere penetrates through the gut wall by means of hooks aided by its proteolytic secretions, into the general circulation, and is carried throughout the body.
5. The oncosphere is finally deposited in a suitable site, usually muscle fibres, where it develops into a small cysticercus, 10 mm in diameter, with a single invaginated scolex.
6. The cysticercus becomes infective in about 8 weeks and can remain viable for 4 to 9 months or even up to 21 months depending on the strain of either the host or parasite.
7. The cysticercus of TT *saginata* is called *Cysticercus hovis* and the infected cattle flesh is called *measly beef.* That of *T. solium* is called *Cysticercus cellulosae* and the infected pig flesh is called *measly pork.*

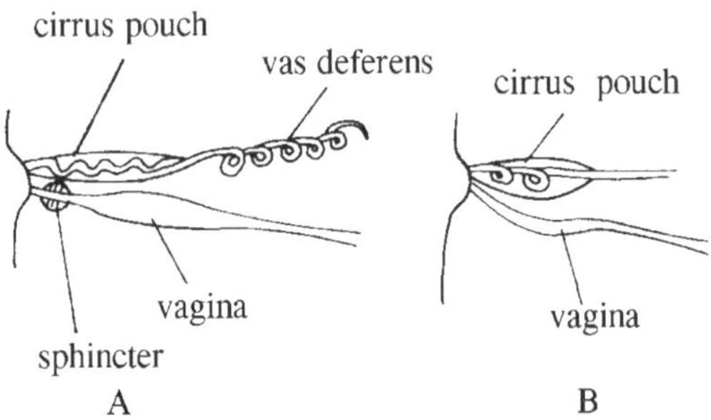

Figure 9.13: Distal portion of vagina showing vaginal sphincter in A. Taenia saginata and none in B. T. solium

8. Man becomes infected by eating raw or partially cooked beef or pork.
9. The scolex then evaginates under the influence of bile salts and the neck starts to budd off proglottids to produce a mature strobila in about 2 to 3 months; the life span of the adult worm is limited by that of the host.

For a comprehensive review of the biology and life cycle the reader is referred to Pawlowski and Schultz.

Hosts of Taenia Saginata

Man is the only significant definitive host of *T. saginata.* In an extensive survey of wild game in Kenya, Nelson, Pester, and Rickman found no *Taenia* infection among the primates. Among the carnivores, only the lion, leopard, hyaena, jackal, and dog were infected, but not with *T. saginata* since their scoleces were hooked.

At least thirteen species of *Taenia* have been encountered in African carnivores. Finally, no suitable experimental hosts have been established for *T. saginata.*

Intermediate Hosts

Although larval cestodes are generally less host-specific than adults, *T. saginata* seems to be restricted to domestic Bovidae as intermediate hosts. In their survey in Kenya, Nelson, Pester, and Rickman found cysticerci widely occurring among the ungulates, but they were not *T. saginata* cysticercus mainly because they possessed hooked scoleces.

Muscle cysticerci have been reported from various herbivores in different parts of East and southern Africa but none of these belong to *T. saginata.* Sachs and Dinnik and Sachs have shown that most of the cysts found in herbivores in Serengeti National Park in Tanzania are larvae of *T. gonyamai* and *T. crocutae* from the lion and *T. hyaenae* from the hyaena, not *T. saginata*.

On the other hand, Graber lists a wide range of intermediate hosts for *T. saginata* in Chad Republic including cattle, sheep, gazelles, camels, and different species of antelopes. Thus while it has been fairly well established that wild animals do not play an important role in the transmission of *T. saginata* in eastern and southern Africa, the possible existence of a secondary cycle in wild animals still needs further investigation in West Africa.

TAENIASIS—PATHOGENESISX AND CLINICAL PATHOLOGY

Adult Infections

'The debilitating effect of taeniasis on humans' claimed by Mann and others does not seem to be borne out by the facts. Most people show little or very mild symptoms and indeed Soulsby states that in most cases 'the host suffers a minimum of untoward effects'y According to Pawlowski and Schultz the most frequent symptom is discharge of proglottids from the anus.

Other obvious symptoms include one or more of the following: abdominal pain, headache, dizziness, nausea, and loss of weight. Some others show conflicting symptoms, e.g. constipation and diarrhoea, loss of appetite and increased appetite. Normally, the worm is located in the duodenum, but it has been known to migrate to unusual sites like the appendix, bile duct, nasopharynx, uterus, etc., causing clinical complications.

Also during vomiting, proglottids may be passed out from the mouth. All these can lead to intestinal obstruction, appendicitis, obstruction of the respiratory tract, etc. In general, the effects are similar to those of other large tapeworm infections except that there is no avitaminosis B_{12} as occurs in the case of *Diphyllobothrium latum* infection.

However, there is verminous intoxication caused by absorption of the parasite's excretory products. Finally, the economic effects of human taeniasis seems to be limited to the cost of diagnosis and treatment of infection.

Larval Infections

The economic consequences of *Cysticercus bovis* infection of cattle, on the other hand, is quite considerable even though cysticercosis does not appear to affect the health and well-being of cattle to any appreciable extent. For a review of pathogenesis of larval cestodes see Smyth and Heath.

TAENIASIS—DIAGNOSIS AND TREATMENT

The following are the diagnostic procedures for human infection

1. Demonstration of scolex and proglottids in the faeces is the most conclusive, although the scolex is very rare in faeces.
2. It is impossible to distinguish eggs of *T. saginata* from those of *T. solium.*
3. Faecal examination for eggs is not reliable and a single examination is not usually sufficient. Scraping of anal region, anal swabs, and cellophane tape method give quicker and more accurate diagnosis, although not even these detect all infections.
4. No completely satisfactory serological or immunodiagnostic tests have been developed for adult tapeworms in the intestine, and they have not been used extensively.
5. Radiological examination of the intestinal tract may reveal tapeworm infection.

Several effective taeniicides have been developed. Concentrated extract of pumpkin seeds and extracts of male ferns have been known as effective taeniicides although their safety has to be established beyond doubt.

Niclosamide is the drug of choice for *T saginata*, with cure rates of 80 to 95 per cent. However, the mode of action of most taeniicides is not well known and medical supervision is necessary for individual and mass chemotherapy.

CYSTICERCOSIS—DIAGNOSIS AND TREATMENT

So far, no rapid and accurate ante-mortem diagnostic tests are available for cysticercosis in cattle. The serological tests which have been developed lack sensitivity in detecting light infections. Also there is the possibility of crossreaction and false positive results when other larval cestodes (e.g. *Echinococcus granulosus* hydatid) and trematode (e.g. *Fasciola gigantica)* infections are present. No treatment is currently available for cysticercosis of cattle.

Although a number of drugs have shown promise of cysticidal activity, their widescale use in the control of larval cestodes in animals is limited because of observed carcinogenic, teratogenic, and other effects.

However, advances in the immunology of cysticercosis indicate some prospects of immunization of cattle against infection.

EPIDEMIOLOGY OF TAENIASIS AND EPIZOOTIOLOGY OF CYSTICERCOSIS

Taenia saginata infection of man is widespread throughout the world. The world prevalence of the disease has been variously estimated at 39 million and 77 million, 32 million of this in Africa, 29 million in the Soviet Union and I million each in Western Europe and North America. However, it is generally recognized that the prevalence of the disease is on the increase in many countries for reasons which Soulsby (1975) and Abdussalam *et al.* have adduced. These include

1. Intensification of animal production.
2. Development of meat industries in several developing countries.
3. Increasing preference for raw beef in the more affluent countries.
4. Consumption of undercooked beef by tourists visiting highly endemic areas.
5. Consumption of semi-cooked meat in manufactured food products like hamburgers, etc.
6. The 'camping explosion' in some countries with the associated increase in promiscuous defaecation.
7. Accelerating urbanization with decreased efficiency of sewerage systems.
8. Sewage farming.

The incidence of human taeniasis in different parts of tropical Africa. As pointed out by Abdussalam *et al.* there is a general dearth of epidemiological information and the little there is, is based on data which is fragmentary, inadequate for statistical analysis, and invariably derived from procedures which are not standardized and thus not comparable.

Furthermore, they do not constitute a fair representation of the entire population either of the localities or the entire nation, being usually restricted to surveys of school children or hospital patients. Finally, they are based on a single stool examination which is not a reliable diagnostic test.

Nevertheless, there is enough evidence from the table to suggest that the prevalence of taeniasis is not as high all over Africa as generally reported. What emerges from the table is that, with the exception of parts of Kenya, Uganda, and Ethiopia in eastern Africa with over 10 per cent prevalence, most other countries have areas which are either free of infection or have very low prevalence.

For example, vast areas of southern Nigeria consistently show no infection, or prevalence of less than 1.0 per cent the same as Zimbabwe, Zaire, Congo, and Cameroon. Even in Kenya there is wide variation ranging from those areas of high prevalence (14 to 65 per cent) in central Kenya to those of low prevalence near the coast and lake shores.

The conclusion is inescapable that there are areas of high endemicity in central Kenya and parts of Ethiopia and Uganda similar to endemic foci in the Soviet Union and Yugoslavia with high prevalences ranging from 7 to 45 per cent as compared to the general figure for Europe which is below 1.0 per cent.

Differences in rates of infection are related to differences in climatic conditions and ethnological factors such as human occupation, habits, behaviour, religion, and beliefs. For example, some authors claim that members of the Masai and Kikuyu tribes of Kenya believe that consumption of measly beef guarantees their virility, while the Suk women of Uganda are said to believe that it enhances their fertility.

Even if these beliefs do exist, it would be difficult to assess the role they play in sustaining transmission, having regard to the fact that most 'tribal groups' in Africa are ignorant about the life cycle of the parasite and the role of cattle in transmission.

A realistic evaluation of the role of social and ethnological factors is indispensable in the development of an integrated, multidisciplinary approach to the study of taeniasis as proposed by Mann. The incidence of *Cysticercus bovis* in cattle in tropical Africa is based on surveys of carcasses in slaughter-houses, usually during routine meat inspection.

Thus there are no data on the incidence in the vast number of cattle slaughtered and consumed in rural Africa. Furthermore, in most abbatoirs, meat inspection facilities are inadequate and procedures are not uniform or standardized, and even where reasonably well developed (like in Kenya), incision is only limited to certain muscles.

Thus, like in the case of taeniasis, it is difficult to obtain accurate figures of the incidence of bovine cysticercosis which can be taken to represent the situation in the countries or even the localities. In the circumstances it is misleading to present data as if they represented nationwide surveys, as done for instance by Urquhart or Soulsby, the latter stating: 'In most of the African countries the prevalence rates reported for bovine cysticercosis have been in excess of 10 per cent.'

Admittedly, many areas in Kenya (from which most information is available) have prevalence rates much over 10 per cent. and the nationwide figure reaches a high of 29.6 per cent. The most that can be said for most other countries is that the rates vary from areas of low prevalence (less than 10 per cent) to high prevalence of over 10 per cent.

However, it is apparent that, on the whole, the prevalence is much higher than in Europe, the Soviet Union, and the United States where it is generally below 1 per cent in most parts, although there is evidence to suggest that it is on the increase in these countries.

Epidemiological and Epizootiological Factors

Basically, man acquires infection by eating raw or undercooked beef infected with cysticerci, and cattle are infected by the ingestion of eggs (hexacanths) which have been passed out with the stool of man, thereby contaminating the pastures in which the cattle feed.

These two principal factors enhancing transmission-the food and feeding habits, and the level of sanitation of the people will now be discussed in greater detail.

Food and Feeding Habits

Obviously, taeniasis due to Taenia saginata is prevalent only among beef-eating people, and, even here, it is restricted to people who have acquired the taste for raw or undercooked beef. The taste for undercooked beef is widespread all over the world.

For example, shashlik in parts of the Soviet Union, shiskebab in the Middle East, and rare steak and barbecues in Europe and the United States are beef dishes which are in no way safer as a source of infection than chunks of beef roasted briefly over an open fire, 'charred on the outside and raw on the inside', eaten by some people in east and central Africa.

In Nigeria, for example, the low prevalence of infection in the south can be related to the practice of boiling beef thoroughly for about one hour before consumption. On the other hand, in northern Nigeria, the people are exposed to greater risk of infection not only because it is the cattle-rearing area of the country where more beef tends to be eaten but also because of the widescale consumption of 'suya', a kebab-like beef preparation which is a favourite dish of the people.

Recent studies by Dada and Usman have shown that the preparation of suya (heating over an open fire at 45°C for 15 minutes) is not sufficient to kill the cysticerci.

Sanitation

Infection of cattle can occur when they feed on pastures and soil contaminated with infected human faeces. Contamination can occur either:

1. Directly, when infected persons defaecate in a pasture, or
2. Indirectly, when insufficiently processed sewage is spread to pastures or used as fertilizer.

The fact that the former more commonly occurs in Africa and the latter is the principal mode in Europe probably prompted the assertion by Pawlowski and Schultz that the reasons for T. saginata infection in the two continents are ironically opposite-'infection is prevalent in developed countries because they are rich, and in developing countries because they are poor!'

The impact of direct defaecation on herbage by herdsmen will be greater under ranching conditions than on cattle raised by nomads, because being constantly on the move the chances of ingesting human faeces are reduced. The difference in incidence in nomadic and settled cattle reported by Graber and Tabo tends to lend support to this view.

Eggs are also spread by birds (e.g. gulls) and insects. In particular, filth flies have been incriminated, although Dipeolu working in Nigeria concluded that houseflies do not significantly influence transmission to man.

Other factors of great epidemiological significance are:

1. Eggs are known to survive for long periods in liquid manure and moist soil, and current sewage treatment procedures are not adequate to kill them. They do, however, succumb to desiccation.
2. Prenatal infection has been reported from Africa with the result that good sanitation may be of little use after the event.
3. Neonatal infection occurs within days of birth when livestock attendants, contaminated with eggs, feed calves with milk from buckets. Neonatal infection is of great epidemiological significance in Africa because:
   (a) The cysticerci remain viable for several years in the animal and
   (b) They induce a state of 'immunological unresponsiveness' which renders the animals susceptible to reinfection.

TAENIASIS AND CYSTICEROCOSIS–ECONOMIC ASPECTS

If human taeniasis in tropical Africa lowers the productivity of infected persons, this is not obvious and the extent has certainly not been extensively investigated. The losses are therefore those resulting from the cost of diagnosis and treatment. Economic losses due to bovine cysticercosis are, however, well defined. It is estimated that developing countries lose about $25.00 per animal and developed, industrialized countries $75.00 per animal. These losses arise from

1. Condemned carcasses,
2. Cost of refrigeration of lightly infected carcasses,
3. Decreased value of the meat so treated, and
4. Indirect costs of setting up facilities needed for meat inspection and processing infected meat.

In most African countries where cattle are reared for local consumption, the losses, if any, are borne by the individual owners. In any case, it is difficult to arrive at an accurate estimate of loss due to cysticercosis because the bulk of cattle slaughtered in rural areas is not inspected. Even when inspected, the infection is either not detected because of defective procedures or they are simply ignored.

However, in East African countries like Kenya where the cattle industry is a substantial foreign exchange earner, cysticercosis is a serious obstacle to national development. Export trade to the European Economic Community, for example, has been seriously affected by stringent regulations which ban meat in which even one cysticercus, live or dead, has been detected.

Annual losses incurred by different nations have been estimated variously to range from US $0.5-3.0 million in general; US $0.25 million by Zimbabwe, £0.5 million by Kenya, $0.5 million by Botswana, and £1.0 million by Kenya. Of even greater consequence is the indirect loss in limiting the further development of modern meat processing and packing plants to handle meat from the already large cattle populations in Kenya and other East African countries.

TAENIASIS AND CYSTICERCOSIS—CONTROL

The life cycle and epidemiology of the parasite suggest that affective control can be achieved by eating well-done beef, maintaining a high standard of sanitation, and treating diagnosed cases. But what are the prospects of success in adopting these strategies?

Beef-Eating

1. *Meat Inspection.* To ensure that only wholesome meat is available for consumption, there should be an efficient meat inspection service and any carcasses found infected should be condemned and destroyed. This is certainly easier said than

done for most tropical African countries. Meat inspection is out of the question outside the main towns because of the vast financial involvement and lack of properly trained personnel. Furthermore, many countries have still to determine the 'predilection sites' (i.e. the sites most favoured by the cysticerci and which should then be selected for inspection). The site probably varies with geographical area, breed of cattle, age, and activity of muscle. For example, while Belino found localization of cysticerci in Nigerian cattle in the tongue (73 per cent), heart (65 per cent), and masseter muscle (63 per cent), Schillhorn van Veen found heavy infection in livers but none in the muscles; Mitchell in Uganda found infection in shoulder muscles (28.9 per cent), tongue (20.5 per cent), heart (15.3 per cent), masseter muscles (12.3 per cent), and diaphragm (15.3 per cent) and Petrovic found the heart most commonly infected in Tanzania. Without establishing the sites to be inspected, many carcasses which are infected may be inadvertently passed for sale and consumption.

2. Lightly infected beef can be rendered safe by freezing. Hilwig, Cramer, and Forsyth have experimentally worked out time and temperature combinations required to ensure death of all cysticerci. Freezing at-10°C for at least 10 days is generally accepted as effective, but the expense and, indeed, the lack of refrigeration facilities puts this out of reach of most parts of tropical Africa.
3. The surest way is to cook meat well before eating. The thermal death-point of cysticerci is 56°C, provided the heat reaches the centre so that it is no longer pink. For most parts of Africa, this constitutes no problem, but there are those who enjoy the flavour and taste of raw and undercooked meat!

Mass Diagnosis and Treatment

Control can be achieved by mass diagnosis of the population and treatment of all infected persons. Farfetched as this may sound, it has actually been tried in the Soviet Union where it resulted in a sharp decline in prevalence rates.

Many African countries are a long way from implementing this at present because of financial and manpower constraints, quite apart from the economic returns to be expected. This has been tried on a limited scale with farm workers in Kenya, but with little success.

Sanitation

No doubt maintaining high standards of sanitation will bring about a reduction in transmission. This can be done in rural areas by the provision and use of latrines and the introduction of health education among the people.

Though these should yield good results in the long term, the numerous problems which loom large in frustrating the successful implementation of these measures have been treated under schistosomiasis. In the urban areas, good sanitation implies proper treatment and disposal of sewage to prevent it contaminating pastures and other cattle-feeding sites.

Considering that sewage systems in most tropical towns and cities are presently at the pioneering stage, this approach appears only to hold promise for the future.

Immunization

Progress has been made in recent times in the search for suitable immunization procedures against bovine cysticercosis. Thus oral infection with attenuated eggs and artificially hatched oncospheres have been observed experimentally to induce immunity in cattle. Also, hatched oncospheres of a heterologous cestode *T. hydatigena* have been found to induce active immunity in cattle.

Unfortunately, these are not effective in endemic areas in tropical Africa where prenatal and neonatal infections are common. There is hope in the future, however, because it has been shown by Soulsby and others that passive immunity can be induced experimentally by oral administration to neonates of serum or colostrum derived from immunized cows.

These are early days yet, and experiments and field trials are still required to establish the effectiveness of passive immunization against bovine cysticercosis in tropical Africa. For excellent reviews and summaries of immunization see Abdussalam *et al.*, Mulligan, and Soulsby.

It would appear, therefore, that extensive research is called for in tropical Africa on the taeniasis/cysticercosis problem. Almost all aspects of the disease require intensive research, but urgent work is required in the following areas:

1. Epidemiology and epizootiology including distribution, prevalence rates, etc., for various countries.
2. Immunology:
   (a) To determine the prevalence of prenatal and neonatal

infection in endemic areas and their role in epidemiology.
   (b) Development of active and passive immunization against infection in cattle.
   (c) The problem of resistance to infection.
3. Development of effective ante-mortem techniques for diagnosis of bovine cysticercosis and more effective post-mortem procedures.
4. Factors involved in the survival of eggs and cysticerci.
5. Clinical pathology, diagnosis, and chemotherapy of taeniasis in man.
6. Development of chemical cysticides.

Details of research needs and recommendations, including the establishment of centres in endemic areas to deal with the problems of taeniasis and cysticercosis are outlined in the WHO Memorandum by Abdussalam *et al.*.

Needless to say, not much is being done in this area in most African countries. In Kenya, where because of the economic demands of the beef industry the problems of this infection have come to the forefront and so given prominence, Mann has described the existence of a 'multidisciplinary Coordinated Research Programme' involving various institutions under FAO/WHO sponsorship.

In spite of the formidable list of institutions and the research and routine work in which they are engaged, it is probably appropriate to conclude this section with a quotation from Mann's footnote which puts the problem in proper perspective, even for Kenya:

> It has to be stressed that the research programme described above is carried out voluntarily by staff already fully committed to their routine work in field laboratories and lecture rooms, under severe financial constraints. Any technical or financial support, any collaborative research programme, visit of scientists to Kenya, assignment of voluntary research workers, or acceptance of Kenyans for training in specialized procedures, will be considered as a direct involvement leading to the eradication of these two parasitic diseases which are threatening the economy and health of many developing countries.

TAENIA SOLIUM

Although potentially more dangerous in its pathogenic effect on man than T. *saginata*, *T. solium* is relatively less common. Its world prevalence is estimated to be about 8 per cent of *T. saginata*, but while effective control measures have rendered it almost extinct in the United States and parts of Europe, some would say its prevalence is increasing in Africa and other tropical third World countries.

Hosts of *T. Solium*

Man is the only known definitive host while domestic pigs are the chief intermediate hosts, although in areas where dogs feed on human faeces and dog flesh is eaten by man, the dog has been known to play a secondary role in transmission. Other intermediate hosts include cats, rats, monkeys, and cattle and even man himself (but more about that later).

Distribution of *T. Solium* in Africa

Knowledge of the status of taeniasis due to *Taenia solium* and cysticercosis due to *Cysticercus cellulosae* infections in man and animals in Africa is fragmentary and limited. Stoll estimated that about 0.5 million people are infected.

While certain parts of Africa undoubtedly have a high prevalence, there is every reason to suspect that vast areas in West Africa whose people embrace the Moslem religion with its ban on pork eating would be relatively free of infection with this particular helminth-just like desert areas of Kenya and Uganda where infection is rarely seen.

Incidence of *Cysticercus cellulosae* in Africa varies a great deal. While certain parts of western Africa have up to 18 per cent of pigs infected, there are areas where the pig population is high but the incidence of cysticercosis is 'unaccountably low'.

Some of the more recent surveys in Africa show that 7 per cent of pigs in Mayo-Kebbi, Chad Republic, and between 0.1 and 8.1 per cent of pigs in four regions of Zaire were infected. There is also the possibility that many of the cysticerci with hooked scoleces seen in the flesh of domestic and wild pigs may belong to other species of *Taenia* of dogs and other carnivores, as cautioned by Nelson, Pester, and Rickman.

Pathogenesis and Clinical Pathology

Like ***T.** saginata*, the effect of the adult ***T.** solium* in man is mild and is no cause for alarm. It is, however, when man is infected with the cysticercus that severe pathological conditions, sometimes with fatal results, develop. Man becomes infected by ingesting eggs (hexacanth embryos) and development proceeds as in any other intermediate host.

Cysticerci may be lodged in any organ, but the predilection sites are skeletal muscles and subcutaneous tissues where they produce no overt symptoms. However, when they become lodged in the eye, they cause varying degrees of ocular disturbances including loss of vision. It is in the brain that their effect is most severe, the most common symptom being epilepsy. Indeed, cysticercosis has been incriminated as the most common single cause of epilepsy in parts of Africa.

According to Cowper, there has been no record of human cysticercosis in Nigeria. It is when they die that the cysticerci elicit severe inflammatory reactions which may prove to be fatal to the host.

Eventually, the cysts become calcified. Sometimes in the brain, the cysts may assume a large size and irregular shape with branches (racemose cyst), which may be confused with coenurus or hydatid cysts. The pathology of human cysticercosis has been reviewed by Smyth and

Heath and Gelfand and Jeffrey have given an account of cerebral cysticercosis in Zimbabwe. It has been suggested that man can acquire infection by *autoinfection* involving a process of anti-peristalsis (during vomiting, for example) in which ripe proglottids or eggs pass back into the stomach, hatch out, and the larvae return to the intestine.

However, from studies on the hatching of eggs, Webbe has shown that autoinfection is a rare occurrence if it does occur at all. In any case, the majority of patients with cysticercosis have no history of *T. solium* adult infection; neither are they from areas where *T. solium* is endemic in Africa. The predilection sites of cysticerci in pigs are the muscles of the jaws, heart, tongue, diaphragm, shoulder, etc., but the incidence in these sites varies from place to place.

Over 40 per cent of infected pigs show cysticerci in the brain as well. The cysts vary in size from 1.0 to 15 mm in diameter depending on age, and they can remain alive for the entire life of the pig. No serious pathological effects have been associated with cysticercosis due to *Cysticercus cellulosae* in pigs.

Diagnosis and Treatment

It is rarely possible to differentiate between *T. solium* and *T. saginata* infection in man by faecal examination, although staining the eggs with Ziehl-Neelson stain gives different results. However, most surveys of helminthic infection by faecal examination in Africa have not tried to distinguish between the two species.

Ante-mortem diagnosis of swine cysticercosis is possible to a limited extent, lacking sensitivity and specificity in light infections. Sometimes visual examination of the lower part of the tongue can reveal cysts. This is a reliable antemortem diagnosis of infection in pigs. In endemic areas immunodiagnostic and X-ray techniques can be used in conjunction to diagnose and locate human cysticercosis. No treatment is currently available for animal cysticercosis. There is particularly an urgent need for the development of suitable cysticides for the treatment of human neurocysticercosis.

Ocular cysticercosis can be treated by surgical removal of the cyst although there are less chances of success with racemose or calcified cysts. Sometimes, misdiagnosis of a cyst in the retina as a malignant tumor has led to the removal of the eye. For the adult worm, Niclosamide, with 90 to 95 per cent cure rates, is the drug of choice. Drugs like quinacrine which induce vomiting should be avoided because of the risk of causing cysticercosis.

Economics of Wwine Cysticercosis

The economic effects of swine cysticercosis are not as serious as bovine cysticercosis. Although most African communities still raise pigs in the backyard or ranging freely in the villages where they could have access to human faeces from which they can acquire massive infection, the fact remains that most of such pigs are found to be free of infection when slaughtered.

Besides, the pork is usually for local consumption and not for export. So the extent of infection remains largely unknown and would be difficult to estimate. However, the practice of raising pigs in sties and modern piggeries where infection is virtually eliminated is on the increase in Africa, as it should if the piggery industry is to thrive.

Control

This is similar to control of *T. saginata* and bovine cysticercosis.

ECHINOCOCCUS GRANULOSUS

Echinococcus granulosus, one of the smallest taeniids, is a parasite of the intestine of carnivores whose larval stage can grow into enormous sizes in the body of intermediate hosts. In man and domestic animals it causes the disease hydatidosis or echinococcosis which is of great medical and economic importance though this is out of proportion to its incidence.

Echinococcus granulosus is cosmopolitan, with major foci in the Soviet Union, Latin America, Australasia, and around the Mediterranean although Nelson, Pester, and Rickman claim that the highest prevalence in the world is in East Africa. A world distribution map of human and animal hydatidosis has been prepared by Matossian, Rickard, and Smyth.

A closely related species, *E. multilocularis*, has not been reported from tropical Africa, being restricted mainly to the holoarctic zone of

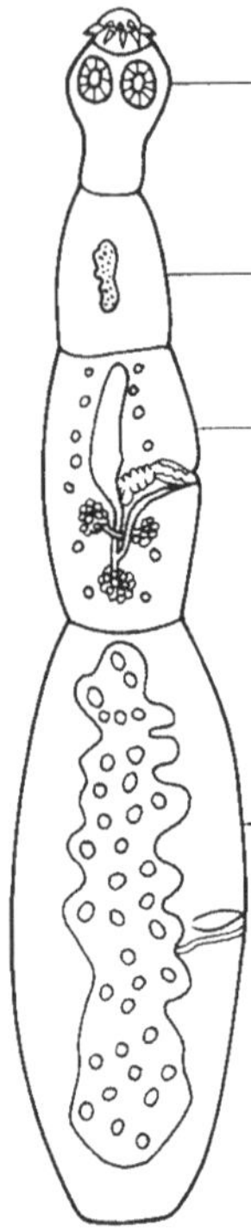

Figure 9.14: Echinococcus granulosus: Adult Morphology

the northern hemisphere. For accounts of world distribution, see Matossian, Rickard, and Smyth and Rausch.

Adult morphology

1. Size is 3-8 mm long.
2. Body is made up of scolex and three proglottids: one immature, the middle one mature, and the terminal one gravid.
3. Mature proglottid are similar to other *Taenia spp. in* morphology.
4. Gravid uterus is an irregular longitudinal sac.
5. Scolex with non-retractable rostellum with two circlets of about thirty to forty hooks.

Echinococcus granulosus closely resembles *E. multilocularis* in adult morphology. Although there are distinct differences in the nature of their cysts and their choice of intermediate hosts, it appears that there exists a 'continuum' of species between the two.

Furthermore, there is considerable infraspecific variation resulting in the development of different biological strains, some of which are not infective to man. This is not surprising when it is recalled that millions of individuals are produced by asexual budding (polyembryony) from a single larva.

This could result in the occurrence of mutation, producing 'instant' strains. The existence of strains could have serious implications on various aspects of the epidemiology of the disease, including the role of wild animals as intermediate hosts.

Life Cycle

1. The gravid proglottid is detached and the eggs are released when it ruptures.
2. Eggs are swallowed by a suitable intermediate host, usually herbivores but also man.
3. Hatching, activation, and migration of the larva is similar to *T. saginata.*
4. Bladderworms develop in a number of organs, but mostly the liver and lungs.
5. Development of a cyst is slow; in 4 weeks it is about 1.0 mm in diameter and reaches 10.0 mm in 6 months. Fully developed cysts can reach enormous sizes ; up to 500 mm has been reported, but average size is 50 to 100 mm in diameter.
6. The bladderworm of *E. granulosus* is known as *unilocular*

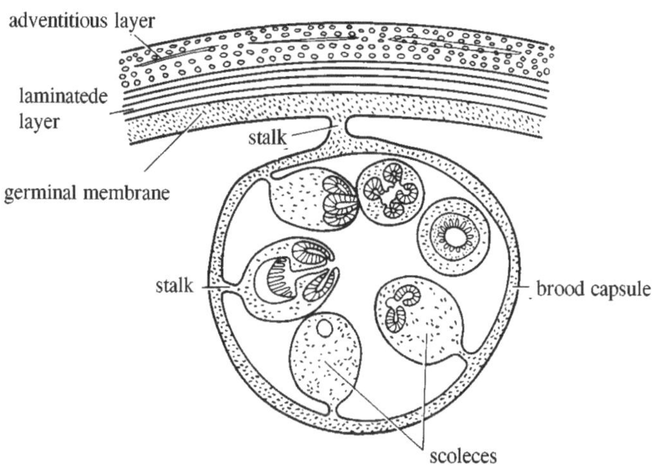

Figure 9.15: Echinococcus granulosus hydatid showing germinal layer budding off brood capsule and protoscoleces

hydatid. The cyst wall is made up of a thick non-cellular laminated layer and an inner nucleated germinal epithelium. The cyst is surrounded by a fibrous adventitious coat of host origin.

7. The germinal layer produces a number of small vesicles known as brood capsules from whose walls ten to thirty protoscoleces are budded. Sometimes, the germinal layer produces daughter cysts which then produce brood capsules and eventually protoscoleces, but this is rare.
8. The brood capsules and scoleces may break free from the wall and float in the hydatid fluid as *hydatid sand*.
9. Large cysts may contain up to 12 to 28 litres of fluid, and each litre may contain up to one million scoleces.
10. Carnivores become infected by eating flesh with cysts and so acquire multiple infection when the protoscoleces evaginate.
11. The cyst of *E. multilocularis* is known as *alveolar* or *multilocular hydatid*. This is a malignant, infiltrative form with no limiting host fibrous coat, with a jelly-like matrix, more like a neoplasm in its presentation than anything else.

For more detailed accounts of the biology of *Echinococcus* spp, see Smyth.

Hosts of *Echinococcus* spp.

Adult *E. granulosus* are found in dogs and allied species. In Kenya, they have been reported from spotted hyaena, jackal, and hunting dogs, but mostly from domestic dogs where the whole of the small intestine is often 'furred' with thousands of worms. The indication from this survey is that wild carnivores may not play a prominent role in transmission of the parasite in Africa, an observation supported by the low incidence or absence in wild carnivores in Chad Republic.

Unilocular hydatid cysts are found mainly in ungulates. In Kenya, Nelson, Pester, and Rickman found over 30 per cent of all cattle, sheep, and goats to be infected, while Mango *et al.* found 24.8 per cent sheep, 21.8 per cent cattle, and 11.6 per cent goats to be infected.

Various surveys have revealed that domestic livestock like sheep, goats, and cattle are the principal intermediate hosts in tropical Africa, with the camel most frequently infected, a prevalence of 37 to 55 per cent having been recorded from Chad and northern Nigeria . Surprisingly, unilocular hydatid cysts have been reported from chickens in Uganda. It appears that wild herbivores do not feature prominently as intermediate hosts in East Africa since surveys of antelopes hardly revealed any infection in Kenya and Serengeti, Tanzania.

Echinococcus multilocularis adults are found in dogs and cats as well as foxes, while the intermediate hosts are rodents. So far, there has been no report of alveolar hydatid cysts in rodents in tropical Africa.

Epddemiology

In Africa, the main cycle involves domestic dog and domestic herbivores. Dogs become infected when they are fed offals from slaughtered cattle, sheep, and goats, which in turn are infected by ingesting eggs along with herbage which has been contaminated with dog faeces. Human involvement comes from too close an association with dogs.

For example, transmission occurs when an infected dog licks the face of a child soon after cleaning its anal region with its tongue, thereby transferring the eggs. Infection also occurs when, as happens in some parts of Kenya, man eats undercooked dog intestine roasted over an open fire. However, human infection is more likely to occur through contamination of food, water, fingers, etc., by eggs from dogs' faeces.

In North America and Australia there is a secondary cycle of *E. granulosus* which is maintained in wild carnivores and herbivores. Domestic dogs become infected when they gain access to meat of wild game. This is known as the *sylvatic cycle* in which man hardly features.

From the result of their survey, Nelson, Pester, and Rickman concluded that if a sylvatic cycle exists, it is not likely to play a significant role in the epidemiology of the disease in tropical Africa. However, the fact that man, his domestic dogs and livestock, and wild animals share the same waterholes in parts of Africa suggests the existence of such a cycle.

The development of hydatid in man represents a dead end in the domestic cycle of the parasite because man is not normally eaten by dogs. Thus man is not a suitable intermediate host, except in situations in which it forms part of the food chain in the sylvatic cycle. Just such a situation exists in the Turkana District of Kenya, where it is reported that dead people are not buried but are left to be 'disposed of by the sanitary police' (e.g. domestic dogs, hyaenas, foxes, vultures, etc.).

Distribution in Tropical Africa

Matossian, Rickard, and Smyth have given an account of the distribution in Africa. Although hydatid disease is frequently reported from domestic animals, it seems that human hydatidosis is rare in West and Central Africa. There have been isolated cases reported from Chad Republic, Nigeria, Ivory Coast, and Senegal. It is, however, in East Africa that high prevalence occurs, especially in the Turkana District, a semi-desert area in northwest Kenya.

It has been estimated that 10 to 15 per cent of the Turkanas who are transhumants suffer from hydatidosis, the highest incidence in the world. Although Mann states that a high prevalence exists in bordering areas of Ethiopia, Sudan, and Uganda, Gemmell reports the rarity of the disease among the neighbouring people, even though hydatidosis of livestock is highly endemic.

Nevertheless, very high prevalence has been reported from the Dassanetch of south-west Ethiopia and from Uganda. The first case from Zambia was reported by Patel. No cases of human hydatid disease have been reported from Somalia, although various serological tests were positive in 4.2 per cent of 740 men investigated.

Pathology

Because of the slow growth of the cyst, the effect of the disease may not be felt for several years. Also, the effect depends on the organ affected and the size of the cyst. In man, the liver is the organ most frequenty affected (about 50 to 75 per cent), followed by the lungs (16 to 40 per cent), skin and musculature (1 to 9 per cent), and other organs like the brain, spleen, kidney, bone, and peritoneum (1 to 2 per cent).

In most of these locations, the cyst exerts pressure on the surrounding tissues but there is generally no serious clinical effect unless the organ is displaced or compressed, thereby interferring with its normal functions. Also, the hydatid fluid may leak out producing severe allergic reactions, including anaphylactic shock which may lead to death.

The effect of the cyst is detected early when it develops in space-limiting areas like the brain and bone marrow. In the brain, it produces neurological symptoms at a very early stage while in the bone marrow great internal pressure builds up which may eventually lead to fracture.

Gajjar and Sinclair-Smith described the case of echinococcosis in which the large cyst (over 12 cm in diameter) virtually replaced one of the kidneys in a child in Namibia. Finally, as a result of the rupture of the cyst which can occur either spontaneously or during surgery, protoscoleces get attached to the peritoneum or are carried by the blood stream to other sites where they develop into new cysts giving rise to secondary echinococcosis.

Diagnosis and Treatment

In most cases, the disease is detected during routine X-ray or exploratory surgery. In endemic areas the chances of a palpable abdominal lump in association with hepatomegaly and local pain turning out to be a hydatid are very high. An intradermal test (Casoni test) has been developed, using an inoculum prepared from hydatid fluid.

While the test is useful for confirming suspected cases, it also gives a false—positive reaction in 17 to 45 per cent of the cases in the presence of other taeniid infections like *T. ovis*, *T. hydatigena*, and *T. saginata*. On the other hand, twenty-five cases in Kenya which had previously shown a negative reaction to intradermal tests were later confirmed to have hydatid cysts by surgery.

A number of other serological tests have been developed with varying degrees of sensitivity. These include complement fixation, haemagluttination, fluorescent antibody, immunoelectrophoresis, latex agglutination, etc. Surgical removal of the cysts is the only sure method of treatment, no reliable drug having been developed.

During surgery, care must be taken not to spill the hydatid fluid. This is quite a difficult exercise because the fluid is usually under pressure. In Turkana it is estimated that there are 96 cases per 100 000 of population per year, and over a five-year period, 789 cases were actually medically seen.

The Flying Doctor Service of Africa carries out twenty-four surgical operations every month in that area, but this hardly solves the problem. There is yet no effective ante-mortem diagnostic technique for hydatidosis in domestic animals; neither is there any treatment.

Recently, the drug mebendazole has been used for treatment in man and animals. The drug devitalizes the cyst causing it to shrink and calcify. Routine post-mortem meat inspection is often not thorough, as was recently shown by Chambers in Zimbabwe where at least as many lungs affected with cysts are missed at routine meat inspection as are detected.

Economics of Echinococcosis

Infection with hydatids results in the condemnation of livers, hearts, etc., which robs the population in Africa of hundreds of thousands of kilograms of first class protein. There are no reliable figures for economic loss due to the disease in man and domestic animals in tropical African countries, but the estimate of US $1.2 million annual loss for Chile gives a fair idea.

Prevention and Control

The lack of reliable chemotherapy or immunization and effective ante-mortem diagnostic tests makes control and eradication of the disease difficult to achieve. Nevertheless, control programmes have been instituted in a number of countries with some measure of success, e.g. Iceland, New Zealand, Tasmania, Cyprus, and some Latin American countries.

However, such programmes are either nonexistent or at a pioneering stage in tropical Africa. Gemmell (1979) has outlined steps to be taken in setting up control programmes. Prevention is, however, possible as follows:

1. Prevention of dogs gaining access to raw offal.
2. Reduction of parasite biomass either by reducing dog population or by mass treatment of dogs with drugs like praziquantel, arecoline hydrobromide, etc.

Theoretically, these should be possible, but, as to be expected, there are problems related to the socio-cultural, economic, occupational, and levels of sanitation of the people which make implementation either unacceptable or impracticable.

MULTICEPS SPP.

Adults of *Multiceps* spp. are found in the intestine of dogs and jackals. They resemble *Taenia spp. so* closely that some authorities regard *Multiceps* as a synonym of *Taenia*. However, they are placed in separate genera because the bladderworm of *Multiceps* known as *coenurus* produces many protoscoleces by polyembryony directly from the cyst wall, while *Taenia* cyst has only one protoscolex.

The intermediate hosts of *Multiceps* spp. are usually herbivores and rodents, and sometimes man. Four species have been reported from man, *M. multiceps*, *M. serialis*, *M. brauni*, and *M. glomeratus* (no longer considered a valid species).

Templeton estimated the world total of coenuriasis at sixty-four, most of them from tropical Africa (half of them from Uganda alone). Other reports are from Nigeria, Ghana, Ruanda-Burundi, Kenya, and Congo. The larva of *M. multiceps*, known as *Cysticercus cerebralis* develops in the brain of ungulates, especially sheep, while the *M. serialis* larva known as *C. serialis* develops in the subcutaneous tissues of the rabbit or hare.

Both of them have been found in man in North and South Africa. In tropical Africa, no central nervous system (CNS) involvement has been reported, implying that none of the coenuriasis cases is due to *M. multiceps*. *Multiceps brauni* is naturally a parasite of dogs and jackals, with various wild rodents serving as intermediate hosts. Fain was able to demonstrate experimentally that the cases of subcutaneous coenuriasis from Ruanda-Burundi were due to *M. brauni*.

Since then most cases from tropical Africa have been referred to that species, although it has been difficult to make specific identification in most cases. There is a great deal of controversy about the taxonomy and identification of *Multiceps spp.* in tropical Africa and this has been well reviewed by Nelson and Wilson and their colleagues.

The pathology of coenuriasis in ungulates, especially sheep, is serious, causing the disease 'gid' or `staggers' which can be fatal. In man, the pathology is similar to that of cysticercosis, but since there is no CNS involvement in tropical Africa, the consequences are not so grave. Wilson, Wayte, and Addae have given a detailed account of the disease in Ghana.

10

Intestinal Nematodes

The nematodes have been said to be the most worm-like of the various groups of parasitic animals lumped under the loose title of worms. This is perhaps a reflection of the fact that they are shaped like the common earthworm, which seems the prototype for all worms. Actually, the earthworm is not a nematode, being a representative of the segmented worms, or annelids.

Nematodes are non-segmented, generally cylindrical in shape, tapering at both ends, and covered by a tough protective covering or cuticle. They have a complete digestive tract, with both oral and anal openings. The sexes are separate; generally males are much smaller than female worms.

Reproductive organs are tubular and lie coiled within the body cavity. In the male there is a single tubule, which at its smaller end consists of testicular cells; it extends into a vas deferens and seminal vesicle and terminates in an ejaculatory duct opening into the cloaca.

The female worm has two cylindrical ovaries, which expand into uteri. The uteri may open to the exterior through a single vulva, or there may be a common vagina between the vulva and uteri. The vulva is frequently located near the middle of the body but varies in position in different species.

In contrast to the trematodes and cestodes, all of which are parasitic, the majority of nematodes are free living. There are an estimated 500,000 species of nematodes. Many are of considerable economic importance as plant parasites, others as causes of disease in animals and a dozen or more are commonly encountered in humans.

The parasitic nematodes are generally a light cream-white color, but the females of the smaller forms may appear darker when filled with darkcolored eggs. Certain structural modifications are of importance in the identification of various species.

The mouth in primitive forms is surrounded by three lips, but in hookworms has become modified into a buccal capsule furnished with cutting plates or teeth. The anterior portion of the digestive tract, or the esophagus, is muscular in most forms.

In one group, of which *Trichuris* and *Trichinella* are examples, the esophagus is much reduced and has the appearance of a fine tubule running lengthwise through a column of large cuboidal cells. The muscular esophagus of certain nematodes is of uniform caliber throughout; this type is called filariform.

If the esophagus is expanded posteriorly into a bulb which contains a valve mechanism, it is referred to as rhabditiform. Male nematodes usually have a pair of copulatory spicules, which lie in pouches near the ejaculatory duct and may be inserted into the vagina of the female. In some forms, the posterior end of the male is expanded into a thin-walled copulatory bursa, supported by thickened rays.

The arrangement of these rays may be of importance in identification of the worms. Stages in the life cycle of nematodes include the egg, larvae which undergo several molts, and adults. The filariform type of esophagus generally characterizes infective stage larvae, which in their free-living stages (or those passed in intermediate hosts) may have been rhabditiform.

As has been mentioned, the majority of nematodes are free living. The parasitic forms include representatives of several different groups of nematodes, which may be assumed to have independently evolved a parasitic mode of existence. The nematodes exemplify, as does no other group, many of the stages which may be considered to lead from a wholly free-living to an obligate parasitic existence.

If one desires to set up such a series, at one end might be placed the vinegar eel, *Turbatrix aceti*. *Turbatrix* is a free-living nematode, which frequently was found multiplying to enormous numbers in vinegar, in the era when that commodity was dispensed from wooden casks and not sterilized when bottled at the factory.

The vinegar eel has been found on occasion in the vagina, where it apparently is able to survive for some time if introduced in a douche.

This organism exhibits some potentialities for becoming a parasite but cannot establish itself permanently in the vagina.

Strongyloides stercoralis is a small nematode which, if conditions are suitable, may pass several free-living generations in the soil but sooner or later produces larvae of a type which must complete their development as parasites of man. The hookworms are invariably parasitic in the adult stage, but their larvae must undergo a free-living developmental period in the soil.

Ascaris eggs must develop for a period outside the body before they mature and become infective, but then they are ingested and no stages of the life cycle are free living. Finally, the filarial worms, such as *Wuchereria,* might be considered perfect examples of obligate parasitism, having larval stages which develop in an insect and adults which live in man or other mammals.

At no time can the worm exist outside the body of one or the other host. The nematode parasites of man are moderately long-lived worms. *Ascaris will* usually die out in about a year in the absence of reinfection, while *Trichuris* lives several times that long, and hookworm infections may persist for as long as eight to 16 years.

Autoinfection is seen in *Strongyloides* (and perhaps *Enterobius),* enabling these parasites to persist for indefinite periods in the absence of reinfection. Diagnosis of intestinal nematode infection is generally made by demonstration of the characteristic eggs in the feces. Occasionally adult worms are found in the stools, but except for *Ascaris* they are so small that they are frequently overlooked unless a special search is made.

ASCARIS *LUMBRICOIDES*

The specific name of the large intestinal roundworm, *Ascaris lumbricoides*, is a tribute to its superficial resemblance to the common earthworm, *Lumbricus*. Female worms range from 20 to 35 cm. in length, while males are seldom over 30 cm. long. The female worms may be as thick as a lead pencil; the males are definitely more slender and may be distinguished by an incurved tail.

Both sexes are creamy-white in color, sometimes with a pinkish cast, and the cuticle has fine circular striations. *Ascaris* infections are found throughout the temperate and tropical areas of the globe, and under conditions of poor sanitation virtually 100 per cent of the population may be found to harbor the parasite.

The per capita worm burden may reach staggering levels, with hundreds or even a thousand or more worms in a single individual. A graphic illustration of *Ascaris* density is given by Stoll, who calculated a total of 18,000 tons of ascaris eggs produced annually by those worms affecting the people of China alone.

The total is perhaps higher today. When fully embryonated eggs are swallowed, they hatch in the duodenum and then undergo an extraordinary migration through the body before returning to settle down in the intestine and grow to adulthood. The larvae first penetrate the wall of the duodenum and enter blood or lymphatic vessels to be carried to the liver, to the heart, and thence into the pulmonary circulation.

They are filtered out by the capillaries of the lungs and break from them into the alveoli. There they grow and molt, and after about 10 days migrate through the respiratory passages to reach the esophagus and eventually once again the small intestine.

Two or three months after ingestion of the eggs, the mature worms commence egg laying in the intestine. There is suggestive evidence that while infection may take place constantly and the larvae undergo a migratory cycle, they will not be able to grow to adulthood in the intestine as long as any considerable number of worms remain from a previous infection.

Batches of adult worms may succeed each other in hyperendemic areas at periods dependent upon the longevity of the adult worms in the intestine. *Ascaris* eggs are unsegmented when passed; under favorable conditions they require a period of about two or three weeks outside the host to develop to the infective stage.

Excessive heat and dryness will soon kill them, but they will remain viable in moist soil for long periods. Mature female worms have been estimated to produce an average of 200,000 eggs daily. In all but the rare infections in which only male worms are present, diagnosis can usually be made with ease on examination of even the unconcentrated stool.

The fertilized egg of *Ascaris* is readily recognized. It is broadly oval, measuring 45 to 75 microns in length by 35 to 50 microns in breadth. The outer covering is an albuminoid coat, usually stained a golden brown by bile as seen in the fresh stool. The outer coat is coarsely mammillated and lies directly on top of a thick smooth shell, which is usually not easily distinguished.

Some eggs will be seen to have lost the outer albuminoid coat and in these the thick yellowish inner shell is obvious. It is thicker than the shell of a hookworm egg, which these decorticated *Ascaris* eggs otherwise resemble. Infertile eggs are longer and narrower than the fertile ones.

They may measure about 90 by 40 microns. Both the inner shell and outer albuminous coat may be thin, and if the latter is absent and the inner shell very thin they may resemble *Trichostrongylus* eggs.

Ascaris infections are sometimes diagnosed roentgenologically, either as worm-shaped radiolucent areas in a barium-filled intestine or more spectacularly with their own intestinal tracts outlined as well by barium which they have ingested.

Symptomatology

Small numbers of adult worms in the intestine often cause no symptoms but may give rise to vague abdominal pains or to intermittent colic, especially in children. Larger numbers of worms can cause problems related primarily to their bulk; they are the commonest cause of intestinal obstruction in children in the tropics.

The worms, irritated by medication into excesses of activity, can penetrate through the wall of the intestine, or into the appendix, and travel up the common bile duct, which they may block or traverse to enter the gallbladder or liver.

They may enter the stomach and be vomited or may even crawl up the esophagus to enter the nasopharynx or trachea. The symptoms caused by migratory worms will depend upon the organs involved. Bustamante-Sarabia et al. review the literature on ectopic ascariasis and describe a case of renal involvement. Large numbers of worms may give rise to more or less severe allergic symptoms.

Eosinophilia is generally present but seldom impressive. Serum IgE has been reported to reach very high levels in children infected with *Ascaris*.

Pathogenesis

Small numbers of infecting larvae will produce no obvious symptoms. Larger numbers may give rise to a transient hepatitis; with rupture into the alveoli, a pneumonitis may develop. Changes shown by x-ray are non-specific, with infiltrates and patchy areas of pneumonitis, increased bronchovascular markings, and widening of the hilar shadows.

These pulmonary findings, when accompanied as is usual by an eosinophilia, fulfill the rather ill-defined criteria for tropical eosinophilia. Later in the course of infection, the presence of large numbers of worms may lead to intestinal obstruction; this complication is most common in smaller children.

Epidemiology

Ascariasis affects more of the world's population than any other parasitic disease—an estimated 650 million persons. It is more commonly seen in areas of poor sanitation or where human feces are used for fertilizer. While the human ascaris and that of swine are distinct, the latter can infect humans and has even been found to cause intestinal obstruction.

Treatment

Pyrantel pamoate (Antiminth) is the most effective drug presently available for the treatment of ascariasis. Its administration requires no special diet or pre- or post-treatment purgation. It may be given with milk or fruit juice. Gastrointestinal reactions, including nausea, vomiting, abdominal cramps and diarrhea, are sometimes seen, and transient elevation of the SGOT has been reported. A cure rate of over 95 per cent is reported.

Piperazine citrate (Antepar) is also effective and requires no special diet or purgation. Side effects are few; dizziness and urticarial reactions are occasionally seen. Visual disturbances are rare; epilepsy may be exacerbated by the drug. Another drug suitable for treatment of uncomplicated intestinal ascariasis is thiabendazole (Mintezol). Nausea, vomiting and vertigo are fairly frequent side effects of this drug. Levamisole is still more effective than any of those just listed but is as yet unavailable in the United States.

Table 10.1: Drugs Effective in Treatment of Ascaris.

Drug	*Dosage*
Pyrantel pamoate (Antiminth)	11 mg./Kg. single oral dose (maximum dose 1.0 gm.)
Piperazine citrate (Antepar)	75 mg./Kg. twice daily x 2 days (maximum dose 3.5 gm./day)
Thiabendazole (Mintezol)	25 mg./Kg. twice daily x 2 days
Tetramisole (Levamisole)	2.5 to 5.0 mg./Kg. single oral dose

In mixed infections of *Ascaris* and other intestinal worms, it is good practice to treat initially with a drug effective against *Ascaris*. Some of the medications specific for other worms, while ineffective ascaricides, are thought to stimulate *Ascaris* to unusual bursts of activity, during which they may cause considerable damage to their host.

Perforation of the bowel wall and invasion of the bile duct are examples of such untoward migratory activity. Intestinal obstruction due to ascarids is treated by nasogastric suction until vomiting is controlled. One or two hours after the suction is discontinued, an initial dose of piperazine is administered through the nasogastric tube, which is allowed to remain in place. This dose may be 150 mg. per Kg. of body weight; the maximum dosage is 3.5 gm.

If vomiting recurs and suction must be resumed, additional doses may be given at the rate of 65 mg. per Kg. (maximum 1.0 gm.) every 12 hours for six doses. If there is no vomiting, the second dose is given by mouth, 24 hours after the first, and is repeated at 12-hour intervals for six doses.

The amount given is again 65 mg. per Kg. If this treatment is not successful or if the obstruction is complete, surgical intervention will probably be necessary.

ENTEROBIUS VERMICULARIS

The pinworm *Enterobius vermicularis* is by all odds the most common helminth parasite of those temperate regions where sanitation is at a high level. Spread of pinworm infection is no doubt facilitated by crowded indoor living in temperate climates, but it is also common in the tropics.

Less attention is paid to pinworm in tropical areas, probably because of the relative prevalence of more important parasites. Conversely, the importance of *Enterobius is* frequently overrated in the United States. The male pinworm is inconspicuous, about 2 to 5 mm. in length, and at most 0.2 mm. in width. The female reaches a length of 8 to 13 mm. and a width of up to 0.5 mm.

They are a light yellowish-white in color; the female is distinguished by a long, thin, sharply pointed tail, which characteristic gave rise to the common name. The adult worms inhabit the cecum and adjacent portions of the large and small intestine. The female worms, when fully gravid, migrate down the intestinal tract to pass out the anus and deposit their eggs.

The worms may migrate several inches out of the anus, depositing eggs as they crawl, or liberating masses of them as the worms dry and literally explode. The eggs are fully embryonated and are infective within a few hours of the time they are deposited; if climatic conditions are suitable they will survive for some weeks outside the body.

The eggs live longest under conditions of fairly high humidity and moderate temperature. Reinfection of the patient by contamination of the hands is common and makes control of the parasite very difficult. Development of the adult worms is stated to require about six weeks; shorter periods have, however, been reported. Infection of others through contaminated clothing, bedding, and so forth is frequently the cause of familial outbreaks. The eggs may survive for some days in dry dust, and air-borne eggs may serve to infect persons at some distance.

A type of autoinfection described as "retrofection" involves hatching of the embryonated eggs after their deposition in the perianal area and subsequent migration back into the rectum and large intestine. Diagnosis of pinworm infection is made on recovery of the characteristic eggs, although it may be suspected in children who have pruritus ani.

Occasionally, the adult female worms will be seen crawling in the perianal region or in the feces. Eggs may be found in the stools, but this is exceptional, as the females ordinarily do not oviposit until they leave the intestinal tract. Various methods of recovery of eggs from the perianal region provide the most efficient means of diagnosis.

The best known of these is the cellophane tape swab or Graham technique. The eggs are 50 to 60 microns in length and 20 to 32 microns in breadth, and have a translucent shell of moderate thickness. They are usually conspicuously flattened on one side, and this flattening and consequent reduction in diameter, plus the thicker shell, serves to differentiate the eggs from those of hookworms.

Symptomatology

The multiplicity of symptoms charged against *Enterobius* are legion and in some cases fantastic. Migration of the female worms from the anus will in some persons produce pruritus, which may at times be severe. In small children, the worms may invade the vagina after leaving the rectum, thereby producing a local irritation.

The local itching undoubtedly may interfere with the sleep of children or adults who are infected, as the worms migrate from the anus during the resting hours. It is probable that *Enterobius* causes no symptoms in the majority of infected adults and children.

Pathogenesis

Enterobius may for all practical purposes be considered a commensal in all save those persons whose hypersensitivity to the secretions and excretions of the worms leads to rectal pruritus. Attachment of the adult worms to the intestinal wall may produce some inflammation. Invasion of the appendix might be expected to be the common occurrence which it is, but any relationship between this invasion and appendicitis remains unproven.

Invasion of the peritoneal cavity via the female reproductive system may result in the formation of granulomas around eggs or worms; these are rarely of clinical significance. Granuloma formation around pinworm eggs in the liver was reported by Little et al. in a patient whose worms presumably gained access to the peritoneal cavity via a necrotic area in an adenocarcinoma of the bowel.

An adult female pinworm found on thoracotomy for a non-calcified pulmonary nodule is thought to have gained access to the lung via the respiratory tract. Chandrasoma and Mendis present evidence that male pinworms (perhaps because of their more slender form) are able to penetrate actively through the intact bowel wall.

Treatment

The worms may be eliminated by a variety of drugs and by means as simple as warm tap water enemas, yet their eggs are so resistant and widespread that their reintroduction into a household containing small children is generally only a matter of time. In a family situation in which reintroduction of the parasite seems probable, only those persons who are symptomatic need generally be treated.

Tap water enemas, repeated as necessary, will control symptoms. For those patients who, for a variety of reasons, need more dramatic treatment, pyrvinium pamoate (Povan) is recommended, as it not only is effective but colors the stools a bright red.

Pyrvinium pamoate is administered in a single dose, at the rate of 5 mg. per Kg. of body weight. Administration of this drug is occasionally accompanied by vomiting or diarrhea; rarely it is associated with photosensitization. Pyrvinium is available in both tablet and liquid form. The tablets are less likely to cause emesis, but they have a coating which contains acetylsalicylic acid.

THE HOOKWORMS

Ancylostoma *Duodenale*

The Old World hookworm, *Ancylostoma duodenale*, is the only hookworm of Europe and the areas bordering the Mediterranean, of the west coast of South America, and of parts of India and China.

It is found together with *Necator americanus* in certain areas in Brazil, a part of India, most of China, and throughout southeast Asia, Indonesia and the islands of the South and the Southwest Pacific. Within these areas, it is generally confined to those parts of the Northern Hemisphere south of the thirty-sixth parallel and of the Southern Hemisphere north of the thirtieth parallel, except where local conditions may be especially favorable, as in mines.

Ancylostoma adults are of a grayish-white or pinkish color. The head has a slight bend in relation to the rest of the body. The male worm measures nearly 1 cm. in length by 0.5 mm. in greatest width; the female is somewhat longer and stouter. The mouth is well developed, with a pair of teeth on either side of the median line and a smaller pair in the depths of the buccal capsule.

The male worm is provided with a prominent copulatory bursa posteriorly. Hookworm eggs when passed in the feces are unsegmented or in the early cleavage stages. Under optimal conditions, when deposited on moist sandy soil, the larva develops and hatches within 24 to 48 hours. Growth and development take place in the soil as the larva feeds on bacteria and organic material and undergoes a first molt.

After about seven days the worm stops feeding and molts a second time, transforming from a rhabditiform to a filariform or infective larva. The infective larvae do not eat and probably can live for only about two weeks if they do not find a host.

They usually live in the upper layers of the soil, and when the soil is cool and moist they climb to the highest point covered by a film of moisture. They extend their bodies into the air and remain waving about in this position until driven down by drying of their surroundings or by heat, or until they come in contact with the skin of a suitable host.

It is probable that man is the only normal host of *Ancylostoma duodenale;* although larval penetration can take place in other mammals, development to the adult stage does not occur. Diagnosis of hookworm infection depends upon recovery of the eggs from the stools. The hookworm egg is unsegmented or in an early segmentation stage when passed.

In specimens which have been allowed to stand at room temperature for a period of hours, especially if the weather is warm, a larva may be seen within the egg shell. Rarely, eggs may hatch and liberate larvae, which are then found free in the stool and must be differentiated from those of *Strongyloides*.

If a stained smear is made of the stool, it is easy to differentiate between hookworm and *Strongyloides* larvae, as the former have a distinct long buccal capsule between the oral opening and the esophagus, while in *Strongyloides* this structure is very short. The eggs are regularly oval and 56 to 60 microns in length by 36 to 40 microns in breadth.

The shell is thin and colorless. Although *Ancylostoma* eggs average somewhat smaller than those of *Necator,* no attempt at differentiation of the two genera is ordinarily made on stool examination. Rough estimates of the numbers of worms present may be made on the basis of egg counts.

In man, larval penetration usually takes place through the feet,

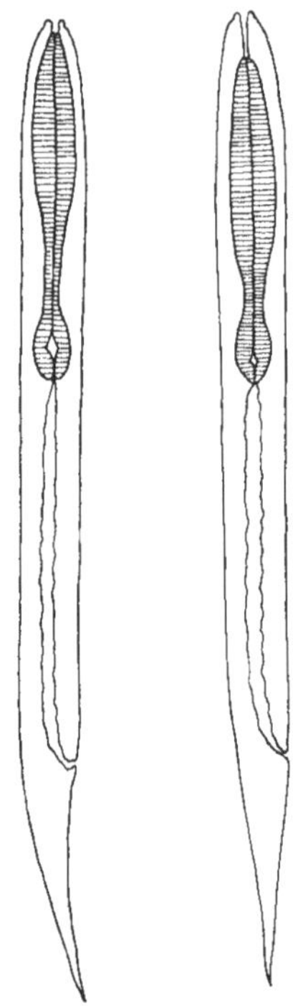

Figure 10.1: Diagram of hookworm and Strongyloides larvae from stool, showing differentiation on basis of buccal cavities.

though the larvae can penetrate through any skin areas or mucous membranes with which they come in contact. The larvae make their way into cutaneous venules and are carried passively to the lungs, where they break out into alveoli.

From the lungs, the larvae migrate up the trachea to be swallowed and reach the small intestine, where they mature. They attach by means of their stout mouth parts to the intestinal mucosa and suck blood and tissue juices of the host. The average prepatent period is seven or eight weeks. However, Nawalinski and Schad report a strain from India having a prepatent period of approximately 30 weeks.

Necator Americanus

The New World hookworm, *Necator americanus,* while prevalent over large portions of the Western Hemisphere, was probably introduced from Africa with the slave trade. In addition to being the only hookworm found in North America and large areas of South America, it is the native hookworm of Africa south of the Sahara and the only one found in parts of India. *Ancylostoma* and *Necator* occur together elsewhere in India, in much of China, in southeast Asia, in Indonesia, in the islands of the South and Southwest Pacific and in parts of Australia.

With increasing rapidity of communications and with the exposure of large numbers of persons to the hazards of infection in various parts of the world, it is probable that the geographical boundaries between the two genera of human hookworms will disappear. Hookworm infection is still prevalent in some parts of the United States.

Gloor et al. reported a 14.8 per cent infection rate in upper elementary grade school students in rural Kentucky, and Martin found that on the coastal plain of Georgia 12 per cent of rural school children were infected. He did not find these infections to be associated with anemia.

Adults of *N. americanus* resemble those of *Ancylostoma* but are slightly smaller. The males range from 5 to 9 mm. in length, while females are usually about 1 cm. long. The head is sharply bent in relation to the rest of the body, forming a definite "hook" at the anterior end, from which the worms derive their common name. The buccal capsule of *Necator* is armed with a pair of cutting plates, *while Ancylostoma* has teeth.

There are also decided differences in the structure of the rays supporting the copulatory bursa in the two genera. However, with a little practice one may be able to distinguish with the eye between adults of *Necator* and *Ancylostoma,* as the anterior hook is very much more pronounced in the former genus.

The life cycles of the two genera of hookworms are very similar. *Necator* larvae are more likely to produce irritation when they penetrate the skin, and ground itch more frequently accompanies infection by this parasite. The adult *Ancylostoma is* larger than *Necator,* and worm for worm it is more likely to bring about iron deficiency.

Eggs of *Necator* closely resemble those of *Ancylostoma,* but are slightly larger, averaging 64 to 76 microns in length by 36 to 40 microns in breadth.

Symptomatology

In penetrating the skin, the larvae may cause an allergic reaction known as ground itch. This is less common with *Ancylostoma* than with the New World hookworm, *Necator americanus.* Hookworm larvae are smaller than those of *Ascaris* and do not usually cause as severe pulmonary symptoms. If the infecting dose was large, pneumonitis may be produced

Figure 10.2: Necator americanus adults: 1, female worm; 2, male worm showing copulatory bursa; 3, frontal view of head showing cutting plates. Male and female worms photographed at same magnification.

by numbers of larvae breaking into the alveoli in a short space of time. Maturation of the worms may be marked by diarrhea, particularly when a previously uninfected person first acquires a heavy infection. This may be seen in persons from non-hookworm areas if they acquire an infection in the tropics.

Other symptoms of early infection may be vague abdominal pains, colic or nausea. In chronic infections, if the number of worms is considerable, blood loss will be serious. If the diet is adequate in protein, and sufficient iron is taken to replace that lost through the activity of the hookworms, there may still be no evident symptoms.

If iron intake is insufficient, symptoms of iron deficiency anemia will gradually develop. Eosinophilia is variable, ranging up to 70 per cent.

Pathogenesis

Roche and Layrisse point out that in any carefully analyzed representative series of patients infected with hookworm, a significant negative correlation between worm burden and hemoglobin level can be demonstrated. When anemia is present, it is of the microcytic hypochromic type. The bone marrow is generally markedly hyperplastic, and there may be erythroid and myeloid hyperplasia of the spleen.

Radioisotopic measurements indicate a host blood loss in the order of 0.15 ml. per day per *Ancylostoma dudodenale* (0.26 ml. daily according to the measurements of Farid et al., 1965); this is considerably greater than the 0.03 ml. per day calculated for *Necator americanus*. Histological changes in the mucosa of the affected intestine appear to be minimal.

Flattening or atrophy of the intestinal villi has been noted on occasion, but more frequently capsule biopsies demonstrate a completely normal mucosal pattern. Malabsorption is apparently uncommon, and malnutrition does not seem to be characteristic of pure hookworm disease in areas where a good diet is available.

Emaciation, and mental and physical retardation frequently associated with this disease, are more properly ascribed to a combination of other nutritional and disease factors which are associated with hookworm anemia and are common in many endemic areas.

Treatment

Bephenium (Alcopara) is the most effective drug presently available for treatment of *Ancylostoma duodenale*. Its administration is simple, as pre-treatment preparation is unnecessary and post-treatment purging is contraindicated. It is administered in the morning on an empty stomach. The dose for both adults and children is a single 5-gm. packet of granules, shaken into one-half glass of water.

A light meal is allowed three hours later, and a second dose may be administered in mid-afternoon. Alternatively, a single daily dose may be given for four to seven days. Vomiting and diarrhea are occasional side effects of treatment. Mebendazole (Vermox) is effective in the treatment of both *Ancylostoma* and *Necator*.

It is administered orally at the rate of 100 mg. twice daily for three days, in both adults and children over 2 years of age. Pyrantel pamoate is likewise effective in the treatment of *Ancylostoma* infections. The dose employed is that used for treatment of ascariasis. Either mebendazole or pyrantel can be used in mixed ascaris-hookworm infections.

Cutaneous Larva Migrans

If man comes in contact with larvae of the dog hookworms *Ancylo-*

stoma braziliense or *A. caninum,* penetration of the skin may take place, but the larvae are then unable to complete their migratory cycle. Trapped larvae may survive for some weeks or even months, migrating through the subcutaneous tissues.

They may evoke a fairly severe reaction, forming serpiginous tunnels through the tissues, erythematous and sometimes vesicular at the advancing end, fading out and becoming dry and encrusted in the older portions. There is often intense pruritus, and scratching may lead to secondary bacterial invasion.

This syndrome is referred to as creeping eruption or as cutaneous larva migrans, to distinguish it from the visceral type of larva migrans discussed in other chapter of this book.

Treatment

The oral administration of thiabendazole, at the rate of 25 mg. per Kg. of body weight, twice daily for five days, is recommended for treatment of creeping eruption.

PHILIPPINE CAPILLARIASIS

This infection, which seems to be restricted to a small area in the Philippines, is caused by the roundworm *Capillaria philippinensis.* The illness is frequently protracted, and the fatality rate is high.

The adult worms are slender, approximately 4 to 5 mm. in length. They live in the intestinal mucosa, primarily in the jejunum, where they may occur in enormous numbers. The finding of larval stages, and of oviparous as well as larviparous females in the bowel, suggests that the parasite multiplies in the intestine and that overwhelming infections are the result of auto-infection.

Eggs voided by infected individuals, and measuring about 45 by 21 μm., develop outside the host and are ingested by fresh-water and brackish-water fish, in which larval stages have been found. The complete life cycle is unknown. Laboratory diagnosis is made by finding the characteristic eggs in the stool.

Symptomatology

Although asymptomatic or mildly symptomatic cases occur, many infected persons exhibit a rather characteristic clinical picture. Abdominal pain, borborygmus (gurgling) and diarrhea appear early.

The diarrhea may be protracted and may be accompanied by anorexia, nausea and vomiting, and hypotension. The patient may become cachectic, with generalized anasarca. Visible peristaltic waves may be seen over the distended abdomen.

Pathogenesis

A pronounced eosinophilia, surprisingly, does not seem to be a consistent feature of this disease. Hypoproteinemia; low blood calcium, potassium, and cholesterol levels; and other features of a protein-wasting enteropathy are encountered and are reflected in the pathological picture.

The villi are blunted, flattened or completely obliterated, with deepening of the crypts of Lieberki hn and an inflammatory submucosal infiltrate. Total thickness of the mucosa is generally reduced. These non-specific changes are seen in various malabsorption stages and have been mentioned in relation to giardiasis and coccidiosis.

Treatment

Mebendazole is the drug of choice for treatment of Philippine capillariasis. The recommended dosage is 200 mg. twice daily for 20 days. This may need to be repeated in some chronic cases. Thiabendazole has also proved effective but may need to be given for prolonged periods (25 mg. per Kg. twice daily for 30 days, followed by 1 gm. every other day for six months).

Protracted anthelmintic therapy may be essential to prevent recurrence of the disease; developmental forms in the mucosa may not be eliminated, and relapses are frequent. In management of the acute illness, fluid and electrolyte replacement and a high protein diet are important. A comprehensive review of Philippine capillariasis was published by Cross et al..

STRONGYLOIDES STERCORALIS

The temperature and moisture requirements of *Strongyloides stercoralis* during the free-living phase of its life cycle are similar to those of hookworm, and their geographical distribution is likewise similar. However, the incidence of strongyloidiasis is generally lower than that of hookworm disease.

A number of species of *Strongyloides* are known, and generally they are quite host-specific. Cats and dogs may both be infected with S. *stercoralis,* and human infection from a canine source has been reported. When environmental conditions are optimal, *Strongyloides* may exist for some time as a free-living nematode, completing two or more generations in this manner.

The adults of the free-living generations, like other soil nematodes, are very small, being only about 1 mm. in length. More frequently, perhaps, there is but a single free-living generation, producing rhabditiform larvae which transform into infective filariform larvae. The

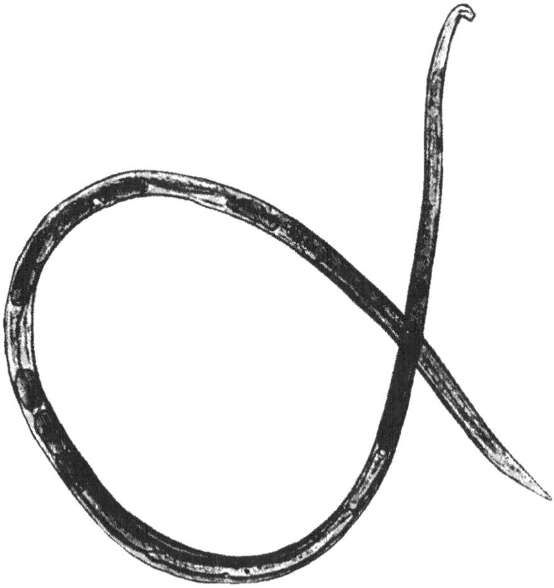

Figure 10.3: Strongyloides stercoralis, parasitic female.

filariform larvae are incapable of further development in the soil and must penetrate the skin of their host to continue the life cycle. Rhabditiform larvae which pass out of the host in the stools may also transform into filariform larvae directly, without developing into free-living adults.

Penetration through the skin and the subsequent migration through the lungs and eventually to the small intestine is similar to that seen with hookworms. The parasitic males are eliminated from the body early in the infection, if indeed they exist. It seems likely that the larvae, produced over a period of months, develop parthenogenetically. The females, which may attain a length of slightly over 2 mm., burrow into the mucosa of the intestinal tract, where they lay their eggs.

The eggs, similar in appearance to those of hookworms, hatch in the mucosa and liberate rhabditiform larvae, which make their way to the lumen of the intestine. The larvae may feed and molt once before being passed in the feces. When they molt within the intestinal tract, they usually retain their rhabditiform characteristics but may transform into infective filariform larvae.

If filariform larvae are formed, they may penetrate immediately into the wall of the gut and enter the blood stream, where they begin the same type of migratory cycle as the larvae which penetrate the skin from the soil. Diagnosis is by demonstration of the characteristic larvae in the stools. Larvae resemble those of hookworms but can be differentiated from them by their possession of a very short buccal cavity.

In severe diarrhea, the embryonated eggs may be present in the stools and can be differentiated from hookworm eggs by the fact that they always contain well-developed larvae. If larvae are scarce, it may be necessary to concentrate the stool.

The larvae may be concentrated with zinc sulfate, but a more efficient means of recovery is the Baermann technique, described in other chapter of this book. Duodenal aspiration will occasionally reveal larvae when the stools remain consistently negative, and the string-capsule method gives good results.

A characteristic x-ray picture is reported in severe strongyloidiasis, with loss of mucosal pattern, rigidity and tubular narrowing.

Symptomatology

Lesions resembling the ground itch of hookworm infection are sometimes seen following penetration of the skin by *Strongyloides* larvae. Pneumonitis may be produced by the larvae, but as in hookworm infection is generally less severe than in ascariasis. The adult worms in the intestine may give rise to no demonstrable symptoms or to moderate or severe diarrhea. A malabsorption syndrome with steatorrhea is described by O'Brien.

Garcia et al. consider malabsorption to be characteristic only of those cases in which there is severe protein malnutrition, to be reversible if the malnutrition is corrected even without elimination of the parasites, and to persist after treatment of the infection if the malnutrition remains uncorrected. Ulceration of the intestinal mucosa may give rise to symptoms resembling those of duodenal ulcer, sometimes with melena and anemia, or ulcerative colitis.

Hyperinfection may lead to severe debilitation or death. It is probable that such heavy internal auto-infections occur primarily in patients whose resistance is lowered by intercurrent disease or immunosuppressive therapy. Such infections may be generalized, with larvae found in virtually all parts of the body, or they may affect primarily the gastrointestinal tract, the central nervous system or the lungs.

Because of auto-infection by larvae which transform to the filariform stage within the gut, strongyloidiasis may persist for many years in nonendemic areas. Gill and Bell report a series of some 600 British former prisoners of war, interned in the Far East during World War II, all of whom were repatriated by 1949. Eighty-eight (15 per cent) were still found to be infected with *Strongyloides* some 30 years after leaving the endemic area.

Gastrointestinal symptoms were noted in only 5 per cent of those infected, but 84 per cent exhibited a characteristic dermal lesion, similar to cutaneous larva migrans caused by dog hookworms. The strongyloid track advances at a much faster rate (5 to 10 cm. per hour) than that of the dog hookworm larva in man, and for this reason the lesion has been referred to as *larva currens*.

Pathogenesis

While local lesions occur on penetration of the larvae into the skin, these are generally minor; chronic cutaneous larval migration (larva currens) is perhaps more common than has been appreciated in the past. More severe skin lesions, including giant hives, are rare.

The pulmonary response to larval migration is generally not severe; in heavy infections there may be a patchy pneumonitis, and larvae may be found in the sputum. The adult female worms may be found in all parts of the intestinal tract, although they are most common in the jejunum.

The young female worms lodge in the intestinal crypts, and as they mature they penetrate the mucosa. They remain embedded in the mucosa, laying eggs from which hatch rhabditiform larvae that migrate to the intestinal lumen. An inflammatory infiltration of the mucosa may lead to such an x-ray picture as is seen in Figure elsewhere in this chpater.

Heavy infections can produce extensive ulceration and sloughing of the mucosa, and fibrosis and inflammatory infiltration of the submucosal layers. In the more severe infections, transformation of rhabditiform to filariform larvae seems to proceed very rapidly, and filariform larvae may be found in many organs and tissues.

Eosinophilia of 10 to 40 per cent is common; in occasional patients it will be higher. Lack of eosinophilic response is occasionally seen; this generally occurs in overwhelming infections. Early in the infection there may be a polymorphonuclear leukocytosis.

Epidemiology

As mentioned previously, strongyloidiasis occurs in much the same tropical and subtropical areas of relatively heavy rainfall as does hookworm infection, though prevalence rates for the former disease seem generally lower. It differs importantly from hookworm in that while the infection will die out over a period of some years in persons with hookworm infection who have moved from an endemic area, strongyloidiasis may persist by virtue of auto-infection, and prolonged absence from an endemic area is no guarantee of freedom from infection.

While percutaneous infection is the rule, Brown and Girardeau report the recovery of larvae of *Strongyloides* from the milk of a nursing mother in Zaire, in an area where the prevalence of strongyloidiasis was found to be 34 per cent in infants under 200 days of age.

In this study, the species of *Strongyloides* not only found in this one mother, but prevalent in the community, was *S. fuelleborni,* a parasite of African monkeys known to infect humans also in the Central African Republic, Cameroun and Ethiopia.

Treatment

Thiabendazole is the drug of choice in treatment of strongyloidiasis. The recommended dose is 25 mg. per Kg. of body weight, twice daily for two days. Nausea, vomiting and vertigo are frequent side effects of this drug.

Renal failure is a relative contraindication to the use of thiabendazole, and Boyd et al. suggest the use of mebendazole, 100 mg. twice daily for three days, in such cases. In patients who are taking immunosuppressive medications, treatment for strongyloidiasis must be prolonged, and may be unsuccessful.

TRICHURIS TRICHIURA

The whipworm, *Trichuris trichiura,* has a worldwide distribution but is more common in tropical areas and in regions where sanitation is poor. The common name of whipworm is most descriptive, the thick posterior part of the body forming the stock, and the long thin anterior portion the lash.

The generic name *(Trichuris* = thread tail) is less fortunate, having been applied under the impression that the attenuated portion of the worm was its posterior end. Subsequently the name *Trichocephalus* was given to the genus and has been adopted by some workers. It is much more apt but unfortunately should not be used, as the name *Trichuris* has priority.

The adult worms are from 3 to 5 cm. in length. As is usual among the nematodes, the females are larger than the males. The thin, almost colorless, anterior three fifths of the body consists of the much reduced esophagus. The expanded posterior part of the worm is pinkish gray in color and contains the intestine and reproductive organs.

Infection is acquired by ingestion of the fully embryonated eggs.

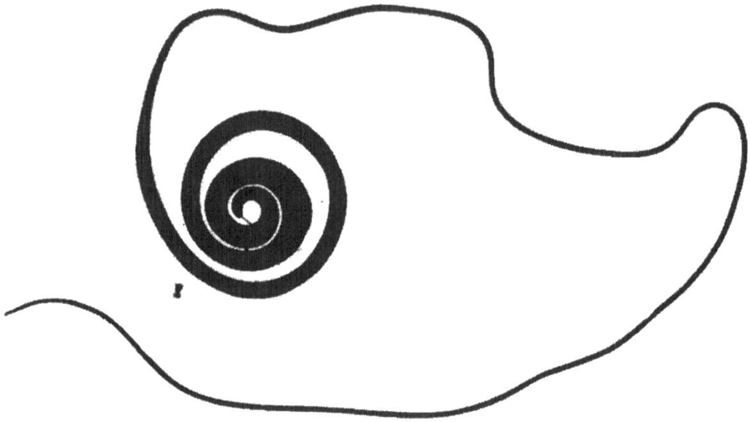

Figure 10.4: Trichuris trichiura, adult male.

These are passed in the unsegmented condition and require a period of 10 days or more outside the body to reach the infective stage. The shell is digested in the small intestine, where the larvae lodge temporarily.

After a period of growth, larvae pass to the cecal area, where they attach themselves permanently with their attenuated anterior ends embedded in the mucosa. In heavy infections, worms may be found as far down as the rectum.

Diagnosis is by demonstration of the characteristic barrel-shaped eggs in the feces. Each female worm produces from 3000 to 7000 eggs daily. The eggs measure 50 to 54 microns in length, with refractile prominences (usually referred to as polar plugs) at either end. The zincsulfate flotation method is extremely efficient in demonstrating them.

Symptomatology

Light whipworm infections are usually asymptomatic. Heavier infections may be characterized by abdominal pain and distention, a bloody or mucoid diarrhea, tenesmus, weight loss and weakness. Prolapse of the rectum is occasionally seen, usually in children with heavy infections. Worms may be visible on the prolapsed, edematous rectum. Anemia and a moderate eosinophilia may be seen in heavy infections.

Pathogenesis

The anterior ends of the worms, interlaced in the colonic mucosa, apparently produce little damage to the host unless present in large numbers. Some authorities consider that bacterial invasion of the mucosa is facilitated by the penetration of the worms. Appendicitis, brought about by blockage of the lumen of that organ by worms, has been frequently reported. Edema of the rectum, produced by numbers of worms embedded in that area, is responsible for rectal prolapse. The blood loss per worm is apparently slight.

Layrisse et al., using radioisotope techniques, calculated it to be approximately 0.005 ml. of blood per worm daily and estimated that infections by 800 worms or more are necessary to produce anemia in children. They did not consider it likely that adults would become anemic from whipworm infections.

Treatment

Mebendazole (Vermox) is the first drug to be relatively effective against *Trichuris*. At a dose of 100 mg. twice daily for four days (children and adults), approximately two thirds of infected patients will be cured; the remainder will exhibit an egg reduction of approximately 90 per cent.

In African children with heavy worm burdens, Scragg and Proctor found that a single course of mebendazole (100 mg. twice daily for three days) eradicated the infection in 43 per cent of patients; a repeat course of treatment increased the cure rate to 74 per cent. The same authors obtained an 88 per cent cure rate with 100 mg. of mebendazole twice daily for six days, and all patients were cured after two such courses.

They suggest that in these diarrheic patients, loperamide hydrochloride (Imodium) helps by increasing contact time between drug and parasites. Both drugs were well tolerated. Noting the prohibitive cost of treatment of all children found to have eggs of *Trichuris* in stool examination, Nagalingam et al. suggest proctoscopic examination, and treatment of those in whom worms are found by this means.

***Trichostrongylus* Species**

The genus *Trichostrongylus* contains a number of species that are primarily parasites of herbivores and are found throughout the world. Human infections have been reported on occasion from many regions and are accidental. *Trichostrongylus orientalis* is fairly common in Japan, Korea, China including Taiwan, and Armenia; a number of other species infecting humans have also been reported from the Soviet Union.

The larvae develop in the soil but do not penetrate the skin; they are ingested with contaminated vegetation. Trichostrongyles are related to the hookworms, and the adults are rather similar in appearance.

The various species reported from man are smaller than the hookw-orms, but their eggs are larger. Identification of the various species of *Trichostrongylus* from the eggs is difficult, but differentiation of the eggs from those of hookworm can be readily accomplished. Trichostrongyle eggs are symmetrical and thin shelled, and differ from hookworm eggs in their size and in having more pointed ends. The size range is from 73 to 95 microns in length and 40 to 50 microns in breadth.

Symptomatology and Pathogenesis

The larvae attach themselves to the intestinal mucosa and grow to adulthood in three to four weeks. They ingest blood, but only in rather heavy infections is the blood loss of clinical significance. Heavily infected patients may become emaciated.

Treatment

Light infections do not warrant treatment. Thiabendazole, in the dosage used in ascariasis, hookworm infection and strongyloidiasis, is effective in treatment of trichostrongyliasis. Bephenium is apparently effective in a single oral dose of 5 gm.

LARVAL NEMATODES ACQUIRED FROM FISH

Anisakiasis

Marine fish frequently are infected with roundworm larvae belonging to the genera *Anisakis, Phocanema* or related genera. In the area of the North Sea, around Japan and on both coasts of the United States, infections have been reported following consumption of such fish, either raw or pickled. The worms may cause acute nausea and vomiting or may penetrate into the wall of the digestive tract, where they give rise to eosinophilic granulomas in the stomach or small intestine.

These infections are frequently misdiagnosed as gastric or duodenal ulcer, carcinoma, appendicitis or other surgical conditions, depending upon their location. Granulomatous tissue obtained at surgery contains nematode larvae which in most instances appear to belong to the genus *Anisakis*. The adult worms occur in marine mammals, which acquire the infection by eating fish.

As far as is known, the larvae do not mature in humans. The disease in humans is accompanied by a low grade eosinophilia, usually less than 10 per cent; occult blood is generally present in gastric juice or stools. A presumptive diagnosis can be made on the basis of the patient's food habits.

Definitive diagnosis rests upon the demonstration of worms in specimens obtained at surgery. Prevention of the disease is by thorough cooking of marine food fishes. A comprehensive review of anisakiasis in Japan, including clinical aspects and treatment, is given by Oshima.

11

Parasitic Arthropods

Members of the phylum Arthropoda possess an exoskeleton with jointed appendages. The body is divided into segments that are variously grouped into functional units such as head, thorax, and abdomen. The digestive tract is complete, and the circulatory system forms a hemocoel that is the body cavity.

The coelom is reduced. Respiration is accomplished by tracheae, gills, book lungs, or body surface. Malpighian tubules serve as excretory organs in most species. The brain is dorsal, whereas the main nerve cord is ventral in position. Paired ganglia usually occur in each somite, and eyes are simple or compound. Sexes are separate.

Some crickets puncture stems of raspberry plants and lay their eggs within the pith. Are these crickets more parasitic than those grasshoppers and crickets that simply chew the stems? No more forceful way to emphasize the difficulty of defining "parasite" can be found than to select a textbook on entomology and to read about the multitudinous methods by which insects have solved the problem of obtaining food.

Among the most destructive plant pests are the chinchbugs, plant lice, mealybugs, and other Hemiptera whose sucking mouth parts, rapid rate of reproduction, and general behavior combine to effect a devastating invasion of plants the world over. But are they not simply plant feeders instead of parasites? The ovipositor of the female of many leaf hoppers is adapted for lacerating plant tissues, and eggs are deposited in longitudinal rows on the stems or under the leaf sheath. Certainly, this habit is as parasitic as the habits of lice.

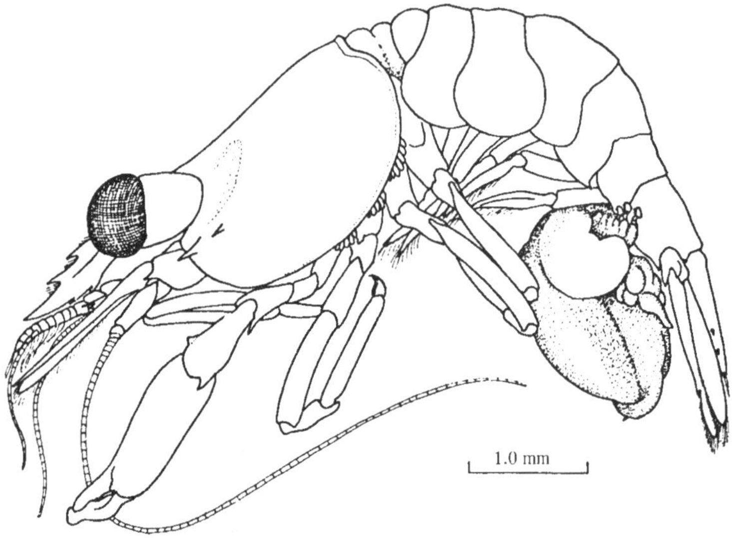

Figure 11.1: Mesophryxus s ventralis, a parasitic isopod belonging to the family Bopyridae. clinging to the ventral surface of the posterior abdomen of a shrimp.

Immune responses of animals to arthropods have been discussed in detail by Gaafar, and the following statements occur in his summary.

> "Reactions of the skin and lymph nodes during primary and subsequent infestations ... [are] physiological means of protection of the host against further invasions with arthropod parasites of the same and possibly closely related species. It is apparent that the role of antibodies in the serum of parasitized or immune animals is not well understood. Immunoglobulins of the precipitating and nonprecipitating classes are apparently found in parasitized animals but no information is available on the types involved."'

Immunity against arthropods involves various physiologic and anatomic characteristics of the epidermis, mucous membranes, and skin. These characteristics are variable, may be adaptive, and should be considered whenever immunologic problems of these hosts arise.

No arthropod antigens in chemically pure form have so far been identified, and the role of antibodies in the serum of parasitized or immune animals is not well understood. Precipitating and nonprecipitating immunoglobulins apparently occur in parasitized animals, but the types are unknown. Some general references are Beesley for control of arthropods, Askew' for parasitic insects, Kabata for crustacea as enemies of fishes, and Salt" for cellular defense reactions of insects.

SUBCLASS MALACOSTRACA

Order Isopoda

These crustaceans possess bodies that are usually flattened dorsoventrally, without a carapace, with sessile eyes, and with a short abdomen the segments of which are often partly fused. Each of the seven characteristically free segments of the thorax bears a pair of legs.

Parasitic species are abundant, and they favor free-living crustaceans and fish as hosts. Most parasitic species have been found in ocean water, although a few freshwater forms have been described. For parasites of decapod crustacea, see Sprague and Couch.'

Suborder Flabellifera

In the family Cymothoidae, a whole range of types exists, with gradations from actively swimming predatory species to parasites that, as adults, are permanently fixed to the host and are incapable of locomotion. The free-swimming species may be exemplified by *Cirolana borealis,* which possesses powerful biting jaws.

The cirolanid isopods are mainly scavengers rather than predators, but they sometimes attack a cod that is caught on a hook or is otherwise at a disadvantage, and gnaw their way into the body, so that the fish is soon nothing but skin and bones. These parasites have even been known to attack humans.

Cymothoa and *Nerocila* represent the genera of isopods that, as adults, cling to the gills or skin of their fish hosts by means of strong hook-claws. *Lirooeca convexa* presumably begins its life cycle as a free-living planktonic individual. Parasitic males enter gill chambers of the host fish, *Chloroscombrus orqueta,* whereas females, probably commensal, may enter the oral cavity of the same fish.

It is not known, however, whether females enter the mouth directly or move there from the gill chamber. Only the adult male, attached to gill filaments, shows evidence of causing direct damage. Other flabelliferan isopods (families Corallanidae and Excorallanidae) are also parasites of fish.

Sexual dimorphism is the rule among parasitic isopods, and the phenomenon of *protandrous hermaphroditism* occurs among the flabelliferans. This phenomenon starts when the parasite first attaches itself as a functional male to a host. Later, the male becomes a female, develops a brood pouch, and produces eggs.

The presence of a female on a fish inhibits further development of the male toward the female phase. The nature of this influence is unknown, but it has been proved experimentally with *Anilocra physodes,* an external parasite that can be removed from the host. Since both male and female are temporary parasites, sexual dimorphism cannot be attributed to the parasitic mode of life.

The protandrous male is not easily recognized, and a young, sexually immature female has probably often been mistaken for the male. Any given species of cymothoid usually has many favored hosts, and it may also be found free in the plankton. Host-specificity, therefore, is often not marked.

Suborder Gnathiidea

Another family of isopods, also containing only temporary parasites, is the Gnathiidae. Unlike those that are parasitic as adults, the gnathiids are parasitic as larvae. These larvae are temporary dwellers on fish and feed exclusively on blood. Adult gnathiids may be found in plankton or in mud dredged from the bottom.

Morphologic differences among the larvae, adult males, and adult females are so pronounced that each type was originally described *as a* distinct genus. Adults of this family do not feed; they possess neither a mouth nor a gut, but the larvae attach themselves to the skin and gills of fish and gorge themselves with blood.

After three larval phases, each phase separated by a molt, the adult stage is reached. The male gnathiid uses its powerful mandibles for digging a burrow into the mud at intertidal levels, and into this burrow the male and female withdraw to end their lives in private.

Suborder Epicaridea

Contrary to the habits of the cymothoids and the gnathiids, which are temporary parasites at either adult or larval stages, the suborder Epicaridea consists of isopods parasitic in both larval and adult stages. This suborder is divided into two superfamilies, the Bopyrina and the Cryptoniscina, both of which are parasitic on crustacea.

Epicarids are particularly interesting because their life cycle involves two hosts and because sexes may be determined epigamic ally, that is, after fertilization, depending on host environmental factors. The first epicarid larva resembles a small isopod and possesses piercing and sucking mouth parts and claw-like appendages with which it attaches itself to the surface of freeswimming copepods.

This kind of larva is called an *epicaridium*, and while it remains on its copepod host, it undergoes six successive molts and changes progressively into two distinct larval stages known as the *microniscus*

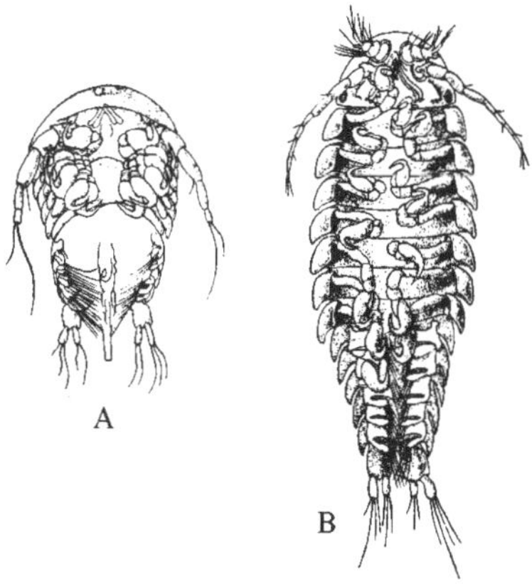

Figure 11.2: A, Cepon elegans, microniscus larva.
B, Portunion kossmanni, cryptoniscus larva.

and the *cryptoniscus* stages. On reaching the latter stage of development, the parasite leaves its copepod host, proceeds to the sandy or muddy seabottom, and there seeks a free-living crustacean, for example, a crab or a shrimp, into whose branchial chamber or brood pouch it enters.

Within this second host, the parasitic cryptoniscium stage develops in one of two directions, according to whether it belongs to the superfamily Bopyrina or to the superfamily Cryptoniscina. If the cryptoniscus larva is a bopyrine, it molts, thereby loses most of its pleopods, and is then known as a *bopyridium*.

This larval stage initially always develops into a female, but successive larvae, either attached to the same host or to the female parasite, all become males. *Stegophryxus hyptius*, a bopyrid ectoparasite on the abdomen of the hermit crab, *Pagurus longicarpu.s,* seeks the definitive host as a sexually undifferentiated and sexually undetermined cryptoniscus larva.

Larvae that settle directly on the host develop into females, and those that attach themselves to a female bopyrid develop into males. *Bopyrus squillarum* lives in the gill cavity of the prawn, *Leander serratus,* and it causes a large swelling on one side of the host carapace. The parasite has a flat and distorted body, with an enormous mass of eggs on the ventral side of the female.

The mouth parts form a short beak with which the parasite sucks the blood of its host. The bopyrine isopods, especially those of the endoparasitic family Entoniscidae, frequently cause complete or partial atrophy of host gonads. *Pinnotherion vermiforme* occurs inside the thorax

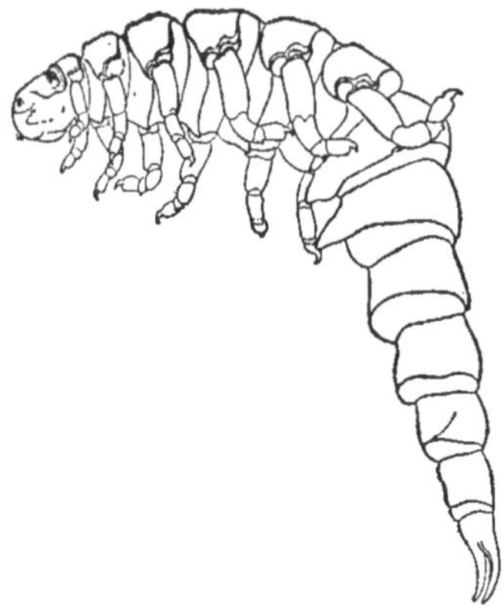

Figure 11.3: Pinnotherion vermiforme, male, showing characteristic ventral curvature.

and abdomen of the pea crab, *Pinnotheres* pisum—itself a parasite of the clam, *Mytilus edulus*. Adult male isopods are found free in the host body. They pass from their normal position among the pleopods of the female through a break in the host cuticle.

Female entoniscids undergo a pronounced morphologic change, and the surface of their pleopods becomes corrugated and filled with numerous blood lacunae that serve as respiratory organs. In the same female, the oostegites form a brood pouch, part of which appears as a hood around the head.

Epicaridian larvae are expelled from this pouch through a secondary opening. Probably all parasitic isopods of the superfamily Cryptoniscina are protandrous hermaphrodites. Males become mature in the cryptoniscan stage. The life history of this group starts in the same manner as that of the bopyrids, and it progresses similarly to the cryptoniscus larval stage.

From here on, the life history is different. On entering the branchial chamber or the brood pouch of' crabs, larvae become protandrous hermaphrodites of a delayed type because males and females are morphologically distinct. An excessive production of eggs causes the gravid female to undergo morphologic, and presumably physiologic, degeneration.

Order Amphipoda

This order is characterized as follows: body often laterally compressed, absence of' a carapace, abdomen flexed ventrally between the third and fourth somites, telson usually distinct, habitat usually marine. The most commonly seen, but not the most common, species are those called "sand fleas." Although many amphipods are associated in a casual manner with marine in vertebrates, few species are parasitic. Some members of the family Gammaridae have suctorial mouth parts and lead a semiparasitic life.

A number of forms burrow into other animals in order to obtain food. The order Amphipoda may be divided into the following suborders, of which the first is the largest: Gammaridea, Hyperiidea, Ingolfiellidea, and Caprellidea.

PARASITIC CAPRELLIDEANS

Five genera of amphipods living on various Cetacea belong to this family. The semiparasites have dorsoventrally flattened bodies, reduced abdomens, and claws on their legs; they cling to the skins of their hosts. *Cyamus,* the whale "louse", is the best known, and it has a wide geographic range. Only a few reports have been made on cyamids of the small, toothed cetaceans commonly known as dolphins and porpoises.

Cyamid mouth parts are not adapted for sucking blood; instead, the animals probably feed on mucus, bacterial and algal growth, and on skin. These amphipods are unique among crustacean parasites in that they are unable to swim at any period of their life history.

The young settle down near their parents, and masses of individuals of all sizes may be seen clinging closely together on the skin of' their host, often intermingled with barnacles.

Figure 11.4: Cyamus ceti, the whale loose.

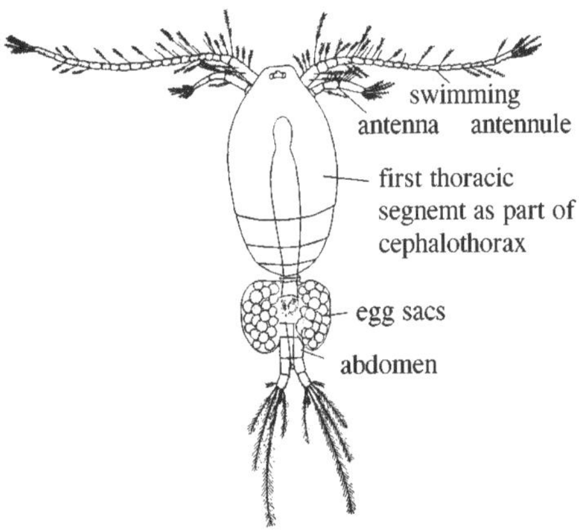

Figure 11.5: Cyclops.

SUBCLASS COPEPODA

A fine plankton net towed through almost any natural body of fresh- or saltwater soon collects multitudes of' organisms whose animal components consist chiefly of' minute crustaceans. The most abundant kinds of crustaceans in such hauls are usually copepods, whose bodies furnish the major basic food supply for all larger aquatic animals.

The best-known freshwater member of the subclass Copepoda is *Cyclops* (order Cyclopoida), which serves as the intermediate host for several helminth parasites of man and of other vertebrates. *Cyclops* is often called a "water flea."

Most copepods are free-living, but many are parasitic, and like so many other parasitic groups, they range in habits from the most casual and temporary contact with a host to a rigid and permanent attachment as adults or larvae within the host body. Most groups of aquatic, especially marine, animals may serve as hosts for at least one species, of' copepod during part of' its life *cycle.*

Echinoderms, annelids, ascidians, molluscs, arthropods, fish, and whales are universally invaded. The parasite may appear to be practically identical to free-living species, or it may be so modified as an adult that, were it not for the larval stages, one would hardly be able to determine even the phylum to which the copepod belongs.

In general, copepods have a high degree of host-specificity. The sexes in copepods are nearly always separate. The male is usually much smaller than the female. The pair of ovisacs ("egg string") is usually conspicuous. Some groups, for example, Harpacticoida, have only one sac. The female of *Chondracanthus merluccii* is 12,000 times larger

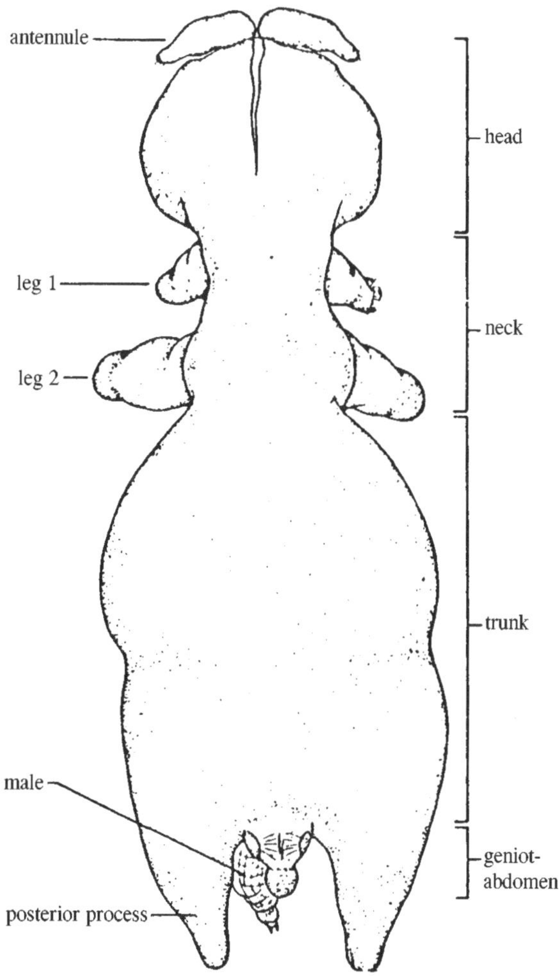

Figure 11.6: Acanthochondria coronet, tamale with attached male, dorsal view.

than the male, but this sexual dimorphism is extreme. Hermaphroditism is rare. Some parasitic species appear to have several breeding seasons each year. In some instances, especially in all the Chondracanthidac and in some of the Lernaeopodidae, the males are sessile on the females.

In such instances, the male loses the power of locomotion on reaching maturity. In still other species, one act of copulation is apparently sufficient to fertilize the female for life, and the male is then not found in persistent association with the female.

The embryos remain attached to the external opening of the oviducts and enclosed in the ovisac until they hatch, a process often requiring several weeks. *Nauplii* larvae are, in the first stage, equipped with three pairs of appendages, one or more pairs of caudal setae (balancers), and two distal antennulary setae.

The three appendages represent the first and second antennae and the mandibles of the adult. Many parasitic forms hatch at a later stage, with more appendages. The endoparasitic copepod, *Mytilicola intestinalis,* parasitizes the edible mussel, *Mytilus edulis,* in British waters and retards the release of host gametes. Variations in host biochemical composition are closely related to the breeding season.

Williams has shown that the biochemical constitution of the copepod also changes with the season and is correlated to its life history." Williams found that carbohydrates and lipids formed important sources of energy, but protein levels were reduced as compared with levels in free-living species.

Copepod larvae normally pass through six nauplius stages (the last three often called "metanauplius") and five copepodid stages, but development may be abbreviated, especially in parasitic species. Copepods of this order are found on freshwater and marine fishes and belong to ten families.

They apparently do not require an intermediate host. The male dies after mating, but may be found holding to the genital segment of the female or lying in the host's cephalic canal. In the family Chondracanthidae, the male is a dwarf symbiont of the female and holds on to one of two vermiform processes on her trunk near the genital somite. Adults attached to fishes are thus all females. For details, see

Order Cyclopoida

Ergasilus is a genus comprising at least 25 species of parasites. The body is similar to that of a free-living copepod. It narrows posteriorly. The abdomen has 4 segments in the male and 3 in the female. After copulation, the male dies, and the female becomes attached to the gills of its freshwater fish host by large clasper-like claws.

Chondracanthus is common on gills and in the mouths of various fish. The female body of C. C. gibbosus within the gill cavity of the marine angler or fishing "frog," *Lophius piscatorius, is* extended into paired lobes and gives the parasite a curious, irregular shape: its appendages are reduced.

The mouth is flanked by sickle-shaped jaws, and the whole body may reach a length of about 2.5 cm. At the posterior end of the female body, just at the point where the egg masses are attached, close inspection reveals a minute, maggot-like creature clinging by means of hook-like antennae. This is the male that is attached, like a secondary parasite, to its enormously larger mate.

Order Notodelphyoida

Notodelphyidae consists of copepods that almost universally inhabit the body cavities of tunicates. The group is a well-defined natural unit because of the preservation of fundamental characteristics in spite of' a high degree of adaptive radiation.

The family is characterized both by a prehensile, modified, articulated hook that is the terminal member of the second antennae and by the development of' a brood sac enclosed within the body. The life cycle probably involves five naupliar stages and six copepodid (subadult) stages.

The second copepodid stage is the infective one, but the sequence of developmental events and the possible metamorphoses in the life histories are almost entirely unknown.

Xenocoeloma (order not definitely known) represents an extreme type of modification involving host tissue. This genus is parasitic on marine annelids, and the adult parasite is so grossly modified that it consists only of' hermaphroditic gonads and some muscles.

The mass is enclosed in a cylindrical outgrowth of the host epithelium that contains a gut-like prolongation of the host coelom. The life history is incompletely known, but the nauplius that emerges from the eggs resembles that of the monstrillids in the absence of digestive organs. The manner of access to the host has, unfortunately, never been observed.

Order Caligoida

The Caligidae is probably the most widely distributed family of copepods parasitic on fish, and it probably contains the largest number of'species, for example, *Caligus* and *Lepeophtheirus*. The family Chondracanthidae, however, contains a greater number of genera.

Caligus is ectoparasitic, chiefly on fish, has a suctorial mouth tube, and retains the power of swimming in the adult stage. The parasites possess two semicircular structures on the frontal margin of the cephalic shield. These structures are probably sensory, rather than attachment devices. *Caligus* does not always remain on one host. It is the most abundant copepod genus parasitic on fishes.

Dinemoura producta is common on the great basking shark, is similar in general appearance to *Caligus,* and has the same structures as does *Cyclops,* but with many modifications related to a parasitic

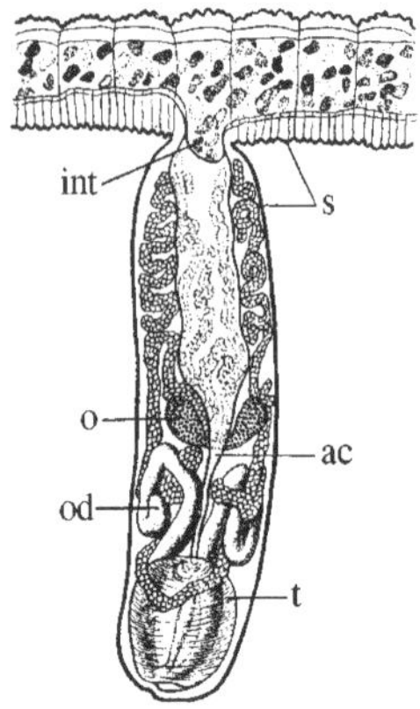

Figure 11.7: Xenocoeloma brumpti C and M, section of' the parasite and the annelid host, ac, Axial cavity formed by the host's coelom. int, Host's gut. od, Oviduct, o, Ovary. s, Skin of both the host and the parasite. t, Testis.

habit. Respiration in copepods is accomplished by a diffusion of gases through the body surface. Obviously, the surface-volume ratio is of vital significance. *Dinemoura* is about 2 cm long, whereas *Cyclops* is only about 2 mm long.

One, therefore, has a mass about a thousand times greater than that of the other, but if its shape were identical to that of *Cyclops,* the external surface of *Dinemoura* would be increased only about a hundred times. Even taking into account the more sendentary existence of the parasitic species, there would not be sufficient surface for respiration.

These considerations probably explain the existence, in *Dinemoura,* of a number of flattened lobes projecting from the dorsal surface of the thoracic segments. Trailing behind the body of the female is a pair of egg strings that may be as many as four times the length of the body.

Lernaeocera, often called the "*gill maggot*", is commonly seen attached to the gills of marine cod, and its bloated, S-shaped and bloodred body looks much more like a worm than it does a crustacean. The larval nauplius stage (unsegmented, three pairs of legs) proves its kinship with the arthropods.

After a free-living period of growth, including several molts, the nauplius is transformed into a "cyclops" or "chalimus" stage, when it becomes parasitic on the gills of certain flatfish, for example, *Pleuronectes,* by means of suctorial mouth parts accompanied by a reduction of its limbs.

The chalimus attaches itself to the host, first by the second antennae, then by a chitinous secretion that is extruded as a laterally flattened thread extending into the gill tissue. This stage is followed by a resumption of the power of movement when the parasite leaves its host and, for a time, lives a free-swimming, adult, sexually mature existence similar to that of *Cyclops*.

At this time, fertilization of the eggs takes place, and the development of the male ceases. The female, however, now seeks a new host, generally a member of the cod family, for example, *Gadus merlangus,* and again, the gills are particularly attractive to the parasite.

The anterior end of the female is buried into the host tissue, and it becomes curiously modified to form a branched anchor resembling short roots. The genital somites become enlarged and vermiform, and the egg mass appears as a cluster of tightly coiled filaments. In proportion, the appendages of the thorax become minute and nonfunctioning.

Salmincola salmonea, the salmon gill maggot, is a common and widespread copepod parasite of the Atlantic salmon *(Salmo salar)*. The mature female parasite, when attached to a gill filament of its host, "somewhat resembles a gymnast hanging from a vertical bar. Attachment to the gill filament is effected by means of 'a secreted "bulla," which is applied to the gill surface.

A thin sheet of living gill tissue partly covers the bulla. A pair of prehensile maxillipeds lies behind an oral cone, and from the sides of the cephalon, the maxillary "arms" (second maxillae) extend and converge on the bulla to which they are permanently fixed. The thorax bears no appendages. The paired egg sacs measure 4 to 11 mm in length. The life history of this copepod has been described by Friends and is used here to exemplify the life history of the group.

Figure elsewhere in this chapter illustrates details of external anatomy of the related genus *Achtheres*. During the first river phase of the fish, and the first sea phase, totalling from two-plus years to seven-plus years, the salmon is not attacked by gill maggots, although it acquires sea lice.

At the beginning of the second river phase, the sea lice are lost, and the maiden fish acquires larval gill maggots, which swim from beneath the gill covers of other and older fish. In the fall, the host reenters the sea, and during its sojourn of up to two years in marine waters, its copepods thrive and grow, but do not breed.

When the salmon reenter the rivers, the copepod parasites begin to breed. The first copepodid larvae of *Salmincola salmonea* may live free for up to six days, but when they come into contact with the gills of a salmon, they attach themselves "by means of a button and thread" and

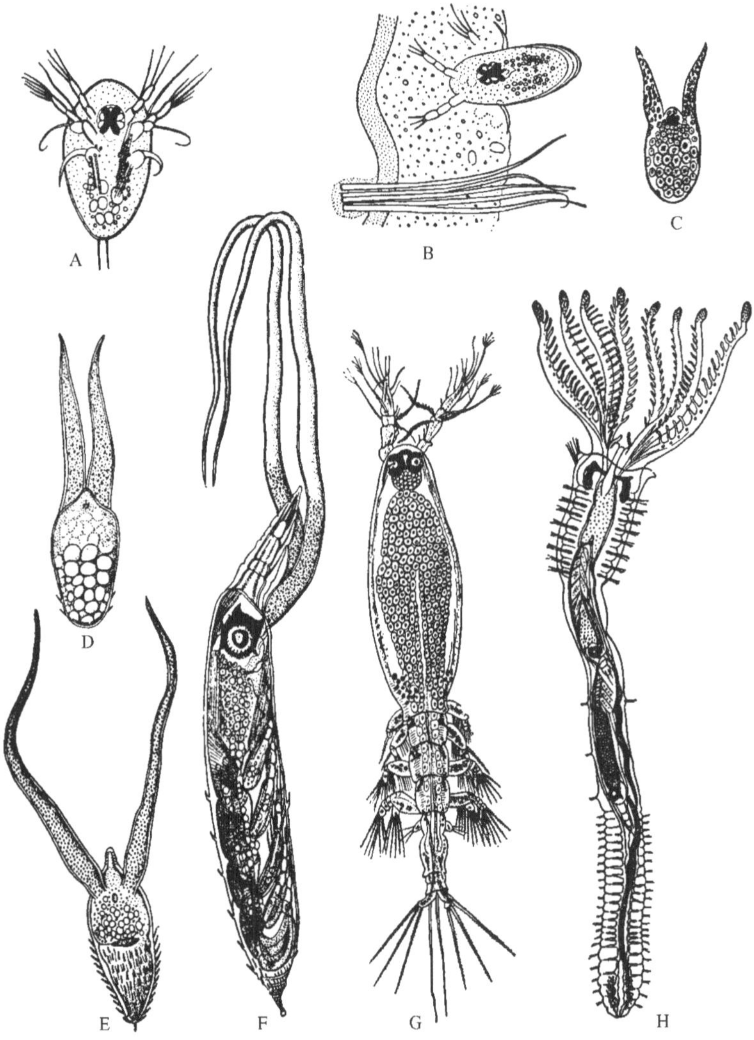

Figure 11.8: Haemocera dance (Clap). A, Nauplius. B, Nauplius in the act of penetrating into the body of its host. C to F, Successive larval stages showing the development of the appendages and also of the spinous sheath enclosing the larva. F, Fully formed copepodid. G, Adult female copepod deyoid of a mouth. H, Annelid with two copepodid larvae in its coelomic cavity

molt to become the second copepodid larvae. The next molt is followed by the sexually mature male or the first stage female, both of which may move freely over the gill surface, or they may attach themselves by means of chelate appendages. During this stage, copulation takes place and the male disappears.

Meanwhile, the frontal gland in the female has been elaborating the attachment bulla, which is planted on the gill tissue in its final position. The female then molts, the distal ends of each second maxilla are forced as plugs into corresponding sockets in the bulla, and permanent attachment is achieved.

The female then grows to mature size. Development to this stage requires about five or six months. One female may produce two or more generations of larvae. *Salmincola californiensis* is a parasite of juvenile sockeye salmon, *Oncorhynchus uerka,* and shows a site preference that differs with the size of the host.

On small fish, the parasites are most abundant in the region of the pectoral and pelvic fins, whereas on larger fish, they are most common in the branchial cavity. Damage to host tissue involves injury to gills, skin, muscle, and bone. The copepods may even burrow through the body wall and may enter viscera.

Order Monstrilloida

The Monstrillidae are copepods that are free-living as adults, but are parasitic during the intermediate stages in the blood vessels of various polychaete worms or in the body cavity of prosobranch snails. The nauplius of *Haemocera* hatches without a mouth or a gut, and it burrows into the body of its host, discards its chitinous exoskeleton, and loses its limbs.

By the time it reaches the host body cavity, it consists only of a naked mass of embryonic cells, which then become surrounded by a thin cuticle and develop a pair of long, flexible processes that apparently represent antennae. The antennae absorb nutrients. Food thus taken lasts the entire remaining life cycle, throughout which no functional mouth parts are present.

The mass of parasitic cells within the host gradually develops mature organs. The adult bores its way outside by means of rows of hook-like spines surrounding the pointed posterior end of the sac. On reaching the surface, the enclosing membrane bursts, and the adult parasite is free and looks like *Cyclops.*

The animal thus passes its whole life cycle without a gut, and between the two free-swimming stages, one at each end of its life, it

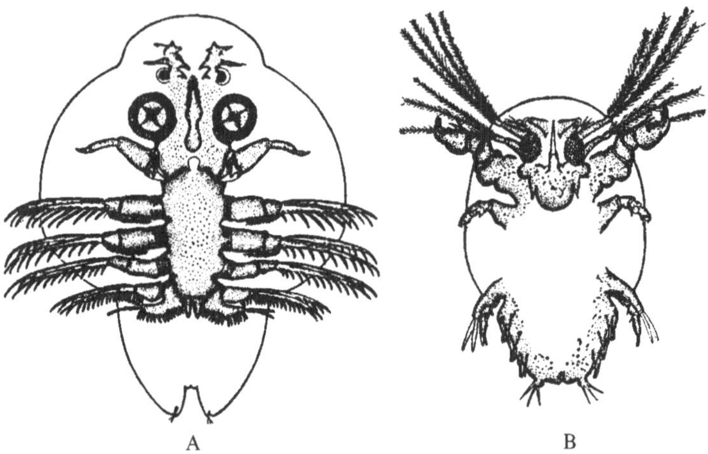

Figure 11.9: Argulus. A, Ventral view of the female. a, Newly hatched larva.

exists as a bag of parasitic cells absorbing nourishment from the internal fluids of its host.

Further details about parasitic copepods may be found in Dudley.

Subclass Branchiura

Branchiurids are crustacea that are temporarily parasitic on fish. They superficially resemble copepods, but differ from the latter in the possession of compound eyes, lateral carapace-like head-lobes fused to the sides of the first thoracic somite, an opening for genital products between the fourth pair of thoracic limbs, and a proximal overhang of some of the thoracic exopodites.

Other diagnostic features include an unsegmented, limbless, bilobed abdomen and four pairs of biramous thoracic limbs. Branchiurids, commonly called "carp lice," or "fish lice," arc found on both fresh and saltwater fish. The females deposit their eggs on stones, bits of wood, and other objects, and the larvae resemble adults.

The most common genus, *Argulus*, has a pair of suction cups. Situated on the second maxillae and a poison spine in front of the proboscis. Both males and females are parasitic and require blood meals. This parasite clings to the skin and gills and appears to have little host preference. See Bowen and Putz for reference to pathogenicity.

SUBCLASS CIRRIPEDIA (BARNACLES)

Barnacles are among the most highly modified crustaceans. They abound in marine waters and attach to rocks, pilings, shells of other animals, or on almost any other solid surface that provides a firm

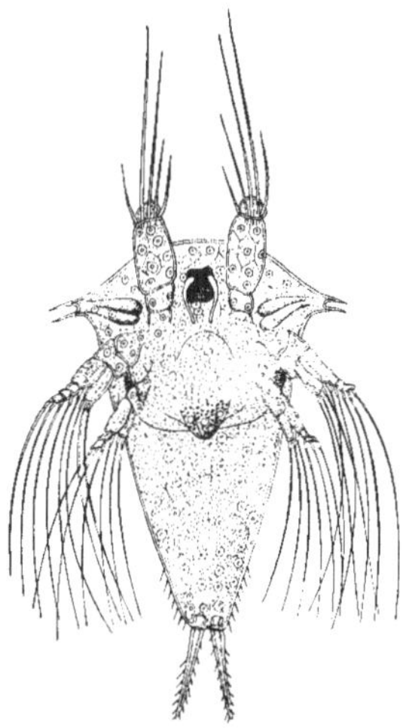

Figure 11.10: Sacculina carcini, nauplius larva.

purchase. Like so many other sessile animals, barnacles, with few exceptions, are hermaphroditic, and their bodies are enclosed in a calcareous shell composed of plates that commonly overlap or are fused to furnish a formidable bulwark against pounding waves or grazing predators.

Cirripedia are crustaceans without compound eves in the adult, with a carapace, except in rare instances, as a mantle over the trunk, with typically six pairs of biramous thoracic limbs, and usually a mandibular palp that is never biramous.

A freeswimming *nauplius* larva hatches from the cirriped eggs, and after a feeding period of a few days, it molts several times and changes into a *cypris* larva (resembling an ostracod) with a bivalve shell. Species of barnacles range in habits from completely free-living to casual commensalism to extreme pathogenic parasitism.

Many forms illustrate phoresis, in which host-specificity is pronounced, as in those species attached only to gorgonian corals, decapods, starfish, sharks, or whales. Examples of commensal cirripeds are: *Chel-onibia,* which has developed a branched system of roots that penetrate into manatees and into the bone of the plastron of marine turtles; *Coronula, Tubicinella, Cryptolepas,* and *Xenobalanus,* whose calcareous shell plates grow into the skin of whales; and

Anelasma squalicola, which becomes partly buried in the skin of sharks. In the last species, a pear-shaped portion is embellished with branched, root-like appendages that apparently secrete an enzymatic

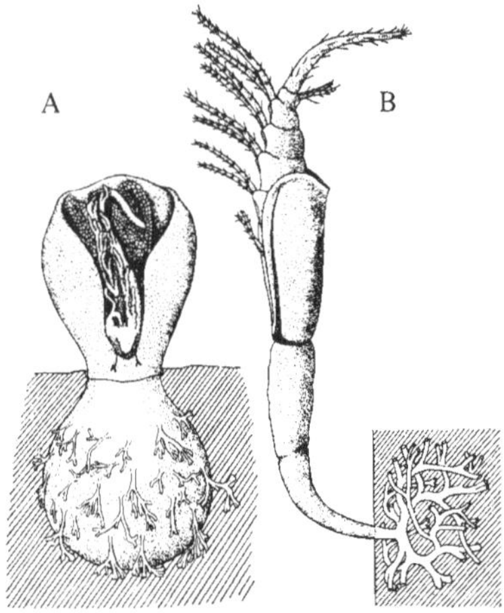

Figure 11.11: A, Anelasma squalicola, partly buried in the skin of a shark. B, Rhizolepas anncllidicola attached to an annelid host.

substance that dissolves the surrounding muscle tissues of the host. *Rhizolepas annellidicola* is another parasitic barnacle that is anchored to its host, the annelid *Laetmonica product,* by a system of foot-like appendages.

Two other examples are *Platylepas* on turtles, manatees, and sea snakes *and Alepas* on various medusae.

Order Ascothoracia

This order contains parasitic barnacles that live on corals. They often are embedded in host tissue.

ORDER RHIZOCEPHALA

The most extremely modified parasitic cirripeds belong to this order. Its members live on or within the bodies of other crustacea, mostly decapods. The larval stages appear to be identical to those of free-living barnacles, but no trace of 'a mouth or gut is present in the parasites.

The adult rhizocephalid possesses neither appendages nor segmentation, and it is anchored to the host by a stalk from which roots proceed into the host tissues. The best-known Rhizocephala are *Sacculina carcini* and *Triangulus munidae.*

The remarkable life history of *Sacculina* starts with a nauplius possessing the characteristic frontal horns of cirriped nauplii. The cypris larva of *Sacculina* is active after dark, and it attaches itself' by its antennae to a crab at the base of a bristle. Soon after attachment, the

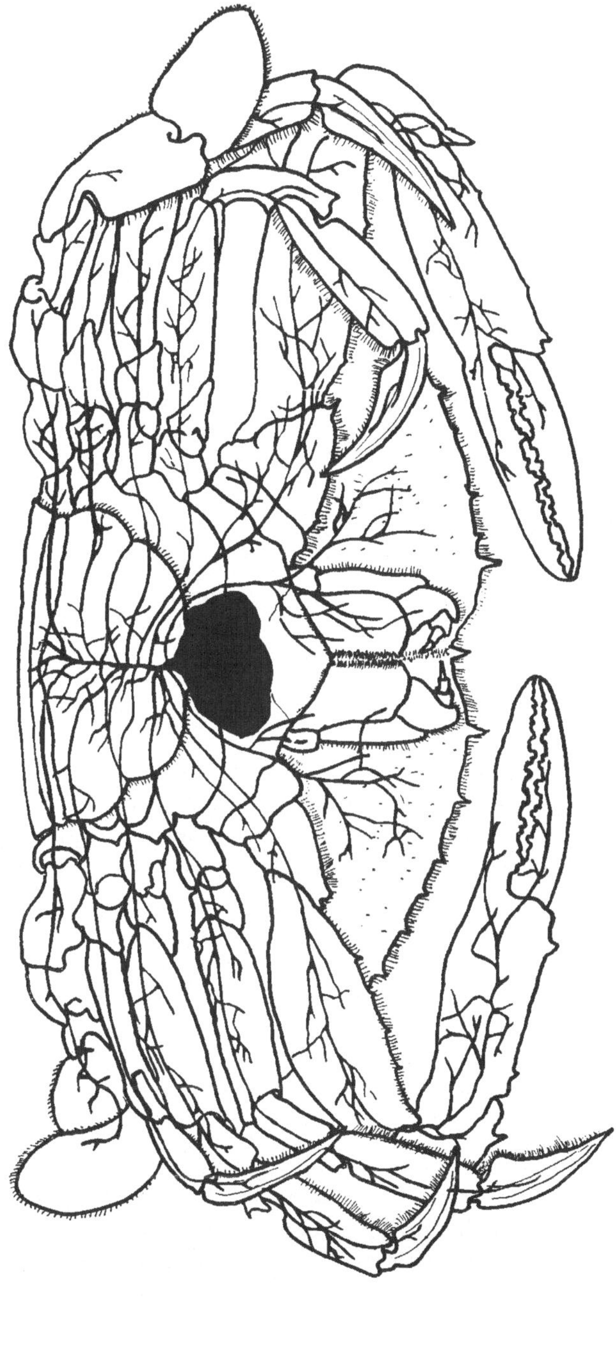

Figure 11.12: The root-like branches of Sacculina permeating the body of its crab host.

whole trunk with its muscles and appendages is thrown off, and a new cuticle is formed under the old one. The body of the parasite becomes an amorphous cellular mass within the two valves of the cypris.

From these cells, the *kentrogon* larva (a mass of embryonic cells) is developed and, by means of a short, dart-like tube that pierces the integument of the host, these undifferentiated cells flow into the body of the crab. The parasitic embryonic cells are carried by the host circulation to the central surface of the gut, where they begin to multiply and spread out in all directions as root-like branches.

A rounded, cellular mass (the future *sacculina externa*), containing the rudiments of genital organs and a ganglion, now appears at the base of the root system, and the parasite migrates to a spot on the ventral side of the crab near the single diverticulum of the gut. The parasite then makes a hole through the new integument.

The external portion of the barnacle thus makes its appearance after the next molt, and it grows into the hermaphroditic adult. The *sacculina interna* continues to grow and may permeate almost the entire body of the host. A "sacculinized" crab may live with its barnacle parasite for at least two years, and it may become infected with two or more individuals. The crab, however, ceases to molt, and its metabolism, particularly that relating to sexual development and activity, is profoundly modified.

CLASS INSECTA I

About three-quarters of terrestrial animals are insects. They live in almost every kind of habitat; this flexibility not only enhances their opportunity to become parasites, but also makes them available for other parasites seeking a home. Some of their habitat choices are amazing.

> "The larva of the petroleum fly lives in pools of petroleum around oil wells in California; other fly larvae breed by the millions in Great Salt Lake; a few flies have been found breeding in the medical-school brine vats in which human cadavers are preserved; and one beetle in the West-often called the 'short circuit' beetlebores into lead cables. A few insects live in hot springs where the temperatures go as high as 120 degrees Fahrenheit (51° C)."

An insect body is characterized by its division into three parts: head, thorax, and abdomen. Eyes, antennae, and mouth parts occur on the head; wings and legs arise from the thorax. Appendages on the adult abdomen may occur at its posterior tip. Other structures and life cycles are discussed in this chapter in relation to parasitism.

For insects and disease, see Snow,' and Weiser. For insect nematolopy, including an illustrated key to the genera of all obligate nematodes of insects, see Poinar and Thomas.

LICE

Lice are parasitic on the surfaces of birds and mammals. In temperate climates, lice are most numerous during February and March and least numerous between June and August. Reasons for this kind of seasonal variation in numbers are not well understood.

The lice are divided into the order Anoplura, which contains species whose mouth parts are adapted for sucking the blood and tissue fluids of mammals, hence often called "sucking lice," and the order Mallophaga, containing the lice whose mouth parts are adapted for chewing epithelial structures on the skins of their hosts.

The chewing habit has given rise to the term "biting lice" for the Mallophaga, but they do not actually bite. Mallophaga have broad heads, at least as broad as the thorax, whereas Anoplura have heads narrower than the thorax. Another readily distinguishable feature is the presence in Mallophaga and the absence from Anoplura of pigmented and heavily sclerotized mandibles.

All lice are wingless, have dorsoventrally flattened bodies, short antennae with three to five segments, and reduced or absent eves. The thorax, indistinctly segmented, bears one pair of spiracles. The short legs possess tarsi whose claws are used for grasping feathers or hair.

The abdomen, always without cerci, generally bears six pairs of spiracles. Unlike most arthropod parasites, all lice spend their entire lives on the bodies of' their hosts, and infestation from one host to another is accomplished by direct contact.

For this reason, host-specificity is well marked. Lice eggs, known as "nits," are attached by the female to the feathers or hairs of the host. Anoplura and Mallophaga possess a simple life cycle with gradual metamorphosis. The first nymph, which develops within the egg, is structurally similar to the adult and differs chiefly in its smaller size, absence of color, and underdeveloped sex organs.

Four nvmphal instars, each separated by a molt (ecdvsis), precede the adult stage. In Co*lunihicola,* each nvmphal stage lasts six or seven days, and between each molt, the body becomes successively larger and darker in color. After the third and final molt, the nymph becomes either a male or a female sexually mature adult. In many species, the

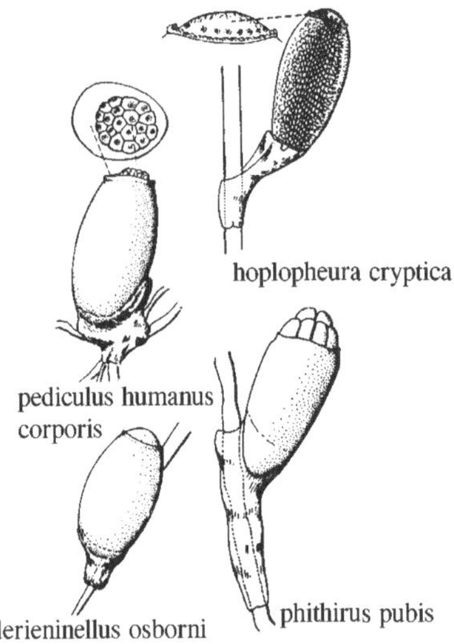

Figure 11.13: Eggs of lice.

female, which is almost always larger than the male, far outnumbers the latter. Sometimes, the male of a species is rare or has never been found. Although parthenogenesis is known to occur in at least one species of mammalian louse, the rarity or apparent absence of males may be attributed to their death immediately after mating.

Many lice, particularly those whose diet consists chiefly of keratin, possess within their bodies symbiotic intracellular bacteria that presumably aid in the digestion of food. The bacteria pass from louse to louse by way of the eggs.

Similar bacteria are found in ticks, mites, bedbugs, and in some bloodsucking Diptera. The bacteria possibly play a role in host-specificity because they are unable to cope with "strange" blood if the louse attaches itself to the wrong host.

Order Mallophaga

This order-contains nearly 3000 known species of lice, primarily parasitic on birds, but also on dogs, cats, horses, cattle, goats, sheep, and other mammals, including marsupials. The Mallophaga have not been convicted as effective carriers of disease-producing microorganisms. Feather lice range in size from the minute males of *Goniocotes,* which scarcely reach 1 mm in length, to the large, hawk-infesting *Laemobothrion,* which attains a length of up to 10 min.

The mouth parts, adapted for chewing epithelial materials, may have severe effects on the hosts. Lice eat the protecting sheaths of growing feathers, feather fiber, down, skin scurf; scabs, blood, their own eggs and cast skins, and probably also mucus and sebaceous matter. The lice on birds apparently can digest keratin (see the foregoing note on symbiotic bacteria).

Some species on mammals ingest hair, and it is possible that these species chew off pieces from the sides in the same manner as a beaver felling a tree. However, mammalian Mallophaga probably prefer a diet resembling that of many of the species parasitic on birds (for example, epidermal scales, skin scurf, wool, wax). Although they possess chewing mouth parts, some species of Mallophaga regularly feed on the freshly drawn blood of their hosts.

For example, *Menacanthus stram*ineus, the body louse of' poultry, actively feeds on its host's blood, but other species prefer blood clots. Some species of Mallophaga parasitic on birds possess piercing mouth parts, and they feed, as do Anoplura, on the blood and tissue fluids of their hosts.

One genus, *Piagetiella,* prefers to live in the throat pouches of pelicans and cormorants. It is possible that certain birds attempt to rid themselves of lice by picking up ants and placing them on their feathers or by perching on an ant hill with wings outstretched. It is presumed that ants eat lice, but this presumption has been questioned.

Another intersting idea is that the birds eat ants, and the resulting formic acid in the bird discourages the lice. We do know that practically all mammals that eat ants are nearly free from lice. Scratching by the host undoubtedly helps to rid the animal of fleas, but the effectiveness of this habit against lice is questionable.

However, Eichler counted 20,000 lice on the skin of one dog that, owing to a defect, could not scratch itself. Damage to feathers caused by lice is probably light, but it is difficult to separate damage caused by lice from that caused by feather mites. Although the Mallophaga are not effective carriers of human disease, one species, *D-ichodectes canis,* acts as the intermediate host for a dog tapeworm, and the genus *Dennyus* on swifts serves as the intermediate host of *Filaria cypseli.*

Suborder Amblycera

Species of lice belonging to this suborder are parasitic on both birds and mammals, and they include the feather, shaft, and body lice of poultry and a number of pests on guinea pigs and other rodents. They may be distinguished by the antennae, which are almost always composed of four segments, the third being stalked.

The antennae always lie in a ventrolateral groove on each side, and

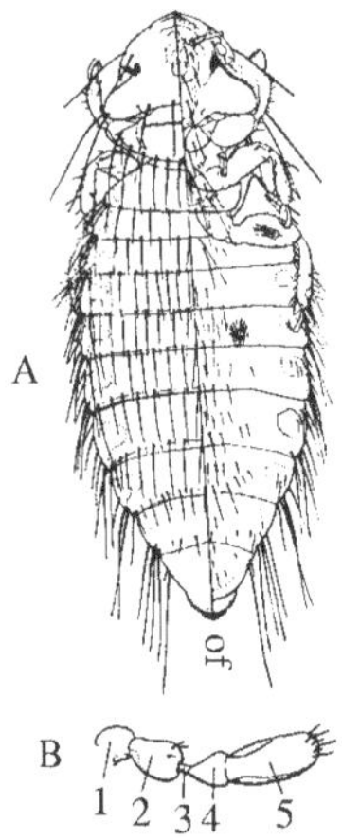

Figure 11.14: A, Menopon gallinne, female. B, The ;intenna of this species, unlike that of most Amblvcera, has five segments.

they may or may not project beyond the sides of the head. The maxillary palps, sometimes absent, may also project beyond the sides of the head in preserved specimens, and, therefore, may be mistaken for antennae.

Menopon gallinae is often called the shaft louse of fowl. The female is about 2 mm long and lays its eggs in clusters on the feathers.

Menaeanthus stramineus (= *Eomenacanthus*) is the chicken body louse of'fitwl and turkeys. The female is *3.3* mm long and prefers the skin to feathers. It may seriously injure adult fowl. One chicken may be infested with more than 6000 lice of several species.

Heterodoxus contains species that occur on dogs in warm countries only, not in Europe, and on kangaroos and wallabies.

Suborder Ischnoeera

Lice belonging to this suborder are commonly found on cattle, equines, goats, sheep, dogs, cats, and also on fowl and other birds. The lice can be distinguished by their easily visible filiform antennae composed of three to five segments. No maxillary palps are present.

Bovicola (= *Damalinia*) is found on cattle, sheep, goats, deer, other two-toed ruminants, and horses. B. hnvi.s is called the cattle-biting louse. It is the most widely distributed louse on cattle in Britain and is also common in North America.

The lice in winter are found at the base of the tail, on the shoulders, and along the back, unless there is a heavy infestation, in which case they may be found all over the host body. Irritation caused by these active pests may be severe, and the infested cattle often try to rid

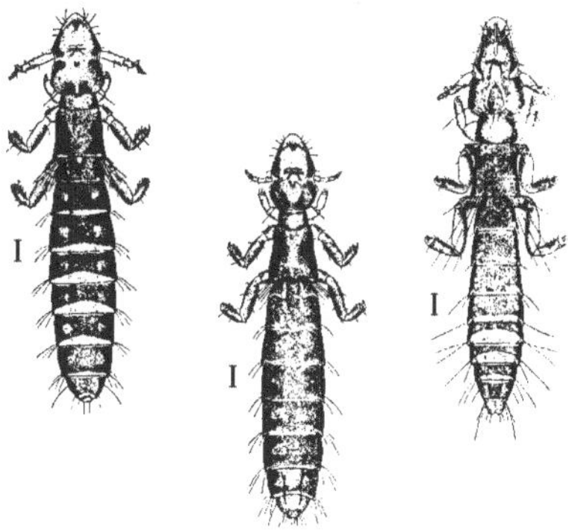

Figure 11.15: Cuclotogaster (Lipeurus), various species.

themselves of the lice by biting the skin and rubbing themselves against tree trunks, fence posts, and rocks.

Trichodectes contains species found on dogs, martins, weasels, badgers, skunks, and other small mammals. Females are almost 2 mm long, and may serve as vectors of the larval stage of a dog cestode.

Cuclotogaster (= *Lipeurus*) *heterographus* is found on the skin and feathers of the head and neck of fowl, partridge, and other birds. It is often called the fowl head louse and may be seriously injurious. The female is about 2.45 mm long, and its eggs are laid singly on the feathers.

Order Anoplura (= Siphunculata)

About 300 species of sucking lice have been described, and they are all parasitic on mammals. In addition to their chracteristic piercing mouth parts, the lice can be distinguished by the small, fused thorax and by their antennae, which are usually composed of 5 segments and are always visible. Eyes are small or absent, and the third pair of legs, often broad and flattened, is usually the largest.

Each tarsus has only one claw. The single pair of thoracic spiracles opens on the dorsal side of the mesothorax. Six pairs of abdominal spiracles are arranged as those of the Mallophaga. Only 7 of the 9 abdominal segments are visible externally.

The mouth parts, adapted for piercing and sucking, are retracted into the head when not in use, thereby obviating the need for a proboscis. The family Linognathidae contains *Linot;nathus vituli,* the bluish black, long-nosed cattle louse. Its first pair of legs is much smaller than the others. The family Neolinognathidae contains only two species, parasitic only on elephant-shrews in East and South Africa. The genus is *Neolinognathus.*

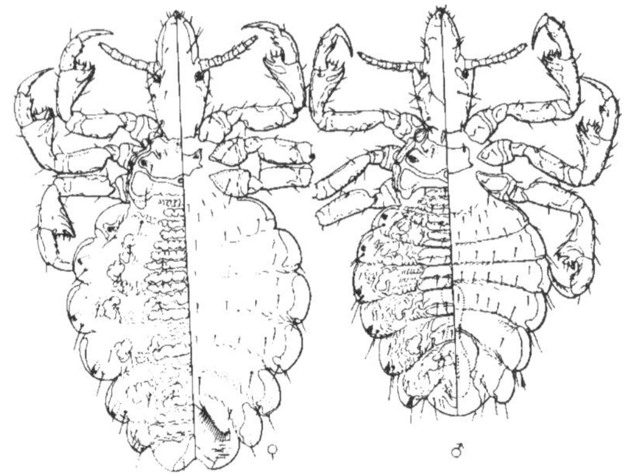

Figure 11.16: Haematopinus suits.

The family Haematopinidae contains *Haematopinus suis,* the largest of all lice to be found on farm stock. Females are 4 to 6 mm long; males are 3.4 to 4.75 mm long. It is the only species of louse that infects the domestic pig.

Human Lice

The family Pediculidae contains the human head louse and the body louse of the genus *Pediculus,* and the human public or crab louse belonging to the genus *Phthirus*. *Pediculus huinanus* occurs in two forms: the head louse, *P. humanus capitis,* and the body louse, *P. humanus humanus (= P. humanus corporis).*

The two look much alike. A typical head louse and a typical body louse are easily distinguished, but they overlap in appearances and movements. Head lice average approximately 2.4 mm long and are smaller than body lice.

Body lice, however, are seldom if ever found on the head, whereas head lice may be found on the body. Head lice are adapted to clinging to hairs, but body lice find refuge in clothing. Head lice and body lice can interbreed and can produce fertile offspring that may possess characteristics intermediate between the two parents.

Females may lay up to 300 eggs during their lives, which last about a month under optimal conditions. The oval eggs, or nits, are laid singly, and they measure about 0.8 by 0.3 mm. At 30^0 C the eggs hatch in 8 or 9 days, and the young nymph is 1 mm long. Adult lice can suck up as much as 1 mg of blood at a time, but they probably prefer to take smaller quantities at frequent intervals.

At 30° C they can survive only about 3 days of starvation. Experiments

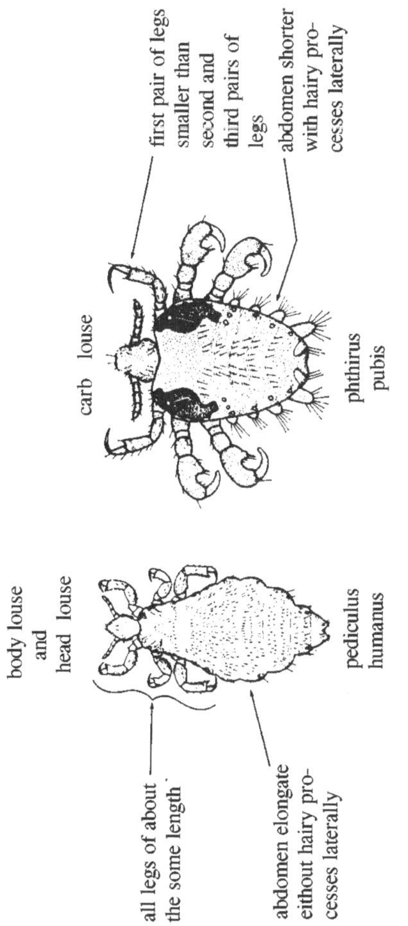

Figure 11.17: Lice commonly found on man.

have shown that lice can move at a rate of 9 inches (23 cm) per minute. They prefer a temperature of 29 to 30° C, and they avoid, when possible, any change in humidity. Their immediate past experience conditions the response to environmental changes; hence different individuals often exhibit different responses.

Movement toward dark areas is chiefly a response to directed light received by the horizontally placed eyes. Phthirus spp. possess a wide thorax that constitutes most of the body, and the coxae are far apart at the margins of the thorax. *P. pubis* frequents the pubic hairs and perianal regions of man, but it may wander to other parts of the body, including the head.

It is smaller and much broader than the other two human lice, and its legs have the appearance of being attached to the edge of the flattened body. The forelegs are slender, with long, fine claws, whereas the middle and hind legs are thick, with thick claws. Adults seem to be unable to survive for longer than a day when removed from the host, and their total span of life is about one month.

Although transmission from person to person occurs by close contact, it is a grave injustice to assume that sexual contact is the only mode of transfer.

Effects of Sucking Lice on Their Hosts

Haematopinus suis probably transmits the virus of swine fever, and lice in general probably transmit tularemia and leishmaniasis. Polypla r spinulosa of black and brown rats transmits the rickettsia that causes typhus. Nevertheless, the sucking lice are not known to be important vectors of domestic and wild animal diseases.

They may be called host irritants, and because they often increase rapidly in numbers, they frequently are the cause of scratching, restlessness, loss of sleep, and interruption of feeding. During the biting process, the saliva injected into the wound prevents the host blood from coagulating as it is sucked through the parasite's slim mouth parts.

The reaction of the host cells to the louse saliva causes the symptoms of irritation. An inflammatory reaction of the skin may be accompanied by a thickening of the epidermis and an increase in tissue lymphocytes, monocytes, mast cells, and fibroblasts.

Lice never seem to be satisfied for long with one meal, but feed all the time. Blood exuding and clotting at the sites of the bites may be a fertile location for the growth of bacteria or an effective attractant for flies, whose larvae may cause serious malady. Cattle lice may be controlled by spraying the animals with growth regulators (insect juvenile hormones).

Pediculus human us can transmit impetigo, trachoma, and cholera by simple mechanical contamination, and this louse is the normal vector of exanthematous typhus caused by Rickettsia prowazekii, trench fever caused by *R. quintana*, and louseborne relapsing fever caused by Borrelia recurrentis.

The rickettsia ingested by the louse with its blood meal multiply in its gut cells, which eventually burst and thus liberate large numbers of these parasitic bodies into the louse feces. Man acquires typhus by rubbing infected louse feces into an abrasion of the skin. The infected louse dies about ten days after acquiring the cellular parasites because of its ruptured gut cells. Hans Zinsser's book, *Rats, Lice aril History*, gives a vivid picture of the manner in which lice and typhus fever have influenced the history of mankind.

Trench fever became widely prevalent during World War I and has since disappeared. The spirochetes of relapsing fever penetrate the louse gut and multiply within the fluid of the body cavity. They remain in this fluid until the louse is crushed, at which time the spirochetes escape and may enter a human host through an abrasion of' the skin.

Obviously, the habit of "*popping*" lice with fingernails and the disgusting practice of biting lice to kill them are hazardous if relapsing fever is prevalent. Head lice, frequently a serious problem among urban children, are much more rare among adults. Body lice are largely confined to those adults and children who do not change their underwear frequently.

Conditions of crowding, especially during sleeping hours, are particularly conducive to the spread of lice. For these reasons, such groups as destitute people, refugees, vagrants, prisoners, and armies provide fertile fields for lice populations.

A chronicler contemporary of the well-known church dignitary St. Thomas a Becket wrote that on the morning after the churchman was murdered, his vestments were removed, and the haircloth underwear was so infested with lice that they "boiled over" as the cloth was stripped from the cold body.

The primary defense against human lice involves personal cleanliness of body and clothing. It is well to remember that even in civilized communities, there are alwavs some chronically lousy individuals whose feeble efforts at personal cleanliness are ineffectual or who have ceased to worry about their condition and passively offer their parasites to every passerby.

Order Hemiptera (Bugs)

Plant bugs and their relatives are predominantly phytophagous (plant feeders) and have piercing and auctorial mouth parts. Many species show a strong tendency toward entomophaLi (insect-eating), and in a number of instances, plant feeding has been abandoned entirely and the predatory role is obligatory.

Here again, the delicate line separating a predator from a parasite defies discovery. The bugs typically possess two pairs of wings, the anterior pair being most often of a harder consistency than the posterior pair. The slender, segmented beak constitutes the most easily recognizable feature of bugs. Palpi are atrophied, and the labium is in the form of a dorsally grooved sheath receiving two pairs of bristle-like stylets (modified mandibles and maxillae). Metamorphosis is incomplete. Probably, no other group of insects is so directly concerned with the welfare of man because of the vast amount of' injury to plants brought about, directly and indirectly, by thousands of species of bugs.

Chinch bugs, leaf-hoppers, plant lice, cotton stainers, whiteflies, tea blight bugs, scale insects, and mealybugs are among the most destructive.

SUBORDER HETEROPTERA

The 3000 or so described species of these bugs exhibit great variation in form. The family Reduviidae, subfamily Triatominae, contains bugs of medium to large size, and usually of' a black or brownish color, but sometimes with bright red or yellow markings. The head is characteristically long, narrow, and with a neck-like portion immediately behind the eyes.

The rostrum (beak) is three-segmented and is bent sharply back under the head when at rest, and the filiform antennae are inserted on the sides of the head between the eves and the tip of the snout. The abdomen is often widened at its middle, exposing the margins of the segments lateral to the folded wings.

Wings of Heteroptera arc generally placed, when at rest, so as to reveal a conspicuous triangular area immediately posterior to the thorax. Reduviids commonly live on the blood of other insects, but a few triatomids ("assassin bugs") attack higher animals, including man.

Rhodnius proli.rus and species of *lriatorna* and of *Paustroncylus* are the natural vectors for *Trypanosoma cruai,* the causative agent of Chagas's

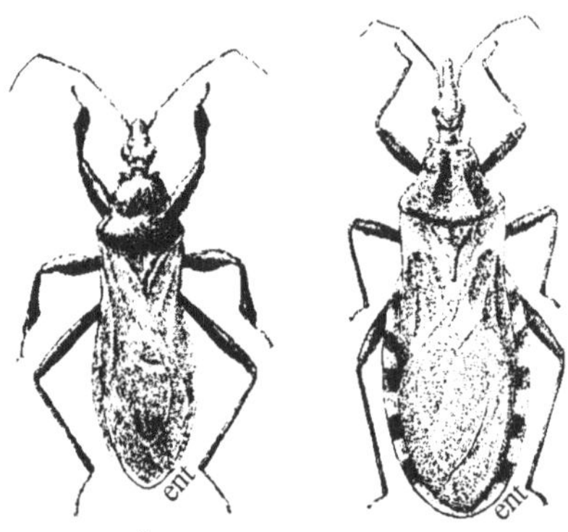

A B

Figure 11.18: Assassin bugs. A, Melanolestes picipes (Herrich-Schaeffer), X 2. B, A blood-sucking conenose, Tiotorno songuisugii UxConte), X 2.

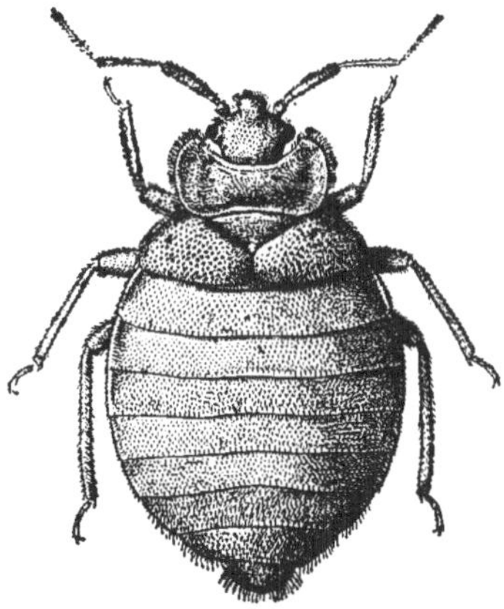

Figure 11.19: Male bedbug.

disease, a frequently fatal form of human trypanosomiasis. Many species of assassin bugs inflict a painful bite if carelessly handled, and severe allergic symptoms occasionally occur. The bugs are regularly found in nests or burrows of rodents or other host animals.

Bedbugs, family Cimicidae, are parasitic on birds and mammals. Characteristic morphologic features are an oval, flattened body about 4 mm long, without wings and covered with many hair-like spines. Compound eyes are conspicuous, but ocelli are absent; the rostrum lies in a ventral groove, and tarsi are three-jointed.

The thorax consists of three segments: an anterior large prothorax extending forward on either side of the head; a mesothorax whose visible portion is a small triangle; and a mesothorax hidden from view dorsally by two small pads, which are rudimentary fore wings.

Members of the genus *Ciuze.r* are associated with birds, bats, man, and other marnlnals and have a worldwide distribution. In North and Central America, *Haematosiplon inodorus* is a parasite of poultry. The two most common bedbugs attacking man *are Cimer lectularius* of temperate climates and *C. hernipterus* of tropical countries.

Both species, colored (lark mahogany or bright chestnut, hide in cracks, crevices, or under rugs by day, and emerge at night to feed on human blood. The bugs are able to endure long fasts, and some have been kept alive without food for over a year. *C. lectularius* is also found naturally on chickens, rabbits, and bats.

Before the female bedbugs can lay fertile eggs, not only must she mate, but also she must feed. The pearly white and curved operculated eggs are normally laid on rough surfaces such as those found in crevices and behind wallpaper. A quick-drying cement fastens each egg (about 1 mm long) securely to the surface of the material on which it is deposited.

When they hatch, in 6 to 10 days, the nymphs, about the size of a pinhead, appear similar to the adult and immediately seek shelter. Five molts take place before the adult stage is reached. For details on the ecology of bedbugs, see Johnson.

Bedbugs and Disease

Bedbugs are not responsible for the transmission, as natural vectors, of disease. Mechanical transmission of infections by means of contaminated feet of the insects may take place, and leptospirosis is known to be transmitted from guinea pig to guinea pig by the bite of bedbugs.

However, in spite of conflicting accounts and persistent suspicion, no clear evidence has indicated that bedbugs are more than harmless pests of mankind. McKenny-Hughes and Johnson, however, have called attention to the fact that "in infested areas it is often possible to pick out children from buggy homes by their pasty faces, listless appearance and general lack of energy.

It can be argued that the house in which bugs are tolerated will also be the home of malnutrition, dirt and other causes of physical infirmity. Such causes cannot be held solely responsible, and sleepless nights with constant irritation due to the injection of the minute doses of bedbug saliva into the blood are liken to contribute largely to the ill health of children and even of certain adults.

Some fortunate people are not affected by the bites of bedbugs; others gain immunity after repeated biting; whilst others, less fortunate, are always susceptible.

See Usinger for a monograph on the Cimicidae.

Order Hymenoptera (Wasps and Ants)

This order consists chiefly of ants, bees, wasps, sawflies, and ichneumon flies. Parasitism is prominently displayed by members of the order, and insects are favored hosts.

Typical parasitic species are entomophagous and are parasites only during their larval stages. In such a situation, they are called "*parasitoids*." The manner and place of oviposition by the female are varied and range from the common placement of the egg within the body of the host to its deposition on foliage or in plant tissues far removed from the animal host.

On hatching, the parasitoid larvae feed on the host, which is usually itself a larva or an egg and is thereby destroyed. That a given larva of

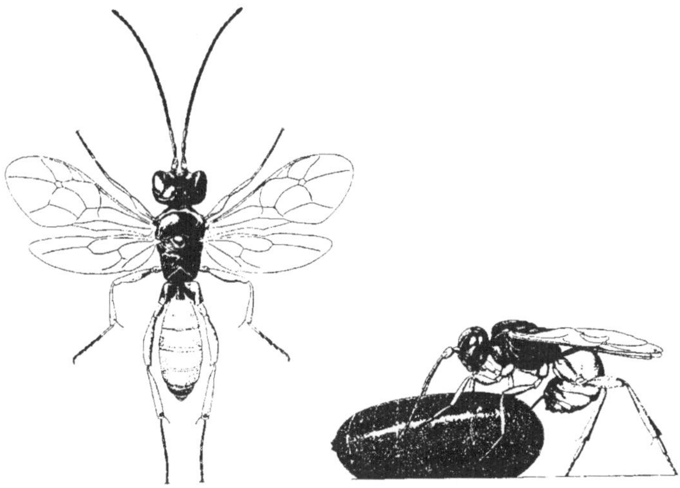

Figure 11.20: A hyperparasitic ichneumon, Phygadeuon subfuscus Cresson(Gelinae). A, Adult male. B, Female ovipositing in puparium of host. The host of this ichneumon is a tachinid fly. Aplornyiopsis epilochnae Aldrich, which is parasitic on the Mexican bean beetle, Epilachno vurivestis Mulsant.

some species may be either ecto- or endoparasitic, according to the host species on which it feeds, indicates that the host is partly responsible for the behavior of the parasitoid.

Larval fruit flies, *Drosophila melanogaster, may* be parasitized by larval braconid wasps, *Asobara tahida*. The fly responds by a cellular immune reaction and encapsulates the parasite with a wall of flattened hemocvtes.

When he had compared parasitoids with parasitic castrators, Kuris made the following intriguing statement: "An analysis of life history features of insect parasitoids and crustacean parasitic castrators suggests that these are similar phenomena, distinct from parasitism and predation.

A parasitoid consumes only one host during its lifetime; parasitic castration causes the reproductive death of only one host. Since population densities of many insect species arc regulated by parasttoids, parasitic castration may also play an important role inl host population regulation.

ORDER STREPSIPTERA (TWISTED-WINGED PARASITES OR STYLOPIDS)

Stylopids are small, endoparasitic insects that exhibit a striking sexual dimorphism in the adult stage. The males have branched antennae, large, protruding eyes, club-like structures (halteres) instead of fore

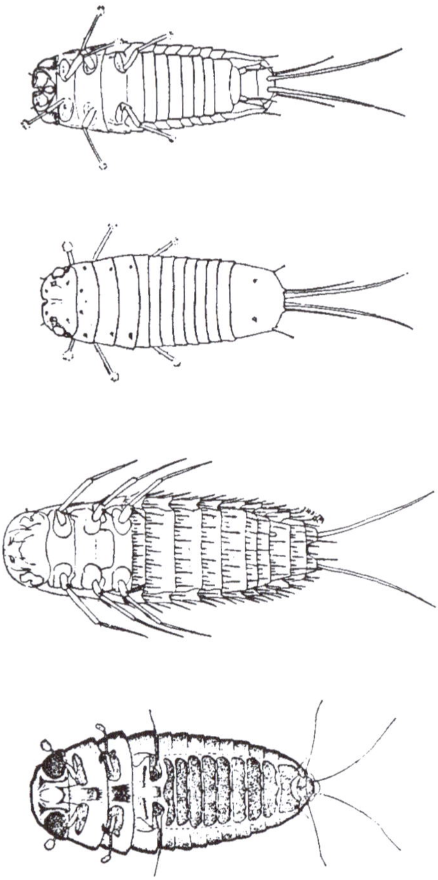

Figure 11.21: First instar larvae of the Strepsiptera.

wings, and large hind wings. The females are wingless and normally remain enclosed in a puparium that protrudes from the body of the insect host. A few females leave the host and have a larviform structure with a terminal gonopore. Only about 300 species are known, and these have commonly been placed within the order Coleoptera.

Allspecies, so far as is known, complete their larval development within the body of the host in a manner similar to that of the beetle *Rhipidius* in cockroaches. The first instar larvae of stvlopids bear a striking resemblance to those of the Rhipiphoridae (Coleoptera).

The minute adult males are not encountered by collectors nearly as often as are the females, and many species have consequently been described on the basis of one sex only. Although a few instances of Orthoptera and Hemiptera as hosts to the Strepsiptera are known, the

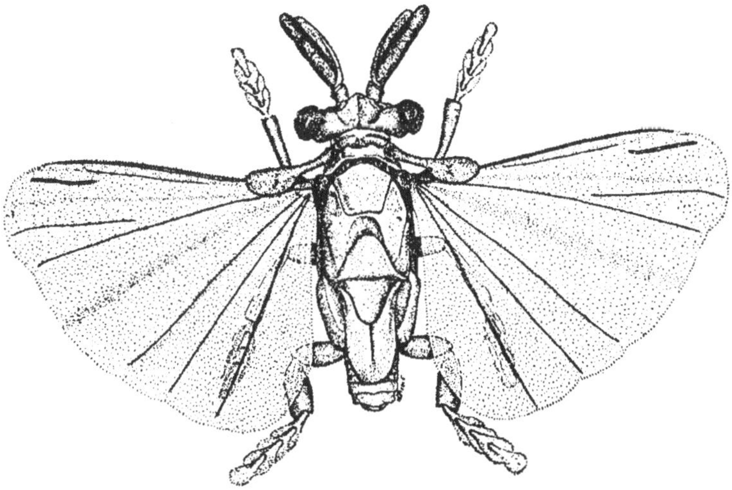

Figure 11.22: Styops slwrntoni, male, enlarged.

preferred hosts are members of the Homoptera (chiefly Auchenorrhyncha) and of the Hymenoptera (chiefly Vespoidea, Sphecoidea, and Apoidea). The following account of the biology and habits of these parasites is based on *Xenos vesparum,* a parasite of wasps and bees.

The male lives only a few hours on emerging from the host, but the female remains permanently endoparasitic, with its cephalothorax protruding through the body wall of the wasp or bee. Copulation takes place when the male alights on the host and inserts the aedeagus (penis plus lateral structures) into the aperture of the brood canal of the female.

Larvae hatch within the body of the female and issue in large numbers, sometimes several thousand, through the genital canals into the brood pouch. Larvae eventually emerge through the brood canal, and they remain as active creatures on the body of the host until opportunity is afforded for escape.

The first instar larvae are known as triungulinids. Larvae probably leave the first or "maternal" host when the latter are closely associated with others on flowers or in the nest. By simple attachment to adult wasps or bees, the larval parasites are transported to larval hosts, within which they speedily burrow through the body wall and take up lodgings in body spaces between the organs, pushing these organs out of position.

Absorption of nutrients from the host blood causes the parasite to grow, and after the seventh instar, the parasitic larva works its way

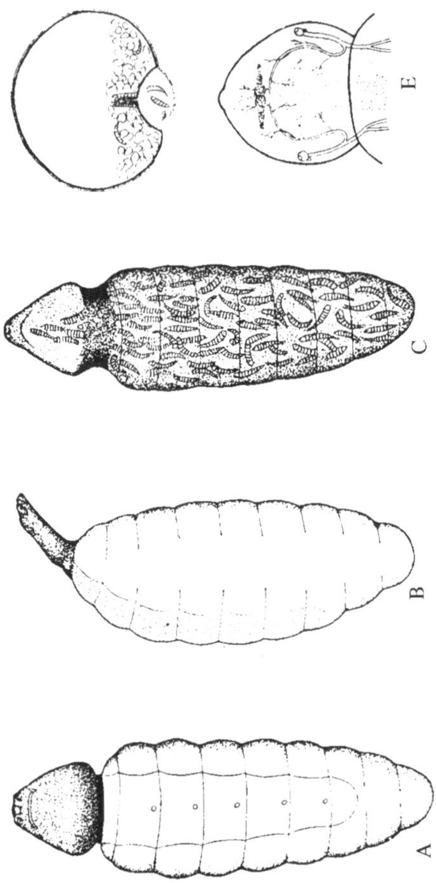

Figure 11.23: Adult females of the Strepsiptera, with details, A, Stvlops melittoe Kirby, showing the genital Openings on the cephalothorax and the brood chamber. B, The same, lateral view. C, A gravid female ofllolictophngus curtisii Dale, showing fully developed triungulinids distributed throughout the body. 1), A diagrammatic cross section through the fourth abdominal segment of S. ruelittoe, showing the outer portion of the genital canal and several triungulinids in the brood chamber. B, Cephalothorax ofXenos vespornin Rossi, dorsal view, showing the single pair of spiracles, the anterior commissure and the longitudinal tracheal trunks, which divide in the first thoracic segment.

outward and protrudes from the body wall of the host, which is by now in the pupal stage of development. Male parasites now undergo pupation, and soon winged insects are liberated. Females become white, grub-like creatures remaining within the host.

Effects of stylopids on their hosts vary, depending on the numbers of parasites within one host, the length of time the parasites spend within the host, the season, and other considerations. Generally, however, changes in the growth and development of the host occur, including pronounced alterations of the secondary sexual characteristics.

CLASS INSECTA II

Order Siphonaptera (Fleas)

Over 1300 species of fleas have been described, and undoubtedly

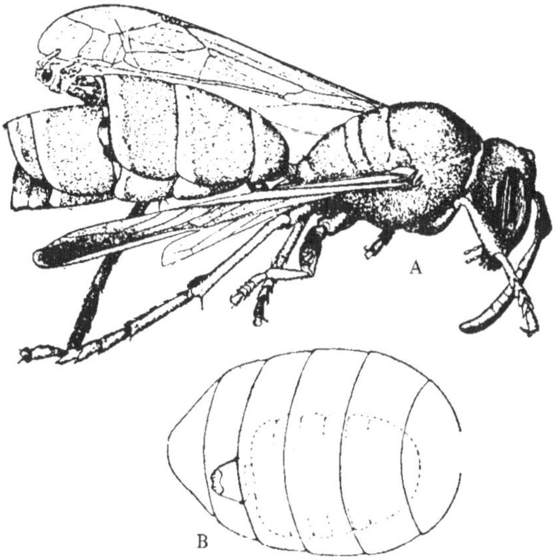

Figure 11.24: A, Polistus Sollicus, with a male Xenos vesparum (a stylopid) hatching from the puparium. B, Abdomen of Andrcoo vogo, with adult female of Stylops sp.

many more have not yet been discovered by man. The adults only are parasitic, and they, like lice, are restricted to birds and mammals on whose blood they feed. Fleas have bodies that are laterally compressed, and the first segment, the coxa, of each leg is large and aids in the jumping ability for which fleas are justly famous.

Most of us may recall how difficult it is to catch a flea. This difficulty is the result of the small size of the flea, its laterally compressed and slippery body, the backward directed spines, and the strong, active legs tipped with claws.

These characteristics enable fleas to jump from one host to another and to move easily among hairs and feathers. The compact structure of a flea is adapted to a forward movement only, and to change even the field of vision requires an alteration in the position of the entire insect.

Probably, the most convenient place to look for a flea is on the body of a domestic dog or cat. Both these hosts may be attacked by the dog flea, *Ctenocephalides canis;* the cat flea, *C. felis;* the human flea, *Puler irritans;* the poultry flea, *Echidnophaga galliruzcea;* or occasionally, by other species of fleas. Many wild animals are infested with *Pular siruulaus*.

Structure

Conspicuous features of the external anatomy of fleas are shown in

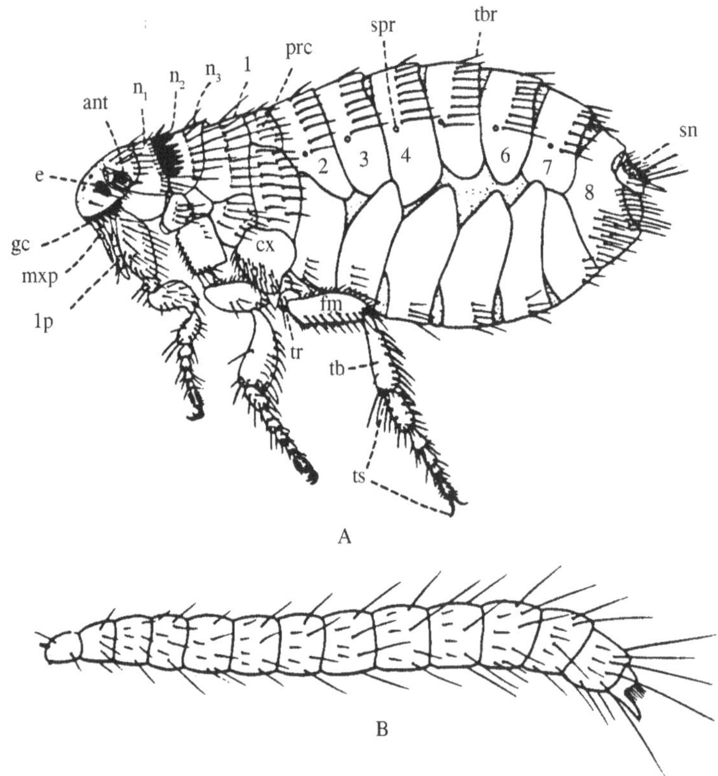

Figure 11.25: A, An adult cat flea, Ctenocephalides fells (Bouche); B, Larva.

Figures elsewhere in this chapter. The antennae of males are nearly always longer than those of females, and during copulation, the male takes up a position underneath the female and holds her firmly with his antennae from below.

Spines along the mouth edge serve to prevent hairs or feathers of the host from interfering with the action of the mouth parts of the flea during feeding. The male body has an upward tilt posteriorly, whereas the female body is evenly rounded terminally.

Fleas are truly encased in a suit of armor, and each segment of the thorax, prothorax, mesothorax, and metathorax may be regarded as a membranous ring of adjoining plates. The notum of the prothorax is often armed with a row (comb) of heave, pi - mented spines (one row on each side) called the *pronotal ctenidium* or *pronotal comb*.

The spines help the flea to move through the feathers or hairs, and they also help to protect underlying parts. The abdomen consists of ten

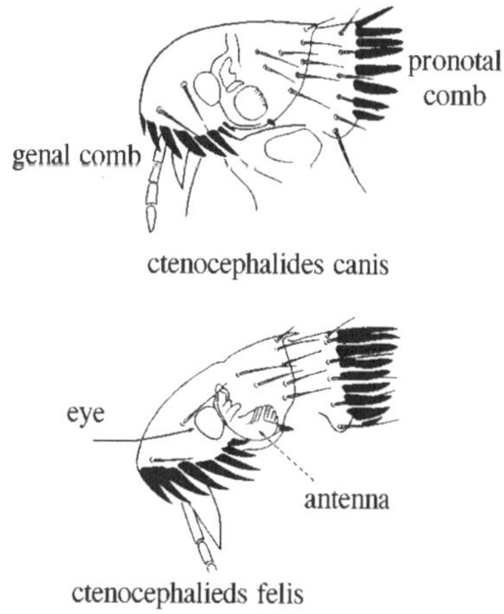

Figure 11.26: Head of Ctenoccphnlidcs cnnis, the dog flea, and of C. fclis, the cat flea.

segments, and each segment, like those of the thorax, has a dorsal sclerite called the *tergum* and a ventral sclerite called the *sternum*, except the first segment lacks a sternum.

On the abdomen, these plates overlap, permitting considerable flexibility inside the abdomen; when a flea has become engorged with a blood meal, the plates appear as islands separated by broad, bare bands of skin. The shape and bristle pattern of the seventh abdominal segment in female fleas has considerable taxonomic importance.

Tergum nine in the male is modified to form a clasping apparatus used during copulation with a female. The clasper is of primary value in the identification of males. The complicated genital structures of the male flea are illustrated in Figure elsewhere in this chapter. The ninth segment of both male and female fleas has on its tergum a dorsal

Figure 11.27: Pules irritáns, the human flea, adult female, greatly enlarged.

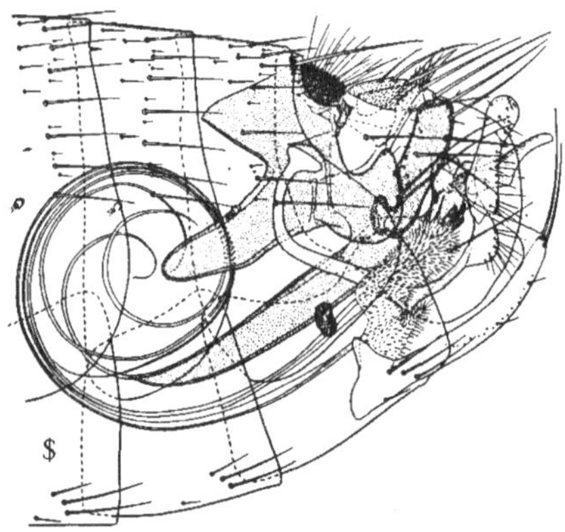

Figure 11.28: Ceratophyllus gdlinae, male, showing clasper, coiled penis, sensilium and other features of the posterior end of the abdomen.

sensory plate called the *pygidium* (sometimes called the *sensilium*), covered with pits, bristles, and hairs. The whole structure suggests a tiny pincushion, and it possibly functions in the detection of air currents. Such a function would assist the flea in finding a host that may be moving about.

The *spermatheca* is taxonomically the most important genital structure of the female flea. It consists of a wide *head* or *reservoir*, and a terminal, long, sausage-shaped *tail* or *appendix*. The alimentary tract is the internal organ system of particular importance in disease transmission. The mouth leads to a thickwalled pharynx equipped with pumping muscles, thence to a narrow gullet or esophagus, which enters a pear-shaped *proventriculus* or *gizzard*.

The gizzard is provided internally with a series of spines that project backward in front of the entrance to the stomach. These spines help to crush the blood cells of the host. Between the gizzard and the stomach is a valve that prevents the food in the stomach from being vomited during the process of digestion. So effective is the valve that pressure applied from behind sufficient to burst the stomach wall does not force food back into the esophagus.

At the posterior end of the large stomach are situated four tubular glands that function as kidneys. The short intestine is equipped distally with six small, oval, rectal glands. A pair of salivary glands lies on each side of the stomach, and they are connected by a common duct that leads to the pharynx. Muscular attachments at the expanded end of the salivary duct constitute a salivary pump.

During the process of biting and feeding, the piercing mouth parts enter the host skin, and the flea thrusts its head downward, elevating the abdomen and hind legs.

The rostrum parts of the palpi lie flat on the skin of the host and apparently serve to check any tendency to warping on the part of the slender piercer; these parts possibly also assist in levering up the mouth parts at the end of the meal. The mouth parts are withdrawn with a sudden jerk.

When a flea bites, the salivary pump pours out a stream of saliva that reaches the host blood vessels through the groove on the inner surface of the laciniac. At the same time, the pharyngeal pump works to draw up the host blood, mixed with saliva, and forces it into the esophagus and stomach, where it is digested.

Life History and Habits

During their lift cycles, fleas pass through a complete metamorphosis from egg to larva to pupa to adult. Eggs are large, smooth, oval, and translucent. If a flea-infested house cat is permitted to sleep on a black cloth during the night, the flea eggs may easily be seen scattered over the cloth the next morning.

Mingled with the eggs are bits of dried blood and hairs. The human flea, *Pule.r irritans*, may lay well over 400 eggs during her lifetime. In 2 to 10 days, the eggs hatch into eyeless and legless but active larvae. The strongly sclerotized head bears 2 short antennae, and the 13 other body segments (3 in the thorax, 10 in the abdomen) bear numerous bristles.

Anal struts consisting of a pair of blunt, hooked processes distinguish flea larvae from those of dipterous insects. Under favorable conditions, the larvae may reach their third stage in about two weeks, but development may be delayed for six months or more. Larvae feed on various organic debris to be found in the host's nest, crevices in floors, and under rugs.

Blood derived from the excreta of adult fleas is sometimes a necessary part of the larval diet. Larvae of bird fleas thrive on broken-down sheaths of feathers and on epidermal scales of young birds. Larvae molt twice before reaching the third stage. Each larva then spins a cocoon within which it pupates.

The larval stage may last from one to 24 weeks. Pupae may live for a week up to a year, depending on the species and such environmental factors as temperature and moisture. The entire life history of a flea may be as short as 18 days, or it may last for many months. The fully formed adult flea may lie quiescent for an indefinite period of time before it begins an active existence. In a pamphlet published by the British Museum of Natural History,' one may find the following interesting observations.

> ... flea's cocoons are extraordinarily sensitive to mechanical disturbance of any kind. Persons entering a loner deserted house sometimes have cause to complain of hordes of fleas appearing 'suddenly' after a short time. It is probable that in such cases fleas resting in the cocoon, beneath floors, in cracks, etc., have come out in response to the vibrations caused by people moving in their proximity. Bird fleas show the same phenomenon."

Bat fleas tend to crowd onto female bats before the hosts migrate to summer colonies. Some fleas, especially small-mammal fleas, have a predilection for male hosts. In contrast, the human flea is more numerous on women than on men.

The explanation for this type of behavior is undoubtedly related to activities of one sex that favor dissemination of fleas and to the influence of host hormones that are circulating in the blood. Some fleas require a blood meal before they copulate. Many males die soon after mating, and the female lives long enough to lay a quantity of eggs that are fertile only if the female has previously had a meal of blood.

Although seasonal changes in climate affect the numbers of eggs laid and the duration of larval stages, bird fleas have a more sharply defined breeding season than do mammal fleas. The moisture requirements of the larvae are of' cardinal importance in determining both survival and transfer to new hosts.

Hormone cycles of the host play an important part in the regulation of the flea breeding cycle and population.'' Minute amounts of' hvdrocortisone injected into a rabbit induce maturation of fleas feeding on its blood.

FLEAS AND HUMAN DISEASE

Bubonic plague, one of the most serious bacterial diseases of' mankind, has, in former years, wiped out hundreds of' thousands of people during a single epidemic. The disease probably retarded western civilization by 200 years.

Although human plague is now largely under control, it is an everpresent danger because the bacterial causative organism, *Yersinia pestis*, is transmitted through fleas from rodents to man. Plague was introduced to man in North America in the year 1900, and since then, hundreds of persons have contracted the disease and a high percentage of those persons have died of it. About 60 different kinds of fleas are associated with the house mouse, black rat, and brown rat, and of these fleas, at least 8 are known to be able to carry the plague bacteria, which lives in the blood of its host.

Rats are the principal culprits in the transfer of infected fleas to man, and the oriental rat flea, *Xenopsylla cheopis,* is the most important transfer host. *Nosopsyllus fasciatrus is* also of' worldwide importance as a carrier of plague bacteria.

Bacilli in an infected flea so congest its gizzard and stomach that blood sucked from a mammalian host fails to pass into the stomach, and when the sucking efforts cease, the blood flows back into the wound and thereby infects a new host.

Xenopsylla cheopis and *Nosopsyllus fasciatius* are also transmitting agents for a nonepidemic typhus of man called "murine typhus." The flea-borne disease is caused by a rickettsia, and it normally occurs in rats.

The etiologic agent of epidemic typhus can also be picked up by the oriental rat flea, and the flea might play a small role in the transmission of this disease to man, but the louse is preeminent as a vector of *typhus*. Other diseases known to be associated with fleas include tularemia (caused by *Francisella tularensis)* in man, rabbits, and rodents; salmonellosis in man (caused by *Salmonella enteritidis);* myxomatosis of wild and domestic rabbits (caused by a virus); anemia; and dermatitis.

Cysticercoid stages of several tapeworms *(Dipylidium coninurn* of dogs and cats, *D. se.rcoronaturn, linniernolepis dirniuuta* of rodents and man) develop in larvae of several species of fleas. Larvae of' a filarial worm, probably *Dipetalonema reconditurn,* found in subcutaneous tissues of dogs develop in dog and cat fleas.

Larvae of the chigoe flea (genus *Tunga)* infest the skin of birds and mammals and cause intense itching and ulceration. *Tundra* and *Neotuoga* are remarkable in that the female burrows beneath the skin of its host and passes its entire adult life as an internal parasite.

Fleas themselves are also parasitized by gregarines and other Protozoa in the midgut and by a hvmenopterous insect larva *(Bairarnlia fuscipes)* in the flea larva.

Order Diptera (Flies)

Structure

Insects belonging to the order Diptera are characterized by the possession of only one pair of wings, hence the name *diptera,* which

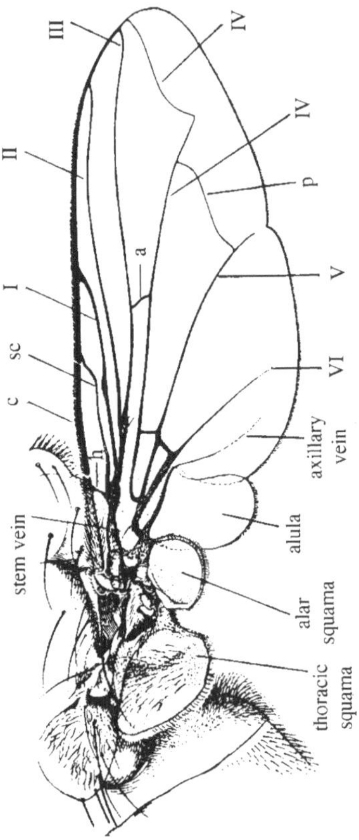

Figure 11.29: Right wing of Calliphora vicina. a, Cross vein ;c, costa; sc, subcosta; p, posterior cross vein. Longitudinal veins numbered by Roman numerals.

means "two wings." Immediately behind the wings is a pair of clubshaped halteres. These organs are considered to be vestigial wings. The three body divisions head, thorax, and abdomenthat characterize insects are especially marked in the Diptera.

The adult head usually possesses prominent eyes and a pair of antennae. The thorax supports legs and wings. Wings are membranous and may be smooth, hairy, or, as in mosquitoes, they may possess scales. Venation of the wings is an important diagnostic feature.

The abdomen is usually distinctly segmented and bears the genitalia at its posterior end. Some major morphologic details of flies are illustrated in Figures elsewhere in this chapter.

The life cycles of Diptera usually involve the egg, larva, pupa, and, adult. Eggs may hatch within the body of the female, but most dipterous insects lay eggs. Larvae of flies are called *tnagcots,* and like other larvae, they undergo a series of molts while growing.

FAMILY CULICIDAE

Mosquitoes transmit the causative agents of such serious diseases as human and avian malaria, dengue fever, yellow fever, fowlpox, elephantiasis and other forms of filariasis. Thus, it is not surprising that, on the basis of weight alone, the literature on mosquitoes is staggering. See Downes" for the ecology of bloodsucking Diptera.

At least 2000 species of mosquitoes occur in the world, and they may be found in almost every country. These insects, belonging to the family Culicidae, are characterized by slender bodies and long legs. Mouth parts of adult females form a bloodsucking proboscis. Antennae of the male are bushier and thus are more prominent than those of the female. Mosquitoes in general may be distinguished from similar flies by their wing venation.

Of special value is the presence of 2 bifurcated veins toward the apex of each wing. These divided veins, separated by a single vein, are covered with scales. The life cycle of mosquitoes involves the usual egg, larva, pupa, and adult stages; the larvae and pupae live in water. Eggs, about a millimeter in length, are laid by members of the genus *Cule.r* in groups on the surface of water.

These eggs are glued together in the form of tiny rafts. Members of the genus *Anopheles* deposit their eggs singly without gluing them together, and they remain afloat by virtue of lateral air chambers. On hatching, the larvae swim about and search for food, for example, minute algae. The larvae, which are called "wrigglers" because of the way they move through the water, come to the surface periodically and obtain air through breather tubes or siphons.

Young insects grow and molt four times, and after the last molt, they become pupae. A pupa is shaped like a comma with a large head

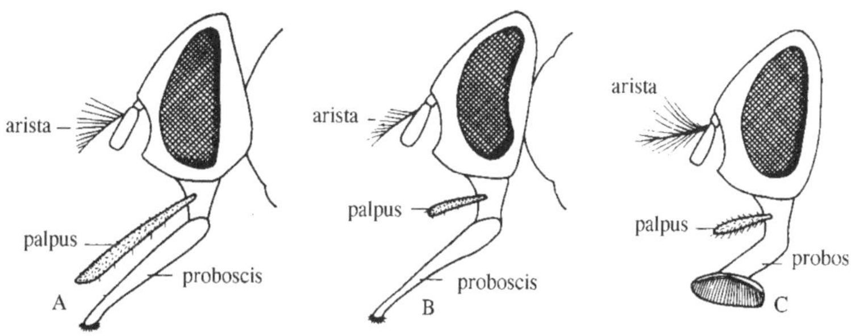

Figure 11.30: Morphologic details of fly heads. A, Siphona irritans. B, Stomoxys calcitrans. C, Mucsca dornestica.

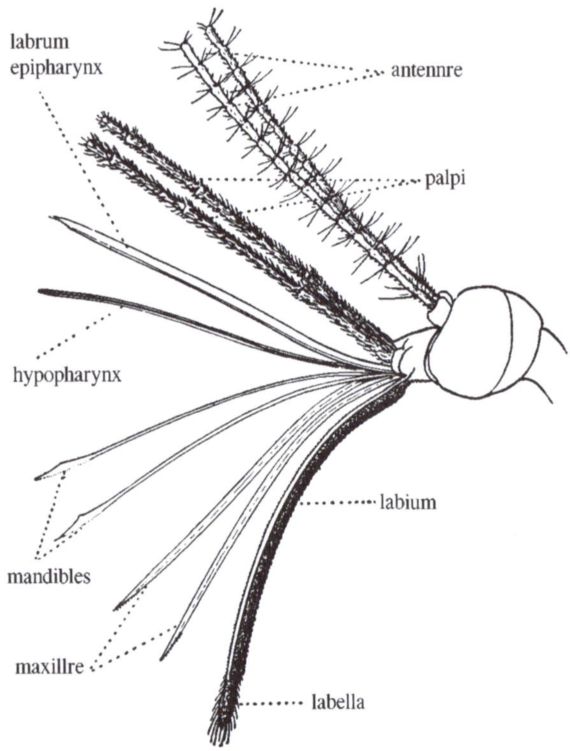

Figure 11.31: Mouth parts of female mosquito, Anopheles qundrinurculatus, dissected out of the sheath. Note that the mandibles have finely serrated, blade-like lips and that the maxillae have pointed chitinous lips with fewer and coarser serrations than the mandibles. The proboscis is made up of all parts labeled, except the antennae and palpi.

equipped with siphons. Pupae are so active that they are called "tumblers." They do not feed, but during the few days of their existence, the adult structures develop. When they molt, the pupae come to the surface of the water, thus permitting the winged adults to take up their aerial and terrestrial life.

After mating, males soon die, but females of some species live during the winter in a dormant condition in protected places such as sheds, barns, and abandoned houses. Sperm within their bodies remain viable, ready to fertilize the eggs that appear in the spring.

Mosquitoes are probably best known for transmitting *Plasmodium,* the causative organism of malaria. The life cycle of this protozoan parasite is described in other chatper of this book. The protozoa undergo greater changes in the mosquito than they do in man; this phenomenon suggests that the mosquito reacts more violently than man to plasmodial infection. Although mosquitoes are probably better adapted to the parasite than is man, we know little about the adjustments a mosquito has to make.

It should be noted that some anopheline mosquitoes, which are the normal vectors of *Plasmodium,* do not become infected even after a meal of parasitized human blood. This fact is not surprising because some people are also refractory to infection, but our knowledge of parasite-host relations *between Plasmodium* and mosquitoes is limited.

At least six species of mosquitoes are known to transmit monkey malaria. Four of these are found in Malaysia and one in India. The species most commonly found in the mangrove forests of coastal Malaysia is *Ariaphels hackeri.* Much has to be learned, however, about the biology of transfer of malaria to monkeys and apes.

These insects may be parasitized by other sporozoa (microsporidia, coccidia) as well as by gregarines *(Lankesteria, Caulleryella),* flagellates *(Herpetomonas, Crithidia), cili*ates *(Lamboruella, Glaucoma),* trematodes *(Agamodistoruurn, Prrewnoucoeces* larvae), filaria, mites (Hydrachnidae) and bloodsucking midges. Immature mosquitoes can be destroyed by adding oil to the water in which they live.

This technique prevents them from obtaining oxygen because they cannot attach to the surface layer of oil with their breathing tubes. The chief destructive effect, however, is due to the volatile toxic substances that occur in most oils used, for example, kerosene and diesel fuel. Various larvicides, such as copper sulfate, Paris green, or naphthalene, may also be added to the water to kill larvae and pupae.

Students should remember that these chemicals may also kill desirable organisms. Insect sprays containing pyrethrum, lindane, or any of a number of other chemicals are effective against adult and immature mosquitoes. Elimination of breeding places is recommended. Swampy areas may be drained and filled, and such containers as cisterns or small vessels may be emptied or covered.

Some of the enemies of mosquitoes may be used in biocontrol. Studies involving the microsporidan *Nosenia* and mermithid nematodes indicate that these parasites may be useful for this purpose. For literature on mosquitoes and mosquito-borne diseases, see Sollers-Riedel."

FAMILY SIMULIIDAE

The family Simuliidae, worldwide in distribution, includes small insects called blackflies or buffalo gnats. The immature stages of these flies are aquatic and normally prefer running water. Both larvae and pupae are attached to rocks or to plants under water. Adults are humpba-

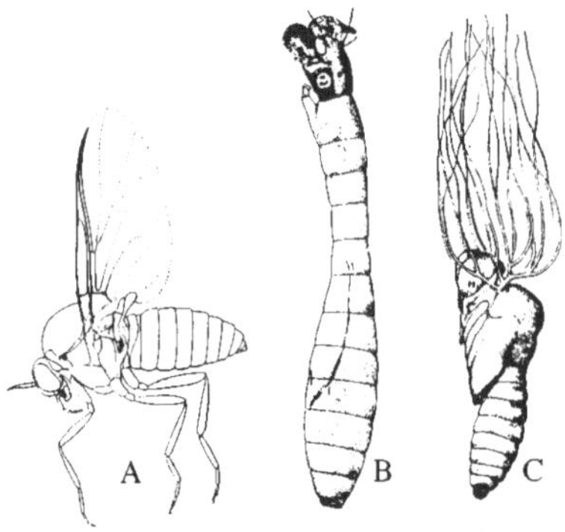

Figure 11.32: Stimuli, a balckfly. A, Side view of adult. B, Larva, C, Pupa.

cked, hence the name "buffalo gnat." They sometimes occur in enormous swarms, especially near water, and they annoy livestock and man by their painful bites. Some species gather in tremendous numbers on domestic mammals and on birds.

Flies may cause such an annoyance to poultry that the birds leave their nests. Aggressive female insects sometimes crawl under the wings of young birds and suck so much blood that the birds die. Danger is not only due to loss of blood and to possible bacterial infection of bitten areas, but also to the toxic saliva of the insect and to parasites that the fly might transmit.

The major parasite of man that simuliid flies carry is the roundworm, *Onchocerca volvulus,* which infects man in warm areas such as Africa, Central America, and Mexico. The flies may also transmit tularemia and the protozoan parasite, *Leucocvtozoon.*

The latter organism is a blood inhabitant of birds, especially of turkeys and ducks. *Leucocvtozoou sirnondi is* found in the peripheral blood of ducks, whereas *L. smithi is* a similar parasite of' turkeys. Common insect vectors are *Sirnulium rucilesi* and *Eusirnuliuw anatinurn.*

The flies attach themselves to the necks of the birds and feed for two or three minutes before flying away. Use of insecticides and other control measures against the fly are only partially effective.

FAMILY TABANIDAE

Tabanidae is another family of flies whose females suck blood. These insects, larger than the Simuliidae, are known as horseflies, deerflies, or clegs. They are stout flies, each with a broadly triangular head, most of which is composed of eves.

Various species of *Tabanus* transmit the flagellate blood parasite,

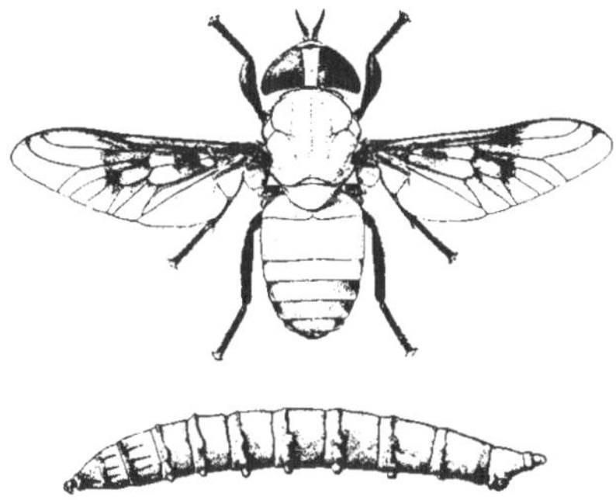

Figure 11.33: Tabanus latipes with its larva.

T typanosoma evaosi, which causes the disease *surra* in horses, cattle, dogs, elephants, and in other animals. Members of this genus of flies also carry anthrax and tularemia to man and animals. Tularemia is also transmitted *by Chrysops,* which, in addition, may carry the filarial worm, *Lou loa*. Different species of the genus *Chrysops* feed at different times of the day. *C. silacea* and *C. dirnidiata* do most of their biting during the morning and late in the afternoon; *C. land* and *C. centurionis* do the bulk of their biting in the evening, at sunset.

FAMILY PSYCHODIDAE

Phlebotomine flies, or sandflies, belong to the family Psychodidae. They occur throughout the tropics and subtropics and are found in some temperate areas of Europe, Central Asia, and North America. The

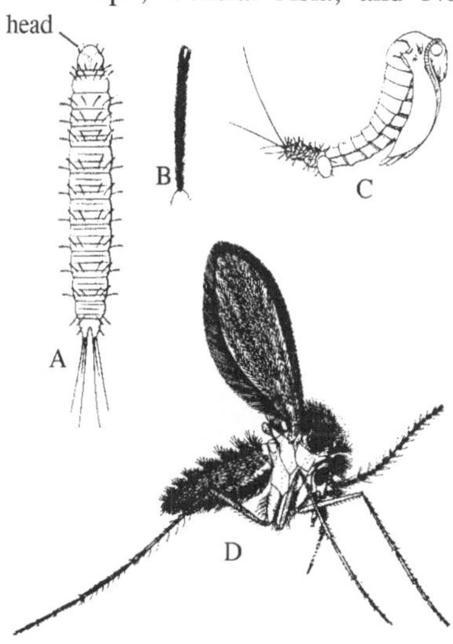

Figure 11.34: Larva, pupa, and adult female of Phlehotomus papatasii.

female is larger than the male and has piercing mouth parts. All species are obligate bloodsuckers.

Sandflies are of considerable public health importance and are vectors of leishmaniasis, bartonellosis, and sandfly fever viruses. The seven or more protozoa they carry include trypanosomes, plasmodia, and hemogregarines parasitic in warm-blooded and poikilothermic animals. Sandflies of the Old World belong to the genera *Phlebotomus* and *Sergentornyia;* those of the New World are included in the genera *Lutzomyia, Brumptomyia, Warileya,* and *Hertigia.*

Most sandflies are nocturnal; during the day, they rest in protected, moist places such as caves, animal burrows, tree buttresses and holes, animal shelters, or houses. Eggs are laid 3 or 4 days after a blood meal in soil, leaf litter, or animal feces. Eggs hatch in about 10 to 12 days. There are 4 larval instars, followed by a pupal stage.

The entire life cycle takes about 6 to 10 weeks, depending on the ambient temperature. The flies are weak fliers, so activity is diminished on windy or rainy nights. For parasites of sandflies, see Ayala.[2] For phlebotomine sandflies of the Orient, see Lewis."'

FAMILY OESTRIDAE

Warbleflies are so called because their larvae usually lie under the skin of their hosts and cause a swelling known as a *warble*. The best-known members of this group are the ox warble, *Hypoderma bovis*, a stout, *hairy fly* that looks a little like a bee, and a similar species, *H. lineatum,* the heelfly. The adult heelfly is hairy, black, and yellow and is several times larger than a housefly.

In the spring, each female fly lays hundreds of eggs on the leg or body hairs of cattle. In a few days, eggs hatch into tiny, white, spiny

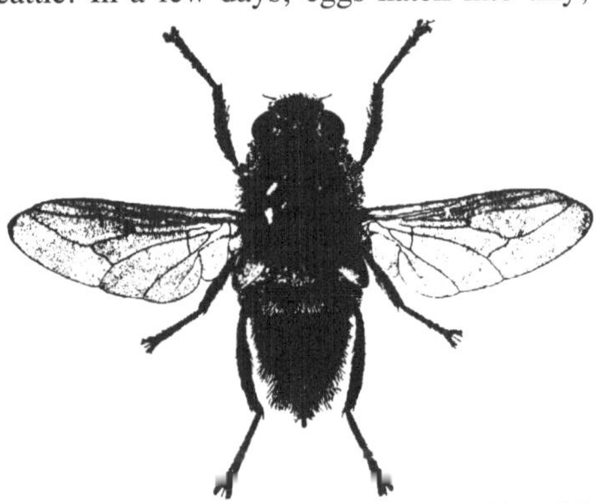

Figuere 11.35: Hypodertua bovis, the ox warble, adult.

larvae (sometimes called "bots," hence the name "botflies") that crawl down the hairs and burrow through the skin. For several months, the larvae wander through the intestines, liver, heart, muscles, or other organs; these larvae apparently enjoy the protection and warmth of their host.

Some of them spend many weeks in the connective tissues of the esophagus. Apparently, the first instar larvae migrate to the vertebral region, where they produce small swellings or warbles in the skin. They make a tiny hole in the skin for air, and then they increase in size to about 25 mm in length. During this period, they turn dark brown. In the spring or summer, the grubs or maggots emerge through the holes and drop to the ground and pupate.

They crawl under loose soil or trash, and in two to seven weeks, depending on the temperature, the adult flies emerge. One to three hundred million dollars are lost annually in the United States because of damage to hides and irritation and annoyance to cattle.

The animals "get off their feed," lose weight, and are generally unthrifty. Milk production diminishes. The holes in the skin make the hide unfit for high-quality leather. *Dermatobia hominis*, a similar fly, though not so hairy, may occur as a maggot in the skin of man in Central and South America.

This warblefly is about 12 mm in length. The nonbiting females attach their eggs to the bodies of mosquitoes *(Fanthinsoma lutzi)*,other flying insects, or even ticks. Eggs thus are given a free ride to a new host. When the mosquitoes alight to feed on man or on other warm-blooded animals, the warblefly eggs hatch, and the larvae penetrate the skin of their new host.

Oestrus ovis, instead of laying eggs, deposits its larvae or maggots in the nostrils of sheep, goats, and a few other mammals such as deer. The maggots crawl into the nasal passages, and during the next few weeks, they molt twice. When fully grown and about 25 mm long, they come out of the nose, drop to the ground, and pupate.

The adult fly emerges from the pupa. It is also called a *gadfly* or *nasalfly*. This fly may attack shepherds or other persons who have recently eaten goat's milk products and whose breath smells of such food as cheese. Larvae are deposited in the shepherd's nostrils, on his lips, or even on his eyes, and sometimes the larvae cause considerable damage.

The names *botfly* and *warblefly* are used interchangeably. Thus, *Gasterophilus intestinalis* may be called a horse bot- or warblefly. This

Figure 11.36: Oestrus ovis, the adult sheep nasalfly.

and related genera are usually placed in a separate family, Gasterophilidae. Adults of' this botfly also look like a bee. The fly attaches its eggs to hairs on the legs or bodies of horses. As soon as the eggs become infective, the larvae pop out when they are brushed by the moist, warm lips of the horse.

These spiny larvae become attached to the horse's lips or tongue and thus are easily swallowed. They may, however, burrow through the mucous membranes of the mouth and make their way to the stomach through various tissues. Larvae attach themselves to the lining of the stomach, sometimes in such large numbers that this membrane is almost covered with them.

After some months of maturing, the maggots pass from the host body with feces, drop to the ground, and pupate. Adult flies emerge from the pupae; when they start laying eggs, the life cycle is complete.

FAMILY TACHINIDAE

The family Tachinidae contains many species of flies, all of which are parasitic on insects or other arthropods, for example, terrestrial isopods. Some of the tachinids look like houseflies, and some appear more like bees or wasps, but most of them possess long bristles on the tips of their abdomens.

A tachinid normally deposits its eggs on the body of its host, for example, larvae of butterflies or beetles, and larvae burrow inside to eat. The larva literally eats itself out of house and home and kills its host. When mature, the fly crawls out of the host and pupates on the ground.

Some tachinids lay eggs on foliage, and when the larvae emerge, they either crawl into a host or become infective when swallowed by the host. For comments on the evolution of the tachinids.

FAMILY CALLIPHORIDAE

Blowflies may look like houseflies, but are often larger and firec]uently arc metallic green or blue. They lay their eggs on organic masses such as dead animals, excrement, open sores, or exposed cooked or uncooked food. The eggs hatch into maggots, which proceed to eat the material around them.

The genus *Calliphora* includes the bluebottle flies whose larvae are commonly found in decaying meat. Eggs are also laid in exposed, foul wounds of man and animals. The maggots eat only the putrid tissues in the wound. Occasionaly, live *Calliphora* maggots are swallowed in cooked meat, and rarely, they pass through the body.

The emergence of these maggots from the intestine accounts for some of the reported cases of myiasis in man. The term *myiasis* refers to the presence of parasitic maggots in or on man or animals. *Phaenicia sericata* and *Phorrnia regina* are two species whose larvae have been used by physicians to clean wounds and to treat such diseases as osteomyelitis in man. ***Lucilia bufonivora*** lays its eggs on the back of a toad or other amphibian.

Eggs hatch within a day, apparently owing to the chemical nature of the skin glands. The tiny larvae crawl to the head region and onto the surface of the eye. By blinking its eyes, the toad carries the maggots to the lacrimal ducts, which lead to the nasal cavity. There the larvae molt and form the second stage, which actively feeds on host tissues and eventually destroys the cartilaginous nasal septum.

When mature, the larvae drop out of this enlarged nasal cavity and pupate in the ground. ***Chrysomya bezziana*** is a green blowfly that seems to prefer wounds and body spaces of man and of wild and domestic

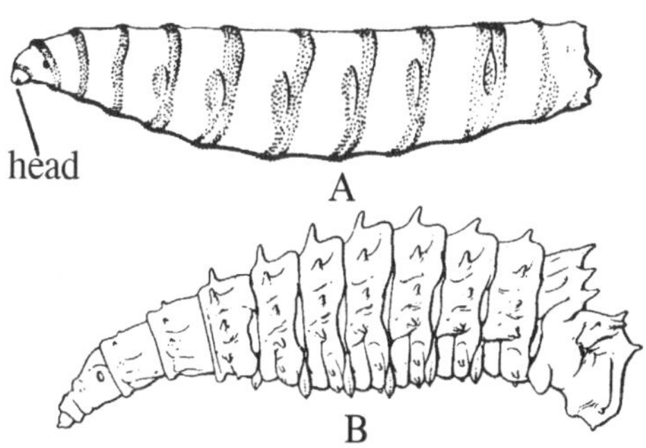

Figure 11.37: A, Chrysomya bezziana, the mature third stage larva. × 4. B, The mature third stage larva of C. albiceps × 4.

animals. Larvae may be found in the nose, eves, ears, alimentary canal, urinary passages, and genital organs, or in tiny cuts or sores in the skin.

Eggs may even be laid in the pierced ear lobes of women. At first, the small maggots are not noticed, but when they grow to a centimeter or more in length and begin to burrow through the skin near the wound, they may produce a tumor of considerable size, especially if many worms are present. This species is found in the Philippines, India, and Africa.

Cochliomyia hominivorax is a bluish blowfly about twice the size of a housefly. It lays its eggs in neat rows on the edges of wounds of mammals, especially on fresh cuts. The eggs hatch in a day or less into maggots that feed on living flesh. These maggots are called "screw-worms." The wound attended by screwworms has a foul odor. In about a week, the maggots drop to the ground and pupate in the soil.

In another week, if the weather is warm, adults emerge. In still another week or less, new eggs, about 200 in a batch, are deposited on the edge of a cut, a sore, the navel of newborn animals, or on some other abrasion. This screwwworm is an obligatory parasite of warm-blooded animals and is responsible for millions of dollars worth of damage annually to United States livestock.

Untreated animals usually die. General control involves doing all that is possible to prevent cuts and scratches on livestock. One method of control consists of releasing laboratoryreared, sterilized male flies in an infected area. Females do not mate a second time, so those that happen to mate with sterile males cannot reproduce.

This trick played on unsuspecting females has resulted in a significant reduction in screwworm infection in isolated areas. Other blowflies, principally *Phorrnia regtna,* the black blowfly; *Cochliomyia niacellaria,* the secondary screwworm fly; and *Phaenicia sericato,* the greenbottle fly, possess larvae that are called fleeceworms. They attack the hair of sheep and goats and also enter wounds. Eggs are usually deposited on soiled fleece or on old or new sores.

In addition to injuring the quality of fleece and aggravating wounds, they may carry the infective organisms of anthrax, plague, undulant fever, tularemia, and enteric diseases. Infestation by larval *Phaeuicia sericata* may start in a normal healthy ear. One such rare case of human aural myiasis was found in Canada. If left untreated, these infestations may lead to pain, deafness, and ringing in the ear if the maggots are in the external meatus. If they enter the middle ear, a bloody, purulent discharge may result.'

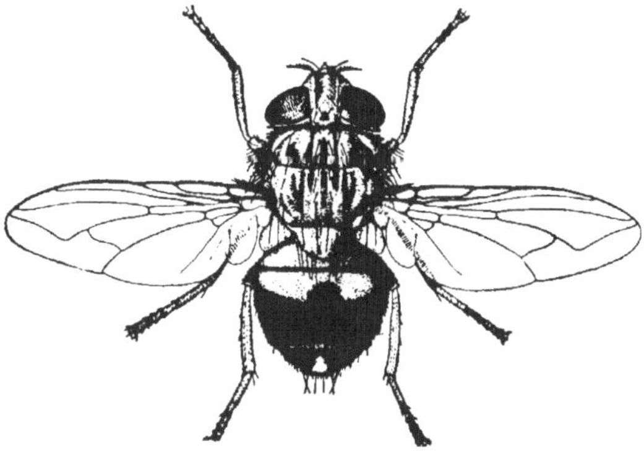

Figure 11.38: Cordylobia anthropophac,a, the tumbu fly, female. × *2.*

The tumbu fly of Africa, *Cordylobia anthropophaga*, measures about 10 mm in length and is yellowish brown. Eggs are deposited on the ground, where they hatch. When the appropriate host (man and other mammals) lies on the ground, larvae burrow through the skin into their new home. As the larva grows, it produces a boil-like swelling in the skin, with a small hole at the top of the lesion.

Through the hole, the maggot breathes and discharges its waste. When mature, the maggot emerges through the hole, drops to the ground, and pupates. Two cases of myiasis caused by this fly have been reported from man in the United States.

FAMILY SARCOPHAGIDAE

The family Sarcophagidae contains the fleshflies, which are large, gray insects with longitudinal black stripes on the dorsal surface of the thorax. Like the blowflies, the fleshflies are scavengers, and the larvae may be found in wounds, carrion, sores, or body cavities of man and animals. Unlike blowflies, most fleshflies do not lay eggs, but are larviparous.

The genus *Sarcophaga* is worldwide in distribution. The genus *Wohlfahrtia* contains species that parasitize man and animals and thus cause myiasis in these hosts. A larva of *Wohlfahrtia magn a* has even been found in the cavity of an infected tooth.

FAMILY MUSCIDAE

The family Muscidae is well known for furnishing man with some of his most serious insect parasites. They include the tsetse *fly, Glossina*; carrier of the causative organisms of African sleeping sickness (Chap. 3); the stablefly, *Stomoxys calcitrans,* which can transmit mechanically the causative organism of Oriental sore.

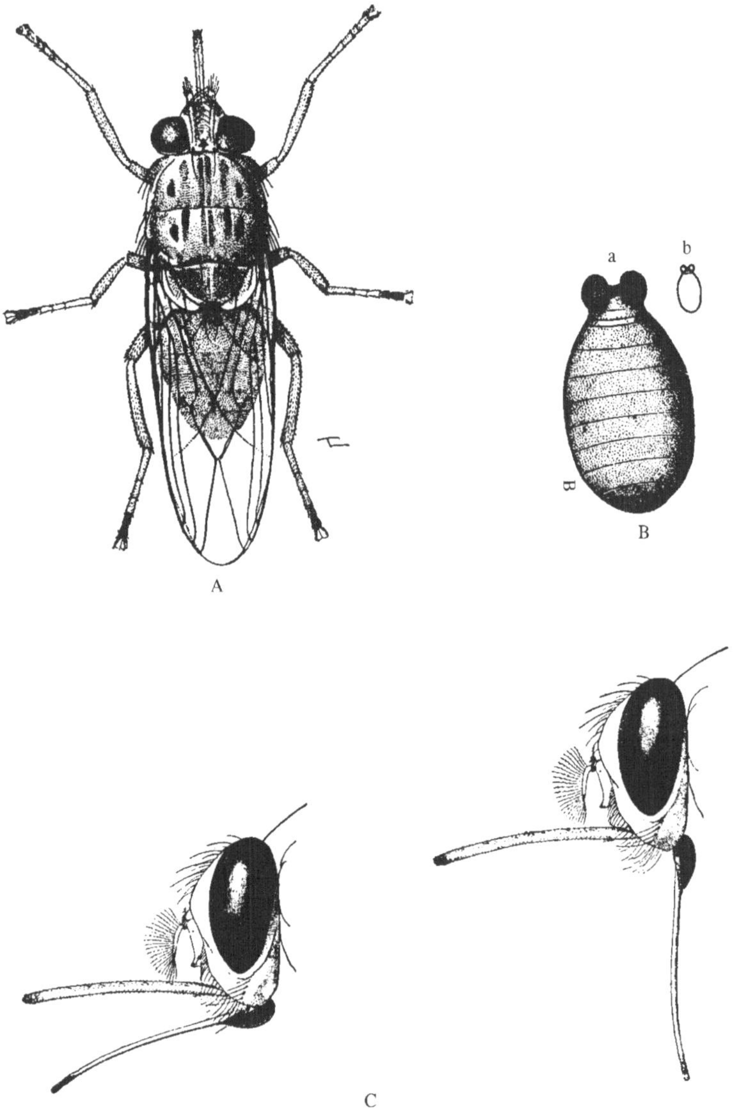

Figure 11.39: A tsetse fly.

PUPIPARA

Pupipara are peculiar looking flies that are ectoparasitic on birds and mammals. They are bloodsucking and are called louse flies, bat flies, tick flies, or keds. They usually are wingless, flattened diptera that can be found on the bodies of animals or in birds' nests or bat roosts. Some of these flies possess and retain wings; others shed them on reaching their hosts. Wild animals are attacked as well as horses, sheep, and other domestic animals.

That ectoparasitic flies are found on bats is not surprising when one considers the probability that ancestral flies deposited their eggs in bat droppings. From this start, the association undoubtedly became progressively closer, until today there are such forms as the completely wingless pupiparous species, *Nycteribia biarticulata,* which at first glance looks more like a louse than a fly. The Pupipara belong to several families.

FAMILY HIPPOBOSCIDAE

The family Hippoboscidae includes the more common species of Pupipara. An important member of the family is the sheep ked or "sheep tick," *Melophnsrus ovitlrzs*, a wingless, leathery, flattened insect that is hardly recognizable as a fly. It is about 6 mm long, and like other Pupipara, does not lay eggs, but gives birth to larvae already advanced almost to the *pupal* stage.

Pseudolyzchia canarietisis, another hippoboscid, is a winged louse fly that lives on pigeons. In addition to causing annoyance to the birds, this ectoparasite carries an endoparasite of birds, the malarial-like blood parasite, *Haerrzoproteus.*

MYIASIS

As defined by Zumpt, myiasis is "the infestation of live human and vertebrate animals with dipterous larvae, which, at least for a certain period, feed on the host's dead or living tissue, liquid body-substances, or ingested food.". At least 187 species of myiasis-producing larvae are recorded in the world literature.

They belong primarily to the families Calliphoridae and Oestridae, but are also found among the Muscidae, Chloropidae, and Gasterophilidae. Several examples have already been given. Those in the intestine produce intestinal myiasis, whereas those in the genital organs or urinary tract produce urinogenital myiasis.

Some maggots occur only in wounds and sores, especially foul and suppurating sores, whereas others actually penetrate living flesh and

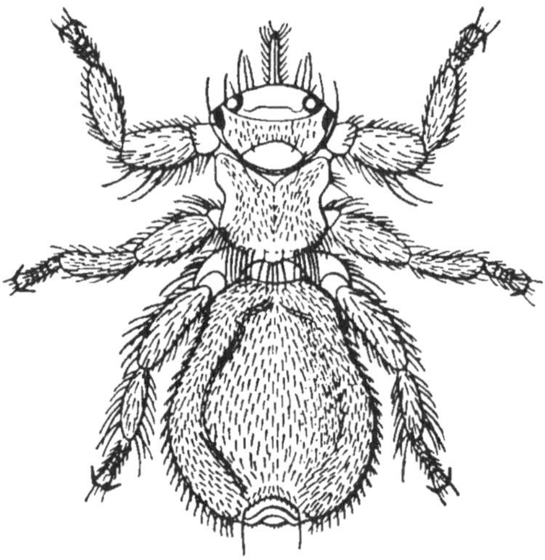

Figure 11.40: Melophagus ovinus, the sheep ked. × 4.

produce boils or weals in the skin or, as we have seen, in the chambers of the nose, mouth, eyes, or ears.

Intestinal myiasis is usually caused accidentally by ingesting contaminated food or drink. Fly eggs or maggots may occur on overripe fruit, raw meats, cheese, salads, dried fish, dirty water, or milk. Urinogenital myiasis is usually also accidental. Flies may lay their eggs on the exposed and unclean pubic area.

Some of the genera of flies involved in accidental myiasis are *Culliphora, Musca, Farinia, Storno.zys, Drosophila, Sep*sis, and *Tipula.* Flies that deposit their eggs in or near foul wounds, and whose larvae thus have an opportunity to invade the wound, belong mainly to the genera *Sarcophagi, Phormia, Cochliornyia,* or *Chrysomyia.* Identification of many of these maggots is difficult.

One of the common diagnostic characteristics is the nature of the posterior spiracles. Figure elsewhere in this chapter illustrates these spiracles as they appear in the larvae of some myiasis-producing flies.

Invertebrates have their share of parasitic fly larvae. Some Hymenoptera may contain maggots that actually attach their spiracular openings to the host trachea in order to breathe. The snail, *Helicella vergata,* may become so infested with fly maggots that the parasites kill their host and eat practically all the dead tissues.

One of the few studies" of the biochemical effect of myiasis on the host involved the white-footed mouse, *Perornyscus leucopus,* and the

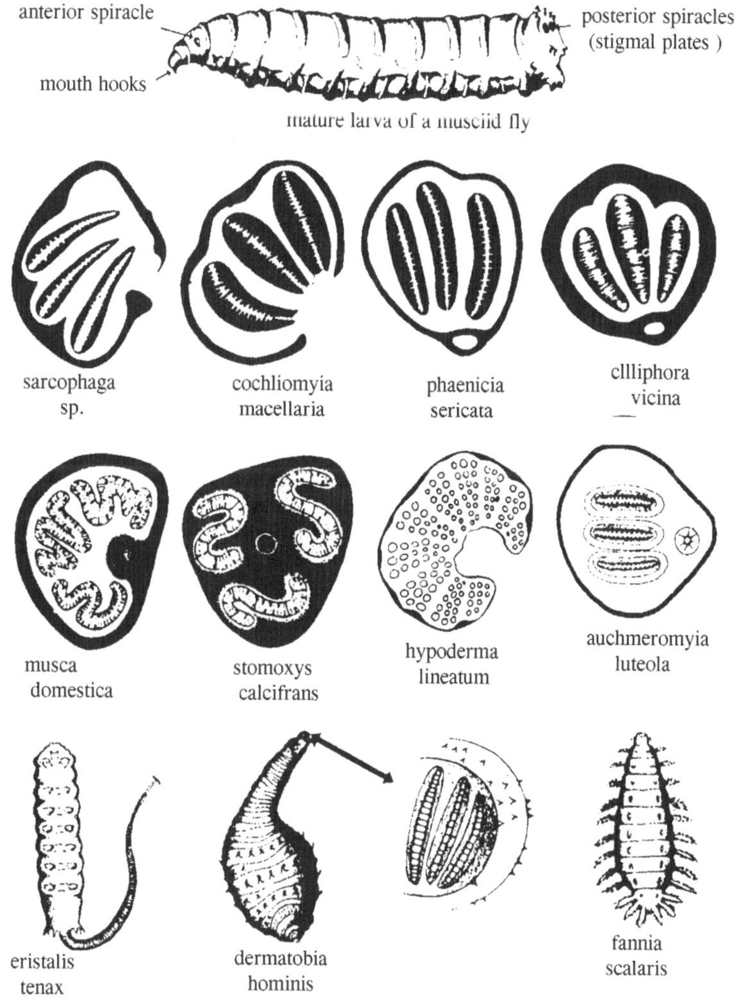

Figure 11.41: Key characteristics of myiasis-producing flylarvae.

botfly, *Cuterebra angustftons*. Development of the larva in the mouse was accompanied by progressive reductions in the albumin-to-globulin ratio of the host. These reductions were correlated with the number of larvae present. Ingestion of albumin by the botfly was proposed as a partial explanation for the reductions.

For a review of insects and disease, see Snow.”’ For flies and disease, see Greenberg.’ For parasitic insects, see Askew.’

12

Symptoms of Parasitic Disease

Very few of the signs or symptoms evoked by infection with *parasitic* organisms can be said to deserve that much-abused term *pathognomonic*. There are but a limited number of ways in which the body is able to react to altered conditions, and therefore it is not surprising that few of these reactions are specific.

However, the presence of certain signs and symptoms should alert the clinician to corresponding diagnostic possibilities, while various constellations of symptoms, or syndromes, are to a greater or lesser degree diagnostic.

It must be emphasized that the following is not intended as a complete differential diagnosis of any of the symptoms discussed. Limitations of space do not permit even mention of the various non-parasitic etiologies of many of these conditions.

ABDOMINAL PAIN

Crampy abdominal pain may characterize amebic colitis, with tenesmus if the ulcerations involve the rectal area. *Diarrhea* or *dysentery* is usually present when the infection is *symptomatic*. If hepatic abscess develops, pain is usually felt in the right upper quadrant (left, if the abscess involves the left lobe), and may be referred to the scapular area.

Pain in giardiasis is usually mild but may occasionally be severe; it is usually crampy and may be accompanied by steatorrhea and a full-blown malabsorption syndrome. Pain is seldom present in intestinal worm infections. Intestinal or biliary obstruction (the former primarily in smaller children) can be the result of *Ascaris* infection, with signs and symptoms which mimic obstruction from any other cause.

Strongyloides stercoralis, invading the mucosal wall, may cause a severe duodenitis or jejunitis, with symptoms suggestive of duodenal ulcer disease. A moderate to heavy eosinophilia generally accompanies either of these worm infections.

ABSCESS, AMEBIC

Amebic invasion of the liver is characterized by tenderness and enlargement of that organ, progressive malaise, an irregularly spiking fever with night *sweats*, *leukocytosis*, elevation and fixation of the right diaphragm, and sometimes development of a right lower lobe *pneumonitis*. With abscess formation, pain becomes more intense and may be referred to the tip of the right (less commonly the left) scapula.

Abscess, Filarial *Abscesses* may develop spontaneously or appear shortly after antifilarial treatment is begun. They occur along the course of lymphatics or at lymph nodes and may be distinguished from *pyogenic* abscesses by the fact that they are generally sterile when first opened and that fragments of the adult worms may be found in the abscess drainage.

Anemia Most frequently associated with malaria, hookworm, and broad fish tapeworm infections, anemia may be seen in kala-azar, trypanosomiasis, schistosomiasis, fasciolopsiasis and trichuriasis. In falciparum malaria the red cell count may fall to 2.5 to 4.0 million in cases of average severity, and under 1.0 million in severe infections.

Anemia is usually not severe in *vivax malaria* and is still less pronounced in quartan infections. The characteristic microcytic hypochromic anemia of *hookworm infection* is the result of blood loss and is thus proportional to the severity of infection, although adequate dietary intake of iron may prevent its development in light or moderate infections.

The small amount of blood ingested per *Trichuris* makes anemia rare in other than massive infections. Persons infected with *Diphyllobothrium latum* may develop a macrocytic hyperchromic anemia on the basis of vitamin B_{12} deprivation if the worm is attached to the jejunal wall. In kala-azar, and possibly also in *Chagas*' disease, anemia may be a consequence of proliferation of infected reticuloendothelial cells in the bone marrow. In the other *trypanosomiases*, *schistosomiasis*, and certain intestinal *helminthic* infections such as fasciolopsiasis, anemia may result in part from nutritional causes.

Appendicitis

Amebic ulceration involving the cecal area or appendix may simulate acute appendicitis; surgical intervention when there is extensive cecal ulceration may be disastrous. *Ascaris* may block the lumen of the appendix and give rise to appendicitis; this is reported also for *Trichuris*. *Angiostrongylus costaricensis* infection may also mimic appendicitis.

Ascites

Circumoval tissue proliferation leading to extensive fibrosis of the liver in *Schistosoma mansoni* and S. *japonicum* infections may lead eventually to a condition clinically very similar to Laennec's cirrhosis, with portal hypertension, splenomegaly and ascites. Although hepatomegaly and splenomegaly occur early in kala-azar, ascites is uncommon. It may occur in chronic cases, probably secondary to a nutritional cirrhosis.

Asthma, Bronchial

Asthmatic attacks may occur in *Ascaris* infection during the stage of migration through the lungs, or later in the course of the infection because of hypersensitization to the absorbed worm antigens. Asthma is not uncommon in visceral larva migrans infections, in which there is usually an accompanying hepatomegaly and marked eosinophilia. See also tropical eosinophilia, under EOSINOPHILIA.

Calabar Swellings

Circumscribed subcutaneous swellings are seen in loiasis. They are usually intensely pruritic and may be quite painful if they develop in areas where there is little loose subcutaneous tissue. They appear rapidly, developing within an hour or so to a diameter of several centimeters, and persist for several days, or if in an area subject to repeated trauma may last for a week or longer.

CALCIFICATIONS, CEREBRAL

Calcification of areas of intracerebral infection in congenital toxoplasmosis may be seen on x-ray, and when intracerebral calcifications are found in a patient who has chorioretinitis, a diagnosis of toxoplasmosis is highly probable. Calcified cysts of *Cysticercus cellulosae* within the brain may be distinguished by their size and uniform rounded or oval shape.

Chagoma

The hard, reddened, raised primary lesion in *Trypanosoma cruzi* infection usually develops on the head or neck and sometimes on the abdomen or limbs, and may persist for two or three months. Although it may occur on or about the eye, the chagoma is not to be confused with the unilateral palpebral edema of Romana's sign (q.v.).

Chorioretinitis

Infection of the retina and choroid by *Toxoplasma* or (rarely) *Entamoeba histolytica* may produce visual disturbances, which can be profound if the macula is involved. On ophthalmoscopic examination, a grayish or yellow-white area surrounded by exudate is seen early; with healing this leaves a white atrophic patch bordered by pigment deposits.

Chyluria

The formation of lymphatic varices, consequent upon repeated attacks of filarial lymphangitis and obstruction of lymphatic drainage, may lead to the passage of lymphatic fluid in the urine, if varices rupture into any part of the urinary tract. Chyluria usually occurs in attacks lasting a few days; the urine may have a milky white color and contain microfilariae.

COMA

The sudden onset of coma in a patient known to be suffering from falciparum malaria, or in an apparently healthy person in, or recently returned from, a malarious area, should always suggest cerebral malaria and requires emergency treatment. While most common as a complication of falciparum malaria, coma may occur with other types of malaria.

In African trypanosomiasis, coma develops after a protracted period of increasingly severe symptoms of meningoencephalitis. It is also seen in primary amebic meningoencephalitis, in which a history of rapidly developing fever, meningeal signs, confusion and coma, and of recent swimming or diving in fresh water will often be elicited.

Cerebral *cysticercosis* may be a diagnostic consideration in persons of Mexican or Latin American origin, or of long residence in those areas, who present with a variety of *neurological* symptoms including headache, alteration of consciousness, focal seizures, coma and internal hydrocephalus. Diagnosis may be difficult, and *eosinophilia* (either peripheral or of the spinal fluid) is not always present. *Serological* tests are helpful.

Conjunctivitis

Chronic conjunctivitis is seen in onchocercal infections, with hyperpigmentation of the conjunctiva, photophobia and gradual development of corneal opacities; acute exacerbations of conjunctivitis and photophobia may be associated with attacks of onchocercal dermatitis (q.v.).

The sheep botfly, *Oestrus ovis,* may lay its eggs in the conjunctivae, and development of the larva in the conjunctival sac is accompanied by considerable pain, localized swelling and conjunctivitis.

Convulsions

Focal convulsive seizures of the jacksonian type are seen in a number of parasitic infections that involve the central nervous system. These are discussed under NEUROLOGIC SYMPTOMS. Convulsions also may be seen in the malarial paroxysm, in acute toxoplasmosis occurring in newborn children, and in *Ascaris* infection in children.

Dermatitis

Dermal leishmanoid is a secondary cutaneous manifestation of *Leishmania donovani* infection, occurring a year or so after supposedly successful treatment of kala-azar. The lesions may be flattened or depressed depigmented macules, or erythematous nodules which, on the face, often occur in a butterfly distribution reminiscent of lupus erythematosus.

Leishmanial amastigotes are found in the lesions. Penetration of schistosome cercariae through the skin causes a localized edema and pruritus, mild in the case of the human schistosomes, more severe in the "swimmer's itch" caused by bird schistosome cercariae.

A similar localized pruritic reaction occurs with penetration of *Strongyloides* larvae through the skin; the reaction to penetration of hookworm larvae is somewhat more severe, often with the formation of papules or vesicles; it may last for a couple of weeks or longer if there is a secondary infection.

The cutaneous larva migrans reaction caused by larvae of *Ancylostoma braziliense* is characterized by a reddened papule at the site of entry; the larva forms a reddened serpiginous tunnel, at first covered with vesicles, later dry and crusted, which advances at the rate of a few millimeters to centimeters a day.

The area itches intensely; without treatment infection may persist for several weeks or months. *Strongyloides* larvae may produce similar cutaneous lesions, but because pf their more rapid subcutaneous movement, they are referred to as "*larva currens.*"

Presence of adult *Loa loa* beneath the skin may be indicated by a thin raised reddened line, a few centimeters in length. The adult female *Dracunculus* also may be visible beneath the skin but usually produces no reaction until about to larviposit, when a vesicle forms over the point at which the worm is about to break through the skin.

In *onchocerciasis*, the presence of microfilariae in the skin sometimes elicits an acute pruritic inflammatory reaction resembling erysipelas and usually confined to the face, neck and ears; repeated acute attacks may result in a chronic lichenification, with hyperpigmentation and fissuring.

The migration of *Sarcoptes scabiei* through the skin produces lesions resembling those of cutaneous larva migrans, but frequently seen in parts of the body that have no contact with soil. This organism is highly infectious, and localized hospital epidemics have been reported.

The mites invade the upper layers of the epidermis, in which they form sinuous burrows. They seem to have a predilection for the interdigital, popliteal and inframammary folds and the groin. Intense itching, with formation of small vesicles and crusting of the chronic excoriated lesions, is typical.

The larvae of the horse botfly, *Gasterophilus,* produce similar cutaneous lesions in man. Pediculosis in hypersensitive persons, usually as a result of repeated exposure, may give rise to a severe localized reaction, with reddish papules at the feeding site, and surrounding vesiculation and a weeping dermatitis.

Bronzing of the affected area may persist following healing. The chigoe flea, *Tunga penetrans,* produces local pruritus as it lies partly buried in the skin of the toes or elsewhere on the body; secondary infections by clostridia are not uncommon. See also RASH.

DIARRHEA

Diarrhea in parasitic diseases may be of diverse etiologies. In kala-azar, infiltration of the submucosa with leishmania-containing macrophages may lead to mucosal ulceration and diarrhea. Plugging of the mucosal capillaries with parasitized red blood cells may lead, in falciparum malaria, to a watery diarrhea so profuse as to suggest cholera. Blood, containing parasitized red cells, may be found in the stools.

The diarrhea or dysentery is usually accompanied by nausea and vomiting. Mucosal ulceration in amebiasis or balantidiasis may produce diarrhea or, if the ulceration is more extensive, dysentery (q.v.). *Isospora* develops within the epithelial cells of the lower ileum and cecum. Infection is self-limited, lasting usually a month or less, and often asymptomatic.

In some cases there is mild abdominal pain, nausea and vomiting, and diarrhea. *Giardia* infections may be asymptomatic, accompanied by a mild mucoid diarrhea, or, like *Isospora,* may give rise to a full-blown malabsorption syndrome with steatorrhea.

Development of the cysticercoids of *Hymenolepis nana* within the intestinal villi may elicit a mucous diarrhea. Maturation of *Trichinella* within the wall of the duodenum and jejunum produces nausea, vomiting, colicky abdominal pain and diarrhea, starting about 24 hours after infection and lasting up to five days.

In *Strongyloides* infections there may be mild diarrhea, alternating with periods pf constipation, or the diarrhea may be severe and prostrating. In heavy infections ulceration and sloughing of the intestinal mucosa may take place, with dysentery and often with secondary bacterial infection and fever. *Capillaria philippinensis* infections may result in profuse diarrhea, malabsorption and a protein-wasting enteropathy.

In schistosomiasis mansoni and japonicum, there is diarrhea, presumably of toxic origin, associated with nausea, vomiting, hepatic tenderness, fever, eosinophilia and an urticarial rash, during the period while the worms are maturing in the liver sinusoids. Somewhat later, with the beginning of egg deposition in the intestinal wall, there may be a profuse diarrhea or dysentery.

In persons previously uninfected, the onset of a heavy hookworm infection may be marked by nausea, vomiting, epigastric or midabdominal tenderness, and diarrhea. The diarrhea is presumably caused by toxicity or hypersensitivity, although mechanical irritation may play some part.

The same may be said of the diarrhea in heavy whipworm infections. In fasciolopsiasis, diarrhea, which usually has its onset about a month after infection takes place, is characterized by the passage of stools containing much undigested food; severe infections are accompanied by symptoms of severe malnutrition, with edema of the face, abdominal wall and lower extremities, ascites and prostration.

The diarrhea sometimes seen in *Taenia* and broad fish tapeworm infections and in infections with the smaller intestinal flukes may be related to local irritation.

Dysentery

Acute amebic dysentery is characterized by the passage of six to eight or sometimes a dozen or more mucoid blood-flecked stools a day. There may be generalized abdominal pain and tenderness if the entire colon is involved, tenderness over McBurney's point, nausea and vomiting with cecal infection, or tenesmus, with relief of the accompanying pain after evacuation if the rectosigmoid is the main diseased area.

An untreated attack lasts a few days to several weeks and usually subsides spontaneously to recur after an interval of some days to several years. Between attacks the patient may be constipated. Balantidial dysentery is similar to amebic, and as in the latter disease, many infections are asymptomatic. Dysentery accompanying kalaazar, falciparum malaria infections, strongyloidiasis and schistosomiasis is mentioned in the discussion of DIARRHEA.

Edema

Circumorbital edema, possibly resulting from vasculitis provoked by the migrating larvae, is frequently seen in the early stages of trichinosis; there also may be edema of the hands. Unilateral circumorbital edema, with local pruritus and sometimes intense pain, results from passage of the adult *Loa loa* across the eyeball or lid.

Passage of the worm across the eyeball takes from less than half a minute to as long as 10 minutes; the resulting inflammatory changes usually persist for several days. Calabar swellings (q.v.) are also seen in loiasis, while localized edema of the face, neck, ears, etc., accompanied by intense pruritus and erythema, may be recurrent in onchocerciasis.

Ocular sparganosis is not uncommon in some areas as the result of poulticing eye lesions with split raw infected frogs. In the subcutaneous tissues around the eye, the sparganum produces a violent tissue reaction with edema; retrobulbar development 4 the sparganum may cause protrusion of the eyeball and consequent corneal ulceration. Areas of localized hard edema, of uncertain etiology, are frequently seen in Chagas' disease, occurring after appearance of the chagoma (q.v.).

The most common type is unilateral edema of the eyelids (Romana's sign) (q.v.). Edematous patches may develop elsewhere on the body, especially involving the abdominal wall, pubic area, scrotum and legs. Of equally obscure origin is the edema of the hips, legs, hands and face that may accompany the acute stage of African sleeping sickness.

Edema of the face and legs, with a protuberant abdomen, is seen in severe hookworm infections, fasciolopsiasis and diphyllobothriasis, and may be related to malnutrition.

ELEPHANTIASIS

Filarial elephantiasis is a chronic enlargement of a limb, the scrotum, a breast or the vulva, with hyperplasia of the connective tissue and skin, a woody non-pitting edema, and thickened, coarsened skin, often with verrucous changes. In Malayan filariasis, elephantiasis is less severe and generally is confined to the lower limbs. Elephantiasis of the external genitalia in both sexes, and hypertrophy of the femoral lymph nodes, producing a peculiar condition known as "hanging groin," have been reported from some areas in Africa where bancroftian filariasis is unknown, and are ascribed to onchocercal infection. In schistosomiasis haematobium, extensive egg deposition may lead to fibrosis, which blocks the lymphatic drainage, and to elephantiasis of the penis.

Eosinophilia

Eosinophilia is a consistent finding in helminth infections, though it may be quite variable in degree. In general, tissue parasites provoke a higher eosinophilia than those that live only in the lumen in the bowel.

As many physicians equate eosinophilia with parasitic disease, it may not be amiss to give the result of a Mayo Clinic study of 418 patients with an eosinophilia of 20 per cent or greater, as quoted by Harris:

Diseases with Eosinophilia of Greater than 20 Per Cent

Disease	*Per cent*
Atopic diseases (vasomotor rhinitis, asthma, hay fever)	28
Lymphoproliferative diseases (lymphoma)	20
Dermatoses (pemphigus, dermatitis herpetiformis)	10
Nonparasitic infections (principally streptococcal)	11
Periarteritis nodosa (with lung involvement)	10
Parasitic infections	4
Nonlymphatic malignant tumors and leukemia	4
Miscellaneous	13

A marked eosinophilia (20 to 70 per cent or higher) is most frequently seen in trichinosis, strongyloidiasis, hookworm infection, visceral larva migrans, filariasis, schistosomiasis and fasciolopsiasis. Moderate eosinophilia (6 to 20 per cent) often accompanies trichuriasis, ascariasis, paragonimiasis, taeniasis and eosinophilic meningitis. It must be realized that eosinophilia is an index of host reaction to the parasite; therefore, it will vary considerably from one patient to another.

Eosinophilia is not characteristic of any of the protozoan infections. Tropical eosinophilia or eosinophilic lung disease is characterized by symptoms of chronic bronchitis or asthma, marked eosinophilia, elevated erythrocyte sedimentation rate, paroxysmal cough or wheezing, malaise, easy fatiguability, anorexia and weight loss. The chest film may show diffuse patchy mottling and transverse branching striations, most prominent in the midlung and basal lung fields, with enlargement of the hilar shadows.

Occasionally there may be unilateral densities in the upper lung field which are suggestive of the picture seen in pulmonary tuberculosis. The disease is reported from such areas as India, Pakistan, Sri Lanka, China, Burma, Thailand, the Philippines, Malaysia and Indonesia, tropical Africa and the West Indies. Its etiology may be diverse.

Filarial infection, with human or non-human species, is considered to be a common cause of this condition. Other agents may be the pulmonary stages of *Ascaris, Strongyloides, Toxocara* or other helminths. Treatment with conventional doses of diethylcarbamazine is often effective; antimonial (stibophen) or arsenical drugs (neoarsphenamine) are sometimes effective when there is no response to diethylcarbamazine.

Epididymitis

An early complication of filarial infection, often associated with orchitis, and with or without accompanying lymphangitis and fever.

Fever

Patterns of fever may be characteristic in malaria and kala-azar, but it is a mistake to suppose that they must conform to the "textbook" pattern. A *quotidian fever is* often seen in the initial attack of vivax malaria, with two or more broods of parasites completing their exoerythrocytic cycle at different times, so that there may be a daily fever peak corresponding to rupture of the infected red cells and liberation of merozoites.

Daily fever peaks usually are seen only for a few days; apparently within this time all broods of parasites become synchronized, and thereafter the fever cycle will exhibit a tertian periodicity. Quartan and falciparum malaria may likewise exhibit a quotidian or irregular periodicity during the first few days of the primary attack.

Tertian fever is characteristic of vivax and ovale malaria. The paroxysm has an abrupt onset, usually initiated with a chill, which varies from a moderate sensation of cold to the intense "bed-shaking" chill usually thought typical of malaria.

The chill lasts up to an hour and the fever (to 104 or 105°) for two hours or longer, followed by a profuse sweat, during the course of which the temperature falls to normal over a period of an hour or so. The sweating stage usually is followed by sleep, and when the patient awakens he usually feels well. The next paroxysm is initiated approximately 48 hours after the onset of the previous one. *Sub tertian fever,* seen in falciparum malaria, is so called because the cycle may more nearly approach 36 than 48 hours.

There is usually no frank chill, and the febrile stage is prolonged, though the fever is not usually so high as in vivax; it may not fall to normal even in the intervals between paroxysms. There may be double peaks of fever in each 24-hour period, resembling the fever curve in kala-azar.

There is often no welldefined sweating stage, though sweating may be continuous, periodic or completely absent. *Quartan fever is* seen in malaria caused by *Plasmodium malariae.* There is often a regular periodicity from the start; the paroxysms recur at 72-hour intervals; while similar to those of vivax malaria, they are generally more severe.

The hot stage often lasts several hours and is frequently accompanied by nausea and vomiting; the sweating stage may be followed by prostration. *Hyperpyrexia* may develop as part of an attack of cerebral malaria or in the course of an apparently uncomplicated attack of falciparum malaria; as the result of injury to the heat-control center in the hypothalamus there is a rapid rise in temperature to 107° or higher, and death quickly ensues.

A doubly remittent or "dromedary" fever is frequently found in kala-azar. Febrile attacks, which last a few days to several weeks, are separated by afebrile periods of equal irregularity. At some time during the course of a febrile attack, there will usually be one or more days during which a double or triple rise to a temperature of 103 to 105° can be demonstrated during a 24-hour period.

An irregularly spiking fever with hepatic tenderness, suggestive of cholangitis, may be seen in amebic hepatitis, fascioliasis and acute *Opisthorchis* infections. The initial period of schistosome infection is likewise marked by irregular fever and hepatic tenderness, with nausea and vomiting, diarrhea and giant hives.

An irregular fever, usually with evening peaks and night sweats, is an early finding in African trypanosomiasis, and a high remittent fever, lasting for several weeks, occurs early in Chagas' disease. A remittent fever, with temperature to 104 or 105°, frequently marks the stage of larval migration in trichinosis. *Filarial fever* may occur very early in the course of a filarial infection.

There is usually a sudden onset, with fever ranging in the neighborhood of 102 to 104° and remaining elevated for several hours to a couple of days, and gradually subsiding in the next several days. Attacks of lymphangitis and lymphadenitis (q.v.) usually accompany the febrile episodes.

Funiculitis

Inflammation of the spermatic cord is frequently an early symptom of filariasis.

Hematuria

In *Schistosoma haematobium* infections, beginning as soon as three months after infection or sometimes not until several years later, there may be intermittent hematuria. There is no dysuria, but there may be some frequency and also bladder pain following urination. Hematuria is often referred to as terminal hematuria, being limited to the last few drops of urine, blood being forced out as the bladder wall contracts.

Hemoglobinuria

Blackwater fever usually is seen in conjunction with an attack of falciparum malaria, generally in patients who have had previous attacks of malaria. The passage of reddish or red-brown urine signals a bout of intravascular hemolysis, which may occur once or repeatedly and may lead to severe renal tubular damage and anuria.

The cause of blackwater fever is unknown; hypotheses include quinine sensitivity, glucose-6-phosphate dehydrogenase deficiency in persons treated with primaquine and related drugs, and autohemolysis on the basis of antibodies formed against altered infected red cells.

Hepatitis

Amebic hepatitis has already been described under the heading of ABSCESS, AMEBIC.

HEPATOMEGALY

Any parasitic infection involving the liver may result in enlargement of that organ. Thus, amebic hepatitis or liver abscess, visceral larva migrans, liver-fluke infections and early schistosomiasis are all characterized by an enlarged and tender liver, which is also seen in some cases of falciparum malaria and acute neonatal toxoplasmosis as well as in kala-azar and Chagas' disease.

Hydatid infections of the liver and *Schistosoma mansoni* and *japonicum* infections may result in an enlarged but usually non-tender liver. The hepatic fibrosis characteristic of chronic schistosome infections produces a clinical picture similar to that of Laennec's cirrhosis, often with splenomegaly.

Those helminth infections involving the liver are characterized also by an eosinophilia. In visceral larva migrans, a leukocytosis of up to 80,000 may be present, with a striking eosinophilia. In amebic abscess of the liver, on the other hand, though the white blood count may be in the range of 25,000, there is no eosinophilia.

Hives

Giant hives and other allergic symptoms, such as bronchial asthma, are commonly seen in ascariasis, and hives often appear during the first few weeks of schistosome infections.

Hydatid Thrill

In large unilocular echinococcus cysts of the abdominal viscera that are situated close to the abdominal wall, a characteristic thrill may be elicited by quick palpation or percussion.

Hydrocele

This is a common finding in areas where filariasis is endemic, developing as a sequel to repeated attacks of orchitis. If lymphatic varices develop in the cord and rupture into the scrotal sac, a condition known as lymphocele results.

Hydrocephalus Although not so intimately associated with congenital toxoplasmosis as are chorioretinitis and cerebral calcifications, hydrocephalus or microcephaly is commonly seen in this condition.

Hyperpigmentation Kala-azar derives its name from intensification of the pigmentation of the skin over the cheeks and temples, and around the mouth. It is most obvious in dark-skinned races.

In onchocerciasis, repeated attacks of allergic dermatitis may result in hyperpigmentation of the area, usually on the face, neck or ears. Bronzing and induration of the affected skin areas may occur in chronic pediculosis (vagabond's disease).

Jaundice Obstructive jaundice may be seen in severe liver fluke infections but is not characteristic of light infections or those of moderate intensity. The symptoms of the falciparum malaria syndrome known as bilious remittent fever include acute epigastric pain, nausea and vomiting, marked enlargement and tenderness of the liver, with jaundice appearing on about the second day.

Diarrhea, a high remittent fever and oliguria are usually seen, and death may result from renal or hepatic failure. Kerandel's Sign Noted in the stage of central nervous system involvement in African sleeping sickness, this sign may be elicited by pressure on the palm of the hand or over the ulnar nerve and consists of severe pain which occurs shortly after the pressure has been relieved. Leukocytosis Leukocytosis seldom continues throughout the course of any of the parasitic infections.

In amebic hepatitis or abscess there may be a white blood cell count of 25,000 to 30,000, with 70 to 80 per cent polymorphonuclear neutrophils. In visceral larva migrans a leukocytosis of up to 80,000 has been reported, with an eosinophilia of 20 to 80 per cent.

Trichinosis may be characterized by a white count of 30,000 early in the infection, and strongyloidiasis by one nearly as elevated; these usually decline and may be followed by leukopenia. Leukocytosis early in the course of infection, followed by leukopenia with a relative monocytosis, is common to many protozoan and helminth infections.

Leukopenia

A white cell count of 4000 or less, with a relative monocytosis, generally is seen throughout the course of kala-azar, sometimes terminating in agranulocytosis.

In malaria, a leukopenia of 3000 to 6000, with a relative monocytosis, characterizes the afebrile periods, while there may be a leukocytosis during the paroxysm.

Lymphadenitis

In filariasis the femoral and epitrochlear nodes are most commonly involved, as are the axillary and inguinals. The nodes are enlarged, painful and tender during an acute attack of lymphangitis and tend to remain enlarged between attacks.

A condition resembling infectious mononucleosis sometimes is seen in the acute stage of toxoplasmosis, with fever, weakness, malaise, generalized adenopathy and sometimes a rash. There may be generalized lymphadenitis without fever or other symptoms.

In the early stages of African trypanosomiasis there may be generalized adenopathy; the glands of the posterior cervical triangle are most conspicuously affected (Winterbottom's sign). Generalized adenopathy is seen in the acute stage of Chagas' disease.

Lymphangitis

Acute lymphangitis is an early symptom of filarial infection. It usually is accompanied by fever and may affect the limbs, breast or scrotum. When it occurs on a limb, it is usually centrifugal in development, starting at a lymph node and progressing distally.

The course of the lymphatic is readily seen because of local distention and erythema. Centrifugal spread of the lymphangitis is the reverse of that seen in bacterial lymphangitis (blood poisoning), in which the infection extends proximally from the point of origin.

Lymphocytosis

A relative or absolute lymphocytosis, unusual in parasitic infections, is, however, generally seen in Chagas' disease. Initially there may be a slight leukocytosis, usually followed by leukopenia.

Lymph Varices

Dilatations of the lymphatic vessels may occur secondarily to lymphatic blockage in filariasis. They are most frequently seen in the inguinal and femoral areas, or other lymphatic tracts may be affected. The soft lobulated swellings may rupture and drain. When this occurs on the scrotum, a chronic condition known as *lymph scrotum* may develop.

Melena

Upper gastrointestinal bleeding of a degree sufficient to produce melena is rare in parasitic disease; it is mentioned here primarily with strongyloidiasis in mind. Infection with *Strongyloides stercoralis* may run the gamut from a complete lack of symptoms to those infections of the duodenum and jejunum which are so extensive as to produce ulceration of the mucosa, with blood loss to the point of clinical anemia, and with melena. Especially in immunosuppressed patients, the coincidental finding of anemia with melena and a significant eosinophilia should stimulate a thorough search for this sometimes elusive parasite.

Meningoencephalitis

Invasion of the central nervous system by trypanosomes is characterized in African sleeping sickness by increasing symptoms of meningoencephalitis. There may be quite variable sensory and motor changes, personality disorders, headache, confusion, drowsiness and finally coma.

Similar but milder symptoms are seen in C4agas' disease. Minor neurologic symptoms are seen during almost any attack of malaria (i.e., headache, disorientation), and cerebral malaria may develop as a complication of any type of malaria. It is characteristic of falciparum malaria, however, and may develop slowly with increasing headache and drowsiness over several days or may present as a sudden coma or other acute mental disturbance.

There may be signs of meningeal irritation; symptomatology is quite varied, depending upon the brain areas affected. If the cord is affected, the symptoms may be suggestive of multiple sclerosis. Amebic meningoencephalitis, caused by invasion of the central nervous system by ordinarily free-living ameboflagellates of the genus *Naegleria* and possibly other amebae, is an acute, rapidly progressive infection, apparently acquired while swimming or diving in fresh-water lakes or pools.

It is characterized by fever, headache, mental confusion and coma, and death frequently occurs within a few days of onset. Eosinophilic meningoencephalitis, seen in various parts of the Pacific area in recent years, is believed, on strong epidemiologic grounds, to be symptomatic of infection with *Angiostrongylus cantonensis* and thus a form of larva migrans infection.

It is characterized by fever, headache, stiff neck, and increased cells (mainly eosinophils) in the spinal fluid. It is generally a mild and self-limited infection.

Monocytosis

A relative or absolute monocytosis is a frequent finding in both protozoal and helminthic infections.

Myocarditis

Myocardial infection is characteristic of Chagas' disease and is seen in about 50 per cent of chronic cases. Cardiac failure may come on slowly, although in infants it tends to occur in the early acute stage. There may be pericardial effusion. Congestive heart failure also has been reported in African *trypanosomiasis*, probably in the Rhodesian form of the disease.

In African trypanosomiasis the etiology of the heart failure is not as apparent. Myocarditis, occasionally severe enough to cause death, has been reported in trichinosis. It is the result of migration of the larvae through the myocardium, in which they do not encyst. Myocarditis also may be seen in acute toxoplasmosis in both infants and adults, the result of invasion of the myocardium.

Myositis Although myositis is a nonspecific symptom of many febrile illnesses, severe myositis is characteristic of the stage of larval migration in trichinosis. If accompanied by circumorbital edema, eosinophilia and a history of consumption of improperly cooked pork, the diagnosis may be made with some certainty. Myositis, usually involving a single muscle group, may also occur in *Sarcocystis* infection.

NEUROLOGIC

Symptoms Neurologic symptoms in trypanosomiasis, malaria and amebic and eosinophilic meningoencephalitis are discussed under MENINGOENCEPHALITIS. Variable neurologic symptoms may occur in schistosomiasis when eggs carried by the bloodstream to the central nervous system lodge there and provoke a granulomatous reaction. Neurologic and other symptoms caused by embolization of eggs are more common in *Schistosoma japonicum* infection than in the other two species, while in *S. mansoni* and *S. haematobium,* eggs are found more frequently in the spinal cord than in the brain, perhaps because of ectopic wanderings of the adult worms.

In *S. japonicum* infection, there may be severe neurologic symptoms, including coma and paresis, during the incubation period or first few weeks after infection. Transitory neurologic symptoms of a variable nature may be caused by the migration of ascarid and trichina larvae in the central nervous system; hemiplegia and focal epileptic attacks have been reported in trichinosis.

Hydatid, coenurus and cysticercus cysts may develop within the central nervous system, where they may produce symptoms related to a space-occupying lesion or, if within the ventricular system, internal hydrocephalus. Cysticercus larvae may give rise to epileptiform seizures, as may *Sparganum proliferum* and adults of *Paragonimus westermani* that have gone astray.

Nodules, Subcutaneous

Lipoma-like subcutaneous nodules include onchocercomas (q.v.) and cysticercus and coenurus larvae. The cysticercus larva of *Taenia solium* develops most frequently in the subcutaneous tissues, where it forms nodules 0.5 to 3.0 centimeters in diameter. In almost half the recorded human cases of coenurus infection, the larvae have been found in the subcutaneous tissues; others have been recorded from the brain, spinal cord and eye.

Echinococcus cysts also may be found in the subcutaneous tissues. Spargana also form subcutaneous nodules, somewhat elongate and several centimeters in length, which may resemble lipomas, but they may move through the subcutaneous tissues at irregular intervals and often cause pain. *Sparganum proliferum* may develop as branched or multiple nodules and invade the viscera. (See also EDEMA for a discussion of ocular sparganosis.)

Larvae of the botfly *Hypoderma* migrate through the subcutaneous tissues, finally coming to rest beneath the skin, where they produce elongate nodules several centimeters in length. Considerable pain may accompany migration, but the resting nodule is seldom painful or pruritic. The human botfly, *Dermatobia hominis,* burrows into the skin and subcutaneous tissues, producing an intensely pruritic papular lesion, which has the appearance of a furuncle.

There is a small central opening, from which comes a serous exudate and through which the posterior end of the larva may protrude from time to time. Secondary infection is common.

Obstruction, Intestinal

Ascaris, especially in children, may produce complete intestinal obstruction, with accompanying abdominal pain, vomiting, distention and hyperperistalsis. Partial or complete intestinal obstruction may also characterize infection by *Angiostrongylus costaricensis.*

Onchocercoma

Adult worms of *Onchocerca volvulus* lie in coiled masses beneath the skin, completely enclosed in a fibrous tissue capsule. They are from a few millimeters to several centimeters in diameter, generally freely movable, and resemble lipomas. In Mexico and Guatemala they frequently occur beneath the patient's scalp; in Africa most of them occur on other parts of the patient's body.

Orchitis

Filarial orchitis may occur early in the disease and at times in the absence of lymphangitis or fever; repeated attacks lead to hydrocele.

Pain

Abdominal pain, generally vague or ill-defined, is said to accompany many of the intestinal parasitic infections. The presence or absence of such tenuous pains is of no value from a diagnostic standpoint. Epigastric pain, sometimes with nausea and vomiting, may be seen in giardiasis, trichinosis and strongyloidiasis; it is related to the duodenitis and jejunitis provoked by these infections.

Moderate to severe abdominal pain is seen in acute amebic colitis; it may be confined to the cecal area or may be generalized. *Angiostrongylus costaricensis* may give rise to similar symptoms. In ascariasis, severe pain may signal intestinal obstruction (q.v.), perforation and peritonitis (q.v.) or bile duct blockage.

Muscle pain in trichinosis is discussed under MYOSITIS, and the delayed pain sensation seen in African trypanosomiasis under the heading of KERANDEL'S SIGN.

Peritonitis

Penetration of *Ascaris* through the wall of the intestine usually leads to generalized peritonitis, with pain, marked distention, generalized abdominal tenderness, and free air under the diaphragm, detectable by x-ray. In severe amebic dysentery, ulcers may erode through the wall of the intestine and cause peritonitis.

PNEUMONITIS

Pneumonitis is characteristic of severe *Ascaris* infection and is caused when the worm larvae break out of the capillaries into the alveoli, whence they are coughed up to be swallowed, beginning the intestinal phase of the disease. Symptoms and signs are first noted one to five days after the eggs are ingested and consist of cough, fever, respiratory distress and the physical and x-ray signs of a bronchopneumonia; in severe cases there may be complete consolidation of one or more lobes.

The pneumonitis usually clears within a week or two; it may be accompanied by high eosinophilia and an urticarial rash. Similar signs and symptoms may accompany the corresponding stage in strongyloides infection, although the pneumonitis is generally not so severe. In hookworm infection there is seldom a clear-cut pneumonitis at this stage, but a cough is frequently present.

In schistosomiasis there may likewise be a transitory cough, sometimes with hemoptysis and frequently with dyspnea, during the stage of migration through the lungs. *Pneumocystis carinii* causes an interstitial plasma cell pneumonia, mainly in newborn and young children. Some cases have been reported in adults. The x-ray picture is that of bronchopneumonia.

Pneumonitis may be a part of acute toxoplasmosis in infants during the neonatal period, and more rarely in adults. Atelectatic pneumonitis may be seen in amebic abscess, the result of pressure from the elevated right diaphragm. The abscess may erode through the diaphragm to produce a right lower lobe infection; infrequently an abscess may develop primarily in the lung. If there is erosion into a bronchus, there may be expectoration of abscess material, a light reddishbrown, or "anchovy paste," color.

Proteinuria

In falciparum malaria, proteinuria, with hyaline and granular casts in the urine, is common. Rarely there may be oliguria or anuria, usually accompanying an attack of blackwater fever (q.v.). The nephrotic syndrome, with proteinuria, is sometimes seen in quartan malaria.

Pruritus Ani

The nocturnal pruritus that accompanies pinworm infection varies considerably in degree, probably depending upon hypersensitivity of the host. In some persons there is no noticeable itching, whereas in others it may be sufficiently severe to interfere with rest. Anal pruritus may be associated with active migration of gravid proglottids of *Taenia saginata* out of the anus.

The spleen is usually tender during an acute attack of malaria, and tenderness may be apparent before the organ can be palpated. Splenic infarction or rupture occurs rarely. In *Schistosoma mansoni* and *S. japonicum* infections, splenomegaly is secondary to hepatic fibrosis brought about by egg deposition in the liver, and portal hypertension.

Splinter Hemorrhages

Sometimes occurring during the stage of active larval migration in trichinosis, these hemorrhages are a sign of vascular injury.

Steatorrhea

Malabsorption, characterized by the presence of fat in the stool, is seen in certain parasitic infections. The most common of these is giardiasis, which may make its presence known by flatulence and the production of foul-smelling fatty stools. The less common and self-limited *Isospora belli* infections are also characterized by steatorrhea, as are those caused by *Capillaria philippinensis*.

Tachycardia

A fast pulse is noted early in both African and American trypanosomiasis. In Chagas' disease it persists into the subacute and chronic stages, where it may be associated with heart block, Stokes-Adams syndrome and fibrillation.

ULCERS, CUTANEOUS

In leishmanial and trypanosomal diseases there is a primary multiplication at the site of infection. In *Leishmania tropica-complex* infections there is first a papule at the site of infection, which gradually transforms into a shallow ulcer with raised edges. The Chiclero ulcer of Southern Mexico and Central America is similar to oriental sore, except when it occurs on the ear, where it may erode the pinna. *L. braziliensis* first produces cutaneous ulcerations, which may, through extension or metastasis, come to involve the nasal mucosa, the soft and the hard palate, the nasal septum, the pharynx and the larynx.

In blacks, granulomatous rather than ulcerative lesions are generally seen. In African sleeping sickness there may be a firm tender raised lesion, up to 2 cm. or more in diameter, at the site of infection. This "trypanosomal chancre" is painful or pruritic, but like the chagoma (q.v.) it does not apparently ulcerate unless secondarily infected. Ulcerative cutaneous lesions rarely are seen in amebiasis, either in the perianal region or in the skin surrounding fistulas or surgical drainage incisions from hepatic abscesses. A rounded ulcer, 2 mm. to several centimeters in diameter, marks the place at which the guinea worm discharges its larvae. In the center of the ulcer, a portion of the worm may be visible. There is often secondary infection, and a painful localized reaction may persist until discharge of the larvae is complete.

Urethritis

Trichomonas vaginalis has been found in up to one third of cases of "nonspecific" urethritis in the male.

Vaginitis

A prolific, irritating, green or yellowish, thin discharge is seen in *Trichomonas vaginalis* infection; the vagina may be diffusely congested, or punctate hemorrhagic spots may be seen.

The organisms may be present in asymptomatic individuals. Pinworms may migrate from the anus and enter the vagina, where they produce a temporary, intense pruritus in some children.

VISUAL DIFFICULTIES

associated with parasitic disease include circumorbital edema (q.v.), conjunctivitis (q.v.) and chorioretinitis (q.v.). Ascarid larvae (both those of *Ascaris lumbricoides* and *Toxocara)* may invade the eye, producing iritis or other symptoms. Patients infected with *Onchocerca* actually may be aware of the intraocular movement of the microfilariae, and lesions of the anterior chamber, iris, ciliary body, choroid, and retina, developing in this condition, may lead to diminution of vision or total blindness. Cysticercus and coenurus larvae may develop within the eye. Ophthalmomyiasis may occur.

X-RAY EVIDENCE OF PARASITIC DISEASE

Amebiasis: Amebic granulomas of the large bowel simulate carcinoma in barium enema studies. Cecal amebiasis tends to produce a funnel-shaped deformity of that portion of the bowel as seen in barium enema studies. In amebic abscess of the liver there may be elevation of the right diaphragm and sometimes right lower lobe pneumonitis.

Intravenous sodium diatrizoate (Hypaque) infusion and tomography of the liver may show the wall of the amebic abscess. *Giardiasis:* Evidence of intestinal malabsorption. *Toxoplasmosis:* Intracerebral calcifications. *Pneumocystosis:* Pneumonitis, typically sparing lateral margins of the bases. *Dracunculiasis, filariasis* and *loiasis:* Calcified worms may be seen in the tissues. *Ascariasis:* Pneumonitis. Adult worms may be *seen* as cylindrical empty spaces in the barium-filled bowel in a small bowel series. *Strongyloidiasis* and *hookworm infection:* Pneumonitis.

Loss of mucosal markings and a tubular deformity of the duodenum and jejunum may be seen in small bowel studies on patients with strongyloidiasis. *Cysticercosis:* Calcified cysts in the subcutaneous tissues, muscles, brain. *Echinococcosis:* Well-defined, rounded masses may be seen in the lung parenchyma; sometimes a fluid level is visible within them.

Hepatic cysts are visible *only* if calcification of the wall has taken place. Sometimes calcified daughter cysts are seen. (Hepatic photoscanning with the use of radioactive isotopes will reveal non-calcified cysts as well.) Hydatid cysts of bone produce extensive intramedullary erosion, demonstrable by x-ray. *Paragonimiasis:* Patchy infiltrates or rounded densities in the parenchyma, pleural thickening, or fluid. *Schistosomiasis:* Pulmonary fibrosis, or a picture suggestive of miliary tuberculosis.

Cor pulmonale with dilatation of the pulmonary artery and its main branches, right ventricular hypertrophy. S. *haematobium* infections: Calcification in the wall of the bladder, hydronephrosis, hydroureter.

INDEX

D

E

I

J

L

O

P

Q

R

S

V

W

X

Y

Z